The Science of Diversity

The Science of Diversity

Mona Sue Weissmark

OXFORD

UNIVERSITY PRESS

Oxford University Press is a department of the University of Oxford. It furthers
the University's objective of excellence in research, scholarship, and education
by publishing worldwide. Oxford is a registered trade mark of Oxford University
Press in the UK and certain other countries.

Published in the United States of America by Oxford University Press
198 Madison Avenue, New York, NY 10016, United States of America.

© Oxford University Press 2020

Library of Congress Cataloging-in-Publication Data
Names: Weissmark, Mona Sue, author.
Title: The science of diversity / Mona Sue Weissmark.
Description: New York : Oxford University Press, 2020. |
Includes bibliographical references and index.
Identifiers: LCCN 2019054197 (print) | LCCN 2019054198 (ebook) |
ISBN 9780190686345 (hardback) | ISBN 9780190686369 (epub)
Subjects: LCSH: Cultural pluralism. | Social justice. | Equality.
Classification: LCC HM1271 .W4545 2020 (print) | LCC HM1271 (ebook) |
DDC 305—dc23
LC record available at https://lccn.loc.gov/2019054197
LC ebook record available at https://lccn.loc.gov/2019054198

1 3 5 7 9 8 6 4 2

Printed by Sheridan Books, Inc., United States of America

I dedicate this book in devoted memory to my parents, who survived Auschwitz, Buchenwald, and Dachau. And I dedicate this book to my aunts, uncles, cousins, and grandparents who were all murdered in the Holocaust. I never knew them. Indeed all that remained of them was two or three tattered photos.

This book is an elegy of sorts; a lament for the dead and for lost love.

I hope that the effort put into writing this textbook may contribute to fostering a more peaceful world.

The wound is the place where the Light enters you.

Jalaluddin Rumi

Ring the bells (ring the bells) that still can ring
Forget your perfect offering
There is a crack in everything (there is a crack in everything)
That's how the light gets in

Leonard Cohen

Contents

Preface   ix
Acknowledgments   xv
Introduction   xix

1. What Is Diversity?   1

2. The Self   28

3. Categorizing   53

4. Judging   82

5. Diversity and Relationships   114

6. Diversity and Groups   151

7. Diversity and Social Justice   189

8. Diversity and Ethnic Conflicts   225

9. Diversity and Nations   309

10. Concluding Remarks   344

References   357
Figure Credit Lines   391
Index   401

Preface

For some fifteen years—at Northwestern and Harvard—I have been teaching a course on the psychology of diversity, and have, since 2014, been teaching the course online via live web conference. When initially invited to write this book, I pictured a text that would be similar to the course. It would be both scientifically rigorous and personally engaging, data driven and thought-provoking.

It would present diversity as an inquisitive researcher might, by portraying diversity as important scientific phenomena, as well as show how researchers uncover and explain such phenomena. It would be realistically wide-ranging, providing a current summary of important research findings, yet would also inspire students' creative thinking—their willingness to probe, to evaluate, to connect diversity principles to themselves, their relationships, and to national affairs.

How does one choose material to include in a practically broad and comprehensive introduction to the subject of diversity—complete enough to allow a full account but engaging enough not to inundate?

I have tried to present theories and findings that are neither too impenetrable for the typical undergraduate nor better fitted to other courses in the field of psychology or related disciplines. Instead, I have selected to present material that puts the study of diversity in the intellectual tradition of the liberal arts and sciences education. Embarking on a sciences education is meant to be transformative—intellectually, socially, and personally.

To this end, *The Science of Diversity* focuses on human behavior and real-world issues. Undergraduate and graduate students taking a course in diversity come from different majors. By choosing to include studies on human behavior and real-world issues, one can present the content that many preprofessional students need in ways that are useful, but also intellectually, socially, and personally stimulating.

The application of the reasoning and of those procedures that we call the "scientific method" to the understanding of human behavior and real-world issues is of relatively recent origin. In any science, the methods of investigation depend on the subject matter. For example, chemistry deals with substances that can be seen, felt, tasted, and manipulated. So, scientists can use direct methods. The chemist can put two substances together in a test tube, see what happens, then measure and analyze the results. By contrast, astronomy has to use methods that are more indirect. It cannot manipulate the stars and planets. So, it must be content to observe them through telescopes.

Because human behavior takes such a wide variety of forms, social scientists have had to improvise. No single method can be applied to all human activities that interest the social scientist. Therefore, social scientists have had to adopt different ways of studying diversity.

In some cases, like astronomers, social scientists can only observe events pertinent to diversity, such as studying the actual behavior of people in various kinds of situations. For example, social scientists might wonder whether the way people interact online is a reflection of cultural tribalism. So in this case, social scientists observe the word usage of users from the social networking site Twitter to see whether each tribal online community can be characterized by their most used words.

Another way to discover how people behave and feel is to ask them; accordingly, social scientists use interview methods, questionnaires, and surveys. For example, social scientists might wonder what can be learned about the automatic visual processing system from people who are unable to see. Social scientists have, therefore, conducted in-depth interviews with blind people to investigate the different ways blind people construct and experience race. In addition, social scientists use physiological measures, the correlation method, experimentation methods, and action research based on real-world interventions to learn about human behavior and diversity.

When choosing material for this book I have tried to select relevant theories and findings from all of these complementary scientific methods of inquiry. Much about human behavior remains a mystery, yet studies on diversity using these different methods of inquiry can now offer partial answers to many intriguing questions:

What is diversity and how do we understand it?
How do race, nationality, and religion influence individuals?
What impact does diversity have on cross-group relationships?
How is diversity related to people's perceptions of fairness and justice and how are these perceptions related to social problems and social change?
Does respect for diversity promote peace and positive change?

Answering those and other questions—my aim in the pages that lie ahead—transforms our thinking and alerts us to the diversity principles influencing us.

Organization

The book opens with a single chapter, "What Is Diversity?," that introduces the definition of diversity and the scientific method. The introductory chapter discusses, in historical perspective, a major theme within the deterministic scientific version of diversity: the claim that differences between people—primarily races, classes, and sexes—arise from inherited, inborn distinctions and that society, in that sense, is an accurate reflection of some predetermined fact.

The introductory chapter attempts to show both the scientific weakness and the historical social context of the deterministic scientific version of diversity. The chapter presents the view that science is a social enterprise, not the work of a computer programmed to collect pure unsullied bits of information. Science, since people must do it, is more like a developmental process that progresses by trial and error. The scientific method cannot escape its interesting dialectic: people studying people.

Scientists, like all people, are susceptible to the human limitations of perception and cognition. By analogy, we can bend our arms forward to the elbow, but not backward. There are physical constraints on how far the human forearm can be bent. Similarly, there are perceptual, cognitive constraints on how much and how we process the world's richness of information.

There are many ways of doing science. Scientists who do science include laboratory experimenters, survey researchers, and field researchers of both the experimental and nonexperimental kind. Whatever their method of inquiry, all attempt to do science in the pursuit of truth. The pursuit of scientific truth is not an automated but a very human, and thus a subjective as well as an objective, process.

Ultimately, it is through the minds and experiences of individual scientists that our world is peeled open for study and understanding. If we hope to have true knowledge of the world, it is helpful to have knowledge of the limitations in the mind of the individual scientist. This assertion of limitations should not dismiss the progress that can be made by using scientific thinking.

In underscoring the limitations, I do not align myself with the now popular, in some circles, relativistic view that truth is a meaningless idea outside cultural assumptions and that science can therefore provide no lasting answers. As a scientist trained at McGill, Harvard, and the University of Pennsylvania, I share the stance of my colleagues: I think that a factual reality exists and that science, by trial and error, can learn about it.

The earth really does revolve about the sun. Galileo Galilei was arrested for his discovery, but eventually the truth behind this factual reality was recognized. This truth required unlearning the view that the earth was the center of the universe and that all heavenly bodies revolved around the Earth.

In terms of the study of diversity, the eye really does draw distinctions. The eye is formed during embryonic development. It is an outgrowth of the central nervous tissue. Because of this, the retina has layers of neurons, internal circuits, and transmitters typical of the brain. In a way, the eye is a bit of the brain that has journeyed out, literally, to have a look at the environment.

And what the eye sees when it looks at the environment are differences, diversities, distinctions. We draw distinctions; that is, we pull them out and then we categorize, judge, and give them subjective meanings.

Science's potential as an instrument for the pursuit of truth cannot be fully realized until scientists give up the myth of objectivity. One must, indeed, locate the brain in one's own eye before interpreting correctly the pervasive blind spots in everybody else's. The blind spots can then become facilitators rather than obstacles.

An important takeaway to consider is that all scientific investigations are subject to error. It is better to be aware of this, to study the causes and assess the importance of such errors in an attempt to reduce it rather than to be unaware of the errors concealed in the data and in the minds of scientists. The scientist's quest is never done. Scientific truth remains always tentative and refutable; subject to possible disconfirmation. The limitations of people studying people does not eliminate the chance to do good research. Instead, it makes us mindful of the errors in research—and the limitations of all human understanding.

The intent of this introductory chapter is to give students the ammunition to be aware and to cast a critical, doubtful eye on the pages that lie ahead. The book then unfolds around the study of diversity at three levels: *diversity at the individual level, diversity at the relational level*, and *diversity at the national level*. Real-world applications of diversity are interwoven throughout the chapters.

Personal Note: Why I Wrote This Book

My mother and father were survivors of Auschwitz, Dachau, and Buchenwald. Apart from my parents, every family member (besides a few cousins) was killed by the Nazis.

In the final weeks of the Holocaust, my father escaped from Langenstein-Zweiberge concentration camp—a Buchenwald subcamp—and found himself at the doorstep of a German pastor and his family in a small village in Germany. Ill with typhus and dysentery, covered in lice and starving, my father was welcomed into the home of the Seebass family, who, despite the risk to their own lives, cared for my father as if he was their beloved son.

Thanks to the altruistic kindness of Pastor Seebass; his wife, Hertha; and their children, my father survived the Holocaust, married my mother, another Holocaust survivor, and immigrated to the United States to raise his family. As the daughter of survivors, I grew up keenly aware that people can choose to exclude others and commit atrocities or can choose to include others and act kindly.

Someone from the Shoah Foundation once asked my mother, "What would you like to tell the world about the pain you suffered in Auschwitz?" My mother paused for a moment and then said, "I want the world to know that no one ever again should suffer as I did."

My mother's answer surprised me. I knew she harbored hatred. It was the cocoon that nurtured her. And she never flew free of it. The pain on her face was always palpable. She lived with the ghosts of the Holocaust every day. Still despite her pain, or maybe because of it, she focused on her desire to ameliorate others' sufferings. It was her final statement about Auschwitz. And it was an act of concern for all humanity.

Many of us who write and teach psychology are inspired to contribute something positive to society and to improve the human condition. So, I write this text gladly offering it to you, and hoping that you will gladly receive the principles related to the science of diversity. The text mainly focuses on the principles (or one might say the mechanisms) of diversity rather than specific diversities in race, religion, nationality, gender, sexuality, ethnicity, disability, physical appearance, political viewpoint, and so forth. I believe the principles of diversity have the potential to expand your mind and enhance your life.

There is a joke where one fish is swimming in the ocean and asks another fish "How's the water?" The other fish replies, "What is water?" The joke reminds us that we are conceptually locked into our own realities. This book aims to expand awareness of us and the nature and place of us in the world. It does not just offer new facts and information. Indeed, I write hoping the text will encourage learning how to think critically; how to think about our thinking; how to refine judgmentalism with compassion; and how to replace illusion with understanding. I try to do my part to reload conceptual certainties with hypothetical possibilities.

If you finish the book with sharpened critical skills and self-awareness, and with a deeper understanding of the science of diversity—then I will be a satisfied author and you, I hope will be a rewarded reader. I trust by sharing these words and my thoughts about them, the book will be meaningful for readers.

Acknowledgments

I owe a large number of debts to those scientists, philosophers, and social thinkers who have made the concern for studying diversity an essential subject.

Next to my desk, I keep a photograph of Hannah Arendt. She is one of the few women philosophers whose scholarly work received acclaim. This was no easy feat.

Aside from being a woman philosopher at a time when women were not recognized for their scholarly contributions, her work was controversial and met with considerable animosity.

Some critics felt she was "disloyal" to her own people (one might say her group or tribe) in her writings on the Holocaust. In addition, her detractors found it difficult to categorize her either as a liberal thinker or as an antiliberal thinker.

But, if there is a tradition of thought with which Arendt can be identified, it is the idea of two-sided thought about all matters affecting a diverse community.

Also, next to my desk, I keep a photograph of Marie Curie. Marie Curie was the first woman to win a Nobel Prize for her scientific discoveries. This was no easy feat either. Marie was principled in her own field, even though, as a woman, she was not initially welcome in its highest ranks.

I am grateful to both these women for their courage, tenacity, originality, and dedication to advancing scientific thinking.

More personally, I owe a debt to my husband, Daniel Giacomo, who spent many hours researching and discussing the topics in this book. For two years, we spent our weekends reviewing and talking about the manuscript. Daniel printed out dozens of articles for us to discuss and generously shared his thoughts. He made substantial contributions to the development of the ideas presented in this book. And I am also very grateful to our precious daughter, Brittany, who inspires me to be a more mindful mother and a better human being.

A program of study and research spanning more than fifteen years is possible only with much help and support. I am grateful to many teachers, colleagues, teaching fellows, research assistants, and students:

To my former teachers at Harvard, Brendan Maher, who taught me the scientific method; Robert Rosenthal, who taught me statistics and how to apply the scientific method; and Jill Hooley, who taught me how to run a research study. To my former teacher at the University of Pennsylvania, Aron Katsenelinboigen, who taught me about diversity and systems theory. I am grateful to my colleagues at Harvard, Myron Belfer and Michael Shinagel, who have encouraged and supported my work for many years; they gave generously of their time and wisdom. I am grateful to them both and to Martha Minow for reading many of the chapters in the manuscript and giving feedback that enhanced it. Also, I am grateful to my colleague at Northwestern, Mark Reinecke, whose support has been invaluable in allowing me to continue my academic career and finish this book. In addition, I am grateful to my colleague at Texas Christian University, Melita Garza, whose help and talent improved the manuscript, and to the journalist, Veronique Mistiaen, for writing about my research.

To my former students and Harvard teaching fellows Jason Ri, who created Power Points for chapters 1, 2, 6, and 8, and Caroline DeVane, who created PowerPoints for chapters 3, 4, 5, and 7. And to my former students and current Harvard teaching fellows and research assistants, Brian Chin, Marilena Dania, Marcelle Giovannetti, Lizbeth Jacobs and Marcelo Soares, who help run and continually improve the Harvard Psychology of Diversity course and the Science of Diversity research projects. Their effort is critical to the successes we have teaching the course and running the projects. This textbook brings together all the concepts from the Harvard class syllabus. My team has spent many hours creating and documenting content for the Harvard Psychology of Diversity course: course trailers, shorts, interviews, presentations, and videos featuring what students around the world are saying about the course in addition to creating the Harvard scholar website *The Science of Diversity*, https://scholar.harvard.edu/weissmark, and my personal website www.weissmark.com.

I would also like to acknowledge the Associate Director of the Career and Academic Resource Center, Chris Davis, at Harvard Extension and my former students, Avanti Bammanhalli, Anubha Tyagiand Humberto Santos for their help and to the many Harvard Ext. Faculty Aide Program research assistants for their help too. And thanks to all my former and current students, from whom I learn every semester and whose curiosity and enthusiasm compel me to study more about diversity.

I am grateful to Johanna Holzhaeur, a special friend whom I met in Israel many years ago when we were teenagers. Johanna produced a TV documentary based on my book, *Justice Matters: Legacies of the Holocaust and World War II*. The film titled *Seeing the Other Side* (Pt. 1 & Pt. 2) has been invaluable for highlighting some of the topics discussed in the Harvard course and in this book. Students have reported that the film has a transformational impact on their lives.

Additionally, I am very grateful to Joan Bossert the vice president and editorial director of Oxford University Press. Joan's belief and support in the manuscript brought it out into the world.

Likewise, to Abby Gross, senior editor at Oxford University Press. Abby's patience and superb editorial skills helped improve and ready the manuscript for publication. Also at Oxford, I would like to thank Sarah Butcher and Katharine Pratt.

I am thankful to Father Tom Liberia for his spiritual guidance. I am also grateful to my close sisterhood of friends Katharine Bensinger, Marcie Dodson, Joan Gelfand, Ilona Kuphal, Mara Lund, Patricia Lebensohn, Beth Roth, and Agnes Seebass for their sisterly love and understanding.

Finally, mere words are but empty expressions in thanking the Seebass family—who showed by their actions what it means to give equal value to all life. They not only saved my father's life but also made my life possible. Their compassion for a stranger's sufferings gives me faith. That faith lies in my heart.

May it help spread the light.

Introduction

What Is the Value of Scientific Thinking in a Polarized Society?

The first woman scientist to win the Noble Prize, Marie Curie, lived by the credo that science, when used responsibly, could be of great value to society. Curie stressed that science education was the key to developing peoples' moral and intellectual strengths, and that this would lead to a better national situation.

"Our society, . . . does not understand the value of science. It does not realize that science is a most precious part of its moral patrimony. Nor does it take sufficient cognizance of the fact that science is at the base of all the progress," Curie wrote (Curie, Kellogg, & Kellogg, 1923, p. 145).

Other noble prize scientists like Albert Einstein and Richard Feynman held similar views on the value of science education to society. Einstein thought the language of science created tools for the possibility of transforming the way the public think. In a speech on education, Einstein emphasized that science education should focus on teaching people how to think scientifically rather than acquiring detailed knowledge.

"The development of general ability for independent thinking and judgment should always be placed foremost, not the acquisition of special knowledge," he said (Einstein, 2010). http://www.cse.iitm.ac.in/~kalyantv/pdf/on_edu.pdf

Also, Feynman stressed that the value of science to society lay in its worldview. According to Feynman, the scientific worldview was a habit of thought, and once acquired one could not retreat from it anymore. In his address to the National Science Teachers' Association, Feynman pointed out that science alone of all subjects contained within itself a valuable way of thinking that could be used for the betterment of educating the public (April 1966).

Curie, Einstein, and Feynman were concerned about the rise in militarism, fascism, and authoritarianism. They witnessed ethnic and national fanaticism bubbling around them, and habits of thought familiar from ages past reaching for the control of peoples' minds. Feynman wrote, "one of the greatest dangers to modern society is the possible resurgence and expansion of the ideas of

The Science of Diversity. Mona Sue Weissmark, Oxford University Press (2020). © Oxford University Press.
DOI: 10.1093/oso/9780190686345.001.0001

thought control; such ideas as Hitler had, or Stalin in his time. . . . I think that one of the greatest dangers is this shall increase until it encompasses all of the world" (Feynman, 1999, p. 98, The Pleasure of Finding Things Out).

Because of such concerns, Curie, Einstein, and Feynman stressed the humanizing power of scientific thinking and its vital role in a democratic society.

Today, once again we are witnessing worries about the rise of militarism, fascism, and authoritarianism. National security experts have testified on Capitol Hill about the rise of authoritarianism, warning lawmakers that in some countries leaders are seeking to gain power by undermining democratic systems. Security experts have said there are troubling signs appearing worldwide that suggest a growing return to despots and dictators.

In his last interview, the famous physicist, the late Stephen Hawkins, cited recent political events in the United States and Britain as indicators of a "global revolt against experts and that includes scientists." Hawkins warned that science was in danger more than ever before. He urged young people to adopt a scientific worldview to overcome global challenges "to look up at the stars and not down at your feet. Try to make sense of what you see, and wonder about what makes the universe exist," Hawkins said. "It matters that you don't give up. Unleash your imagination. Shape the future."

Because of the current political environment, many scientists, like Hawkins, have been galvanized by what has been dubbed the "post-truth" era to speak out on the importance of science. Oxford Dictionaries (Simpson, 1993) defines "post-truth" as "Relating to or denoting circumstances in which objective facts are less influential in shaping public opinion than appeals to emotion and personal belief."

To counteract the effects of post-truth discourse (and Internet-based campaigns of disinformation and misinformation) scientists have been urged to get training in communication skills to persuade the public that they should trust science, rationality, and objective facts rather than appeals to emotions and beliefs.

For the past few years, the National Academy of Sciences has held a series of colloquia in an effort to identify ways that might help scientists to communicate more effectively with the public.

To date, most efforts in the scientific community have centered on improving the content, accessibility, and delivery of scientific communications and also developing online strategies to counteract the effects of misinformation. This communication skills approach relies on a "knowledge deficit model," the idea that the lack of support for science and "good policies" merely reflects a lack of scientific information.

According to this model, the post-truth disregard for objective facts reflects this lack of scientific information and if the public were just given more facts there would be more support for science and "good policies." The Netflix show *Bill Nye Saves the World* (a.k.a. Bill Nye the Science Guy) is billed as communicating real objective facts in an age of alternative facts. "Each episode will tackle a topic from a scientific point of view, dispelling myths, and refuting antiscientific claims that may be espoused by politicians, religious leaders or titans of industry," Netflix said in a statement.

Though it is important to supply the public with more scientific information on a range of topics, the question remains whether conveying knowledge using a top-down model—which is still the way most scientific, information is communicated—works. There is some evidence suggesting that efforts to persuade the public often fail. For instance, communication strategies on vaccines and genetically modified organisms intended to persuade the public that their religious or personal beliefs do not align with scientific facts––often wind up backfiring. Telling people they are wrong and uninformed may result in people being less likely to vaccinate or choose GMO foods.

Likewise, telling people they are biased and therefore they need to attend a mandatory diversity training program can activate bias rather than stamp it out. If people feel forced to accept scientific information they may do the opposite to assert their autonomy. https://www.psychologytoday.com/us/blog/justice-matters/201802/outlawing-bias-is-doomed-fail

When areas of science are contentious, a missing fact is not the sole core of the problem, and supplying the public with more scientific information is not the sole solution. As Curie, Einstein, and Feynman stressed equally or more important is also teaching the public to think scientifically, and to learn to evaluate the scientific information contained in the communication. https://www.psychologytoday.com/us/blog/justice-matters/201808/evaluating-psychology-research

For nearly twenty years at Harvard––I have been teaching a course on advanced research methods and on the psychology of diversity, and have, with my team of researchers, been conducting research on the science of diversity using the scientific thinking approach. As a professor and researcher, I have had a ringside seat to the power of scientific thinking. I have also seen how attainable this skill is. Yet, when I first began to delve into the research on scientific thinking, I was surprised by the striking gap between science education and specific teaching on the actual process of scientific thinking. Surprisingly little is known about improving this critical skill.

So what is scientific thinking? How is scientific thinking different from everyday thinking and from appealing to emotion and personal belief? And how can scientific thinking be used to educate the public in a polarized society?

First, scientific thinking involves reliance not on armchair theorizing, political conviction, or personal opinion, but instead on methods of *empirical research* (external observations) independently available to anyone as a means of opening up the world for scrutiny. All opinions are hypotheses to be tested empirically rather than appeals to emotion. This does not mean "everyone is right" or all truths are morally equivalent; rather, it means that our opinions are hypotheses to be tested.

For instance, recent high-profile police shooting deaths of black men and women have raised contentious questions about the extent to which law enforcement officers are affected by racial biases. Some people think there are racial differences in police use of force due to racial bias and discrimination. Other people think racial differences in police use of force are not due to bias and discrimination but rather can be explained by other factors. So, researchers set out to test these working hypotheses.

Second, there is a feature of scientific thinking that is often not talked about explicitly. We might term this feature *scientific integrity* or honesty, and we just hope that students will catch on by example. When researchers are conducting a study, we are expected to report everything that we think might make it invalid and unreliable, not just what we think is right about it. We are expected to give alternative interpretations of the data; specific details that could cast doubt on our interpretations must be given; we are expected to report anything that is wrong, or possibly wrong with our conclusions.

For instance, if a researcher is reporting on police shootings and claims studies have shown no racial bias in shootings and minorities are not in mortal danger from racist police, such a report would be incomplete. Yes, some high profile studies have shown that there is no evidence of racial bias in police shootings. But other studies have come to the opposite conclusion.

Though "factfulness" can be useful for persuading the public, reporting only half the facts is not useful if our intention is to educate the public to think scientifically. If our aim is to encourage scientific thinking the researcher would ask the public to consider the question, why did studies on racial bias in police shootings reach such different conclusions?

The researcher would encourage the public to review meta-analyses or systematic reviews that combine the results from multiple conflicting studies.

Meta-analyses can provide more credible evidence and can suggest reasons why results differ. An awareness of the conflict in scientific findings and reasons for the conflict is a part of education in scientific thinking. Guiding policy or activism by citing one-sided facts in support of an opinion without reference to conflicting data, would then come to be seen as suspect by the public.   https://www.psychologytoday.com/us/blog/justice-matters/201808/evaluating-psychology-research

Third, scientific thinking considers all the facts and information to help others evaluate the value of the research not simply the information that persuades judgment in one specific way. Scientists have learned that the truth will ultimately come out when other scientists repeat our experiment. So, we are encouraged to examine our own assumptions and to be honest with ourselves.

For instance, if I reported only on the studies showing that there is no evidence of racial bias in police shootings, why did I do so? Was my intention to convince the public that racial bias does not exist? Or if I reported only on the studies showing that there is evidence of racial bias in police shooting, why? We might term this principal of scientific thinking *self-awareness*, the ability to see our intentions and ourselves clearly.

Fourth, scientific thinking remains always *tentative and refutable*, subject to possible disconfirmation. The limitations of scientific thinking do not eliminate the chance to do good research. Instead, it makes us mindful of the errors in research—and the limitations of all human understanding.

Fifth, all scientific thinking is *subject to error*. It is better to be aware of this, to study the causes and assess the importance of the errors rather than to be unaware of the errors concealed in the data and in the mind of the scientist.

Sixth, scientific thinking takes discipline and *diligence*. Thinking like a scientist keeps us constantly open to new ideas and questions before we believe. The scientific method encourages us to change our minds when the data suggest doing so. And it encourages us to be persistent and study it again. When the results are not what we expected, we are pressed to find out why and to figure out a better approach.

In today's polarized society, conversations on so many topics often end up being politicized debates and arguments. By contrast, scientific thinking is designed to facilitate conversations on contentious topics, between divergent viewpoints, and to foster understanding. Students take away the experience that the scientific thinking approach to contentious topics is a prerequisite for productive conversations. Data from many years of our course evaluations show that facilitated conversations using scientific thinking may have a transformational impact on peoples' lives.

When conversations in our classes on diversity get bogged down by opinions, my teaching fellow at Harvard, Lizbeth Jacobs, likes to say, "Let's use our scientific thinking life raft." It is an apt analogy. A raft can help us from sinking and becoming stuck in the workings of our own mind.

It is a universal truth that diversity is a feature of nature. This is true of individuals, families, social classes, religious groups, ethnic groups, and nations. There will always be diverse polarized opinions with which people are passionately identified. Scientific thinking is a fair two-sided method for evaluating polarized views, fake news, misinformation, and disinformation.

But do not take my word. I may be wrong. So test it yourself and see if it works.

I invite you to tell me about your findings.

1
What Is Diversity?

The Tower of Babel

The Tower of Babel narrative in the Book of Genesis is among the most famous in the bible. Whether we read the bible as a true religious text or as a fictional literary text, the Tower of Babel story describes the origin of linguistic and cultural diversity and its influence on human relations. The Tower of Babel narrative highlights a turning point in history as it relates to human relations because it symbolizes the end of the universal.

According to the story as it appears in the Authorized King James Version of the Holy Bible, before the Tower of Babel, there was linguistic and cultural unity and homogeneity among all people on earth. All humans were descendants from Noah and his wife and their three sons and their wives. Noah's descendants multiplied over the generations into many nations still speaking one language. "And the whole earth was of one language, and of one speech" (Genesis 11:1).

According to the narrative, the descendants of Noah migrated from the east to the land of Shinar. And there they decided to build a city and a tower, "whose top may reach unto heaven; and let us make us a name" (Genesis 11:4).

God saw that the descendants of Noah were planning to build a city and tower and remarked that as one people with one language, nothing that they sought would be out of their reach: "And the Lord said, Behold, the people is one, and they have all one language; and this they begin to do: and now nothing will be restrained from them, which they have imagined to do" (Genesis 11:6).

So seeing this, God decided to confound their speech so that they could no longer understand each other and scattered them around the world: "Go to, let us go down, and there confound their language, that they may not understand one another's speech. So, the Lord scattered them abroad from thence upon the face of all the earth: . . . Therefore is the name of it called Babel; because the Lord did there confound the language of all the earth: and from thence did the Lord scatter them abroad over the face of all the earth" (Genesis 11:7–9).

The Science of Diversity. Mona Sue Weissmark, Oxford University Press (2020). © Oxford University Press.
DOI: 10.1093/oso/9780190686345.001.0001

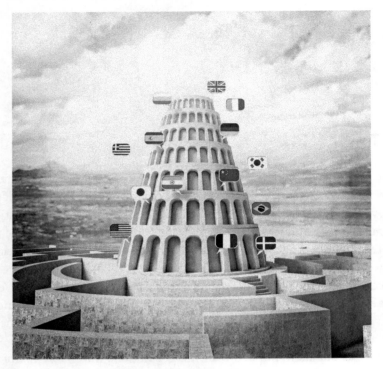

Figure 1.1 Babel tower with flags of different countries

Interpretations of the Tower of Babel explain the building of the tower as a hubristic act of defiance against God. Noah's descendants wanted to build a tower that was to reach to heaven, to make them equal to God. Therefore, God punishes them for their unrestrained pride and makes it difficult for them to understand each other and communicate and cooperate.

Thus, the biblical story presents the origin of linguistic and cultural diversity as a punishment that hindered developing harmonious human relations.

Greek Mythology

Besides the biblical story that explains the origin of diversities, early Greek myths and later philosophers and scientists attempted to explain the origin of diversities too. For example, the story of the legendary character Phaethon is famous in Greek mythology. According to the legend, Phaethon, the son of the god Helios, convinced his father to let him drive the sun chariot. The god was reluctant, but conceded to his son's wishes and handed him the reigns. The boy's inexperience proved fatal. Phaethon was unable to control the horses and drove the sun chariot too close to earth in some regions, burning the people there black. And in other regions, he drove too far from earth, whose inhabitants turned pale from the cold.

Hippocrates

Later, Hippocrates, a famous Greek physician who lived in the fifth century B.C., who may have been aware of this Greek legend, explains the origin of racial differences on climate and geography. Hippocrates believed, as many thinkers throughout early history did, that factors such as climate and geography played a significant role in the physical appearance and temperament of different peoples.

In his essay *On Airs, Waters, and Places*, written 2,000 years ago, Hippocrates wrote that the forms and dispositions of human beings corresponded with the nature of the country. He attributed physical and temperamental differences among different peoples to environmental factors such as climate, water sources, elevation, and terrain. For example, he wrote that people who "inhabit a country which is mountainous, rugged, elevated, and well watered, and where the changes of the seasons are very great, are likely to have great variety of shapes among them, and to be naturally of an enterprising and warlike disposition;" whereas people who "dwell in places which are low-lying, abounding in meadows and ill ventilated, and who have a larger proportion of hot than of cold winds, and who make use of warm waters-these are not likely to be of large stature nor well proportioned, but are of a broad make, fleshy, and have black hair; and they are rather of a dark than of a light complexion, . . . are less likely to be phlegmatic than bilious; courage and laborious enterprise are not naturally in them" (Hippocrates, part 1 to part 23).

Greek Philosophers

Next, the classical Greek philosopher Socrates attempts to explain the origin of class diversities. In *The Republic*, Plato, speaking through his teacher Socrates, explains that the citizens of *The Republic* are born with one of three kinds of soul: gold, silver, or bronze, and therefore, a citizen's class and function in the city is determined by what kind of soul he possesses.

Figure 1.2 Statue of Socrates

Socrates states that although the citizens of *The Republic* are all brothers god created them differently: "'but the god, in fashioning those of you who are competent to rule, mixed gold in at their birth; this is why they are most honored; in auxiliaries, silver; and iron and bronze in the farmers and the other craftsmen . . . for the most part you'll produce offspring like yourselves'" (Plato, 1968, p. 94).

According to Socrates, an explanation for the origin of the different souls is necessary to keep strict class separation and to eliminate factionalism. The gold-souled people are best suited to rule, the silver-souled people (the warrior class) assist the rulers in their plans for the city, and the bronze-souled people are to obey. In addition, according to Socrates, the classes must never intermarry, as those who "by nature" are superior cannot be ruined by a lower class. For the good of the city, the bronze-souled people must accept their natural inferiority to the silver- and gold-souled classes. Also, they must be willing to obey and carry out orders since they are intellectually inferior to the silver- and gold-souled rulers and cannot properly direct their lives without the leadership of their natural superiors.

Later, Plato's student the Greek philosopher Aristotle builds on Socrates's theory of the natural endowed differences between people. Aristotle is sometimes called "the father of natural law." Natural law is law whose content derives naturally from human nature ("Natural Law," n.d.).

For Aristotle, not all humans are equal even though humans are all of the same basic atomic species. Aristotle maintained that some people are masters by nature, some slaves by nature, each "right from birth" (1981,1254a17, p. 67). In his book *The Politics*, Aristotle develops a theory of natural slavery that claims humans have natural differences in mental and physical capacities, and should live according to their given and fixed nature.

Aristotle states that slaves are by nature slaves because nature's purpose was to make their minds and bodies different from free men. A slave, according to Aristotle, is intended by nature to be governed, since natural slaves are those who understand reason but possess no reasoning ability (1981,1254b16, p. 69). And Aristotle maintains that slaves, unlike free men, have strong bodies designed with the purpose to carry out necessary physical tasks. "It is, then, nature's purpose to make the bodies of free men to differ from those of slaves, the latter strong enough to be used for necessary tasks, the former erect and useless for that kind of work, but well suited for the life of a citizen" (p. 69). Aristotle concludes that these naturally occurring mental and physical differences indicate that masters are better off having slaves and slaves are better off having masters.

In addition to his theory of natural law, Aristotle is acknowledged as the first biologist in the Western tradition and the first to start to classify all living things. Aristotle used a simple system of classification. He divided all living things into two groups: plants and animals. He maintained that everything exists for a purpose and that the lower exits for the sake of the higher. Aristotle is widely credited with devising the concept of the "great chain of being" that would dominate Western thought until the time of Darwin.

The idea of the "great chain of being," starting with Aristotle's classification system of living organisms, assumes that living organisms can be classified hierarchically, with plants at the bottom, moving through lesser animals, and on to humans at the pinnacle of creation, each becoming progressively more perfect in form. God is the designer of all creatures, and everything has a purpose and a place as ordained by god. In short, the idea of a great chain of being assumes every species of life, including humans, had its fixed place in a hierarchical order.

Scientists Devise Classification Systems

François Bernier

Though Aristotle did not explicitly demarcate the diversity of the human species on this hierarchical scale, later scientists would reinvent the scale, using explicit divisions and classifications of human races. François Bernier (1620–1688) was a French physician. He is credited with devising the first post-Classical comprehensive classification of humans into distinct races.

Bernier's *Nouvelle division de la terre par les différents espèces ou races qui l'habitent* (A New Division of the Earth according to the Different Species or Races of Men Who Inhabit It), published in 1684 in the respected *Journal of the French Academy of Sciences*, seems to be the first racial classification system. The article has been cited as the first scientific presentation of the modern concept of race (Stuurman, 2000).

Bernier's new classification system marked an intellectual break from all former explanations of human diversity in terms of biblical genealogy, geography, climate, souls, and natural law. Bernier's new system attempted to explain the origin of human diversities based on distinct species or races. According to Bernier, his scientific, objective way of classifying human beings into distinct races based on physical characteristics such as skin color, facial type, and bodily shape was more fundamental than the traditional geographical division of the world.

Bernier states,

> The geographers up until this point have divided the world only according to different countries or regions. The remarks which I have made upon men during my long and numerous travels, have given me the idea of dividing it in a different way.... I have remarked that there are four or five species or races of men in particular whose difference is so remarkable that it may be properly made use of as the foundation for a new division of the earth. (Bernier, 1684, pp. 360–361)

Bernier maintained that there are four general classifications of races including the "first" race (the Europeans), the African negroes, the East and Northeast Asian race, and the Lapps (1684, p. 361). Bernier discusses the "first race" before the other races and uses it as a benchmark against which the others are compared.

Bernier does not describe the first race in much detail, but does describe the other races in undesirable terms. For example, he says the Far Easterners have a peculiar turn to their faces and oddly shaped eyes and the Lapps are nasty creatures, have faces similar to bears, and are frightful looking. The Africans have a peculiar sort of hair, "which is not properly hair," and oily skin (1684, p. 362). And, he points out, "The blackness which is peculiar to them, and is not caused by the sun, as many think; for if a black African pair be transported to a cool country; their children are just as black. . . . The cause must be sought for in the peculiar texture of their bodies, or in the seed, or in the blood" (p. 361).

Later in the 18th and 19th centuries, as the idea of separate races grew, so did scientists efforts to classify the human races. The study of differences among human races became a major focus of scientific investigations. And the idea of the "great chain of being" (that there was a hierarchical structure of life from the most fundamental elements to the most perfect) encroached on the concept of race.

Scientists started devising classification systems that included not just physical characteristics, as Bernier did, but also behavioral and psychological traits in their observations assuming the traits were innate and unchangeable. The scientific classification of phenotypic variation became frequently coupled with ideas about innate predispositions of different groups, mostly attributing the desirable features to the white, European race and arranging the other races along a continuum of progressively undesirable attributes.

Carl Linnaeus

Carl Linnaeus (1707–1778) was a Swedish botanist, physician, and zoologist. He is known as the father of modern taxonomy. Linnaeus is credited with being the first scientist to define the human races in modern taxonomic terms and to mix character with anatomy.

In the first edition of his major work *System Naturae,* published in 1735, Linnaeus classified man and monkeys under the same category *Anthropomorpha,* meaning "manlike." Linnaeus observed that monkeys and man had many similarities. He noted that except for speech both species had the same anatomy. So, he classified man and monkeys under the same category. But his colleagues were critical of this classification. If man and monkeys were put at the same level this would mean that man was not spiritually higher in the great chain of being, and that both man and apes were created in the image of God. This idea was unacceptable to his colleagues.

So, in the 10th edition of *Systema Naturae* (1758) Linnaeus introduced new terms, including *Mammalia* and *Primate* that would replace *Anthropomorpha*. Also, Linnaeus gave humans the new full binomial name *Homo sapiens* (Latin: "wise man"). This revised classification received less criticism. Still some of his colleagues were concerned that Linnaeus lowered humans from their superior place to rule over nature to placing humans as part of the animal kingdom.

Linnaeus subdivided the human species, now named *Homo sapiens*, into four and then five separate races that he named the *Europeanus albus* (white European), *Americanus rubescens* (red American), *Asiaticus fuscus* (brown Asian), and *Africanus Niger* (black African). Later he added the fifth race, the *Monstrosus* (abnormal and unknown humans).

Linnaeus proclaimed that each race possessed innate characteristics. For example, the *Europeanus albus* were white-skinned, of gentle character and inventive mind, and bellicose; the *Americanus rubescens* were red-skinned, of stubborn character, and angered easily; the *Asiaticus fuscus* were yellow-skinned, avaricious, and easily distracted; and the *Monstrosus* were wild. These views into what Linnaeus proclaimed as racial character, personality traits, behavior, and intelligence categories were further developed by other scientists in an attempt to devise a science of racial classification (Haller, 1970).

Johann Friedrich Blumenbach

Johann Friedrich Blumenbach (1752–1840) was a German physician, naturalist, physiologist, and anthropologist. Blumenbach expanded on the work of Carl Linnaeus. Blumenbach's central questions, like Linnaeus's, focused on whether humans comprised one or more species and on the varieties of humans. Blumenbach gave credit to Linnaeus for being the first to arrange the diversity of the human species into separate racial varieties. Like Linnaeus, Blumenbach maintained a monogenic view of the origin of the diversity of races. He agreed with Linnaeus and maintained that the races had a single origin. But Blumenbach wanted to devise a more scientific, accurate description of the different races.

Blumenbach proclaimed that Adam and Eve were Caucasian and that all other races came about by degeneration from environmental factors, such as the sun and poor dieting. For instance, Blumenbach claimed that the heat of the tropical sun caused Negroid pigmentation. The tawny color of the Eskimos was caused by the cold wind. Living in towns protected from environmental factors caused the fair skin of the Chinese compared to the other Asian stocks.

Blumenbach believed that this degeneration in skin color could be reversed in proper environmental conditions and that all contemporary forms of man could revert to the original Caucasian race. Blumenbach did not consider his degenerative theory an example of an idea that a particular race is superior to another. Nevertheless, Blumenbach proclaimed that white people set a standard, from which all other races must be viewed as departures.

Blumenbach applied his knowledge of comparative anatomy to the classification of what he called the natural human races, of which he determined there to be five natural races all belonging to a single species. Blumenbach was the first to use facial configuration as well as skin color in his classification of races. His scientific methods for his categorization system included examining skulls, fetuses, hair, anatomical preparations, pictures and drawings, and giving examples of people fitting his five varieties of races.

Blumenbach emphasized his scientific observations of different skulls. He categorized and reduced his extensive skull collection to five main racial varieties. In the third edition of his book *The Natural Varieties of Mankind*, Blumenbach lists the primary five races that he devised and labeled: Caucasians, Mongolians, Ethiopians, Americans, and Malays.

Surprisingly, as Bhopal points out (2007), although Blumenbach mentions that environment influenced skull shape, Blumenbach drew definite conclusions from his study of skulls. Blumenbach wrote,

The meaning and use of this will easily be seen by an examination of plate III, which represents, by way of specimen, three skulls disposed in the order mentioned. The middle one (2) is a very symmetrical and beautiful one of a Georgian female; on either side are two skulls differing from it in the most opposite way. The one elongated in front, and as it were keeled, is that of an Ethiopian female of Guinea (3); the other dilated outwardly toward the sides, and as it were flattened, is that of a Reindeer Tungus (2). In the first, the margin of the orbits, the beautifully narrowed malar bones, and the mandibles themselves under the bones, are concealed by the periphery of the moderately expanded forehead; in the second, the maxillary bones are compressed laterally, and project; and in the third, the malar bones, placed in nearly the same horizontal plane with the little bones of the nose and the glabella, project enormously, and rise on each side. (as cited in Bhopal, 2007)

Though Blumenbach's research retained a scientific stance based on his examination of skulls, his interpretation of the data went beyond the evidence. His conclusion that the Caucasian skull of a white Georgian female was the "most handsome and becoming" is evidence of an "interpreter effect."

While interpretation of data is part of any research process, it is difficult to state the rules for accurate interpretation of data. However, inconsistency of possible interpretations that can be offered in explanation of the same data, in this case determining which skull is the most beautiful, imply that a researcher 's interpretation of the data may turn out to be incorrect.

Blumenbach (1825) interpreted his data with the firm conviction that white people set a standard of beauty from which all the other races should be viewed as degenerate departures: "The Caucasian must, on every physiological principle, be considered as the primary or intermediate of these five principal Races. The two extremes into which it has deviated, are on the one hand the Mongolian, on the other the Ethiopian [African blacks]" (as cited in Gould, 1981, p. 38).

Blumenbach's work was a turning point in the history of the study of racial differences. His attempt to devise a scientific description of the verities of racial differences based on his skull collection was a standard model for other scientists in the field of craniometry. The Blumenbach Skull Collection can still be viewed at the Centre of Anatomy at the University of the Medical Centre in Göttingen, Germany.

Samuel George Morton

Samuel George Morton (1799–1851) was an American physician and natural scientist. He is known as the father of American physical anthropology. Like Blumenbach, Morton collected and studied skulls in an attempt to explain the origin of racial differences. Morton expanded on Blumenbach's study of skulls and went beyond just describing the skulls.

Instead, Morton decided to measure the cranial cavity, or intracranial space, which is the space formed inside the skull.

The brain occupies the cranial cavity. So, Morton reasoned that if he measured the cranial cavity it would provide him with an accurate measure of the brain it once contained. He filled the carnal cavity with mustard seed, and poured the seed back into a cylinder and then read the skull's volume in cubic inches. But later he was dissatisfied with using mustard seed because they were too light and yielded inconsistent results. The measurements of the skull capacity would vary when he measured it with mustard seeds. So, Morton changed methods, used one-eighth-inch-diameter lead shot to get readings that are more reliable, and was pleased with his reliable measurements.

Morton explains his measurement procedure and states,

These measurements have been made by the process invented by my friend Mr. J. S. Phillips, and described in my Crania Americana, p. 253, merely substituting leaden shot, one-eighth of an inch in diameter, in place of the white mustard-seed originally used. I thus obtain the *absolute capacity of the cranium, or bulk of the brain in cubic inches*; . . . I have restricted it, at least for the purpose of any inferential conclusions, to the crania of persons of sixteen years of age and upwards, at which period the brain is believed to possess the adult size. Under this age, the capacity-measurement has only been resorted to for the purpose of collateral comparison; nor can I avoid expressing my satisfaction at the singular accuracy of this method, since a skull of an hundred cubic inches, if measured any number of times with reasonable care, will not vary a single cubic inch. (1849, p. 1)

Morton ended up measuring the skull capacity of 623 human skulls "with a view to ascertain the relative size of the brain in various races and families of Man" (1849, p. 1). Morton took great pains to obtain accurate measurements and to gather his data objectively.

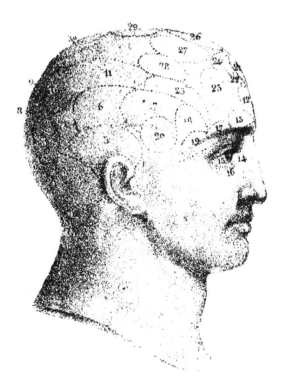

Figure 1.3 Side profile

Morton states,

> All these measurements have been made with my own hands. I at one time employed a person to assist me; but having detected some-errors in his measurements, I have been at the pains to revise all that part of the series that had not been previously measured by myself. I can now, therefore, vouch for the accuracy of these multitudinous data, which I cannot but regard as a novel and important contribution to Ethnological science. (1849, p. 1)

Morton gathered these data to support his hypothesis that skull volume indicated high intellectual capacity whereas a small skull indicated a small brain and decreased intellectual capacity. Morton then set out to formulate a systematic ranking of human races according to mental capacity. Morton published his findings in several books between 1839 and 1849.

In each book, Morton provided a table summarizing his results for the average skull volumes arranged by race. Morton's summary tables showed that the Caucasians had the biggest brains, averaging 87 cubic inches; Indians were in the middle, with an average of 82 cubic inches; and Negroes had the smallest brains, with an average of 78 cubic inches (Morton, 1839).

Morton interpreted his data claiming that it showed "the whites as the most intelligent race, the American Indian to be less intelligent, the Hindus to be more inferior still, and the negro to be the stupidest of the lot" (Bates, 1995, p. 6). Unlike his concern for the reliability of his measurements, Morton was unconcerned with the validity of his conclusions. He did not consider alternative hypotheses nor did he question whether his data actually measured the construct "intelligence."

Instead, Morton used his data to claim each race had a separate origin and that the descending order of intelligence he discerned, placing Caucasians at the top and Negroes at the lowest point (with the other racial groups in the middle), proved that each race was created separately with irrevocable characteristics. Morton claimed the skulls of each race proved the races were so different that the "creator" from the start had created each race and put them in separate homelands to reside.

Morton argued against the Bible's single creation story and the monogenic theory of human origins that posits a common descent for all human races. Instead, Morton supported the theory of polygenism that is opposite to the idea of a single origin of humanity. Polygenism is a theory of human origins that posits that humans are different races from different biological origins.

From his measurements of skulls and study of mummies, Morton concluded that Caucasians and Negroes were already distinct three thousand years ago. Since the Bible indicated that Noah's Ark had washed up on Mount Ararat only a thousand years before this, Morton claimed that Noah's sons could not possibly account for every race on earth. Morton maintained that humans belonged to different races and had evolved separately in different continents and shared no common ancestor. Morton's followers carried his ideas further. They tried to collect more "scientific" evidence to prove there are innate differences between races.

Robert Bean

Robert Bean (1874–1944) was an American physician and professor of anatomy and ethnologist. He expanded on Morton's work by measuring not just skull capacity as Morton did, but rather by measuring the actual brain.
Bean states,

> From time to time in the past hundred years attempts have been made to determine the distinctive points of difference between the Caucasian and the Negro brain. While differences in skull capacity, in brain weight and size—especially of

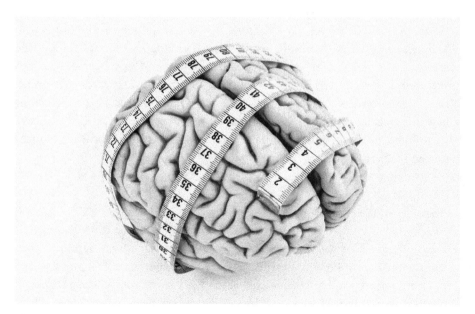

Figure 1.4 Brain with measuring tape around it

the frontal lobes—or in the gyri have been demonstrated by Gratiolet, Tiedemann, Broca, Manouvrier, Peacock, Marshall, Parker, and others,—more recently Waldeyer in Germany and by Elliott Smith in Egypt,—yet no exact measurements of the brain, such as we have of the skull, are to be found. (1906, p. 353)

So, Bean set out to measure the brains of black and white people. Bean obtained most of his brain specimens from the Anatomical Laboratory and the Pathological Department at Johns Hopkins University. Bean obtained "one hundred and fifty-two, of which one hundred and three are from American Negroes and forty-nine are from American Caucasians" (1906, p. 354).

Following a basic belief of craniometry, that higher mental functions reside in the front of the brain and sensorimotor capacities toward the rear, Bean reasoned that he might rank races by the relative sizes of parts within the corpus callosum. Therefore, Bean measured the length of the genu, the front part of the corpus callosum, and compared it with the length of the splenium, the back part.

He plotted genu versus splenium and obtained virtually complete separation between black and white brains. Whites had a relatively large genu compared to blacks. Hence, Bean concluded that whites have more brain up front in the seat of intelligence, and therefore blacks were intellectually inferior to whites. Also, Bean claimed that within each race, women had a smaller genu than men and hence were intellectually inferior.

Bean published his results in a series of scientific papers. "Some Racial Peculiarities of the Negro Brain" is the title of one paper he published in the *American Journal of Anatomy* in 1906. In this paper, Bean provides his copious detailed measurements of the brains of blacks and whites to demonstrate that the genu is smaller in blacks than in whites. Besides, his conclusions concerning racial intelligence, Bean stated that the differences in brain size also pointed to the origins of innate personality and behavioral differences between blacks and whites.

Bean states,

The relative differences found in the association centers of the two races is suggestive in relation to the known characteristics of the two. . . . The Caucasian is subjective, the Negro objective. The Caucasian-more particularly the Anglo-Saxon, which was derived from the Primitives of Europe, is dominant and domineering, and possessed primarily with determination, will power, self-control, self-government, and all the attributes of the subjective self, with a high development of the ethical aesthetic faculties. The Negro is in direct contrast by reason of a certain lack of these powers, and a great development of the objective qualities. The Negro is primarily affectionate, immensely emotional, then sensual and under stimulation passionate. There is love of ostentation, of outward show, of approbation; there is love of music, and capacity for melodious articulation; there is undeveloped artistic power and taste—Negroes make good artisans, handicraftsmen—and there is instability of character incident to lack of self-control, especially in connection with the sexual relation; and there is lack of *oldentation,* or recognition of position and condition of self and environment, evidenced by a peculiar bumptiousness, so called, that is particularly noticeable. (1906, p. 379)

Bean's work was not restricted to only academic journals. He was popular in the public as well. In 1907, a year after the publication of "Some Racial Peculiarities of the Negro Brain," an editorial in *American Medicine* discussed the implications of Bean's findings for a democratic society:

The editorial states "the anatomical basis for the complete failure of the negro schools to impart the higher studies—the brain cannot comprehend them any more than a horse can understand the rule of three . . . [and] leaders in all political parties now acknowledge the error of human equality. . . . It may be practicable to rectify the error and remove a menace to our prosperity—a large electorate without brains." (Cited in Gould, 2007, p. 497)

In addition to measuring the brains of blacks and whites and relating brain size to intelligence and personality characteristics, Bean was also interested in racial/religious classifications based on anatomical features such as ears, nose shape, facial muscles, and so forth. He measured anatomical parts then published the copious details, and sometimes pictures. For example, in 1913 he published an article titled "The Nose of the Jew and Quadratus Labii Superioris" (a facial muscle) in the reputable journal *The Anatomical Record.*

In the article, Bean states, "The quadratus muscle is said to produce expressions of the face that indicate a great variety of emotions, all of which may be grouped as related to indignation. It is essentially the muscle of disgust, contempt, and disdain, which lead to scorn, acknowledging guilt" (1913, p. 48). "The expression of the Jew is that which would result from very strong contraction of the quadratus muscle. . . . it is more pronounced on Jews than on other peoples, and that it is a Jewish feature cannot be doubted" (p. 49). Bean did not offer an explanation for the validity of his interpretation that the Jew harbored disgust, contempt, disdain, and guilt.

By the time Bean died in 1944, he had the most copious collection of recorded measurements of anatomical parts of any scientist.

The Theory of Evolution: On the Origin of Species and Descent of Man and Selection in Relation to Sex

Charles Darwin (1809–1882) was an English naturalist and geologist. He is famous for his contributions to the theory of evolution. Darwin published his book *On the Origin of Species* in 1859. This book is considered as the foundation of evolutionary biology. In the book, Darwin introduced the theory that populations evolve over generations by a process of natural selection. He included evidence he got on his travels in the 1830s and later findings from his research and experimentation.

Darwin presented empirical evidence to support his theory that the origin of the diversities of life resulted from a common descent by a branching pattern of evolution. He argued that all species of life descended over time from a common ancestor.

Figure 1.5 Darwin (could not find the original image)

Darwin introduced the theory that the branching pattern of evolution ensued from natural selection. (Alfred Russell Wallace was also a British naturalist who independently conceived of the theory of evolution through natural selection. Russell's paper titled "On the Tendency of Varieties to Depart Indefinitely from the Original Type" was jointly published with Darwin's a year before Darwin published his book *On the Origin of the Species*.)

In *On the Origin of Species*, Darwin includes just one illustration—an abstract diagram of a Tree of Life, with no names given to species. Darwin uses the image of a Tree of Life to explain the concept of natural section, common descent, and the branching pattern of evolution. In his book, Darwin explains his reasons for including the image of the tree of life:

> The affinities of all the beings of the same class have sometimes been represented by a great tree. I believe this simile largely speaks the truth. The green and budding twigs may represent existing species; and those produced during each former year may represent the long succession of extinct species. At each period of growth all the growing twigs have tried to branch out on all sides, and to overtop and kill the surrounding twigs and branches, in the same manner as species and groups of species have tried to overmaster other species in the great battle for life. . . . As buds give rise by growth to fresh buds, and these, if vigorous, branch out and overtop on all sides many a feebler branch, so by generation I believe it has been with the great Tree of Life, which fills with its dead and broken branches the crust of the earth, and covers the surface with its ever branching and beautiful ramifications. (1859, pp. 129–130)

Like the scientists before him, Darwin was interested in explaining the origin of diversities of living beings and devising a classification system. However, unlike his predecessors (and unlike the "great chain of being" concept that his predecessors endorsed) Darwin devised a new concept and classification system that was relational and nonhierarchical.

Fundamental to Darwin's concept of natural selection is the idea of change by common descent. This suggests, according to Darwin, that all living organisms are related to each other. Darwin maintained that for any two species, if we search back far enough, we would find that all are descended from a common ancestor. This is a radically different view from Aristotle's concept of the "great chain of being," in which each species and living thing is formed individually with its own purpose and hierarchical place in nature.

No one before Darwin had ever proposed the image of a tree with interconnected branches and a nameless species to understand the origin of the diversities of living beings. In his notebooks, when he first set out to formulate his theory, Darwin explains how he devised his nonhierarchical classification system.

In 1838 in one his early notebooks, Darwin explains the classification system he was looking for: "We now know what is the natural arrangement," he declared in his "C" notebook, "it is the classification of relationship, latter word meaning descent" (Darwin, 1838, cited in Barrett, Gautrey, Herbert, Kohn, and Smith, 1987, p. 286). Thus, Darwin invoked the Tree of Life image to help his readers envision the interconnected history and relationships of the diversities of all living beings.

In truth, Darwin was critical of his colleagues' attempts to classify humans according to a hierarchical racial classification system. In *Descent of Man and Selection in Relation to Sex* (1871), Darwin states that such attempts were futile. He writes,

> But the most weighty of all the arguments against treating the races of man as distinct species is that they graduate into each other, independently in many case, as far as we can judge, of their having intercrossed. Man has been studied more carefully than any other animal, and yet there is the greatest possible diversity amongst capable judges whether he should be classed as a single species or race, or as two (Virey), as three (Jacquinot), as four (Kant), five (Blumenbach), six (Buffon), seven (Hunter), eight (Agassiz), eleven (Pickering), fifteen (Bory St. Vincent), sixteen (Desmoulins), twenty-two (Morton), sixty (Crawfurd), or as sixty-three, according to Burke. This diversity of judgment does not prove that the races ought not to be ranked as species, but it shows that they graduate into each other, and that it is hardly possible to discover clear distinctive characters between them. (1871, p. 147)

The publication of Darwin's work occurred within the fervent debates between advocates of monogeny, who as mentioned before, held that all races came from a common ancestor, and advocates of polygeny, who held that the races were separately created. According to Darwin's biographers (Desmond & Moore, 2009), Darwin had come from a family with strong abolitionist ties and Darwin was opposed to slavery. His biographers argue that Darwin's writings on evolution were influenced not only by his abolitionist tendencies but also by his belief that nonwhite races were equal in regard to their intellectual ability as white races, a belief that had been strongly disputed by polygenists and scientists.

By the late 1860s, however, Darwin's theory of evolution had been thought to be compatible with polygeny theory. So, Darwin decided to publish the

Descent of Man and Selection in Relation to Sex in 1871 in a further attempt to discredit polygenism and to end the debate between polygenists and monogenists conclusively. Darwin also attempted to disprove other hypotheses on racial difference that had persisted since the time of ancient Greece, for example, that differences in skin color and body constitution occurred because of differences in geography and climate.

Darwin states,

> The question whether mankind consists of one or several species has of late years been such discussed by anthropologists, who are divided into the two schools of monogenists and polygenists. Those who do not admit the principle of evolution must look at the species as separate creations, or as in some manner as distinct entities; and they must decide what forms of man they will consider as species by the analogy of the method commonly pursued in ranking other organic beings as species. But it is a hapless endeavor to decide this point. . . . Those naturalists, on the other hand, who admit the principle of evolution, and this is now admitted by the majority of rising men, will feel no doubt that all the races of man are descended from a single primitive stock; whether or nor they may think fit to designate the race as distinct species, for the sake of expressing their amount of difference. (1871, p. 148)

Darwin concluded that the biological similarities between the different races were too great for the polygenist thesis to be plausible. So, he sought to demonstrate that the physical characteristics that were being used to define race for centuries (e.g., skin color and facial features were superficial and had no utility for survival (1871, p. 166). According to Darwin, any characteristic that did not have survival value could not have been naturally selected. Darwin devised another hypothesis for the development and persistence of these characteristics. The mechanism Darwin developed is known as "sexual selection."

Briefly, Darwin defined sexual selection as the struggle between individuals of one sex, generally the males, for the possession of the other sex. According to Darwin sexual selection consisted of two types, the physical struggle for a mate, and the preference for some color or another, typically by females of a given species. Darwin asserted that the differing human races, insofar as race was conceived phenotypically, had arbitrary standards of ideal beauty and that these standards reflected physical characteristics sought in mates.

In sum, generally speaking, Darwin's view of what race was and how it originated in the human species are ascribed to his two claims: that all human beings share a single, common ancestor, and that phenotypic racial differences are superficially selected via sexual selection and have no survival value. Given these two claims, Darwin attempted to establish monogenism as the dominant paradigm for racial origin, and to invalidate the views of his predecessors including the Greek philosophers Hippocrates, Socrates, Plato, and Aristotle and scientists such as Bernier, Linnaeus, Blumenbach, Morton, and Bean (as described previously).

It is important to highlight here that Darwin's nonhierarchical, relational classification system took into account differences. Darwin states,

> There is, however, no doubt that the various races, when carefully compared and measured, differ much from each other—as in the texture of hair, the relative proportions of all parts of the body, the capacity of the lungs, the form and capacity of the skull, and even the convolutions of the brain. But it would be an endless task to specify the numerous points of difference. The races differ also in constitution, in acclimatization, and in liability to certain diseases. Their mental characteristics are likewise very distinct; chiefly as it would appear in their emotion, but partly in their intellectual faculties. (1871, pp. 141–142)

However, although Darwin mentions there are many differences between humans, he emphasizes that the differences do not add up to the idea of distinct species or races. He states,

> the existing races of men differ in many respects, as in color, hair, shape of skull, proportions of body, etc., yet, if their whole structure be taken into consideration, they are found to resemble each other closely in multitude of points. Many of these are so unimportant or of so singular a nature that it is extremely improbable that they should have been independently acquired by aboriginally distinct species or races. (1871, p. 150)

The major point Darwin makes throughout his work is that his intention, unlike his predecessors, is not to classify the differences between the so-called races; but rather "to inquire what is the value of the differences between them under a classificatory point of view, and how they have originated" (1871, p. 140). Darwin concluded that the differences between people, from an evolutionary viewpoint, were unimportant and had no inherent value. Despite Darwin's conclusion, evolutionary theory did not put an end to the scientific idea of a hierarchical natural classification system that supposedly reflected inborn differences and measures of value between people.

The Use of Classification Systems

Science does not exist in a social vacuum. Ideas advanced by scientists regularly make their way into the social consciousness of a nation. One such "scientific" idea that made its way into the consciousness of many nations, including the United Kingdom, the United States, Canada, and South American, Asian, and European nations was the idea of "eugenics." The idea was used to promote laws and social policies to "improve" human populations by stopping the reproduction of supposedly inferior genes (Nourse, 2016).

The word "eugenics" comes from the Greek word *eugenes*, meaning "well born," and from *genos*, meaning "race, stock, kin." The eugenic scientific movement maintained that some set of humans were genetically superior to other humans. Supporters of the eugenic movement advocated improving human genetic traits by promoting higher rates of sexual reproduction for people with superior traits (positive eugenics) and reducing rates of sexual reproduction for people with inferior trait by sterilization (negative eugenics).

Francis Galton (1822–1911) was an English statistician, psychologist, and sociologist. He was the first to apply statistical methods to the study of human differences and inheritance of intelligence. Galton is credited with developing the ideas for a scientific "eugenic" program using statistical methods.

After reading *Origin of Species*, Galton built on Darwin's ideas. Galton maintained that the mechanism of natural selection was potentially blocked by human society. Galton reasoned since many human societies protected the underprivileged and weak, those societies were at odds with the natural selection responsible for extinction of the weakest; and only by changing these social policies could society be saved from a "reversion towards mediocrity," a phrase he first coined in statistics, which we more charitably refer to today as "regression toward the mean."

In his book *Inquiries into Human Faculty and Its Development* (1883, pp. 24–25), Galton explains that the intention of his work "is to touch on various topics more or less connected with the cultivation of race, or, as we might call it, with 'eugenic' [and here Galton adds a footnote that reads: "That is, with questions bearing on what is termed in Greek *eugnes*, namely, good in stock, hereditarily endowed with noble qualities . . . "], questions, and to present the results of my own separate investigations."

Galton then devises a method of how to improve the human stock so that, paraphrasing Galton, "more suitable races or strains of blood have a better chance of prevailing speedily over the less suitable than they otherwise would have had." Galton concluded that it was possible to produce a "highly gifted race of men" by the process of selective breeding and by discouraging the re-production of "undesirables." Therefore, Galton actively began to promote eu-genics and gained important followers.

The United States eugenics movement of the 19th and 20th century was rooted in the ideas of Galton. Followers of the eugenic movement in the United States were mostly university-trained biologists and doctors affiliated with Harvard, Princeton, Columbia, Stanford, and the Museum of Natural History. Eugenic research programs received extensive funding from foundations to advance their research goal to "improve human populations by halting the reproduction of lesser genes." Also, the eugenics research program influenced governmental social policy and used science to expand the power of the state over social issues.

Ultimately, in the United States the eugenics program of research led to the enforced sterilization of thousands of human beings, immigration restrictions, marriage prohibitions, and segregation policies, as primary methods of "improving" the human population." In the United States, the Supreme Court's 1927 *Buck v. Bell* ruling made sterilization of "undesirable" citizens the law of the land. Undesirable citizens deemed unfit to reproduce included people with mental or physical disabilities, people who scored in the low ranges intelligence tests, criminals and deviants, and members of disfavored minority racial and ethnic groups (Cohen, 2016).

After the eugenics movement was well established in the United States, it spread to Germany. The eugenics research in Germany before and during the Nazi period was similar to that in the United States. However, its im-portance rose under Adolf Hitler's leadership. Briefly, the eugenic programs in Germany were designed to implement Nazi racial policies. The Nazis declared that the Nordics or Aryans (now known as the Germanic peoples) were superior in an assumed racial hierarchy to all other races. The actual legal policy that was implemented by the Nazi government resulted in the Aryan certificate. The law required all German citizens to get an official Aryan certificate that required the citizen to trace his or her lineage through baptism, birth certificates, or certified proof that all grandparents were of "Aryan descent."

German citizens including Jews and Gypsies, and some Slavs, Poles, Serbs, and later Russians were defined by Nazi policy as being non-Aryan and *Untermeschen* or "subhuman and inferior people." These subhuman people were considered a danger to the Aryan (Germanic) *Übermenschen* or master race. So to improve the German population it was deemed best to reduce the number of inferior, subhuman people by mass murder, enslavement, starva-tion, expulsion, or extermination.

Also, other people targeted for destruction under Nazi eugenics policies were a group categorized as *Lebensunwertes Leben* "life unworthy of life." Most of these people were living in private and state-operated institutions, including prisoners, degenerates, dissidents, people with congenital cognitive and physical disabilities (including feebleminded, epileptic, schizophrenic, manic-depressive, cerebral palsy, muscular dystrophy, deaf, blind) homosexuals, idle, insane, and the weak. These people were sterilized or euthanized by the Nazi state.

It is an understatement to say that the Nazi eugenic programs failed at improving the superiority of some human race. Rather the eugenic programs resulted in violence, mass destruction, and untold sufferings.

Changed Focus on the Origin of Diversities: From Biology to Culture

In the decades following the collapse of the Nazi regime, countries gradually ended eugenic national policies. The violence of the Nazi rule and World War II changed the whole focus and discussion of the origin of the diversity of races and ethnicities. The racial policies implemented during the Nazi regime created a popular moral change against racial hierarchies.

In 1945, partly as a response to the Nazi genocide and the rise of mass democracy, the United Nations Educational, Science and Cultural Organization (UNESCO) was formed and released several statements on the origins of diversities.

The UNESCO 1945 constitution declared: "That since wars begin in the minds of men, it is in the minds of men that the defenses of peace must be constructed; That ignorance of each other's ways and lives has been a common cause, throughout the history of mankind, of that suspicion and mistrust between the peoples of the world through which their differences have all too often broken into war" (UNESCO Constitution, 1945).

Between 1950 and 1978, UNESCO issued five statements on the origin of diversities. The first statement included a rejection of a scientific basis for theories of racial hierarchies and proclaimed, "all men belong to the same species" (UNESCO, Paris, July 1950). Also, the statement argued that there was no scientific basis for believing that there are any innate differences in intellectual, psychological, or emotional potential among races. The statement, however, did not reject the idea of a biological basis to racial categories. It defined the concept of race in terms of a population defined by certain anatomical and physiological characteristics as being divergent from other populations.

The statement pointed out that people use the term "race" incorrectly:

> To most people, a race is any group of people whom they choose to describe as
> a race. Thus, many national, religious, geographic, linguistic or cultural groups
> have, in such loose usage, been called "race," when obviously Americans are not a
> race, nor are Englishmen, nor Frenchmen, nor any other national group. Catholics,
> Protestants, Moslems, and Jews are not races, nor are groups who speak English
> or any other language thereby definable as a race; people who live in Iceland or
> England or India are not races; nor are people who are culturally Turkish or Chinese
> or the like thereby describable as races. National, religious, geographic, linguistic
> and cultural groups do not necessarily coincide with racial groups: and the cultural
> traits of such groups have no demonstrated genetic connection with racial traits.
> Because serious errors of this kind are habitually committed when the term "race"
> is used in popular parlance, it would be better when speaking of human races to
> drop the term "race" altogether and speak of ethnic groups. (UNESCO, Paris,
> July 1950)

The first UNESCO statement proved to be controversial. Biologists and physical anthropologists criticized the statement for confusing the "biological fact" and the concept of race as a social phenomenon. They declined to acknowledge as a proved fact that there are no mental differences between racial groups. For example, the famous English statistician and biologist Ronald Fisher (who was a member of the Eugenics Society at Cambridge) opposed the statement, believing that evidence and everyday experience showed that human groups differed in their innate capacity for intellectual and emotional development (UNESCO, 1952).

In response to the criticisms, UNESCO formed a new committee and in 1951 published a revised statement. The second statement focused on race as a "biological heuristic" and maintained that equality of opportunity and equality in law did not depend on the view that human beings are in fact equal in endowment.

Later in 1964, a new commission was formed to draft yet a third statement. This statement broke more clearly with the idea that there are endowed genetic differences between races. The statement proclaimed, "The peoples of the world today appear to possess equal biological potentialities for attaining any civilization level. Differences in the achievements of different peoples must be attributed solely to their cultural history" (UNESCO, 1965).

The 1950, 1951, and 1964 statements focused on dismissing the scientific foundations for racial categories. However, the statements did not consider other factors contributing to racial differences. So, to this end, in 1967, a new committee was assembled. It included representatives of the social sciences who were asked to prepare a statement addressing the social aspects of the problem.

The new statement asserted, "The human problems arising from so-called 'race' relations are social in origin rather than biological" (UNESCO, 1969).

The statement was the first to give a definition of racism. It stated "A basic problem is racism, namely, antisocial beliefs and acts which are based on the fallacy that discriminatory intergroup relations are justifiable on biological grounds" (UNESCO, 1967).

In 1978, the general assembly of the UNESCO considered the four previous statements and published a final collective statement titled, "Declaration on Race and Racial Prejudice." It stated that all human beings belonged to a single species, that the division of the species into "races" is arbitrary and does not imply a hierarchy, that all peoples of the world possess equal faculties for attaining the highest level in intellectual development, and that the

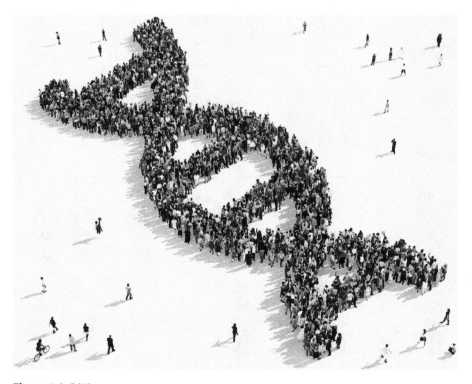

Figure 1.6 DNA

differences between peoples are "entirely attributable to geographical, histor-ical, political, economic, social and cultural factors" (UNESCO, 1979). The statement declared that human problems arising from so-called race relations are social in origin rather than biological.

Today, the question of whether racial and ethnic differences are biological or cultural is still debated. But the general scientific consensus is that race is a social concept, not a scientific one.

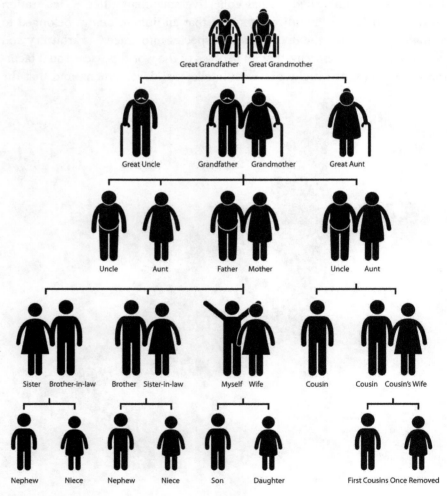

Figure 1.7 Family tree

Although research into the structure and sequence of the human genome is still in its infancy, geneticists have compiled an outline of human genomic history, called the "Out of Africa" hypothesis.

By this theory, modern *Homo sapiens* originated in Africa 200,000 to 100,000 years ago at some point a relatively small number of them, about 10,000 or so, began migrating into the Middle East, Europe, and Asia and across the Bering land mass into the Americas.

So, scientists have concluded that people everywhere descended from a single migration of early humans from Africa. Because of that, humans are strikingly homogeneous, differing from one another only once in a thousand subunits of the genome. Because all humans descended from a single family tree, on average any two people share 99.9% of their genomes.

The fraction of sequence difference between any two genomes shows how far back in time they had a common ancestor. The chief conclusion of genetic studies is the single story of evolution and evidence in the genetic structures that all humans are admixed (Chakravarti, 2015, p. 6).

However, despite the consensus among scientists that the origins of diversities are not reflected on a biological or genetic level the fact remains people are attuned to recognizing differences. And people are attuned to identifying with each other based on similarities, such as a common language, or cultural or religious or national experiences. People are social beings.

Hence, if our goal is to undermine the idea that one group is superior to another group it is insufficient to show its biological fallacies. We need to understand the social, psychological subconscious factors that explain our propensity to connect to a group. So, we turn now to consider the development of the self.

2
The Self

Development of the Self in the Womb

The self develops in a set way (as with intellectual development), by a series of stages merging one into another. The overture to the development of the self plays out in the mother's womb. Developmental psychologists and researchers concur that the self is shaped to a degree during development in the womb. Analyses of fetal behaviors in healthy populations show that the process of functional development starts in the prenatal period with behaviors emerging and developing continuously over gestation and childhood.

Simultaneously, the central nervous system that will eventually form the foundation for the child's mental and physical capacities is taking root. During each minute in the womb, the brain of the infant-to-be gains tens of thousands of new cells. By the time the fetus is 20 weeks old, the nervous system is mature enough to make the developing baby sensitive to touch, pain, and change in temperature. The brain is clearly "turned on" and responsive to the environment.

Researchers have been interested in fetal development since the late 1800s. Systematic studies, however, only started by the early 1980s after fetal physiological monitoring technology and inventions in ultrasound technology were created, offering new prospects for the study of fetal behavior (Kisilevsky & Low, 1998).

With the use of new technology, it is known that from about 30 weeks of gestational age fetuses react to auditory stimulation. They show cardiac and body movement responses to white noises (Querleu, Renard, Versyp, Paris-Delrue, & Crepin, 1988). Also, by the third trimester human fetuses are actively reacting and retaining information about specific auditory stimuli detectable from the uterine environment and actively responding to these stimuli. They are not passive and neutral listeners, as previously thought (Hepper, 1988; Mennella & Beauchamp, 1999; Molina., & Molina, 1995; Pedersen & Blass, 1982; Smotherman, 1982; Smotherman & Robinson, 1987).

The findings from studies using monitoring technology suggest that auditory stimuli are an important developmental link, delivering clues from the

The Science of Diversity. Mona Sue Weissmark, Oxford University Press (2020). © Oxford University Press.
DOI: 10.1093/oso/9780190686345.001.0001

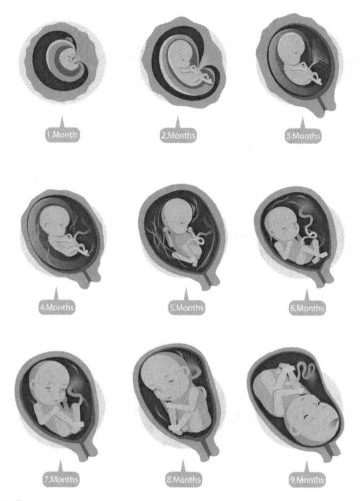

Figure 2.1 Fetus

outside world to the womb. The mother's voice is conducted through bone and tissue to create a unique reverberation that differs from other voices entering the amniotic wall, and is reported to be the most intense acoustical signal measured in the amniotic environment (Ferrari et al., 2016).

Studies on fetal voice recognition show that fetuses can distinguish their own mother's voices from stranger's voices. It is important in developmental research to determine whether such findings are culturally based or universal and applicable to all cultures. So, studies on fetal voice recognition have been conducted in Canada and China (because of the vast differences between Canadian and Chinese culture), and the studies have yielded similar results. The heart rates of both Chinese fetuses and Canadian fetuses increased in response to their mother's voices and decreased in response to stranger's voices (Kisilevsky et al., 2003).

Researchers have pointed out that the deceleration of the heart rate is "an attention mechanism." The heartbeat among fetuses that heard an unfamiliar voice slowed down because they were paying close attention to a voice they did not recognize. In other words, they were trying to figure out who was talking. The fact that the heartbeat changed in both cases—up for the mother's voice down for a stranger's voice—shows the fetuses "noticed both voices," and could tell one from the other (Kisilevsky et al., 2003).

The findings of differential physiological reactions in response to a familiar versus a novel voice provide evidence that in utero experiences shape the developing brain. It suggests that while still in the womb, fetuses' brains are learning and remembering their mother's voice and can distinguish it from other voices. It shows that even before birth humans can recognize their mother's voice and distinguish it from other voices. Furthermore, according to researchers, the findings lend support to the "epigenetic" model of the self,

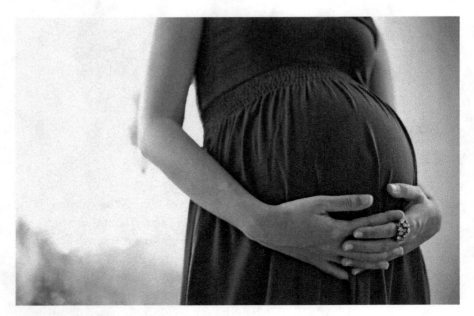

Figure 2.2 Pregnant woman

which presumes an interaction between fetal neural development and social experiences (Kisilevsky et al., 2003).

The theory of epigenetics is relevant here to our discussion of the development of the self. Briefly, "epigenetics" means "above genetics" and Conrad Waddington originally conceived it. Waddington (1905–1975) was a British developmental biologist, paleontologist, geneticist, embryologist, and philosopher. He laid the foundations for systems biology, epigenetics, and evolutionary developmental biology.

In 1956, Waddington published a paper in the journal *Evolution* in which he demonstrated the inheritance of a characteristic acquired in a population in response to an environmental experience. Waddington regarded himself as a Darwinist because Darwin also, in *The Origin of Species*, included the inheritance of acquired characteristics. Waddington proposed an evolutionary process, "genetic assimilation" as a Darwinian mechanism that allows certain acquired characteristic to become heritable.

Waddington maintained that cells acquired their identities just as humans do—by letting nurture (the environment and experiences) change nature (genes).
"For that to happen, Waddington concluded, an additional layer of information must exist within a cell—a layer that hovered, ghostlike, above the genome. This layer would carry the "memory" of the cell, recording its past and establishing its future, marking its identity and its destiny but permitting that identity to be changed, if needed. Waddington termed the phenomenon '*epi*genetics'—'above genetics'" (Mukherjee, 2016, pp. 4–5).

As Mukherjee (2016) points out, Waddington had left-wing political leanings. He was an ardent anti-Nazi and Marxist. So more than a biological interest in epigenetic theory may have motivated him. "The Nazis had turned a belief in absolute genetic immutability ("a Jew is a Jew") into a state-mandated program of sterilization and mass murder. By affirming the plasticity of nature ("everyone can be anyone")," Waddington hoped to eliminate the notion of innate distinctions and allow for the possibility of change (Mukherjee, 2016, p. 5). Thus, according to Waddington, the genome is not a passive blueprint, but rather the selective activation or repression of a gene that allows an individual cell to acquire its identity and to perform its function.

The findings on the effects of experience on fetal voice recognition fit Waddington's epigenetic theory because they demonstrate that fetal voice discrimination is influenced by in utero experiences. The fetal experience of hearing the mother's voice affects the developing nervous system; in turn, new synaptic connections are formed in response to the events providing the

Figure 2.3 Human and DNA

information to be stored. Such experience-dependent learning is open to later changes.

According to researchers, experience plays a critical role in the differential behavior observed in human fetuses because the same voices were presented to both groups of fetuses, the only difference being the familiarity of their mother's voice and the novelty of the stranger's voice. Thus, fetuses learn to recognize their mother's voice during repeated exposure. This suggests that neurological modifications based on hearing their mother's voice takes place during fetal development. Also, the researchers contend, the differences in heart rate exhibited in response to the familiar maternal voices versus the stranger's voices suggest that memory and learning has taken place, which in turn modifies the synaptic connections (Kisilevsky et al., p. 223).

In addition to the effects of experience on fetal voice recognition, other studies have demonstrated that near-term fetuses not only recognize their mother's voices but also change their behaviors in response to their mother's voices. Studies have demonstrated that near-term fetuses displayed a behavioral orienting response to their mothers reading aloud, shown by a reduction in motor activity after she began reading. And other studies have demonstrated that fetuses displayed more arm, head, and mouth movements when the mother touched her abdomen (Marx & Nagy, 2015).

Additionally, other studies have focused on the detailed behavioral analysis of fetuses' mouth movements in response to their mother's speech. Because newborns at birth can respond with matched behaviors to the social signals produced by their mothers, the researchers hypothesized that such responses could possibly emerge in the prenatal period.

So, by means of a two-dimensional ultrasonography, researchers assessed whether fetuses at 25 weeks of gestation, showed a congruent mouth motor response to maternal acoustic stimulations. Mothers were asked to provide different stimuli, each characterized by a different acoustic output (e.g., chewing, yawning, and nursery rhymes). The researchers then recorded the behavioral responses of the fetuses.

The findings showed that when mothers sang a nursery rhyme, the fetuses significantly increased mouth openings. Other stimuli provided by the mother did not produce significant changes in the fetuses' behaviors. The researchers concluded that the findings showed that fetal matched responses are rudimentary signs of early mirroring behaviors that become functional in the postnatal period (Ferrari et al., 2016).

Taken together, the findings on fetal development suggest that fetuses are sensitive to the communicative input of the mother. Fetuses actively regulate their behavior in response to the external environment, specifically to maternal stimulation. They become "familiar" with their mother's voice, which implies that a sensory stimulus has been experienced frequently over time so that it is recognized (no longer strange and unfamiliar). These findings not only provide evidence of the onset of development of the self in the womb, but also have implications for theories of the early development of attachment and emotional regulation, as we will see.

Development of the Self After Birth

The data show that just hours after birth newborn babies are responsive to their mother's voices, suggesting that they recognize and remember the sounds from the womb (DeCasper & Spence, 1986; Fifer et al, 1987; Fifer & Moon, 1995; Granier-Deferre, Ribeiro, Jacquet, & Bassereau, 2011; Moon, Cooper, & Fifer, 1993; Spence & DeCasper, 1987).

The findings demonstrate that newborns actively change their sucking behavior to hear their mothers' voices rather than voices of other women.

They ramp up their sucking bursts to prompt an audio recording of their mother's voice over that of a stranger's voice (DeCasper & Fifer, 1980; Fifer & Moon, 1989).

Also, newborns show a physiological orienting response to the maternal voice, displaying heart rate decelerations and fewer movements while listening to a recording of their mother's voice versus a stranger's voice (Ockleford, Vince, Layton, & Reader, 1988).

In addition, the data show that newborn infants rapidly learn about faces and show preference for their mother's face. Newborn infants are unable to see very well. Their vision is blurry and visual acuity is sharpest at the edges, rather than the center of their visual field. Still, the findings show that newborns, ranging from 12 to 36 hours of age, produce significantly more sucking responses in order to see an image of their mothers' faces as opposed to an image of strangers' faces (Walton, Bower, & Bower, 1992). Researchers have suggested that despite their poor vision these data indicate newborns can distinguish differences in face shape, hairstyle, and color (Pascalis & DeSchonen, 1994).

In addition to the infant's preference for the mother's voice and face over a stranger's voice and face, infants also show a preference for their mother's individually distinctive odor.

Research suggests that olfactory preference is one of the most developed senses at birth, and the data show that newborn infants prefer the smell of their mother's breast milk to any other olfactory stimulus. As early as a few minutes after birth, breast odor elicits preferential head orientation by newborns to guide them to the nipple as they turn their heads toward the odor source.

Figure 2.4 Newborn baby asleep

Also, the data show that newborns recognize and prefer the smell of their own mother's breast milk to that of a stranger's. For example, the findings show that when 6-day-old breastfed newborn infants had two pads placed on either side of their head, they were more likely to turn to the one that their mother had worn next to her breast than the pad worn by a stranger. They also spent more time oriented to the pad infused with their mother's scent versus a stranger's scent (Todrank, Heth, & Restrep, 2011).

In addition to the studies that demonstrated infants could identify their mothers by their odor, other studies have provided evidence for the complementary observation; mothers can identify their infants using a similar cue (Macfarlane, 1975; Russell, 1976; Russell, Mendelson, & Peeke, 1983). The data show that mothers of newborns can identify their infants by smell alone at 6 hours postpartum after a single exposure to their babies.

In summary, researchers have concluded that an infant's ability after birth to recognize their mother's voice, face, and smell plays an important role in the communication between infant and mother and helps lay the ground for attachment and emotion regulation.

Early Mother–Infant Attachment

The relationship between a mother and her newborn starts with mutual recognition. As previously mentioned, recognition takes place through auditory, visual, and olfactory learning, which occurs very early during the so-called critical periods. In animal species, recognition between individuals is an essential requirement for any kind of further interaction. Thus, it seems that recognition between mother and newborn is a fundamental relational process.

Recognition involves more than just perceptual identification between mother and child. It also involves physiological responses including changes in heart rate and neural development in the fetus and later the infant. The familiarity of the mother's voice, face, and smell is registered, so to speak, as a positive biological experience.

As an analogy, consider the immune system. The immune system is a host defense system consisting of many biological structures and processes within a person that protects against disease and can recognize a wide variety of "unfamiliar" agents (pathogens) from the person's own familiar agents (antibodies). Similarly, one might consider the development of the self a recognition defense system for detecting unsafe, unfamiliar people from safe, familiar people. The ability to recognize a safe, familiar person is needed to develop a close relational bond or attachment to facilitate the survival of infants and children.

Studies show that in human infants during the first years of life, attachment takes the form of a strong tendency to approach familiar people, to be receptive to care and consolation from them, and to be secure and unafraid in their presence. Human babies seem to be born with a tendency to become attached to the familiar adults who care for them. They show a strong preference for those who have served as continuous caretakers—especially when they are bored, frightened, or distressed by the unfamiliar or unexpected.

The attachment relationship between infants and their caregivers is vital for human development and is universal across cultures, enabling infant survival as well as social, emotional, and cognitive development (Insel & Young, 2001, Sroufe et al., 2005). (Though infants are biologically inclined to form an attachment relationship to their caregivers, the type of bonds they form will depend on the conditions and cultural context in which they are raised.)

The attachment relationship is so deeply ingrained in development because it provides a solution to a difficult adaptive problem that our ancestors encountered—how to increase the probability of survival through the hazardous years of social and physical development. Compared to most other

Figure 2.5 Mom holding baby in arms

species, human infants are born in an underdeveloped and premature state. Attachment behaviors serve the evolutionary function of keeping vulnerable infants in close physical proximity to their mothers or caregiver, thereby increasing their chances of survival (Kaplan, Lancaster, & Hurtado, 2000).

Since caring for an infant is necessary for the perpetuation of the species, and therefore is of crucial evolutionary importance, researchers have become increasingly interested in the neurobiology of maternal attachment. The neurobiology of maternal attachment behaviors has been studied extensively in animal models (Insel & Young, 2001; Swain et al., 2007), and more recently in humans using functional magnetic resonance imaging (fMRI) (Lorberbaum et al., 2002; Bartels & Zeki, 2004; Swain et al., 2007; Strathearn et al., 2008).

The studies show there are several interconnected brain regions that influence maternal mood and attachment behaviors. Although researchers have suggested there is likely to be a complex interaction of multiple neuroendocrine systems, two specific systems have been shown to consistently play a role in promoting and maintaining maternal attachment behavior: the dopaminergic reward-processing system (Champagne et al., 2004 ; Ferris et al., 2005; Strathearn et al., 2008) and the oxytocinergic system (Bartels & Zeki, 2004; Champagne et al., 2001; Levine et al., 2007).

The findings from studies on the dopaminergic reward-processing system suggest that the rewards system of a mother's brain will light up, so to speak, just by staring at their babies. The data show that infant cues such as smiling or crying facial expressions are strong stimuli of human maternal behavior that activate dopamine-associated brain reward circuits in mothers.

Researchers point out that neurobiology of maternal attachment employs a push–pull mechanism that overcomes social distance by deactivating networks used for critical social assessment and negative emotions, while it bonds mothers through the involvement of the reward circuitry to care for their infants (Bartels & Zeki, 2004). The researchers conclude that the rewarding neural basis of maternal attachment ensures the experience is a deeply positive and pleasurable experience, thereby guaranteeing its survival and perpetuation.

In addition to the dopaminergic reward-processing system, researchers have studied the oxytocinergic system. Oxytocin has been described as the "hormone of attachment." Oxytocin is a hormone that is made in the brain, in the hypothalamus. It is transported to, and secreted by, the pituitary gland, which is located at the base of the brain. In chemistry, oxytocin is classed as a neuropeptide (a peptide containing nine amino acids), while its biological classification is as a neuropeptide. It acts both as a hormone and as a brain neurotransmitter.

Oxytocin has been found to be critically important for maternal attachment behaviors. The results from studies on human mothers suggest that the oxytocin system is associated with bond formation. Higher levels of oxytocin are related to higher levels of maternal attachment behaviors including proximity seeking, touch, contact, and repeated checking. Also, higher levels of oxytocin are related to higher levels of maternal behaviors such as gazing at the infant, "motherese" vocalizations, positive expressions, and responsiveness to the cues expressed by the infant (Feldman, Zagoory-Sharon, & Levine, 2007).

In summary, researchers have concluded that the neurobiological basis of the mother–infant attachment suggests the importance it serves for the continued propagation of the human species. The mother–infant bond, the primary attachment across mammalian species, is a dynamic relationship that establishes the foundation of our social nature.

Attachment and Interactive Emotion Regulation

The inborn tendency to attachment is a valuable advantage in survival. It helps infants find the nurturance and protection from distress, real or imagined. And later in development, it makes children more receptive to parental and social standards (Kagan, 2015).

Studies have found that strongly attached children are more likely than others to obey the request and commands of their mothers (Londerville & Main, 1981). Around the age of two, children develop a sense of right and wrong—inner standards and the desire to live up to them. Children can discern even from the changes in father's voice or the shape of mother's eyes—that their own behavior elicits judgmental, emotional responses from others. So, children will change their behavior to elicit a positive emotional response from others (Kagan, 1981).

Generally, psychologists have focused on emotion regulation as happening within the person. But the interpersonal nature of emotion regulation has been discovered in research on mother–child interactions. In this context, the emphasis moves from a focus on self-regulation to the complex ways in which emotions are regulated via attachment in social interactions.

Research on mother–child emotion regulation demonstrates that the mother's emotions systematically influence the child's emotions and the child's emotions influences the mother's in reciprocal fashion. The quality of such exchanges is hypothesized to result in a variety of developmental outcomes, including the child's growing ability to self-regulate emotions and to meet parental standards and social demands.

Early studies on mother–child emotion regulation focused on observing the moment-to-moment interactions between infants and mothers. Researchers hypothesized that spontaneous interactions would be regulated by reciprocal emotional communications (e.g., Cohn & Tronick, 1988; Field & Fogel, 1982; Fogel, 1993; Gianino & Tronick, 1988; Stern, 1985; Trevarthen, 1984; Tronick, 1989).

To test the hypotheses, researchers observed mother's and infant's emotional expressive behaviors and recorded them. Later they were coded continuously and independently and analyzed to examine the timing and sequencing of changes in mother and infant emotional behaviors. To further provide evidence of the mother–infant emotion-regulation process the researchers included multiple and synchronized measurement strategies (e.g., time-linked facial and cardiovascular recordings).

In general, the findings show mothers regulate infant emotional states by reading infant emotional signals, providing appropriate stimulation, modulating levels of infant arousal, and reciprocating and reinforcing infant reactions. Infants regulate their mothers' emotions through their receptivity to mothers' initiations and stimulation, approaching and withdrawing from stimulation, and responding contingently to maternal emotion.

Researchers concluded that the findings suggest "synchrony" between mother and infant emotional expressive behaviors (facial activity, vocal activity, and physiological responses). According to the researchers, the data demonstrates that healthy mothers and infants are sensitive to each other's emotional signals. They reciprocate by matching emotion or modifying behavior to amplify or modulate the other's emotion, and maintain an up and down pattern of emotional interaction that sustains the relationship in an ideal and sensitive way.

Emotion regulation does not just occur between infants and mothers. Researchers have observed it in parent interactions with toddlers and with preschoolers as well (e.g., Cole, Teti, & Zahn-Waxler, 2003; Denham, 1993; Dumas, LaFreniere, & Serketich, 1995). These studies use laboratory procedures to present mother and child with challenges that children confront in their everyday lives.

The procedures are set up to incite a child's desire for an activity or object and then block access to it. Typical procedures of this kind are designed to activate frustration and anger (e.g., asking a child to clean up toys, to wait for mother to finish work to get a toy, to resist touching prohibited toys, or to persist at a difficult task). The typical procedures also include tasks that support positive emotional exchanges (e.g., snacks, free play, receiving the toy).

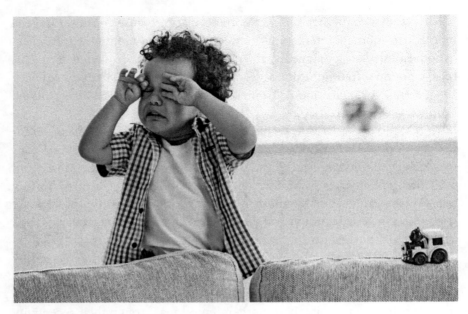

Figure 2.6 Boy crying and rubbing eyes

The procedures elicit social interactions that are then coded for emotional cues. Mother and child emotion, as observed by facial and vocal cues, are coded independently but are time synchronized to reveal emotion regulation relations between each person's reactions (Cole et al., 2003; Denham, 1993). The findings demonstrate contingencies in mother–child emotion displays, with results suggesting that mothers and children responded emotionally to each other in predictable, systematic, and temporally dependent ways.

Taken together, the data on parent–child emotional interactions provide evidence for emotion regulation by showing reliable, conditional changes in mother's and child's emotional expressive behaviors. The changes are dependent on the pair's emotional communication and are not a function of individual expressivity. They are bidirectional and unrelated to periodic cycles in either person's behavior (e.g., Cohn & Tronick, 1988). The emotional changes in mother–infant face-to-face interaction involve coconstructed synchronization, including matching of positive emotions and repairing of negative or mismatched emotions (Field, Healy, Goldstein, & Guhertz, 1990; Stern, 1974; Trevarthen, 1984; Tronick & Cohn, 1989). Moreover, changes in the mother's and child's emotional expressions and behaviors are associated with changes in physiological activity in each person. Thus, researchers have concluded that the findings on mother–child emotion regulation show that one person's emotions are regulated and regulatory.

Another method researchers have used to investigate emotion regulation capitalizes on the effects of *disruption* of the expected course of social interaction. The famous "still face experiments" reveal how infants and young children react to a suddenly unresponsive parent. The experiments demonstrate the systematic changes in a child's emotions as a function of change in maternal affect, thereby offering another avenue for demonstrating interactional emotion regulation. The findings from still face experiments are one of the most replicated findings in developmental psychology (Mesman, van IJzendoorn, & Bakermans-Kranenburg, 2009).

Briefly, in 1975 researchers presented the results from a still face experiment at a professional meeting of the Society for Research in Child Development that was later published in an article (Tronick, Als, Adamson, Wise, & Brazelton, 1978).

The highlight of the presentation was the illustration of the still face paradigm using then innovative videotape technology (Adamson, & Frick, 2003). First, a split screen image of an infant and her mother appeared on the conference ballroom's screen as they engaged in the pleasant recurring back-and-forth of a face-to-face interaction. Then, the infant and mother reappeared in a "still face" during which the mother remained completely unresponsive, with an expressionless face for 3 minutes.

Here is a link to the still face video experiment—follow the link so you can see the interactions between the infant and mother for yourself—though be prepared some people find it disturbing and uncomfortable. But if you can watch the still face video you may experience a sense of relief when the mother finally breaks her stony impassive expression and starts laughing and talking to her noticeably upset infant again. (Tronick, 2009, https://www.youtube.com/watch?v=apzXGEbZht0)

The still face experiment uses a three-part procedure. First, mother and infant engage in spontaneous, reciprocal emotionally expressive interactions. They are cooing, babbling, smiling, pointing, talking, and laughing. Next, the mother is instructed to be emotionally unresponsive for a short period, keeping her face still and neutral. Finally, the mother is asked to resume her spontaneity.

The findings show that when the mother is still, infants will change their emotional expressive behaviors. Specifically, infants will decrease smiling and increase signals of distress. They will behave as if they are trying to reengage the mother by vocalizing and gesturing at her.

In the video, you see the infant coo, gurgle, smile and reach out to her mother, only this time, there is no response. The mother looks at the child with a blank expression. The infant stops for a moment, as if not understanding what's going on, then starts to shriek a little, kick her feet, and arch her back as if to get that loving attention back. The mother does not respond; she continues looking at her child with a blank expression on her face. Then, very quickly the infant gets upset. She fusses, turns away, and starts to cry. The infant withdraws and turns her gaze away from her mother as efforts to reengage her mother have failed. During the final relief phase of the procedure when mother reengages, the infant resumes looking at her mother with increased positive emotional expressions.

The findings from studies using the still face procedure suggest that in addition to the emotional and behavioral changes across episodes there are changes in the infant's physiological reactions as well. During the still face phase, the infant's heart rate increases (Weinberg & Tronick, 1996). Also, in studies that examined the reunion phase, the findings show that there are carryover effects. The data from second-by-second coding show that the disruption of the interaction when maternal emotion is constrained blocks the mutual regulation of the dyad. There is a carryover of negative emotion from the still face phase as well as changes in mother–infant coordination compared with previous phases. Also, the data suggest that 4-month-old infants exposed to the still face will remember it 2 weeks later, rapidly showing physiological changes to negative responses that infants exposed to it for the first time do not (Weinberg & Tronick, 1996).

The findings from still face experiments are reported to be very robust (Mesman et al., 2009). The results of a meta-analyses of about 80 studies confirmed the classic still face effect of the child's reduced positive affect and gaze, and increased negative affect, as well as the partial carry-over effect into the reunion episode consisting of lower positive and higher negative affect compared to baseline.

What is striking about the still face experiments is that it suggests how deep the need to connect is, and how painful when it fails. Infants and children will go through repeated cycles where they try to elicit attention from their mothers, fail, turn away, sad and disengaged, then they turn back and keep trying again. They continuously seek approval and connection. When it goes on long enough and they fail to connect you see infants withdraw, disengage, lose postural control, and literally collapse in their seats.

Scientists have referred to these constellations of effects as sobering, comparing the infant's reaction to those of abused and neglected children, and noting, that advances in brain research show that child neglect damages not only the way a developing child's brain functions, but also changes in the structure of the brain itself, in such a way that makes clear thinking, controlling emotions and impulses, and forming healthy attachments and social relationships more difficult.

Studies on children raised in orphanages show that if a child lacks a reliable source of emotion regulation via attachment the result can be damaging to the brain. Researchers using a technology known as electroencephalography (EEG) that measures electrical activity in the brain show that young children living in orphanages have low levels of brain activity. And in later studies, as the children grew older, researchers used MRI to study the anatomy of their brains, and the results show damaging effects on brain development. The data revealed a dramatic reduction in what is referred to as gray matter and in white matter, areas of the brain involved in vision, language, and emotion. Consequently, researchers have noted that children raised in orphanages display a variety of behavioral and psychological symptoms (Vanderwert, Marshall, Nelson, Zeanah, & Fox, 2010).

Figure 2.7 Boy on skateboard

Psychological Theories of Attachment

Much psychological thinking on attachment stems from the pioneering research of John Bowlby, who studied the behavioral and psychological effects of institutionalized care on children. John Bowlby (1907–1990) was a British psychologist, psychiatrist, and psychoanalyst. He is famous for his pioneering work on the psychological theory of attachment and child development. His psychological theory of attachment laid the groundwork for the neurobiological and mother–infant emotion regulation studies reviewed earlier.

A few years after World War II ended, in 1949, Bowlby's work on the effects of institutionalized care on children led to his being asked to write the World Health Organization's report on the mental health of homeless children in postwar Europe (Bowlby, 1951). During and after the War, Bowlby studied children who were separated from their families.

These included Jewish children who were rescued from Germany, children from London who were evacuated to keep them safe from air raids, and children living in group nurseries. So, from the start of his career Bowlby was interested in the problem of separation. By the late 1950s, Bowlby had gathered enough observational and theoretical work to demonstrate the central importance for human development of attachment from birth (Bretherton, 1992).

Bowlby postulated that early childhood attachments play a critical role in child development and psychological functioning.

Some biographers have speculated that Bowlby's interest in the psychological aspects of attachment stem from his own early losses. Bowlby's mother, like other mothers of her social class in England, thought parental attention and affection dangerous and would spoil a child. So, a nanny who was his primary caretaker and with whom he was much attached raised Bowlby. When Bowlby was about 4 years old, his nanny left the family. According to biographers, Bowlby described this separation as being as tragic as the loss of a mother. A few years later after the nanny left, Bowlby was sent to a boarding school, which he regarded as psychologically damaging.

So, perhaps, as his biographer has speculated, these events were the driving force behind Bowlby's interest in studying the psychology of children: specifically child development and maternal deprivation that gradually led to his theoretical conception of attachment theory (Van Dijken, 1998).

The central idea of Bowlby's attachment theory is that mothers who are responsive to their infant's needs during critical biological periods establish a sense of security in the infant. The baby knows that the caregiver is dependable, and that creates a secure base for the child to then explore the world.

Bowlby postulated that the earliest bond formed by children with their mothers or caregivers had an important impact that continues throughout the life cycle. Bowlby was interested in family dynamics and on how attachment patterns were transmitted from one generation to the next.

Bowlby defined the attachment bond as a "lasting psychological connectedness between human beings." While mothers are often associated with this role as primary caregiver and attachment figures, Bowlby maintained that infants could form such bonds with others. The formation of the attachment bond offers comfort, security, and nourishment, but Bowlby noted that physical nourishment itself was not the purpose of this attachment. Rather, the development of a sense of trust was the main purpose of attachment. When attachment figures are available and reliable, the child develops a sense of trust in the world. The child can then rely on the mother (or caregiver) as a psychologically secure base from which the child can separate and develop autonomously.

Bowlby suggested that psychological attachment proceeds in a series of developmental stages. During the first stage, there is a preattachment phase. Infants recognize their primary caregiver but do not yet have an attachment. Their crying and fussing draws the attention and care of the parent that is mutually rewarding to the child and the caregiver. As this stage progresses through about 3 months, infants begin to recognize the parent more and develop a sense of trust. During the second stage, there is an indiscriminate attachment phase. Infants demonstrate a clear preference for the primary caregiver as well as certain secondary caregivers in their lives. During the third stage, there is a discriminate attachment phase. Children form a strong attachment to one person and will experience separation distress and anxiety when parted from that person. And, during the fourth stage, there is a multiple attachment phase. Children start to develop strong attachments to people beyond the primary caregivers.

Bowlby's psychological theory of attachment had an influential effect on clinical practice. Psychotherapeutic approaches were developed using attachment concepts and then applied to clinical practice. For example, in attachment-oriented psychotherapy, a therapist is trained to establish a secure attachment relationship with an adolescent or adult patient providing a secure base from which the patient can explore both self and others who are subjects of relational bonds.

If the adolescent or adult patient grew up having had an insecure attachment relationship this would be characterized by extremes of connection or autonomy, that is, by intense enmeshment or by avoidance of intimacy. So, by contrast, the therapist–patient relationship can help provide a patient, for the first time, a context for a smooth balance between attachment-connection and exploration-autonomy. The patient can start to experience the comfort and security of a close therapeutic relationship without the loss of self-boundaries with the other person. The patient can also move away from the relationship, gaining autonomy, without risking a total break and loss of the close relationship. The experience of this attachment dynamic in the context of the patient–therapist relationship is thought to be an important step in the achievement of the patient's autonomy that preserves connection.

Unlike other schools of psychotherapy (e.g., psychoanalytic or cognitive), in attachment-oriented psychotherapy, the therapist–patient relationship is viewed as a real one.
Bowlby (1977) assumed that progress in therapy could not be expected without such a relationship. Rather than acting as a "blank screen" on which the patient projects past or current relationships or talks about distorted thinking processes, the attachment-oriented therapist enters into a real and genuine relationship with the patient and the patient's family, regardless of the duration of therapy. And, rather than hiding hurt or angry feelings evoked by the patient, the therapist conveys them to the patient. Bowlby postulated that such genuine and congruent communication is particularly important

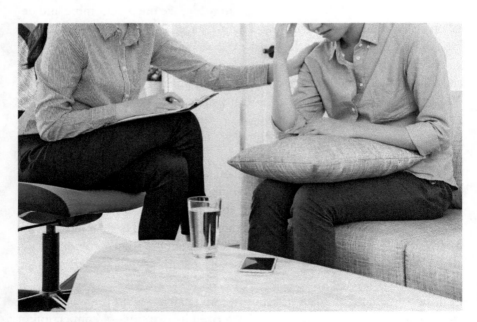

Figure 2.8   Therapy session

for patients whose attachment figures displayed pseudoaffection and thus fostered insecure attachments (Bowlby, 1977).

In attachment-based psychotherapy, termination is exceptionally important. In the context of the secure patient–therapist relationship, the patient has the opportunity to review past separations from other attachment figures, and can make changes in his or her reactions to the impending separation from the therapist. When an insecure attachment is lost, self-worth may have been lowered. So, when a secure attachment, like that with a therapist ends, the patient has the opportunity to experience it with less distress (Bowlby, 1979). It is particularly important that the termination not be viewed as a loss or a rejection or abandonment and thus become a repetition of old relationships.

In attachment-oriented psychotherapy, because the patient–therapist relationship is viewed as continuing over time, even if only in memory, termination does not have the final quality that frequently typifies other modes of psychotherapy. In attachment-oriented psychotherapy, the therapist is not just an observer of the patient's emotional journey or even a neutral guide, but a fellow traveler, resonating with the patient's sadness, anger, and anxiety. And rather than withdrawing from the intensity of the client's experience, the therapist provides the stability and security to keep the client feeling not only understood, but safely supported by tone of voice, eye contact, expression, and posture as well as words and, if needed, contact after termination (Diamond, Russon, & Levy, 2016).

Several clinical trials and process studies of attachment-based therapy have demonstrated empirical support for the approach and its proposed mechanism of change. There is some research evidence suggesting the importance of establishing what Bowlby called a safe haven and a secure base within a therapeutic relationship. There is also empirical evidence that psychotherapy, viewed as a corrective attachment experience, can move patients away from insecure and toward secure attachments, and that this change is a good indication of effective treatment. However, there are few controlled studies that examine the long-term effects of security-enhancing therapeutic figures on patients' attachment patterns, and the extent to which changes in these attachment patterns are associated with therapy outcomes (Mikulincer, Shaver, & Berant, 2013).

In addition to Bowlby's psychological theory of attachment having an influential effect on clinical practice, it also had an influential effect on the research programs of other famous psychologists, including Bowlby's colleague Mary Ainsworth. Ainsworth made significant contributions to attachment theory, coming up with a more nuanced view of several types of insecure attachment (Ainsworth & Bowlby, 1991).

Another famous psychologist who further developed the psychological concept of attachment was Abraham Maslow (1908–1970). Maslow was an American psychologist who is best known for his hierarchy of needs. Maslow wanted to understand what motivates people and postulated that all people possess a set of motivational needs.

Maslow formulated what he termed "a positive theory of motivation which will satisfy these theoretical demands at the same time conform to the known, facts, clinical and observational as well as experimental" (Maslow, 1943, p. 371). Maslow theorized that the "need to belong" was one of five human needs in a hierarchy of inborn needs, along with physiological needs, safety, self-esteem, and self-actualization (and later Maslow added spiritual needs). These needs are arranged on a hierarchy and must be satisfied in order. After physiological needs and safety needs are met, an individual can then work on meeting the need to be loved and belong.

Although the meaning of love and belonging needs are not operationalized or clearly spelled out, Maslow hypothesized that people have a need for affectionate relations with other people and a need to belong to a group.

"If both the physiological and the safety needs are fairly well gratified, then there will emerge the love and affection and belongingness needs . . . the

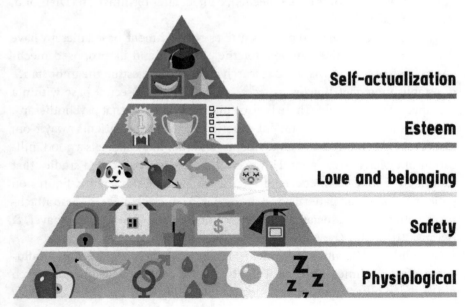

Figure 2.9 Maslow Pyramid

person will feel keenly, as never before, the absence of friends, or a sweetheart, or a wife, or children. He will hunger for affectionate relations with people in general, namely, for a place in his group, and he will strive with great intensity to achieve this goal. He will want to attain such a place more than anything else in the world and may even forget that once, when he was hungry, he sneered at love. In our society the thwarting of these needs is the most commonly found core in cases of maladjustment and more severe psychopathology" (Maslow, 1943, p. 380–381).

Most clinical psychologists before Maslow were concerned with the abnormal aspects of behavior. By contrast, Maslow was interested in positive mental health. His hierarchy of needs theory produced several different psychotherapies. All were directed by the idea that people have the inner resources for growth and healing, and that psychotherapy could help people remove obstacles so they could achieve positive psychological growth and advance to the highest need, self-actualization. Maslow assumed that the need to belong is most often an "unconscious rather than a conscious" motivation, but he suggested that with "suitable techniques" belongingness needs could become conscious in some people (Maslow, 1943, p. 389).

Biographers have speculated that Maslow's interest in "belongingness needs" stem from his own childhood experiences growing up in New York. His parents were Jewish immigrants from Russia who escaped from Czarist persecution in the early 20th century. They had decided to live in Brooklyn, New York, in a multiethnic, working-class neighborhood. According to Maslow's biographer, Maslow experienced anti-Semitism from his teachers and from other children around the neighborhood. He was one of the few Jewish boys in his neighborhood, and other boys bullied him because of his religion. So, perhaps, as his biographer has speculated, these events were the driving force behind Maslow's theory that the need to belong was a major source of human motivation (Hoffman, 2008).

More recently, social and personality psychologists following in the footsteps of Bowlby and Maslow have suggested that the need to belong can be used to understand and integrate a great deal of the existing psychological literature on human behavior. Baumeister and Leary (1995) reviewed a large body of the psychology literature in an effort to integrate the literature and to provide the empirical findings to support the theory of the need to belong. Briefly, they searched the empirical literature of social and personality psychology for findings relevant to the belongingness hypothesis, and claim they found much evidence to support predictions about the need to belong.

For example, they cite empirical studies that show forming social bonds arises easily.

In addition, they cite studies showing that belongingness appears to be a powerful factor shaping human thought. Also, they cite studies showing that many of the strongest emotions people experience, both positive and negative, are linked to belongingness needs. In addition, they cite studies showing that the deprivation of stable, good relationships has been linked to a large array of aversive and pathological consequences. And they cite studies showing that people resist losing attachments and breaking social bonds (Baumeister & Leary, 1995).

Baumeister and Leary conclude their literature review suggesting that the field of psychology has underestimated the need to belong. Although they note that most of the studies they reviewed are correlational and many rival explanations can be suggested, they maintain that their review of the literature demonstrates the many links between the need to belong and emotional patterns, behavioral responses, and health and well-being. They conclude their review asserting that the existing literature supports the hypothesis that the need to belong is a basic and universal motivation (Baumeister & Leary, 1995).

Building on the research that has identified the importance of belongingness and the links to positive outcomes, more recently researchers have studied whether the need to belong can be derived from the use of social networking sites. To study belongingness in online contexts, researchers have devised measurement scales for the online contexts (Leary, Kelly, Cottrell, & Schreindorfer, 2013; Mellor, Stokes, Firth, Hayashi, & Cummins, 2008; Pickett, Gardner, & Knowles, 2004; Sanquirgo, Oberle, & Chekroun, 2012). From basic bulletin boards and discussion forums to current user-generation sites, such as Facebook, MySpace, YouTube, and Flickr almost all user-generated content sites provide a way for users to connect and communicate online.

Studies of belongingness in online contexts are still new. So, the findings, therefore, are preliminary and have not been replicated. And the few studies that have been conducted have yielded mixed results. Still there is some data to suggest that Facebook use may provide the opportunity to develop and maintain social belongingness in the online environment, and that Facebook connectedness is associated with lower depression and anxiety and greater satisfaction with life (Nichols & Webster, 2013).

Other recent research has focused on attachment theory as a framework for explaining engagement with Facebook. This line of research uses attachment theory to study individual differences in styles of Facebook engagement. As social media has become a popular way of social interaction, self-expressive profiles and postings on sites such as Facebook have become an outlet for social behavior.

Figure 2.10 2 men high-fiving

People display different patterns of social media behavior. For example, some people post status updates frequently that may include reporting everyday activities to promoting opinions. Other people take a restrained approach, going on Facebook to view others' activity, but not engaging much beyond that. Researchers have hypothesized that attachment style can explain the difference between these two types of social media engagement.

To test this hypothesis, subjects were asked to complete an online questionnaire that assesses attachment style and a measure that assesses Facebook engagement. Again, this type of research is new and has not been replicated.

Still the data suggest that attachment style is related to how a person engages on Facebook. The findings show that insecure attachment anxiety was related to feedback sensitivity, feedback seeking, and other aspects of active Facebook engagement. Individuals who scored high on attachment anxiety behave actively on Facebook and are motivated to seek positive feedback from others (Hart, Nailling, Bizer, & Collins, 2015).

In sum, this chapter analyzes research on the development of the self in relation to others. Studies show that even in the womb the fetus is sensitive to maternal stimulation. Through experience and memory, the fetus gets "familiar" with their mother's voice. This sets the stage for mother–child

Figure 2.11 Aerial view of 2 people on laptops

attachment and emotional regulation that forms the foundation of our so-cial nature. The neurobiological basis of attachment and the need to belong ensures our survival.

But alongside the development of attachment is the development of cogni-tion. So, we turn now to consider the self in relation to cognitive development and categorizing.

3

Categorizing

Background

To understand diversity, an important concept to grasp is "categorizing." Without categorization we would not differentiate groups and consider "the other." Some researchers have maintained that categorization underlies prejudice, the negative side of diversity.

George Miller (1920–2012), a psychology professor at Harvard, was one of the founders of the cognitive psychology field and one of the most influential experimental psychologists of the 20th century. In his famous paper titled "The Magical Number Seven, Plus or Minus Two," Miller (1956) demonstrated why categorizing is such an essential cognitive skill. Miller's research established a new way of "thinking about thinking" and opened a new field of research known as "cognitive" studies." Prior to Miller's work, the dominant paradigms of psychological study were Freud's psychoanalytic theories of the mind, which were untestable, and behaviorism, which rejected the study of the mind altogether.

In his pioneering work on personality and prejudice, Gordon Allport stated everyone must categorize in order to function. Allport maintained that this propensity lies in the normal and natural tendency to form generalizations, concepts, and categories. "The human mind must think with the aid of categories . . . we can not possibly avoid this process. Orderly living depends upon it" (Allport, 1954, p. 20).

The ability to categorize is vital to intellectual development. It is an essential cognitive skill. Our world has a vast amount of stimuli and diverse information that is constantly changing. Categorizing is important for handling information. It allows us to efficiently sort an otherwise overwhelming amount of data. The cognitive ability to categorize ensures that we can manage the diverse information with order, coherence, and organization.

According to the Freudian psychoanalytic view, the remedy to eliminate prejudice associated with categorization entailed understanding childhood experiences and the unconscious motivations and defenses that motivated a person's prejudices. People could be cured of their prejudices by making

The Science of Diversity. Mona Sue Weissmark, Oxford University Press (2020). © Oxford University Press.
DOI: 10.1093/oso/9780190686345.001.0001

Figure 3.1 Wooden blocks

conscious their unconscious thoughts and motivations. By releasing repressed emotions and experiences people could make the unconscious conscious and in so doing gain insight into their pathological prejudices.

In the 1980s and more recently in the 2000s, theories on the authoritarian personality have resurfaced to explain prejudice (Altemeyer, 1988, 1992; Hetherington & Weiler, 2009). *The Authoritarian Personality* (1950) is a book by Theodor Adorno and his colleagues who were working at the University of California, Berkeley, during and after World War II. A central idea of *The Authoritarian Personality* is that authoritarianism is the result of a psychoanalytic developmental model.

Adorno had fled Nazi Germany and was interested to uncover the unconscious motivations and defenses that motivated anti-Semitism. In studies of American adults, Adorno and his colleagues (1950) found that hostility toward Jews was associated with hostility toward other minorities. Prejudice appeared to be a symptom of a personality trait. Adorno and his colleagues concluded that prejudiced adults shared authoritarian personality traits.

Adorno and his colleagues provided a set of criteria by which to measure the authoritarian personality traits and then ranked the traits in any given person on what it called the F scale (F for fascist).

Figure 3.2 Sorting shapes

The personality type traits that were believed to cluster together as the result of childhood experiences included such things as conventionalism, authoritarian submission, authoritarian aggression, and anti-intellectualism.

Adorno and his colleagues hypothesized that as children, authoritarian people were harshly punished. And excessively harsh and punitive parenting was thought to cause children to feel anger toward their parents. But fear of parental disapproval and punishment caused people to avoid confronting their parents, and instead to identify with and idolize authority figures. This was revealed in their agreement with such statements on the F scale as, "Obedience and respect for authority are the most important virtues children should learn" and "What this country needs most, more than laws and political programs, is a few courageous, tireless, devoted leaders in whom the people can put their faith."

Scholars have criticized the research on the authoritarian personality for focusing on right-wing authoritarianism and overlooking dogmatic authoritarianism of the left. Still, though strongly criticized for bias and a flawed methodology, *The Authoritarian Personality* was highly influential in

Figure 3.3 Finger pointing to crowd

American social sciences and continues to be influential today. The right-wing authoritarianism scale is the most frequently used, contemporary descendant of the F scale. And some researchers have maintained that contemporary studies of right-wing authoritarians confirm there are individuals whose unconscious fears and hostilities appear as prejudice (Altemeyer, 1988, 1992, 2012).

In addition to the authoritarian personality traits, theories on social dominance orientation (SDO) suggest another example of other personality traits that may explain a person's prejudice (Altemeyer, 1998; Pratto, Sidanius, Stallworth, & Malle, 1994; Sidanius, et al., 2000; Sidanius & Pratto, 1999).

Although the psychoanalytic view dominated psychological thought in the early 20th century, another school—behaviorism—arose out of experimental psychology to dispute Freudian theory. One of the pioneers of behaviorism, B.F. Skinner (1904–1990), a psychology professor at Harvard, believed that the study of the unconscious mind did not provide acceptable scientific data because such observations were not open to verification by other researchers.

Figure 3.4 Art mannequin addressing seven others

Figure 3.5 Nails

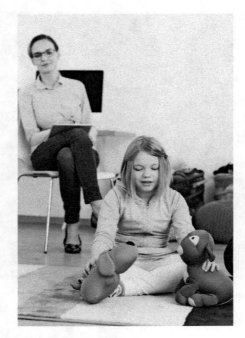

Figure 3.6 Girl playing with stuffed animals

In Skinner's view, only the study of directly observable behavior—and the reinforcing conditions that "control" it—could serve as a basis for formulating scientific principles of human behavior.

According to the behaviorist view, prejudice behaviors are the result of faulty conditioning. Therefore, the remedy to eliminate prejudice entails eliminating prejudicial behaviors by conditioning unprejudiced behaviors via reinforcements techniques. According to Skinner, it is possible "to shape . . . behavior almost as a sculptor shapes a lump of clay" (Skinner, 1951, pp. 26–27).

George Miller criticized the psychoanalytic and behaviorist views. Miller has been credited with revolutionizing the field of psychology by showing that the human mind, though invisible, could also be observed and tested in the lab. Miller and a colleague, Jerome Bruner, gave a name to the new research field when they founded a psychology lab at Harvard, the Center for Cognitive Studies. Just by using the word "cognitive," considered taboo among behaviorists, Miller and Bruner indicated a break with the behaviorist school. Miller stated that using the word "cognitive" was an act of defiance: ".'cognitive

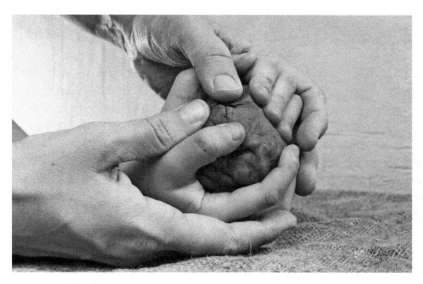

Figure 3.7 Molding clay

psychology' made a definite statement. It meant that I was interested in the mind" Hunt, 1993).

This new approach to psychological research came to be known as the cognitive revolution. Miller demonstrated an idea that was to become a basic tenet of cognitive science: that the brain was an information-processing system that followed computational rules that could be empirically measured.

Miller's research demonstrated the computational limitations of the human mind for processing information. "There seems to be some limitation built into us either by learning or by the design of our nervous systems, a limit that keeps our channel capacities in this general range. On the basis of the present evidence it seems safe to say that we possess a finite and rather small capacity" (Miller, 1956, p. 86). Miller concluded that this small capacity imposed severe limitations on the amount of information that we are able to receive, process, and remember (Miller, 1956).

Thus, Miller concluded, because the mind had a limited capacity to process information, categorization was an essential cognitive skill. By organizing an overload of information into a category of one or so dimensions, a person can manage to break (or at least stretch) the informational bottleneck (Miller, 1956). So, according to Miller, to categorize is to simplify the bottleneck of information in the environment.

Studies on Categorization

The cognitive approach exemplified by Miller's research has inspired hundreds of researchers to further investigate how the mind categorizes information. For example, some studies show that rather than considering people in discrete terms of their unique attributes, a person categorizes other people by some similarity (e.g., race, gender, age). Having done so, a person can think about other people more easily. Categorizing people into groups can provide useful information with minimal effort. Studies show that categorization is helpful both for reducing and organizing information (Bodenhausen & Macrae, 1998; Brewer, 1988; Bruner, 1957; Fiske & Neuberg, 1990).

In addition, other studies show that categorization is helpful for retrieving information from memory. These studies note that if a person were to record each separate event or each other person they encountered in the environment in their memories in no particular arrangement, then recognition would be slow and mistakes more frequent because it would require comparing each new person or event to a huge number of stored items on a trial-and-error basis. It would be like looking for a book in a library without a catalog database system. By contrast, recognition is faster and more accurate if a person has organized and stored the events in their memories as categories. The studies show that categories provide an organized storage system for banking the information and an efficient way for retrieving the information (Quinn & Bomba, 1986).

Other studies show that another advantage of categorization is the ability to respond quickly and consistently to a large number of examples from multiple categories including many events never before experienced. For example, a person may encounter novel stimuli like feathered vertebrates with wings and toothless beaked jaws that fly, and new four-legged creatures that meow, and a printed work consisting of pages glued together along one side and bound in a glossy cover. Yet, mostly a person does not interact with the environment trying to figure out what is this or how should they respond. Instead, they bring to mind the categories, "This is a bird" and that is a "cat" and a "book." So, categorization allows a person to respond to novel situation quickly without mental effort (Murphy, 2002; Smith & Medin, 1981).

Studies on categorization (and the cognitive approach in general) have had a great influence on research about prejudice, and they continue in the 2000s. More than 19,300 articles (Source: Psych INFO) on stereotyping and prejudice apply the research on categorical thinking (e.g., Andersen & Glassman, 1996; Banaji & Hardin, 1996; Bargh, 1999; Bodenhausen & Macrae, 1998; Brewer,

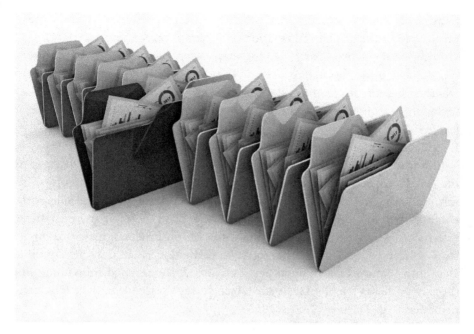

Figure 3.8 Open file folders

1988; Bruner, 1957; Devine, 1989; Dovidio et al., 1986; Fiske, 1989; Fiske & Neuberg, 1990; Gilbert & Hixon, 1991; Hamilton & Sherman, 1994; Lepore & Brown, 1997; Dijksterhuis et al., 1999; Sherman et al., 1998; Smith & Decoster, 1998; Srull & Wyer, 1989; von Hippel et al., 1995; Zarate & Smith, 1990).

The cognitive approach transformed not only how prejudice and stereo-typing researchers did their studies but also the kinds of questions they asked. For example, some studies conceptualized stereotypes as cognitive structures and focused on questions about the processes that give rise to stereotype formation. They investigated issues like how groups are categorized and how categorical features might influence judgments, behaviors, and stereotype change (e.g., Bodenhausen et al., 1994; Brewer & Caporael, 2006; Dovidio & Gaertner, 2010; Mackie et al., 1996; Ostrom & Sedikiedes, 1992; Park & Banaji, 2000; Rokeach & Mezei, 1966; Taylor, 1981, Wilder, 1978).

Other studies focused on exploring whether stereotypes are prototypes within a hierarchical categorization system (Rosch, 1978). And some studies looked at whether stereotypes are instead judgmental generalizations based on stored exemplar information (Smith & Zarate, 1992). Still other studies focused on whether stereotype structures are best represented by a mixture of prototypic and exemplar information (e.g., Hamilton & Sherman, 1994).

Additional studies, using the cognitive approach, explored how stereotypes affect information processing. They focused on questions related to whether stereotypes lead to selective processing of available evidence. They included questions on attention, such as whether people attend more or less to stereotype-consistent or stereotype-inconsistent information (e.g., Bodenhausen, 1988; Hamilton & Sherman, 1994).

In addition, other studies focused on questions that examined people's interpretation of others' behavior. These studies showed that stereotype information creates hypotheses about a stereotyped individual. These hypotheses are often tested in a biased fashion that leads to their false confirmation, referred to as stereotype-confirming information processing. For example, studies have suggested that stereotype information such as socioeconomic class information creates hypotheses about the stereotyped individual. But these hypotheses are often tested in a biased way that leads to their false confirmation (e.g., Darley & Gross, 1983).

Additionally, further studies found that peoples' stereotypes can lead to others behaving in "self-fulfilling prophecy" ways or "expectancy-confirming" ways (Snyder, Tanke, & Berscheid, 1977; Word, Zanna, & Cooper, 1974). The term "self-fulfilling prophecy" has a long history, starting with the 20th-century sociologist Robert Merton, who is credited with coining the expression and formalizing its scientific meaning (Merton, 1948).

Briefly, Merton defined a self-fulfilling prophecy as a "false definition of the situation evoking a new behavior which makes the originally false conception come true" (Merton, 1948, p. 195). Merton used the term to explain ethnic and racial conflict, suggesting that, "As a result of their failure to comprehend the operation of the self- fulfilling prophecy, many Americans of good will are sometimes (sometimes reluctantly) brought to retain enduring ethnic and racial prejudices. They experience these beliefs not as prejudices, not as prejudgments, but as irresistible products of their own observation" (Merton, 1948, p. 196).

To illustrate how a self-fulfilling prophecy relates to racial prejudice, Merton gave the example of a "fair minded white citizen" who strongly supported a policy of excluding "Negroes" from labor unions because he used "facts" to support the belief that " 'Negroes are undisciplined in traditions of trade unionism and the art of collective bargaining' " (Merton, 1948, p. 195.) According to Merton, these so-called facts often produced a "vicious, circle of self-fulfilling prophecies" (Merton, 1948, p. 196).

Merton and later other sociologists applied the concept of self-fulfilling prophecies to the categorization of out-groups and in-groups. For example,

Langmuir (1996) proposed that when in-groups (non-Jews) are the powerful group and categorize out-groups (Jews), the out-group might be forced to comply in important ways to the in-group's categorization.

The origin for this idea of self-fulfilling prophecies as the categorization of an out-group by a powerful in-group has been credited to the philosopher Sartre, who famously asserted, "It is the anti-Semite who makes the Jew." According to Sartre, a Jew is a person whom others have categorized to be a Jew. Therefore, a Jew's Jewishness exists only to the extent they are categorized Jewish by those around them (Sartre, 1948).

Later, the famous social psychologist Robert Rosenthal of Harvard University conducted experimental research on self -fulfilling prophecies. More specifically, Rosenthal's studies focused on the influence that a researcher's categorization labels can exert on the outcome of research investigations that he termed "expectancy effects" (Rosenthal, 1994). Rosenthal's interest in this question started when he feared that he nearly ruined the results of his 1956 doctoral dissertation.

Rosenthal speculated that he had probably treated research participants differently depending on the categorization label of the experimental condition. He realized that his categorical expectation or prediction for participants' performance might have become a self-fulfilling prophecy. So, to find out whether these experimenter effects might be produced experimentally, Rosenthal and his colleagues conducted a series of studies in which they randomly assigned different categorical expectations for research results to different experimenters (Rosenthal, 2003).

For example, in one early study Rosenthal and Fode (1963) tested the effects of experimenter expectancy on maze-running performance.
Briefly, they had two groups of students (the students were the experimenters) test rats, wrongly informing them either that the rats were categorized as especially bred to be "maze dull" or "maze bright." In actuality, all rats were standard lab rats, and were randomly assigned to the categories "dull" and "bright" conditions.

The results showed that the rats categorized as "bright" learned the mazes more quickly than those categorized as "dull." Apparently, the student experimenters had unconsciously influenced the performance of their rats, depending on what they had been told (Rosenthal & Fode, 1963).

Rosenthal reasoned that a similar effect might occur with teachers' expectations of students' performances. So, he conducted a series of experiments in which teachers were informed that some of their students scored very high on a measure of academic "blooming" and were entering a year of high achievement, and other students were not. In actuality, the measure had no such

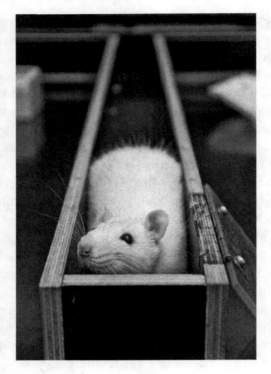

Figure 3.9 Rat in maze

predictive validity. Rosenthal and Jacobson's results showed a self-fulfilling prophecy. That is, students who were categorized to be on the verge of great academic success performed in accordance with these expectations; students not categorized this way did not.

Meta-analyses (i.e., statistical analyses combining results of separate studies) in different research fields (e.g., studies of human and animal learning, of reaction time, and of the perception of inkblots, carried out in various laboratories) showed that the phenomenon of categorization and interpersonal expectancy effects in laboratories and in classrooms was replicable (Rosenthal, 2002; Rosenthal & Rubin, 1978).

Other researchers have conducted experiments on the cognitive phenomena termed "accentuation effects." Studies on accentuation effects suggest that people are influenced by category labels and exemplars (e.g., Corneille, Klein, Lambert, & Judd, 2002; Tajfel, 1959; Tajfel, Sheikh, & Gardner, 1964; Tajfel & Wilkes, 1963, 1964).

For example, Tajfel and Wilkes (1963) demonstrated in their now-classic experiment in which they asked participants to estimate category exemplars (i.e., lines) that varied continuously along a physical dimension (i.e., length) that people exaggerate the differences between stimuli from different categories, and minimize the differences between stimuli falling under the same label.

Studies on the accentuation effect gave rise to an abundant body of research in cognitive social psychology. It has played a role the study of the cognitive processes involved in stereotyping and prejudice, and later in the elaboration of social identity theory (see, e.g., Hogg & Abrams, 1981; Tajfel, 1969, 1978). Also, studies have been conducted on the occurrence of accentuation effects when a place, thing, or person is placed into a category.

In the case of a person, the accentuation effect has been found to be similar to stereotyping and social categorization in that when classified as part of a group, a person's features appear to closely match their categorical classification rather than any particular differences they have.

For example, some studies suggest that when people look at ethnically ambiguous faces, certain ethnic features that stood out caused people to falsely remember the individual more toward an ethnic category than they actually were (Corneille et al., 2004). When researchers used Caucasian or North African faces, and morphed them to be either low, moderate, or high on stereotypical features the faces that were moderately stereotypical of either a Caucasian or North African faces person were falsely recollected in memory as more Caucasian or North African than they actually were. So, researchers have concluded that distortions in memory are due to stereotypical representations that are held about certain ethnicities. And researchers have claimed that memory of anything that can be categorized is subject to an accentuation effect in which the memory is distorted toward typical categorical examples (Corneille et al., 2004).

To sum up, according to the cognitive approach, stereotyping that underlies prejudice is a byproduct of categorical thinking—a person's way of simplifying information. So, according to the cognitive view, prejudice stems not from pathological personality traits or conditioned behaviors but rather from faulty categorical thinking. Thus, according to the cognitive view, the remedy to eliminating prejudice is not by understanding childhood experiences, unconscious defenses, or conditioned behaviors, but rather by understanding the cognitive processes and "redirecting them" (Jones, Dovidio, & Vitze, 2014, p. 134).

To this end, some researchers have asserted that certain strategies can be used to redirect the cognitive processes. For example, some have suggested that "combating" prejudice requires cognitive "decategorization strategies" and "recategorization strategies."

Decategorization strategies are defined as getting "people to stop thinking about others primarily in terms of group boundaries ("we" vs. "they") and instead encourage them to regard one another primarily as distinct individuals ("me and you") (Fiske, 1998, 2000; Jones et al., 2014, p. 134).

According to some researchers, "personalization strategies" can help strengthen decategorization. Personalization is defined as conveying information that expresses a person's unique qualities. According to this view, personalization can help people recognize that their stereotypes of another group are incorrect, which can then undermine their bias against the group as a whole (e.g., Brewer & Miller, 1984; Davies, Tropp, Aron, Ensari, & Miller, 2002; Ensari & Miller, 2002; Davies et al.,2011).

Some researchers have maintained that personalization is one reason why having friendships with people of another group is effective for reducing bias toward the group (e.g., Aberson, Shoemaker, & Tomolillo, 2004; Binder et al., 2009; Eller & Abrams, 2004; Levin, Van Larr, & Sidanius, 2003; Paolini, Hewstome, Cairns, & Voci, 2004; and meta-analytic studies: Pettigrew & Tropp, 2006; Davies & Aron, 2016).

Figure 3.10 Handshake

In addition to the cognitive decategorization strategies, "cognitive recategorization" has been suggested as a remedy as well. Cognitive recategorization strategies are defined as getting people to produce a superordinate common identity or a "we" category to replace the way people ordinarily categorize others into separate groups (e.g., Jones et al., 2014, p. 134; Dovidio, Gaertner, & Saguy, 2009; Levine, Prosser, Evans, & Reicher, 2005; Nier, Gaertner, Dovidio, Banker, &Ward, 2001).

Some research on cognitive recategorization suggests that when members of different groups view one another as part of a "we" superordinate category that includes both groups then positive group relations can be achieved (e.g., Gaertner & Dovidio, 2000; Gaertner, Mann, Murrell, & Dovidio, 1989; Gaertner, Rust, Dovidio, Anastasio, & Bachman, 1996). Other research shows that positive effects between groups occur when people categorize themselves and others in terms of both the "we" superordinate group and their subordinate group memberships (e.g., Gonzalez & Brown, 2003; Hornsey & Hogg, 2000).

When the cognitive approach became popular in the United States, researchers observed that prejudice had changed from the old-fashioned blatant type that involved overt negative attitudes to a more subtle form of prejudice. It became less acceptable to express prejudice or act in biased ways in a society that endorsed the rights of equality. Researchers became aware of this change as they observed inconsistencies between self-report measures of prejudice and continuing evidence of behavioral racial bias.

Researchers noted these were not typical of people whom one would normally think of as, for example, racists. In fact, researchers noted that these people might say they think it is wrong to be prejudiced. For example, white participants in studies might write down on a questionnaire that they are positive in their attitudes toward black people, but when given a behavioral measure of how they respond to pictures of black people, compared with white people, that is when, researchers claimed, the negative effects come out (Devine, 1989; Crandall, Eshlemann, & O'Brien, 2002; Karpinski & Hilton, 2001).

So, some researchers became interested in studying "implicit" prejudice, where people harbor subconscious biases, of which they may not even be aware, but that come out in controlled psychology experiments. As the cognitive and technological revolutions converged in the 1990s, measures were developed to measure these unconscious biases. The most common measure of this type is the Implicit Association Test (IAT) (Greenwald, Poehlman, Uhlmann, & Banaji, 2009). The IAT measures strengths of associations between concepts by observing response latencies in computer-administrated categorization tasks.

A typical IAT procedure involves a series of tasks asking people to categorize stimuli into categories. For example, people have to categorize different groups (e.g., Latinos or whites) in conjunction with positive or negative words. If people have an implicit, automatic bias favoring one category (e.g., Latinos over whites) over another, they will be quicker in pairing positive words and Latino names.

Because these categorical responses occur in a split-second, researchers have asserted they are difficult to control. In a meta-analysis of 122 studies, some researchers have concluded that scores on IAT reliably predict people's behavior and attitudes, and that the test is a better predictor of interracial behavior than self-description (Greenwald, Poehlman, Uhlmann, & Banaji, 2009).

However, some critics of the IAT have reached a different conclusion (Tetlock & Mitchell, 2008). Their research underscores both the psychometric flaws of implicit bias measures and the weaknesses in claims that such measures predict prejudiced behavior in real-world settings. After reanalyzing the data, some researchers say the findings are inconsistent and frequently demonstrate the reverse of what has been reported.

Also, some researchers maintain that the unresolved construct-validity disputes over whether reaction-time differentials in implicit measures, such as the IAT, actually tap into stable mental associations indicative of unconscious prejudice is not supported by the data. They suggest that other interpretations for such quick categorizations may be related to more benign constructs such as unfamiliarity with minority or out-groups.

They maintain that it is possible people may fail the IAT not because of unconscious negative associations to some group but because they are less familiar with minority or out-group stimuli used in the test, or because these stimuli are less accessible. In any case, the critics underscore both the psychometric flaws of implicit bias measures and the weaknesses in claims that they predict behavior in realistic settings. Also, they maintain that the only valid conclusion one can draw is that the testing has generally showed that most people display an unconscious preference for their own group over the out-group who is different from them.

Although there are controversies about how to explain unconscious biases and how to organize them researchers have come up with a list of about 175 cognitive unconscious biases that have been grouped into different types including, racial biases, decision-making biases, social biases, and memory biases. They range from the popular confirmation bias to the attention bias, omission bias, automation bias, in-group bias, consistency bias, zero-sum bias, and so forth. The cognitive bias cheat sheet has a summary of the 175 cognitive unconscious biases that can be found online at the Better Humans website (Benson, 2016).

In sum, then, starting with the work of Miller there was the assumption that cognitive processes operated and produced their effects without people's awareness. For instance, as mentioned before, when a person encounters some novel stimuli like a new, feathered, four-legged creature that meows, it is assumed that the person is not aware they are ignoring the distinctive features of the particular cat when they bring to mind the stereotyped category "cat." The categorization "cat" allows the person to respond quickly without conscious mental effort.

Another example of responding without awareness comes from the research when stereotyped targets adopted behavior that matched with perceiver's expectancies without necessarily having the knowledge that they were doing so. Likewise, experimenters' categorization labels were found to exert influence on the outcome of their research investigations without their awareness. So, the idea of unconscious influences was taking form in the cognitive approach—a perspective that would become critical to cognitive researchers.

As Eric Kandel, the Noble Prize–winning neuroscientist, explained, "Most aspects of our cognitive processes are based on unconscious inferences, on processes that occur without our awareness. We see the world effortlessly and as a unified whole—the foreground of a landscape and the horizon beyond it—because visual perception, the binding of the various elements of the visual image with one another, occurs without our being aware of it. As a result, most students of the brain believe, as Freud did, that we are not conscious of most cognitive processes, only the result of those processes (Kandel, 2006, pp. 374–375).

Consequently, researchers wanted to better understand the unconscious processes underlying categorical thinking. Note that the term "unconscious processes" does not refer to Freud's concept of the unconscious, in which primitive emotional conflicts are thought to fester. Instead, the term "unconscious mental processes" as studied by cognitive researchers is a descriptive term for mental processes that occur without our being aware of them.

Researchers in social psychology mainly investigated how people categorized from written tests, behavioral descriptions, and computer measures. But to better understand the unconscious influences on categorical thinking, developmental researchers and later cultural neuroscientists turned their attention to the developmental determinants underlying categorizations and the neurobiological processes, such as genetic expression and brain function that give rise to categorizations in an effort to better understand the hidden factors.

Categorization and Development

Developmental researchers have described categorization as "the primitive in all behavior and mental functioning" and have concluded that people are born to categorize (Thelen & Smith, 1994, p. 143). For nearly three decades, researchers have studied categorization in human infants to better understand how prelinguistic infants categorize their environment, as they have suggested that it may be from these abilities that the more complex categorization abilities of the adult develop.

Studies show that categories are especially helpful in infancy and childhood, when many new objects, events, and people are encountered. Without the ability to categorize, children would have to learn to respond anew to each novel entity they experience (Bornstein, 1984; Rakison & Oakes, 2003). In this sense, researchers maintain that insights into how categorization initially develops are fundamental to understanding children's cognitions as well as other emerging related mental functions, such as memory.

In the preverbal infant, studies on categorization traditionally have been operationalized through patterns of looking and orienting behavior. Given that researchers cannot verbally ask infants about their categorization skills, researchers have made use of looking-time procedures or behavioral expressions, and categorization is then inferred if infants display differential responsiveness (Younger, 2010).

The results from these types of studies show that categorization starts when a newborn is just a few hours old. For example, the data show that newborns can categorize different smells and show response preferences for their mother's milk. Also, within hours after birth, infants show a visual preference for their mother's face over a female unfamiliar face (Bushnell, 2001; Bushnell, Sai, & Mullin, 1989; Field, Cohen, Garcia, & Greenberg, 1984; Pascalis et al., 1995).

By the end of the first year, a child's behavior is marked by mother preference and stranger wariness or avoidance. This behavior signals the emergence of the categorical distinction mother-stranger. The child displays behaviors indicating not all adults are the same; mother is the most valued social stimulus. The emergence of the category mother-stranger involves a developmental learning process that includes approaching mother, learning to recognize mother, forming a preference for mother, and avoiding nonmother adults.

Development psychologists have termed these behaviors "stranger anxiety" behaviors.

Among children everywhere, stranger anxiety behaviors first appear at about 4 or 5 months, increase to around the first birthday, then decline. It is a normal part of development.

Babies will usually smile if the mother shows her face above the crib. But if a stranger's face appears, they often show anxiety by turning away and perhaps breaking into tears. These behaviors show that babies have acquired some sort of categorical representation of the mother's familiar face that is violated by the stranger's unfamiliar face.

At around 7–8 months infants become more aware of their surroundings, so stranger anxiety is more frequent and clearly displayed. As a child's cognitive skills develop, typically around 12 months, their stranger anxiety can become more intense. They display behaviors like running to their mother, grabbing at their mother's legs, or demanding to be picked up.

The scientific study of the infant's categorization mother-stranger has a long history. For most of this time, the focus has been on the cognitive and behavioral processes that mediated the categorization as described earlier. But, within the past decade, considerable attention has shifted to the study of the neural basis of categorization in children and adolescents.

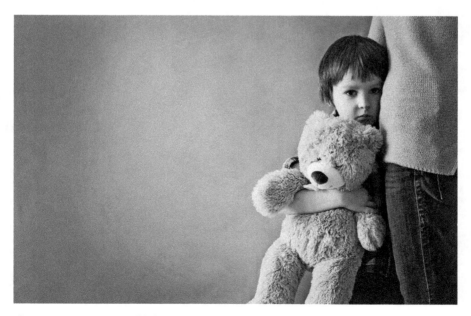

Figure 3.11 Boy with teddy bear

As discussed in an earlier chapter, there is a neurobiological basis of the mother-infant attachment. This suggests the importance it serves for the propagation of the human species. Here we will look at studies showing the neurobiological basis of the categorization familiar versus stranger. This suggests the importance it serves for the propagation of group survival.

Recent studies have examined how the mother-stranger category is represented at the neural level and how neural responses translate into motivated behaviors (Olsavsky et al., 2013; Ono et al., 2008).

Results from these studies suggest that the amygdala (a brain region that plays an important role in emotional reactions) plays an important role in representing the affective relevance of the mother or caregiver. For example, when typical children are shown pictures of their mothers, the response in the amygdala is much greater than when they see a stranger.

The data show that the amygdala is necessary for the expression of mother preference; infants with amygdala lesions, for example, show a lack of maternal preference. Also, the findings show that children's amygdala is preferentially engaged by the mother stimulus over and above that for an unfamiliar adult, and this amygdala response has been found to mediate specific

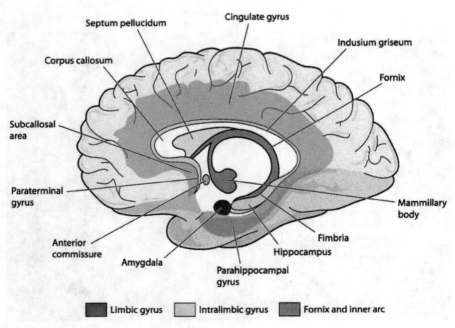

Figure 3.12 Diagram of cross section of brain

approach behaviors to caregivers. Maternal stimuli had powerful effects on amygdala development, attachment-related behaviors, and the categorical representation mother-stranger.

Studies show an altered amygdala development in children who were raised in orphanages and later adopted compared to children raised by mothers or caregivers. When children who were raised in orphanages and later adopted were shown pictures of either an unfamiliar woman or their adoptive mother, the amygdala signal was not discriminating mother from strangers (Tottenham et al., 2010).

Also, the findings showed that prolonged institutional rearing was associated with "indiscriminate behaviors" and difficulties in emotion regulation toward strangers and teachers. The researchers noted that indiscriminate behaviors was often a source of complaint from teachers, as the children engaged in attention-seeking behaviors, attempting to engage in social approach toward teachers too frequently and at inappropriate times, in a way that disrupted the classroom environment.

The finding that amygdala activity supports attachment-related behaviors and the categorical representation mother-stranger is substantiated by findings that mothers also show increased amygdala activation by their own child. Taken together, these data suggest a role for amygdala in the dyadic and intense interaction between mother and child and in recognizing affective salience of the primary caregiver over a stranger. The findings show that the mother-stranger distinction is represented at the neural level and these neural responses translate into motivated behaviors (Olsavsky et al., 2013).

Cross-Race Effect

In addition, to the studies on the categorization mother-stranger, other studies have examined the categorization own-race face versus other-race face (also known as the cross-race effect and own-race-bias effect). All these terms indicate that people are more accurate at recognizing faces from their own racial, ethnic group than faces from other racial, ethnic groups (e.g., Bothwell, Brigham, & Malpass, 1989; Meissner & Brigham, 2001).

The cross-race effect has been noted for having applied significance. The criminal justice system, for example, often uses eyewitness identification (Sporer, 2001). And it has been estimated that other-race eyewitness misidentifications account for a third of wrongful convictions in the United States (Scheck et al.,2003).

The cross-race effect is one of the best-replicated findings in science (Chance & Goldstein, 1996) and has been shown to generalize across a number of research paradigms (Meissner & Brigham, 2001) and participant populations (e.g., Ng & Lindsay, 1994; Sporer, 2001). A meta-analysis on the cross-race effect based on over 90 independent samples (almost 5,000 participants) concluded that indeed the cross-race effect exists. The cross-race effect is not limited to African Americans and Caucasians; in fact, it occurs across borders and across races (see Meissner & Brigham, 2001; Sporer, 2001). The cross-race effect has been and continues to be a robust phenomenon in and out of the laboratory.

Studies show that in the first few days of life, newborn infants demonstrate a visual preference for faces (Fantz, 1963; Goren, Sarty, & Wu, 1975; Johnson, Dziurawiec, Ellis, & Morton, 1991; Maurer & Young, 1983; Valenza, Simion, Macchi Cassia, & Umiltà, 1996), a preference for their mother's face over a stranger's face (Bushnell, Sai, & Mullin, 1989; Field, Cohen, Garcia, & Greenburg, 1984; Pascalis, deSchonen, Morton, Deruelle, & Fabre-Grenet, 1995), and the ability to distinguish between faces from their own ethnic groups (Pascalis & de Schonen, 1994).

And studies show that at 3 months old infants show a significant preference for faces from their own-ethnic groups (Kelly et al., 2005). The same-race preference has been demonstrated with behavioral studies involving a wide variety of protocols, face stimuli, participants, and cultural settings. For example, some studies have assessed the own-race recognition preference in 3-month-old Caucasians using face stimuli protocols. Infants were first habituated to a single face. Then, at test, the same face was presented together with a novel face of the same race. Looking times at the novel face were longer for Caucasian than for Asiatic faces, suggesting that the infants were better at recognizing their own-race than other-race faces. Researchers have suggested that these findings demonstrate an own-race processing advantage (Sangrigoli & de Schonen, 2004; Pascalis, de Haan, & Nelson, 2002).

Other studies have used standard visual preference tasks to examine 3-month-olds' looking times at own-race versus other-race faces as a function of environmental exposure to faces from different categories. For example, researchers have studied Caucasian infants living in a Caucasian environment, African infants living in an African environment, and African infants living in a predominantly Caucasian environment. The results indicate that preference for own-race faces is present as early as 3 months of age, but that this preference is modulated by cross-race attachment relationships. That is, the results suggest that intensive cross-race relationships may block the development of own-race preference in infants (Bar-Haim, Ziv, Lamy, & Hodes, 2006).

Additional studies have further underscored the role of the intensive attachment relationship in shaping the own-race effect by showing that early intensive contact with other-race faces can influence the effect. For example, findings from one study showed that adults of Korean origin who were adopted by European Caucasian families between the ages of 3 and 9 years identified Caucasian faces better than Asian faces. They performed exactly like a control group of French participants, identifying the Caucasian faces better than the Asiatic ones. In contrast, a control group of Koreans showed the reverse pattern. The researchers suggest that the results indicate that the face effect remains plastic and open to learning during childhood to reverse the other-race effect (Sangrigoli, Pallier, Argenti, Ventureyra, & De Schonen, 2005).

Other researchers have been interested in studying the neural substrates of the same-race effect using functional MRI (fMRI). In one study, adult European American males (EA) and African American (AA) males underwent fMRI while they viewed photographs of EA males and AA males. The results suggested that white adult males were better at identifying faces of whites; black adult males were better at identifying faces of blacks. Also, they displayed greater activation in specific brain areas for faces of their own race than for faces of the other race. And greater activation predicted better memory for faces (Golby, Gabrieli, Chiao, & Eberhardt, 2001).

There are many theories as to why the cross-race effect occurs, however, after almost 40 years of empirical study, researchers still do not know the underlying cause of this robust phenomenon nor do they know if the own-race face effect may contribute to race-related biases later in life (Meissner & Brigham, 2001).

Learning Processes: Assimilation and Accommodation

What researchers do know, however, is that people are quicker at categorizing out-group faces than categorizing in-group faces. When categorizing out-group faces, people tend to think more generally about out-group members whereas people tend to think more individually about in-group members. For example, when categorizing out-group faces people may connect a general facial feature with a certain race or ethnicity, and may not categorize the differences in hair texture, skin tone, and eye color that in-group people categorize. So, for example, to Caucasians, all East Asian people may look alike, while to East Asian people, all Caucasian people may look alike.

By contrast, same-race faces are categorized using individualized information involving a higher level of mental processing requiring more time, and involving brain areas such as the right hemisphere and frontal lobe (Bruce & Young, 1986; Perett et al., 1992). Whereas other-race faces, as mentioned earlier, are categorized for general information requiring lower level, rapid mental processing more akin to action-based fight- or-flight response.

The different speeds for categorization (slow for in-group and fast for out-group) that occurs for in-group and out-group faces suggest the operation of different learning processes. Learning—which can be defined as an increased mental ability to adapt to new information and situations—takes place because of two key mental processes that the Swiss psychologist Jean Piaget calls *assimilation* and *accommodation* (1947/1972).

Assimilation is the faster learning process of categorizing new information into one's existing categorizations. Accommodation is the slower learning process of changing one's categorization when new information dictates such a change. Piaget called the ability to categorize the basic building block of intelligence—a way of organizing knowledge.

Piaget emphasized that categorizing is a *dynamic learning process* not a static mental event. In Piaget's theory, categorization includes both a category (or schema) of knowledge and the process of obtaining that knowledge. According to this view, creating categories is an inherently active process. Piaget was opposed to the view of categorization as a passive copy of reality. He maintained that categorization meant acting on our experiences.

As experiences happen, new information is used to modify, add to, or change previously existing categories. There is always tension, Piaget concluded, between assimilation (which in essence represents the use of old categories to meet new situations) and accommodation (which in essence is a change of old categories to meet new situations). The resolution of this tension results in what Piaget called cognitive development.

According to Piaget, we can develop our cognitive abilities only through active interaction with the objects, information, and other people in our world. As a simple example (taken from Kagan & Segal, 1968), consider a young girl who has many toys. To these familiar toys, we add a new one—a magnet. The girl's first impulse will be to quickly assimilate the new toy into her category of her other toys. She may decide to try to bang it like a hammer, throw it like a ball, or blow it like a horn. But then slowly she comes to realize that the magnet has a new quality—the power to attract iron—so she may accommodate her categorization of "toys" to include this previously unfamiliar information. She now plays with the magnet according to her modified categorization that some toys are not designed to bang, throw, or make noise but to attract metal. So, the girl changes her original categorization to fit her experience.

We can see, then, that accommodation involves modifying one's existing set of categories when dealing with new events. This new toy produced an unfamiliar, conflictual experience. So, the girl's first response is to limit her categorization of toys to include only those that she is already familiar with: toys that bang, throw, or make noise. Later, however, she enlarges her category of toys to include ones that also attract metal. So, the girl enlarges her category to include this new information. We can see, then, that accommodation involves modifying one's existing set of categories in dynamic interaction with a situation.

Piaget describes how—as a child gets older—his or her categorizations become more numerous and elaborate. The child's categorizations continue to evolve, incorporating familial and cultural categories. According to Piaget, the final period of cognitive development, which starts at around the age of 12 and continues throughout the life cycle, involves the stage of formal operations. In Piaget's words, "Thoughts take wings." Adolescents, unlike children, no longer categorize with trial-and-error techniques. Instead, they try to think about possible solutions, and they think about their own thoughts. This inquiring attitude may cause conflict with the categories of the adult world and later in the life cycle with one's own children.

For example, the play *Fiddler on the Roof*, based on a series of stories by Sholem Aleichem, illustrates the difficult experience of adapting one's categories to fit new information. *Fiddler on the Roof* tells the story of the conflict between a father, Tevye, and his five daughters.

The story takes place in prerevolutionary Russia in the largely Jewish community of Anatevka, Ukraine, whose residents are ruled by community and cultural traditions.

For the poor dairy farmer Tevye and his wife, Golde, those traditions include asking the town matchmaker, Yente, to find their three oldest, daughters Tzeitel, Hodel, and Chava, who are approaching marrying age—proper wealthy husbands, especially important since the girls will have no dowries. For Tevye the category "proper Jewish marriage" means the matchmaker arranges the match for his daughter and he the father approves it.

Tevye tries to maintain this categorization of the Jewish religious and cultural marital tradition. But Tevye is forced to adapt to the actions of his daughters. When the local matchmaker Yente arranges a match between his older daughter Tzeitel and an old widow, the butcher Lazar Wolf, Tevye agrees to the wedding and is thrilled that his oldest daughter will be marrying a rich Jewish butcher. But, his daughter Tzeitel falls in love with a poor tailor, Motel

Figure 3.13 Fiddler on the Roof

Kamzoil. Motel asks Tevye for permission to marry his daughter. Tevye struggles to incorporate this new information into his category "proper Jewish marriage." He has never heard of the idea of marrying for love and is unsure whether it properly fits into the category. Eventually, with much deliberation he accommodates his category "proper Jewish marriage" to include this unfamiliar concept of "marrying for love." Tevye eventually accepts the marriage and does so to please his daughter.

Then his other two daughter's choices of a husband move him even further away from the customs of his Jewish faith. His second daughter, Hodel, and the revolutionary student Perchik decide to marry each other. However, they do not ask Tevye for his permission. Instead, they just inform him they plan to marry. Tevye has never heard of this idea of marrying without asking one's father for permission and is unsure whether it properly fits into his category. Eventually, again with much deliberation, Tevye accommodates his category "proper Jewish marriage" to include this unfamiliar concept of "marrying without asking for permission." Tevye accepts the marriage and does so to please his daughter.

But when his third daughter Chava decides to marry a Christian man named Fyedka, Tevye is unable to accommodate this information of marrying a Christian to his category "proper Jewish marriage." Instead, he breaks off his relationship with his daughter and considers her dead. He refuses to speak to her or her husband. When his daughter and her husband plead with him and try to explain they share similar human values, Tevye still refuses to accommodate his category "proper Jewish marriage" to fit this new information. He remains steadfast in his refusal to acknowledge his daughter or her husband.

At the end of the play when the family is forced to move away from Anatevka because of anti-Semitic programs, Chava and her Christian husband Fyedka stop to tell the family that they are leaving Anatevka too. They inform the family they are unwilling to remain among anti-Semitic people who could do such things to others. Still, Tevye will not talk to his daughter or her husband. But when one of her sister's shouts out goodbye to Chava, Tevye prompts her to add "God be with you." We do not know what the meaning of this is. Has Tevye accommodated his categorical view of "proper Jewish marriage" to include the possibility that God will look favorably on this interfaith marriage? In any case, the play is a good illustration of Tevye's struggle to think about his thoughts and to modify his categorical thinking to adapt to new events.

Another recent illustration on the difficulty of adapting one's categories to fit new information is depicted in the award-winning documentary titled *Meet the Patels*. Like *Fiddler on the Roof*, the film explores the categorizations and expectations surrounding marriage in the Patels' first-generation Indian immigrant family and in wider American society.

The film is directed by siblings Geeta Patel and Ravi Patel. Neither Ravi nor his sister is married, to the concern of their parents. However, without his parents' knowledge Ravi has been dating Audrey, a redheaded American woman with whom he recently broke up but still cares for.

Ravi's parents are eager to find him a proper Indian wife by means of an arranged marriage. So, on a family trip to India, Ravi agrees to make a serious effort to find a suitable Indian wife by the matchmaking process organized by his parents. His parents continue to lament his lack of commitment to the process and high Indian standards of an arranged marriage.

Ravi discusses his conflict with his sister. On one hand, Ravi understands his parent's categorical view of the "right way of an Indian marriage" but on the other, he embraces the American idea wanting to be free to choose his own wife. Unlike his parents, Ravi revised his categorical view of the "proper

Figure 3.14 Indian wedding/hand with henna

Indian" marriage to accommodate to the idea of choosing one's own marital partner.

Ravi discusses his feelings about the matter with his sister Geeta. Meanwhile Geeta notices that Ravi has resumed seeing his girlfriend Audrey. Ravi eventually recognizes his frame of reference for a relationship is always Audrey, his first love. And so, Ravi concludes that an arranged marriage would be a failure because it would deny his true feelings.

Ravi tells his parents the truth that he has been dating a white American woman. His parents (like Tevye in *Fiddler on the Roof*) struggle to incorporate this new information into their category "proper Indian marriage." Though they are familiar with the idea of marrying for love, they assumed their son would follow the proper ways of an arranged Indian marriage. Ravi's mother tells him that she is worried her deeply held Indian values would be lost.

Eventually, with much deliberation, Ravi's parents accommodate their category "proper Indian marriage" to include the concept of "marrying for love." Though at first they are reluctant to revise and accommodate their views to the new information, they end their matchmaking activities and expectations. Ravi's parents accept their son's wishes to be with someone he loves. Ravi ends up back with Audrey, who eventually wins the affection of his parents and adopts Indian traditions.

In conclusion, categorizing is an ongoing dynamic process that evolves throughout the life cycle. Often, there is a tension between assimilation and accommodation. Initially, assimilation and accommodation are opposed to each other, since assimilation is conservative and tends to subordinate new events to the person's set of categorizations as it is, whereas accommodation is the source of changes and bends the person's categorizations to the new events and experiences. But if in their rudiments these two processes are antagonistic, according to Piaget, it is precisely the role of mental life and intelligence to coordinate them.

This coordination, according to Piaget, presupposes no special force of organization, since from the beginning assimilation and accommodation are inseparable. They are two poles of an interaction between a person and the new events and experiences he or she must face. Such an interaction presupposes a dynamic equilibrium between the two tendencies of opposing poles. That is, there is reciprocal movement between the two learning processes. Accommodating new events and experiences is extended eventually into assimilation. It is a matter of conserving new categories and of reconciling them with old ones.

An increasingly close connection thus tends to be established between the two processes. Sometimes, however, the relation between assimilation and accommodation loses its mutual dependence. When this occurs, assimilation may prevail. And the reciprocal movement between the two processes is stuck. This may be due to any number of reasons including biological, social, or cultural factors. When this occurs, the relation between assimilation and accommodation loses its mutual dependence, and shifting from assimilation to accommodation may become impaired. Whatever the cause, the net result is the same—a loss of flexibility to shift from assimilation to accommodation.

The cognitive view of categorization assumes the mind is like a computer, an information-processing system. But the data reviewed previously on the significance of attachment relationships and the influence it has on our brain development and our nervous system suggests that the cognitive view is too limited. People have a cultural history, a developmental history, and an experiential history that are uniquely marked. Learning is a personal process rather than a static mindset.

The world is not presented to the brain like a set of a random list of letters, words, or numbers that we can neatly categorize. Rather, we judge what the world presents and these judgments create a value system.

So, we turn now to consider our ability to judge.

4

Judging

The Genesis of Judging

Much like the Tower of Babel narrative, the Garden of Eden narrative in the Book of Genesis is among the most famous in the bible. As mentioned in chapter 1, whether we read the bible as a true religious text or as a fictional literary text, the Garden of Eden story describes the genesis of judging and its influence on human beings.

Whereas the Tower of Babel narrative highlights a turning point in history as it relates to human relations because it symbolizes the end of the universal, the Garden of Eden narrative highlights a turning point as it relates to human beings because it symbolizes the end of unity.

Figure 4.1 Serpent with apple

The Science of Diversity. Mona Sue Weissmark, Oxford University Press (2020). © Oxford University Press.
DOI: 10.1093/oso/9780190686345.001.0001

The story of Adam and Eve starts in the garden of paradise. Life in the garden is a perfect whole. There are no categories, no distinctions, no pairs of opposites, no time. Man and woman are unaware they differ from God and from each other. "And they were both naked, the man and his wife, and were not ashamed" (Genesis 2:25).

In the garden, man, woman, and God have a singular identity. "So God created man in his *own* image, in the image of God created he him; male and female created he them" (Genesis 1:27). All was singular, perfect, whole, and complete in the garden. "And God saw every thing that he had made, and, behold, it *was* very good" (Genesis 1: 31).

But the situation soon changes radically. Adam and Eve eat the apple from the tree of knowledge of good and evil. After eating the forbidden apple, Adam and Eve judge their differences and evaluate them negatively. They notice they are naked and feel ashamed.

Judging and valuing happen together. They go hand in hand, forming a subjective evaluation process.

For instance, Adam and Eve might have evaluated their differences positively and felt curious or proud or delighted. The narrative might have included a sentence saying "And the eyes of them both were open, and they knew they were naked; and they went to take a closer look and revel at what

Figure 4.2 Adam and Eve under an apple tree

they saw." Or the narrative might have mentioned that Adam and Eve evaluated the situation differently and had an argument about it.

For example, the narrative might have included a sentence stating, "Adam's eyes were open and he saw he was naked and was embarrassed at what he saw; and Eve's eyes were open too and she was proud of what she saw. And they argued about who was right."

But the story plainly indicates that Adam and Eve both evaluated their differences negatively and felt ashamed. "And the eyes of them both were opened, and they knew they *were* naked; and they sewed fig leaves together, and made themselves aprons" (Genesis 3:7).

According to the narrative, before eating the apple Adam and Eve were unaware of their nudity and their differences. But after eating the apple, the categorical oppositions male and female, naked and clothed, human and God, good and bad, life and death emerge from human awareness.

Some interpretations of the narrative have suggested that Adam and Eve are symbolically expelled from the "garden of the timeless whole" into the "world of reality." And this change symbolizes a major shift in the human mind's awareness. In the beginning of creation, human awareness has a singular identity. But after eating the apple, human awareness changes and has a dualistic identity. The human mind becomes aware of differences and judges and evaluates the differences.

In other words, Adam and Eve give value to their experiences. They are not just impartial observers. Rather, their minds by means of their brains and emotions construct value from the information and experiences available to them. This story illustrates that the human mind judges experiences in relative and subjective terms, rather than absolutely. It suggests, therefore, that to understand people one needs to understand the process of how judging arises in the mind. The mind is more than an input-output machine.

The Limitations of the Cognitive Approach

As mentioned in chapter 3, the cognitive revolution intended to bring "mind" back into psychology in reaction to the limitations of behaviorism. But, according to one of the founders of the cognitive revolution, Jerome Bruner, ironically the cognitive approach dehumanized the very concept of mind it had sought to establish (Bruner, 1990). In part to gain experimental control, the cognitive approach views the mind as an information-processing system. In place of stimuli and response behaviors, there is input information

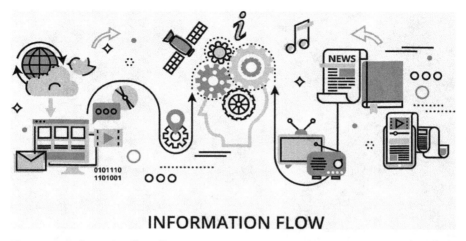

INFORMATION FLOW

Figure 4.3 Information flow diagram

and output information, and the "mind" is viewed as a computational system grounded in the physical world by the concepts of information, computation, and feedback.

Bruner points out that the cognitive view of the mind is indifferent with respect to judging information subjectively. In traditional computational terms, information is an already precoded message in the system. Judging and evaluating is preassigned to the information. It is not an outcome of the system. In other words, the traditional cognitive approach focuses on studying objective "information" not on the human process of judging and evaluating the information.

The cognitive approach views the individual as a processor of information, in the same way that a computer takes in information and follows a program to produce an output.

Cognitive researchers assumed that by studying and developing successful functions in computer science and artificial intelligence it would be possible to make testable inferences about human mental processes, including prejudiced and stereotyped thinking.

So, the study of cognition historically excluded subjective process like judging, evaluating, feeling, emotions, and meaning-making and instead focused on objective processes like memory, attention, perception, problem-solving, and categorical representations. The cognitive approach of information processing does not deal with anything beyond well-defined inputs strictly governed by a consistent and complete program of

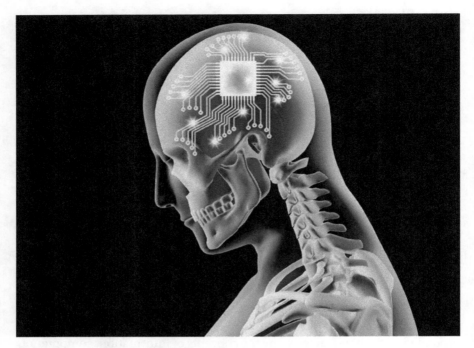

Figure 4.4 X-ray of human with computer chip in brain

computational operations. Computing is the model of the mind, and in place of judging and evaluating information, there is the concept of computing information.

A computing information system needs exact rules. Such a system cannot handle subjective mental processes. So, the traditional cognitive approach to studying the mind precludes such questions as "How do Adam and Eve evaluate their nakedness before and after eating the apple? "Or "How does the evaluation of a "proper Jewish marriage" change in Tevye's mind? Or "How does the evaluation of a 'proper Indian marriage' differ in Ravi's mind and in his mother's mind?" Or "How are evaluations of affirmative action policies organized in the minds of working-class white and black people?" Or "How are evaluations of injustice transmitted from one generation to the next generation?" Or "How do the evaluations of slavery and the Holocaust influence relations among the disparate descendants today?"

The cognitive approach prefers questions like "What is the average cognitive limitation in memory span?" or "What is the level of categorization and content of gender and racial stereotypes in the brain?" or "Do stereotypes function

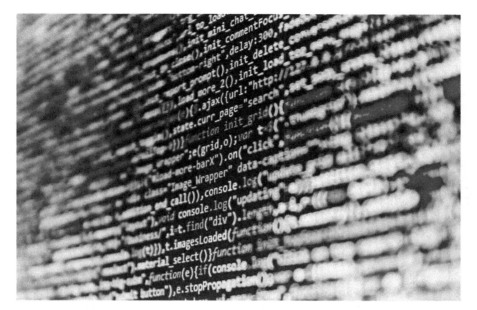

Figure 4.5 Programming code on computer screen

as resource-preserving devices in mental life?" or "Does free recall and recognition memory for stereotype-consistent and stereotype-inconsistent information differ as a function of attentional capacity during encoding?" or "What does it take to activate stereotypes?" Or "What is the relationship between implicit stereotyping and implicit race bias and their respective effects on instrumental versus consummatory forms of race-biased behavior?"

In addition to Bruner, other postcognitive researchers and philosophers have criticized the limitations of the cognitive approach and the types of questions it generates. These postcognitive researchers have carried forward some of the work of Martin Heidegger, Jean Piaget, Maurice-Ponty, Lev Vygotksy, and others.

Though most postcognitive researchers agree that the cognitive approach made important contributions to understanding how information is stored, circulated, and processed, they claim that the cognitive approach leaves out and obscures the very issues that inspired the cognitive revolution in the first place. Issues of how to develop a mental science around the concept of judging, evaluating, and meaning-making.

Many scholars in the field saw raising these issues as an attack on the emphasis on experimentation in psychology, and it provoked opposition among some scholars. But Bruner and others had become disillusioned with the reductionist approach in cognitive psychology that ignored the contexts in which people live and function.

Critics of the traditional cognitive approach maintained that it failed to account for the larger scope of what it means to be human, how humans got that way, and how they could become more so. They argued that starting with behaviorism the psychological sciences tried to deny the existence of human subjectivity, but with little success. They pointed out that a major limitation of the cognitive approach is that the mind is equated to a program with no place for subjective processes.

For example, John Searle, an American philosopher at the University of California, Berkeley, in a famous article posed the query, "Is the Brain's Mind a Computer Program?" And unequivocally states, "No. A program merely manipulates symbols, whereas a brain attaches meaning to them" (Searle, 1990, p. 26).

According to Searle, cognitive researchers mistakenly believed that by designing the right programs with the right inputs and outputs they were creating minds. "The mind, they suppose, is something formal and abstract, not a part of the wet and slimy stuff in our heads" (Searle, 1989, p. 31).

Other critics predicted that the cognitive revolution would fail because the conception of mental functioning was so naïve. Hubert Dreyfus, an American professor of philosophy at the University of California, Berkeley, is an outspoken critic of the cognitive approach. In a series of papers and books, Dreyfus criticizes the underlying assumptions of the cognitive approach.

According to Dreyfus, a key limitation of the cognitive approach rests with the assumption that human cognition is simply the manipulation of internal symbols by internal rules and that, therefore, the human mind and behavior are context-free. Dreyfus argues that the idea that "internal" rules of the human mind can be studied in the same way as the laws of physics is an incorrect assumption.

Dreyfus and other postcognitive researchers argue that a science of the mind will never be able to understand the human mind and behavior in the same way scientists understand objects in, for example, physics or chemistry: that is, by considering people as things whose mind and behavior can be predicted via objective (context free) scientific laws.

According to Dreyfus and other postcognitive researchers, a context-free psychology is a contradiction in terms. They argue that much of what people "know" about the world consists of subjective judgments and tendencies that make people lean toward one judgment and evaluation over another. Postcognitive researchers claim that even when people use explicit symbols,

Figure 4.6 Tree shaped as human face, one side with leaves, the other side dead

they are using them against an unconscious background of subjective, commonsense knowledge and that without this background symbols cease to mean anything.

Postcognitive researchers argue that human mental life depends mainly on unconscious, subjective judgments rather than conscious, objective information manipulation, and that these unconscious phenomena can never be captured in formal computational rules as suggested by the traditional cognitive approach. Postcognitive researchers assert that to get a computer to have a human-like mind requires computers to have a human-like being-in-the-world and to have bodies more or less like humans, and social acculturation (i.e., a society) more or less like humans.

A human-like mind, according to postcognitive researchers, is based on unconscious judgments and knowledge about the world. This "context" or "background" is a type of knowledge that is not stored in a person's brain, but rather occurs intuitively in interaction with the world and other people. It affects what a person notices and evaluates and what they do not notice.

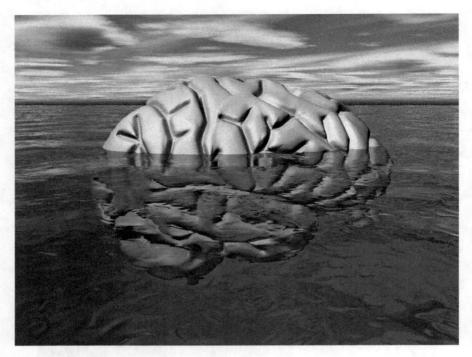

Figure 4.7 Brain underwater

Beyond the Traditional Cognitive Approach

In general, the traditional cognitive approach considered society, the body, culture, relationships, anything outside the brain as peripheral to understanding the nature of mind and cognition. Postcognitive researchers attempted to replace this traditional view of cognition with the idea that mind must be understood in the context of its relationship to a physical body that interacts with the world.

The terms "embodied cognition," "ecological psychology," "acts of meaning," "enaction," "situated cognition," "embedded cognition," and "extended cognition" are some examples of the terms postcognitive researchers introduced. The terms are meant to suggest a new framework that places emphasis on the idea that cognition should be thought of as a brain-body-world mutual interaction occurrence.

Starting with the well-known books *The Embodied Mind* (Varela, Thompson, & Rosch, 1991) and *Being There: Putting Mind, World, and Body Back Together* (Clark, 1998), and in recent publications (Thompson, 2010,

2014) and (Clark, 2005, 2008), postcognitive researchers argue that the standard division between pregiven, external features of the world and internal symbolic representations should be dropped, as it is unable to explain the interactions of being-in-the-world. They argue that the fundamental differences between the embodied view of cognition and the traditional cognitive view lies in the answers to the questions of what cognition is and how it works.

Whereas the traditional cognitive approach views the mind as disembodied from the body and separated from culture and society, the term "embodied mind" is intended to express the idea that cognition should be understood in the context of its relationship to a physical body that interacts with other people and society.

Postcognitive researchers introduced the concept of "enaction" to underline the idea that the embodied mind is determined by mutual interactions between the physiology of the organism, its sensorimotor circuit, and the environment. The concept of embodied mind encourages a view of enaction as distinct from computation, as traditionally conceived.

The concept of enaction focuses on the structural coupling of brain-body-world. This idea builds on the classical phenomenological concept that

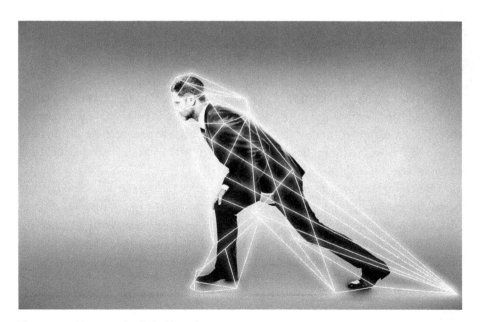

Figure 4.8 Man runs in digital interface

cognitive beings bring forth a world by means of experiences and interactions in the world. According to the post-cognitive view, as the metaphor of "bringing forth a world" implies, the human mind is viewed as emerging from engagement with the environment, rather than being determined by symbolic computations (Stewart, Gapenne, & DiPaolo, 2010).

The postcognitive approach views cognition as a dynamic sensorimotor activity, and the world that is given and experienced is not only conditioned by the neural activity of a person but also essentially enacted in that it emerges through the bodily activities of the person. The postcognitive view challenges the standard position in the traditional cognitive sciences that the mind is identical to and realized in the brain.

Rather, the postcognitive view asserts that people do not passively receive information from their environment that they then translate into internal representations. Instead, according to the postcognitive view, people participate in the generation of meaning by judging, evaluating, and engaging in transformational (and not merely informational) interactions: they enact a world (e.g., Fuchs & De Jaegher, 2009; Di Paolo, Rohde, & De Jaegher, 2010).

The concept of enacting the world is closely related to the ideas of cognitive development of Piaget and the social constructivism of Vygotsky. As mentioned in chapter 3, Piaget focused on how children construct knowledge (via the processes of assimilation and accommodation). And in a cultural context, Vygotsky and other researchers have emphasized the role of dialogue and social interaction in the construction of knowledge and meaning making (Vygotsky, 1978; De Jaegher & Di Paolo, 2007; Di Paolo & De Jaegher, 2012; Thompson, 2012).

Researchers in social neuroscience have borrowed the concepts of "enacting the world" and "embodied mind" to develop the social interactive brain hypothesis. According to this hypothesis, the social neuroscience field has been limited by its exclusive focus on the individual brain as a detached interpreter of social stimuli (e.g., Van Overwalle, 2009).

Whereas traditional neuroscience views cognition as arising solely from events in the brain, the interactive brain hypothesis argues that social cognition requires, in addition, causal relations between the brain and the social environment. Researchers suggest, therefore, that more studies need to be conducted that focus on the neural mechanisms involved in "embodied social interactions" in addition to studies that view cognition as a unidirectional process (Dumas et al., 2010; Lindenberger et al., 2009; Redcay et al., 2010; Pfeiffer et al., 2011; Schilbach et al., 2006; Tognoli et al., 2007).

In summary, a main factor that influenced the development of the traditional cognitive approach was the limitations of the behavioral approach. The

Figure 4.9 2 smiley faces intertwined in an infinity symbol shape

behavioral approach focused on visible behavior without studying the mental, internal processes that created it. When the US government wanted to develop educational programs to combat prejudice, behavioristic research could provide little insight into peoples' mental processes.

So psychologists conducted studies to learn more about the mental, cognitive processes related to prejudice. As mentioned in chapter 3, in the landmark book *The Nature of Prejudice* Allport (1954) brought the subject of prejudice and racial and ethnic stereotyping into the mainstream of behavioral science by treating this phenomenon as a special case of ordinary cognitive functioning. The traditional cognitive approach has since become the dominant theoretical perspective in research on prejudice and discrimination. And Allport's book remains one of the most influential and often-cited publications in the field of prejudice reduction.

Also, as mentioned in chapter 3, George Miller, one of the founders of cognitive psychology, studied the relationship between short-term memory capacity and categorization. After first adopting the behavioristic framework that dominated experimental psychology, Miller came to find it too limiting to study memory capacity. Whereas classical behaviorism viewed the mind as impossible to study scientifically because it is not directly observable, Miller asserted that mental phenomena were a reliable subject of psychological research and could be studied through empirical, objective methods.

In his landmark paper, "The Magical Number Seven, Plus or Minus Two: Some Limits on Our Capacity for Processing Information" Miller (1956) showed as a law of human cognition that humans can effectively process no more than seven units or chunks of information, plus or minus two pieces of information, at any given time. That limit applied to short-term memory and to several other cognitive processes, such as distinguishing different sound tones and perceiving objects at a glance.

Miller emphasized the importance of categorizing—the reorganization of information into fewer units with more bits of information per unit—as a central feature of human cognitive processes. Categorizing, Miller showed, increases the quantity of data that one can process effectively and can help to overcome the seven-item information-processing limit. Thus, Miller's empirical work helped support Allport's claim that categorization is a normal cognitive process, and that stereotypes are normal cognitive representations of how members of a group are similar to one another and different from members of other groups.

Following Miller and Allport's research, social psychology researchers viewed prejudice and stereotyping as the product of adaptive processes that simplify an otherwise complex world so that people can devote more cognitive resources to other tasks. But, researchers noted that despite any cognitively adaptive function stereotypes might serve, using these mental cognitive shortcuts when making decisions about other individuals could have serious negative results. The mistreatment of groups of people in recent

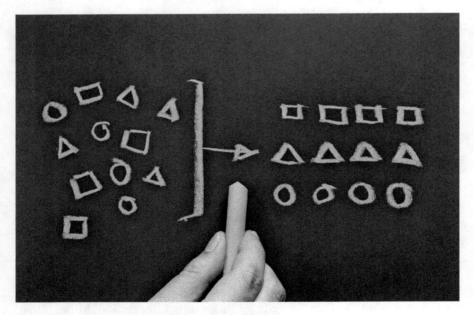

Figure 4.10 Shapes drawn with chalk on chalkboard

history, such as the Jews, the Romani people, African Americans, women, and homosexuals, among others, was the major impetus for the social psychological study of prejudice and stereotyping (Fiske, 1998; Kite & Whitley, 2010).

Allport and other researchers' studies were initially concerned almost entirely with conscious, negative attitudes and explicitly prejudicial actions. But, as mentioned in the previous chapter, according to social psychology researchers, as the societal acceptability of prejudice changed, the displays of prejudice and stereotypes also changed. The social and political movements to eliminate racism in society decreased the mistreatment of people and overt displays of racism. But social psychologists hypothesized that forms of implicit racism may have come to replace the overt expressions of prejudice (Stangor, 2000; Dovidio et al., 2005; Dovidio et al., 2010).

Because of this new view of prejudice, there were methodological adaptations in the study of prejudice and stereotyping that went beyond studying conscious cognitions, attitudes, and behaviors of individuals to studying implicit cognitive prejudices and stereotypes. In place of giving people questionnaires to measure their hidden prejudicial attitudes, tests such as implicit association tests were developed to test automatic cognitive associations that measure semantic concepts comparing speed and error rates on categorizing common stereotypes (e.g., Greenwald et al., 1998; Greenwald & Banaji, 1995).

Although traditional cognitive research has made important contributions to understanding the relationship between categorizations and explicit stereotyped thinking, and categorizations and short-term memory limits, and categorizations and implicit stereotyped thinking, critics assert that the traditional cognitive approach is too limited. Critics claim that traditional cognitive research does not help explain how a person judges information or creates meaning out of encounters with the world.

Because the traditional cognitive approach views the mind as a computer and cognitive processes as rule-governed manipulations of internal symbolic representations, it is unable to account for value-laden judgments. Traditional cognitive research focuses on information processing that goes on inside people's minds. This means that all mental phenomena no matter how complex are reduced to simple cognitive processes.

In addition to studies using tests to measure an individual's explicit and implicit categorization, typically, social psychologists using the traditional cognitive approach conduct laboratory experiments to also study cognitive operations such as categorizing in-groups and out-groups and to test prejudice interventions as well.

The Limitations of Laboratory Studies

Although research using the traditional cognitive approach continues, and yields insightful findings, some postcognitive researchers maintain that a variety of difficulties and limitations have become increasingly apparent. Some critics maintain that a major limitation is the widely used laboratory experiment. Postcognitive researchers have criticized laboratory experiments for lacking ecological validity. Ecological validity refers to the extent to which the findings of a research study can be generalized to real-world settings (e.g., Paluck, 2012; Stangor, Sechrits, & Jost, 2001).

Critics assert that controlled laboratory experiments conducted in artificial settings that lack realism have little in common with real-life settings and relationships, and therefore, are likely to have low ecological validity. There is usually a trade-off between ecological validity and experimental control.

The more researchers try to control a study or experiment, the less ecological validity they have. This is because when researchers control an experiment, they are changing the conditions under which the experiment occurs. These changes are different from what one would find in people in a natural setting in real relationships in the real world.

Figure 4.11 Microscope man

For example, recently, social psychology researchers using the traditional cognitive approach were interested in studying how people categorize out-group members. So they designed online lab experiments and recruited volunteers to play online games that involved giving and receiving money where the online volunteers witnessed one player stealing another player's money (e.g., Yudkin, Rothmund, Twardawski, Thalla, & Van Bavel, 2016).

The results showed that when volunteers made their decisions quickly, they were biased in their punishment decisions. They punished out-group members more harshly, and treated members of their own group more leniently. The researchers asserted that people (the volunteers in the studies) could overcome their "biased instincts" if they engaged in rational deliberation. When the researchers gave the volunteers the chance to reflect on their decisions, the researchers reported the volunteers were largely unbiased, handing out equal punishments to in-group and out-group members.

The researchers concluded that people can learn how to "override their worst instincts" if they are taught to think about their decision-making as

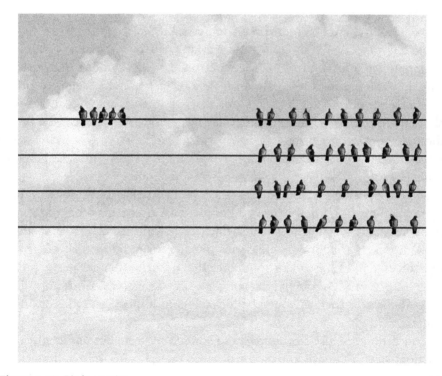

Figure 4.12 Birds on wire

opposed to acting on their first impulse. And they concluded that the results from the online studies could be applied to real-world situations to help people overcome their "biased instincts" (Yudkin et al., 2016).

Postcognitive researchers have pointed out that although such studies can provide insightful research into the nature of mental operations like categorizing in-groups and out-groups, they do not reflect real-world relationships. Social psychologists conducting research on prejudice reduction have noted that these types of controlled online studies may lead to internally valid conclusions on the causal impact of an intervention. And they may include creative and meticulous experiments using a wide range of prejudice reduction interventions, such as cognitive training manipulations. But, it is an open question whether laboratory interventions yield reliable and lasting strategies for prejudice reduction in the real world.

According to Paluck (2012), who conducted extensive reviews of the prejudice reduction literature, this question is largely unaddressed because few laboratory-derived interventions relevant to prejudice reduction have been tested in field trials. So, the conclusion reached is that without evidence, there are reasons to suspect that laboratory findings might not generate pragmatic knowledge to change prejudice and conflict in the real world.

Paluck notes that laboratory interventions generally use quick solutions for prejudice and conflict such as controlled manipulations like wearing similar t-shirts and reading differing sets of instructions meant to prime different attitudes. Paluck points out that while such manipulations may show the minimal conditions necessary to demonstrate change, the prejudice and conflict reduction laboratory's focus on these types of individually targeted techniques means that it is not testing the interventions offered in the real world.

Moreover, Paluck and other researchers point out that the removal of these manipulations from their real-world occurrence disregards other contextual influences and social processes in which real-world factors are embedded. In addition, the laboratory does not include a typical sample of people, prejudices, and expressions of prejudice that occur in the real world, preferring American racial prejudice, volunteers, college sophomores, and low-stakes behaviors such as nonverbal behaviors or implicit attitudes or online game activities.

Concerning the use of volunteers in studies on prejudice and conflict reduction, scientists have known for decades that persons who volunteer for behavioral research may be different from those who do not. Rosenthal and Rosnow (1997, 2009) published an extensive empirical review of the literature suggesting that, in general, volunteers tend to be better educated, of higher social class, more intelligent, more sociable, more unconventional, less authoritarian, more arousal seeking, and more approval-motivated than nonvolunteers.

Rosenthal and Rosnow concluded that the use of volunteer participants might seriously affect any statistical findings. For example, if researchers wanted to conduct an experimental laboratory study to assess the validity of a new prejudice intervention that was supposed to make people less rigid in their thinking and randomly assigned volunteers to an experimental group that received the new procedure or to a control group that did not receive the procedure, we would predict that the controls would already be unusually low on the dependent variable because volunteers are low in authoritarianism.

Or suppose researchers wanted to find out how persuasive an online program was to influence the reduction of prejudicial attitudes by using a sample of volunteers, half of whom would receive the online program, the experimental group, and half of whom would not, the control group. Given that volunteers tend to be higher in the need for social approval, and that people who are high in the need for social approval are more readily influenced than people low in this need, we would predict that participants exposed to the experimental program would be more responsive to it.

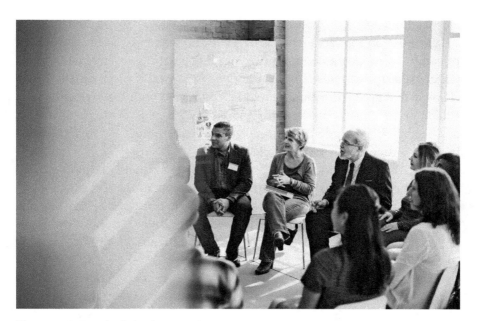

Figure 4.13 People sitting in a meeting

Comparing their pre-to-post scores with those in the control group would exaggerate the true impact of the prejudice reduction program (Rosenthal & Rosnow, 1997, p. 112).

Another major limitation of laboratory experiments, according to Paluck, is that experiments on prejudice and conflict reduction have thus far focused only on testing individual-level theories and on just one or two aspects of individual prejudice at a time (such as attitudes and beliefs or implicit and explicit cognitions), ignoring an examination of how various aspects of "cognitive, affective, and behavioral prejudice are functionally interdependent" (Paluck, 2009).

Action Research and Real-World Interventions

In response to the limitations of laboratory-controlled studies, some social psychology researchers have called for integrating field experimentation, qualitative methods, and action research (e.g., Nagda & Zúñiga, 2003; Paluck, 2010; Paluck & Cialdini, 2014; Weissmark, 2004; Weissmark, Giacomo, & Kuphal, 1993). Action research leads back to the work initiated by a group of researchers led by Kurt Lewin, a German American psychologist (1890–1947) who is known as the father of action research and the founder of modern social psychology.

Lewin was an applied researcher and a practical theorist. He viewed action research as a collaborative enterprise engaging practitioners, researchers, and policymakers in partnerships that addressed critical societal issues. Lewin claimed that applied research could be conducted with rigor and that one could test theoretical propositions in applied research. He had a deep concern for social problems and a commitment to use his resources as a social scientist to do something about social problems.

Lewin, then a professor at MIT, published a paper titled, "Action Research and Minority Problems." In that paper, Lewin coined the term "action research" and discussed what he called the triangle of research, training, and action in producing social change. He underscored that action research was no less scientific or "lower" than what would be required for pure science in the field of social psychology.

According to Lewin, basic action research was needed to develop deeper insights into the laws that govern individual and social life in the real world. As an example, he cited a study that he conducted as a "change experiment on minority problems" (Lewin, 1946, p. 39). The study was an experimental workshop designed cooperatively by social scientists, practitioners, and

Figure 4.14 Businessman stick figures

governmental officials for a group of community workers, aimed at improving race relations.

Based on the findings from the workshop, Lewin concluded that future research focused on the improvement of intergroup relations needs to consider intergroup relations as a two-way affair. This according to Lewin meant both interacting groups must be studied. Also, Lewin emphasized that the results from his study suggested that intergroup relations could not be solved without taking into consideration group tensions and the emotionality of the individuals (Lewin, 1946, p. 44). Due to the inherent groups' tensions and emotionality, Lewin referred to intergroup relations as potential dynamite.

Recently, Paluck and other social psychology researchers who draw their roots from Lewin have reiterated Lewin's suggestion that more studies need to be conducted focusing on real-world interventions. But, to date only about 108 field experiments on prejudice and conflict reduction have been conducted on interventions in the real world. And, unfortunately, they have not yielded any reliable, durable, or observable evidence of the effects of these interventions in the world (Paluk, 2012, p. 185).

According to social psychologists, this is because most of the prejudice and conflict reduction research has used theories that separate individuals from environments and theories that separate various cognitive phenomena like prejudiced attitudes, beliefs, and norms (Adams, Biernat, Branscombe, Crandall, & Wrightsman, 2008; Christie & Louis, 2012). Paluck and Green's (2000) review of the intervention literature shows that most research into prejudice and conflict reduction is influenced by traditional cognitive theories of the mind.

Thus, the data from such studies are unable to account for phenomena like personal histories, traumatic memories, attachments, and value-laden judgments, all of which people incorporate in their self-identities to judge the social world in a particular way and to act on their judgments. So, to date, what has been missing are studies based on theories of prejudice and conflict reduction that are grounded in the embodied view of cognition. (Later in the book, we will look at a few exploratory real-world studies that have attempted to examine how people's personal histories, traumatic memories, and attachments influence racial and ethnic relationships.)

As mentioned before, the concept of embedded cognition and enactivisim emphasize the growing view that cognition is not the representation of a pregiven world by a pregiven mind but is rather the enactment of constructing the world on the basis of personal histories, memories, and attachments. The world people inhabit is constructed by judging their experiences in addition to categorizing information. A core concept of the postcognitive theory is derived from the Chilean biologist Humberto Maturana (1990, 2004) who came up with the concept "biology of cognition."

What this means is that people are biologically equipped with a set of predispositions to judge other people and other groups of people in the social world in a particular way. Not surprisingly, then, as the postcognitive revolution matured, there was the growing recognition of the need for a parallel "affective revolution" to help understand how the emotions are related to the biology of cognition and more specifically to judgments.

Emotions

Both neuroscience and cognitive science have neglected the emotions until recently. Neuroscientists and cognitive scientists for some time had been much more interested in cognitive aspects of the mind than in emotions.

Indeed, one main feature of the cognitive revolution was the lack of emphasis on the affective, emotional aspects of brain functions. The traditional cognitive approach viewed the emotions as mental states that were outside the field of cognitive explanation.

The emotions were left out of the cognitive scientific mainstream because they were viewed as too subjective, elusive, and vague. The emotions were considered too much at the opposite end of what scientists considered the finer human ability, rational reason. They were thought of as animal energies or primal impulses wholly separate from cognition (Damasio, 2000).

The view that emotions are primitive and irrational goes back as far as the Greek philosophers. Socrates and the "pre-Socratics" who preceded him viewed the emotions as a threat to reason and a danger to philosophy and philosophers. And later the Stoics adapted the Socratic view that virtue is nothing else than knowledge, adding the idea that emotions are essentially irrational beliefs, and the good life required rooting out of all emotions.

The Greek philosophers stressed the overarching value of "ataraxia," the absence of any emotional disturbance. Philosophy was viewed as therapy, the function of which was to purge emotions from the soul. The Stoic philosophers

Figure 4.15 Cartoon of 2 men sitting; one man has head detached

believed that ungoverned emotions could destroy one's character (Nussbaum, 1994, 2016).

For instance, anger in the name of justice was considered "furor brevis"— temporary insanity, in the Roman Stoic philosopher, Seneca's phrase. "The wise man will not be angry with wrongdoers. Why? Because he knows that the wise man is not born but made, he knows that very, very few turn out wise in the whole expanse of time, because he has come to recognize the terms that define human life—and no sane man becomes angry with nature" (Seneca, 2010).

Later, throughout the Middle Ages, the study of emotion was typically attached to ethics, and it was central to Christian psychology and the theories of human nature in terms of which the medievals understood themselves (Hyman & Walsh, 1973). There were elaborate, quasi-medical studies of the effects of the various "humours" (e.g., gall, spleen, choler, and blood) on emotional temperament. Emotions were essentially linked with desires, particularly self-interested, self-absorbed desires.

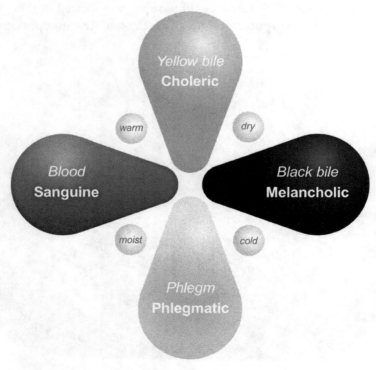

Figure 4.16 Diagram of blood categories

The Christian concern with sin led to elaborate analyses of those emotions, passions, and desires designated as sins (notably greed, gluttony, lust, anger, envy, pride, and sloth). The tight connection between the study of emotion and ethics is suggested in the view that the highest virtues, such as love, hope, and faith, were not classified as emotions, but rather were elevated to a higher status and often (e.g., by Thomas Aquinas) linked with reason. Since some emotions were seen as sins, the highest virtues were not counted among the emotions.

Reviewing the ancient and medieval literature on emotion, René Descartes (1596–1650), the French philosopher, mathematician, and scientist considered the father of modern Western philosophy, concluded that the mind is a separate substance from the body. And he concluded that cool reason existed in a separate province of the mind, where hot emotions should not be allowed to intrude. Descartes reached this conclusion by arguing that the nature of the mind is completely different from that of the body.

Descartes's separation of mind and body and reason and emotion was made famous in his proclamation, "I think, therefore I am." Descartes's philosophical thesis that mind and body are distinct—a thesis now called "mind-body dualism" has had a deep and lasting influence on psychology and science in general.

Since Descartes, science has often overlooked emotions as the source of a person's true being. And the legacy of René Descartes' dualism of mind and body extends even beyond academia into everyday thinking, as reflected in common statements like, "There's nothing wrong with you physically or your body—it's all in your mind."

Robert Solomon (1942–2007), an American professor of philosophy, points out in his essay on emotions that two features of Descartes's thesis still determine much of the view of emotion today. First, there is the inferior role of emotion—the belief that emotion is more primitive, less intelligent, more bestial, less dependable, and more dangerous than reason, and therefore needs to be controlled by reason. Second, there is the reason–emotion distinction itself—as if human beings contain two conflicting and antagonistic characteristics. According to Solomon, even those scientists who tried to integrate reason and emotion kept the distinction and continued to insist on the superiority of reason.

So, the classical view that reason is superior to emotion partially explains why cognitive scientists did not include the study of emotions among the research interests of the cognitive neurosciences. Cognitive researchers preferred to focus on the analysis of mental states that could be translated in terms of computational operations, such as perception, learning, and memory (Almada, Pereira, & Carrara-Augustenborg, 2013).

In agreement with the classic view that emotion ruins human rationality, the emphasis for years in psychology and the cognitive sciences has been on cognition and rationality, and on ways of eliminating the influence of subjectivity and emotion in prejudicial thinking and in general in decision-making and behavior. The assumption dating back to the ancient Greeks has been that so-called higher forms of human existence—rationality, foresight, and decision-making—can be hijacked by the sway of emotions.

The attempt to complement and overcome these classical views inherent in the cognitive revolution—gave rise to the emergence of an affective revolution. The new approach to the issue of emotions highlighted the limits of the cognitivist conception (Berridge & Winkielman, 2003; Dubois, 2010). Researchers associated with the affective revolution focused on studying the neural basis of emotion and how emotions indeed play a key role in intelligent life (Davidson & Suton, 1995; Panksepp, 2001, 2004, 2005). The classic belief that emotions were a disruptive force in rational thought and separate from reason was shown to be an oversimplification.

In the well-known book, *Descartes' Error: Emotion, Reason, and the Human Brain* (1994) Antonio Damasio, a leading neurologist and professor at the University of Southern California, challenged the traditional view that emotions disrupt reason. The book is widely acknowledged to be a work with far-reaching implications for understanding mental life. To explain the importance of emotions and the close link between emotions and reason, Damasio presents several neurological clinical cases.

For example, consider the case of Elliot reported by Damasio (1994). Elliot was a businessman who developed a brain tumor that impaired his prefrontal cortex. Elliot began behaving irrationally. But testing showed that his intelligence, attention, and memory remained unaffected by his illness. Instead, Elliot had lost the ability to experience emotion. And the lack of emotional guidance made decision-making an unpredictable, dangerous game of chance.

Additionally, citing other neurological cases, Damasio and his colleagues (1999) demonstrated that people who have damage to the ventromedial prefrontal cortex and lose the ability to integrate emotions into their judgments can perform well on tests of moral reasoning and know the moral norms of society. But, when unregulated from the input of emotions, they do not become superrational people who can apply moral principles objectively. Rather, they actually lose the ability to know intuitively that some ethically dubious actions should not be taken.

Deprived of feelings of right and wrong, such people are unable to decide which course of action to take, and they wind up making poor choices or none at all. According to Damasio and his colleagues, as illustrated in the famous case of Phineas Gage, they often show a decline of moral character (Damasio, 1994). And, if the damage to the cortex occurred early in childhood, depriving the person of emotional learning while growing up, the outcome goes beyond moral cluelessness to moral callousness with behaviors similar to that of a psychopath. Psychopathy is a serious personality disorder characterized by persistent antisocial violent behaviors, lack of empathy and remorse, and bold, disinhibited, egotistical personality traits (S. Anderson, Dechara, Damasio, Tranel, & Damasio, 1999).

These clinical findings illustrate that certain aspects of the process of emotion and feeling are indispensable for rationality. The clinical cases suggest that pure reason—reason uninfluenced by emotion—appears to occur only in pathological states that are characterized by impairment of day-to-day decision-making and social interaction.

According to Damasio, both emotion and reason are needed for rationality and to presume otherwise was Descartes's error. The error was the separation between body and mind, between reasoning and emotion and the suggestion that the suffering that comes from emotional upheaval or pain (as compared to physical pain) might exist separately from the body.

According to Damasio, the operations of the mind and the body are intertwined in a biological organism and are connected by nerve cells, lending support to the concept of the embodiment of mind. Damasio presents the somatic marker hypothesis, a proposed mechanism by which emotions guide behavior and decision-making, and suggests that rationality requires emotional input. Somatic markers, according to Damasio, are feelings in the body that are connected with emotions, such as a rapid heartbeat with anxiety or nausea with disgust, and strongly influence decision-making. Somatic markers are thought to be processed in the brain in the ventromedial prefrontal cortex (VMPFC) and the amygdala.

The somatic marker hypothesis has had a major impact in contemporary science and philosophy in the United States and Europe. As the notion that emotions contribute to an intelligent life took hold, researchers investigated the physiological processes; the biological (e.g., Boiten et al., 1994; Cacioppo et al., 1997; Davidson, 1994; LeDoux, 1995; Levenson, 1996), the biochemical (e.g., Rubinow & Schmidt, 1996), and neural substrates (Davis, 1997; LeDoux, 1995; Neafsey et al., 1993); and the neuropsychological aspects of emotions (e.g., Borod et al., 1997). Taken together, the results from all these studies strongly suggest that the brain is organized in part as an affect, emotional, system. The affect system is what allows people to judge and give value to information and to experiences.

The Evolution of Emotions

Damasio and other scholars maintain that the scientific neglect of emotion was in part due to the lack of an evolutionary perspective in the study of the brain and mind. They claim that neuroscience and cognitive science have proceeded as if Darwin never existed (Damasio, 2000; Haidt, 2010).

But the situation changed as more data accumulated providing evidence of the ubiquity of emotion, with the influence of emotions extending to all aspects of cognition and behavior. Scientists turned to evolutionary theory to help to provide a paradigm for understanding the function of emotions.

According to an evolutionary perspective, the evolutionary advantage of an affective system is initially evident as a danger signal system. Evolutionary theory suggests that to survive in an unpredictable environment, humans had to have a decision-making mechanism that is body-mind based and survival-oriented. An affective system allowed people to recognize dangerous, threatening things in the environment quickly and hence increased the probability of survival. Emotions motivated people to respond quickly to events in the environment, which helped improve the chances of success and survival. So, an affective system flowed directly from evolution's first imperative to survive.

The evolutionary perpective viewed our emotions as having developed as a quick way to respond to the environment (Dimberg & Ohman, 1996; Ohman & Soares, 1993). According to Ohman, an orienting response was the way evolution sculpted an emotional affective system to provide preferential access to those classes of things with adaptive significance for organisms (Ohman et al., 1998). Based on comparative data, Hunt and Campbell (1997) have further suggested that orienting responses to neutral things may have evolved from earlier, more motivationally basic responses, answering the questions "Is it friendly or dangerous?" or "Is it poison or food?"

From an evolutionary perspective, scholars have speculated that the early human nervous systems evolved innate patterns of emotional activity to reliably control basic reflexes and drives promoting survival such as respiration, feeding, fight–flight behavior and species perpetuation such as attachment, sexual behaviors, care of kin, and later belonging to groups. Emotions and feelings were patterns of neural activity that evolved as indicators and facilitators of these basic functions. Several researchers have covered in detail some of the neural substrates of the affect system (e.g., LeDoux, 1995).

According to an evolutionary perspective, evolutionary forces value species survival and therefore a system to differentiate between hostile and

Figure 4.17 Anetlope and 2 cheetahs

hospitable things was necessary. So, according to evolutionary theory, the human brain and body have been shaped by natural selection to perform affective judgments and to act accordingly. Affective judgments and actions are so critical that organisms developed rudimentary reflexes for judging and approaching or withdrawing from certain classes of things and for providing metabolic support for these actions (Davis, 1997; LeDoux, 1995).

As humans evolved, the affective system was shaped by learning and cognition. As several authors have noted, an additional adaptive advantage is given to species whose individual members can learn based on the unique environmental events to which they are exposed, can represent and predict events in their environment, can manipulate and plan based on representations, and can exert some control over their attentional and cognitive resources (Berntson et al., 1993; Kahneman et al., 1998).

A number of studies have suggested that the affective system shaped by learning to deal with an unpredictable environment resulted in the propensity to react more strongly to negative events and experiences than to positive ones. Exploratory behavior can provide useful information about a person's environment, but exploration can also place a person in contact with dangerous and hostile experiences.

Because it is more difficult to reverse the consequences of an injurious or fatal assault than those of an opportunity unpursued, the process of natural selection may also have resulted in the tendency to react more strongly to negative than to positive events. Termed the "negativity bias," this heightened judgment to negative events and information is a robust psychological phenomenon (e.g., Cacioppo & Berntson, 1994; Cacioppo et al., 1997, Peeters & Czapinski, 1990; Rozin & Royzman, 2001; Taylor, 1991).

Miller's research on rodent behavior provided some of the earliest evidence for a negativity emotional bias by demonstrating that the slope for an avoidance gradient was steeper than the slope for an approach gradient (Miller, 1961). Forty years later, data supporting a negativity bias has been shown in areas as wide-ranging as impression formation (e.g., Skowronski & Carlston, 1989), person memory (e.g., Ybarra & Stephan, 1996), hiring decisions (e.g., Tucker & Rowe, 1989), personnel evaluations (e.g., Ganzach, 1995), voting behavior (e.g., Klein, 1991, 1996), friendships, marital relationships, and ethnic and social class relationships (Baumeister, Bratslavsky, Finkenauer, & Vohs, 2001).

The negativity bias has been found to characterize the judgments of children as well as adults (e.g., Aloise, 1993, Robinson-Whelen et al., 1997). Taylor summarized a wide range of evidence showing that negative events in a context evoke stronger and more rapid physiological, cognitive, emotional, and social responses than neutral or positive events (e.g., Taylor, 1991; Westermann et al., 1996).

As further evidence, researchers studying event-related brain potentials (ERPs) uncovered evidence consistent with a negativity bias in the affect system. Negative information tends to influence evaluations more strongly than comparably extreme positive information. To test whether this negativity bias operates at the evaluative judgment stage, researchers recorded ERPs, which are more sensitive to evaluative judgments than the response output stage, as participants viewed positive, negative, and neutral pictures (Ito, Larsen, Smith, & Cacioppo, 1998).

According to the researchers, the results revealed larger amplitude late positive brain potentials during the evaluative judgments of (1) positive and negative stimuli as compared with neutral stimuli and (2) negative as compared with positive stimuli, even though both were equally probable, evaluatively extreme, and arousing. The researchers concluded that these results provided strong support for the hypothesis that the negativity bias in affective processing occurs as early as the initial judgment into valence classes (Ito et al., 1998).

In sum, negative emotions have been described as playing a fundamental role in regulating the affective system; they serve as a judgment for mental and behavioral adjustments.

Positive emotions, in contrast, serve as a judgment to stay the course or as a judgment to explore the environment. This characterization may help account for evolutionary forces shaping distinctive judgment and activation functions for positive and negative affect; the separable activation functions serve as complementary, adaptive motivational organization. Species with a positivity offset and a negativity bias enjoy the advantages of exploratory behavior and the self-preservative advantages of a predisposition to avoid or withdraw from threatening events.

According to Darwin, as humans evolved they inherited social emotions as well. In *The Descent of Man and Selection in Relation to Sex*, Darwin included a chapter in which he outlined an account of the evolution of social, moral emotions that has often been cited in social psychology. Darwin discussed several stages in the evolution of the emotional roots of morality.

First, Darwin suggested people are social beings that inherited social emotions motivating them to affiliate with members of their group and to care deeply about their approval and disapproval. Next, Darwin suggested that people experience conflicts between selfish emotions and social emotions, and in many cases, selfish emotions win out.

However, Darwin underscored that when early humans acquired the ability to remember what they had done and to care about the opinions of others, they ended up feeling guilty and bad about violating their social feelings and treating others poorly. This, argued Darwin, marked the origin of a moral conscience.

Darwin maintained that this human moral sense or conscience is the supreme principle of human action and can be summed up "in that short but imperious word *ought*, so full of high significance. It is the most noble of all the attributes of man, leading him without a moment's hesitation to risk his life for that of a fellow-creature; or after due deliberation, impelled simply by the deep feeling of right or duty, to sacrifice it in some great cause" (Darwin, 1871, p. 79).

Next, Darwin suggested that as humans evolved, their intellectual and language abilities expanded their moral emotions, and their sense of right and wrong evolved too. Darwin pointed out that after people acquired the power of language, "and the wishes of the community could be expressed, the common opinion how each member ought to act for the public good would naturally become in a paramount degree the guide to action" (Darwin, 1871, p. 80).

According to Darwin, people's moral emotions were acquired in a very rude state and probably even by their apelike progenitors. Darwin argued that people's moral emotions and sense of ought were influenced to a high degree by the wishes and judgments of one's fellow tribespeople. Like all social animals, humans inherited the tendency to obey the wishes and judgment of the community and to aid and defend their tribe members. Darwin maintained that people valued the strong feeling of the approval of their fellows, and even more so the still stronger feelings of horror of disapproval, scorn, and infamy.

However, Darwin argued that people would eventually evolve to the point of being the supreme judge of their own conduct and would adopt the Kantian moral imperative "I will not in my own person violate the dignity of humanity" (Darwin, 1871, p. 90). Darwin argued that the moral emotion of sympathy was the most important emotion for the advancement of humankind.

The feeling of sympathy, Darwin maintained, lies in a person's strong retentiveness of former states of pain or pleasure. So, for example, the sight of another person enduring hunger, cold, fatigue, revives in the person some recollection of these states, which are painful even in idea. Thus, according to Darwin, people will be impelled to relieve the sufferings of another, in order that their own painful feelings may be at the same time relieved. In like manner, people will be led to participate in the pleasures of others (Darwin, 1871, p. 86).

Darwin maintained that as people advanced in civilization and small tribes are united into larger communities, people's feelings of sympathy would extend to all of humanity, extending to all people of all nations and races and to all living beings. The very idea of humanity, Darwin thought, was one of the greatest virtues that eventually would be spread through instruction and example to the young and eventually become incorporated in public opinion (Darwin, 1871, p. 100).

In conclusion, the emphasis for years in psychology has been on cognition and rationality and on ways of diminishing the influence of subjectivity and emotions in rational thinking. But research suggests that emotions are a part of our evolutionary past, and are fundamental to reason, social living, and morality.

Studies suggest that emotions are not merely primal impulses wholly separate from cognition. Rather, emotions are intelligent responses to the perception of value. They proceed from judgments people make concerning objects and other people and are part and parcel of the system of general and moral reasoning.

Human beings enter the world dependent on objects beyond their control, most notably attached to their mothers, and emotional development starts in relation to this fact. As mentioned in chapter 2, research suggests that emotions are intelligent responses to the perception of value that starts even before birth. Emotions are a personal value-laden mode of judgment.

People are participants in the social world, not just observers of it, and the emotions help guide our judgments. As we will see later, people acquire mindsets consisting of their judgments, of their individual way of experiencing the world. Thus, if our mindsets and judgments contain in themselves an awareness of value or importance, they cannot easily be ignored in studies on prejudice and conflict reduction.

In the next chapter, we will look at diversity and relationships.

5

Diversity and Relationships

Relationships in Evolutionary Perspective

The question of life's beginnings—one of those existential questions that people have pondered since ancient times—has been explored by physicists, chemists, and biologists. Physicists have their Big Bang theory, chemists have their chemical reaction theory, and biologists have Charles Darwin's evolution by natural selection theory.

Darwin tried to answer the question "How did life in all its forms get underway and evolve?" As mentioned in chapter 1, Darwin concluded, and scientists generally agree, that all life today evolved by common descent from a single primitive life form. Scientists claim there is a compelling list of evidence—for example, the universal genetic code and statistical evidence corroborating the monophyly of all known life—to support Darwin's theory of a universal common ancestor. Scientists, however, do not know how this early form came about. But they agree with the Darwinian view that it was a natural process that took place approximately 3.5 billion years ago (e.g., Steel & Penny, 2010; Theobal, 2010).

In the final chapter of his book *Descent of Man and Selection in Relation to Sex*, Darwin plainly states, "The main conclusion here arrived at, and now held by many naturalists who are well competent to form a sound judgment, is that man is descended from some less highly organized form" (Darwin, 1871, p. 545).

A few pages later, Darwin describes the process of descent:

By considering the embryological structure of man,—the homologies which he presents with the lower animals,—the rudiments which he retains,—and the reversions to which he is liable, we can partly recall in imagination the former condition of our early progenitors; and can approximately place them in their proper place in the zoological series. We thus learn that man is descended from a hairy, tailed quadruped, probably arboreal in its habits, and an inhabitant of the Old World. This creature, if its whole structure had been examined by a naturalist, would have been classed amongst the Quadrumana, as surely as the still more ancient progenitor of the Old and New World monkeys.

The Science of Diversity. Mona Sue Weissmark, Oxford University Press (2020). © Oxford University Press.
DOI: 10.1093/oso/9780190686345.001.0001

The Quadrumana and all the higher mammals are probably derived from an ancient marsupial animal, and this through a long line of diversified forms, from some amphibian-like creature, and this again from some fish-like animal. In the dim obscurity of the past we can see that the early progenitor of all the Vertebrata must have been an aquatic animal, provided with branchise, with the two sexes united in the same individual, and with the most important organs of the body (such as the brain and heart) imperfectly or not at all developed. This animal seems to have been more like the larvae of the existing marine Ascidians than any other known form. (Darwin, 1871, p. 548)

What is interesting here is that Darwin proposes that our earliest progenitor, the origin of all life, was an aquatic animal with the *two sexes united in the same individual*. So, according to Darwin, the evolution to separate sexes took place later in the process of natural selection.

Since hypotheses for the origins of separate sexes are difficult to test experimentally, most current research has focused on understanding the evolutionary advantage of sexual reproduction. Why are two sexes needed?

Figure 5.1 Big bang theory artwork

Figure 5.2 2 moths

Biologists have concluded that the advantage of two sexes and sexual reproduction derives from the recombination, where parent genotypes are reorganized and shared with the offspring. This stands in contrast to single-parent nonsexual replication, where the offspring is genetically identical to the parents. Many jellyfish, sea anemones, and marine worms reproduce by nonsexual means, giving rise to new populations, but the individuals are identical. If some hostile environmental change should happen, all the individuals would be equally affected and none might survive.

By contrast, sexual reproduction not only replaces individuals within a population but also creates a new population that is more likely to survive under changing environments. The major difference is that organisms resulting from sexual reproduction have two parents that are never exact genetic replicas of either.

When two reproductive cells from different parents come together and combine, the product of development is not the same as either parent. So, sexual reproduction generates novel and diverse genotypes. It creates controlled diversity and the variability necessary to adapt to new environmental

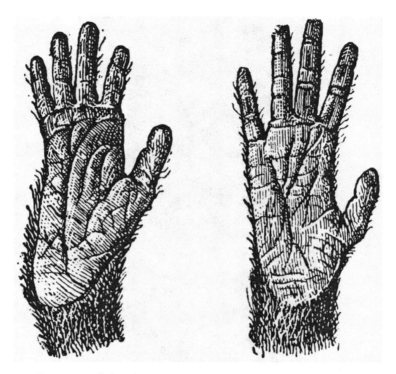

Figure 5.3 Illustration of 2 hands

changes. Because of the range of genetic differences, some individuals have the possibility of surviving under changing circumstances.

In essence, sexual reproduction is a process that double guarantees that individuals within a population will be replaced, and that the population will be better suited to survive under changing circumstances. The diversity resulting from sexual reproduction is vital for the process of evolution to work. Sexual reproduction is responsible for diversity, without which evolution could not take place.

Recent research supports the conclusion that sexual reproduction improves population health and protects against extinction. According to researchers, sexual reproduction ultimately dictates who gets to reproduce their genes into the next generation; therefore, it is a widespread and powerful evolutionary force (Lumley et al., 2015).

Because sexual reproduction is necessary for survival of the species, Darwin sought to describe the mechanisms by which it operates. As mentioned in chapter 1, Darwin hypothesized that sexual selection operates when males

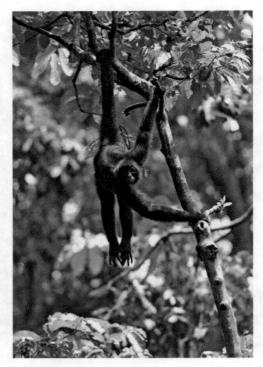

Figure 5.4 Monkey hanging on tree

compete for reproduction and females choose, and the existence of two different sexes encouraged these processes. Since many structures and behaviors in individuals could not be explained by natural selection, Darwin felt he needed to invent the concept of sexual selection (Darwin, 1871, p. xviii).

Drawing on Darwin's sexual selection hypothesis, social and evolutionary psychologists have been interested in studying its influence on human behavior and close relationships. In this regard, psychological research on sexual selection is in the general tradition of understanding how evolutionary processes have shaped the human mind (e.g., Dawkins, 1976/1989, 1982, 1986; Dennett, 1995; Miller, 2000; Pinker, 1997, 2003).

Psychologists who study sexual selection have purported that the human mind evolved not just as a survival machine but also as courtship and relationship machine. They claim that evolution is driven not just by natural selection for survival but also by the equally important process of sexual selection through mate choice (e.g., Buss, 1995; Kenrick, 1987; Miller, 2000). Evolutionary psychologists maintain that the human mind's most impressive,

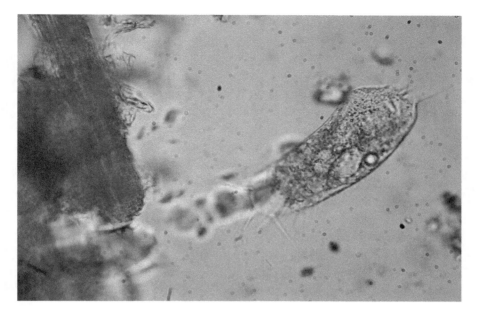

Figure 5.5 Microscopic photograph

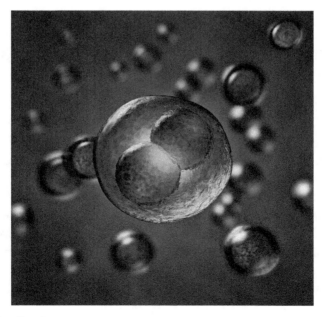

Figure 5.6 2 cell embryo

enigmatic abilities are courtship and relationship tools that evolved to attract and maintain sexual partners. So, according to evolutionary psychologists the psychological process of sexual selection has played a causal force in evolution.

The theory of mate choice was not very popular in the scientific literature and has only been revived in biology and psychology in about the last 15 years or so. Many journals including evolution, animal behavior, and biology have featured research on mate choice in the study of animal behavior. The topic passed by psychology and social sciences almost completely, and little research attention was paid to understanding how sexual selection could have shaped human behavior. But the revival of research in sexual selection in animal behavior and biology suggested that sexual selection functioned the way Darwin proposed (e.g., Hosken & House, 2011).

Evolutionary psychologists claim that sexual selection in humans can explain many human behaviors related to mating and relationships. They hypothesize that men and women faced different adaptive challenges throughout human history that have shaped behavioral differences in males and females today. Women, they claim, face the challenges of surviving through pregnancy and lactation and then rearing children.

Men face the challenges of paternity uncertainty, with its related risk of misallocating parental resources and of maximizing the offspring onto which they pass their genes.

Because insemination and pregnancy occurs inside of the female, males cannot be certain they are investing in their genetic offspring.

Evolutionary biologists have proposed that the relative parental investment of the sexes influences the processes of sexual selection and mate preference (Trivers, 1972). Specifically, parental investment theory posits that the sex that invests more in offspring is selected to be more discriminating in choosing a mate, whereas the sex that invests less in offspring is more competitive with members of the same sex for sexual access to the high-investing sex.

In theory, a male from such a species can produce a large number of offspring over the course of his life. In contrast, a female from said species typically can have a much smaller number of offspring during her reproductive life, partly due to an obligatory parental investment including gestation and delivery. This suggests that females will be more selective ("choosy") of mates than males will be, choosing males with good fitness (e.g., genes, high status, resources, and so forth), to help offset any lack of direct parental investment from the male, and therefore increase reproductive success.

Whereas a female brings one fetus to term and then nurses it, a male can spread his genes be fertilizing many females. Women's investment in childbearing is

Figure 5.7 Family portrait

at least nine months; men's investment may be shorter. Thus, say evolutionary psychologists, females invest their reproductive prospects carefully, by looking for sign of resources and commitment. Males compete with other males for chances to win the genetic draw by sending their genes into the future, and look for healthy, fertile soil in which to plant their seed. To maximize their offspring, men have adopted a short-term mating strategy of attracting and impregnating many fertile mates rather than one long-term mate.

To test sexual differences in heterosexual mate preferences, evolutionary psychologists surveyed 10,047 people from all races, religions, and political systems across 37 countries on six continents and five islands (Buss, 1994). The researchers wanted to determine the different characteristics each sex looks for in a mate. They sought to answer the questions: "Is there anything consistent about human behavior when it comes to the search for a mate?" "Would a Gujarati of India be attracted to the same traits in a mate as a Zulu of South Africa or a college student in the Midwestern United States?" (Buss, 1994, p. 238; Buss, 2007).

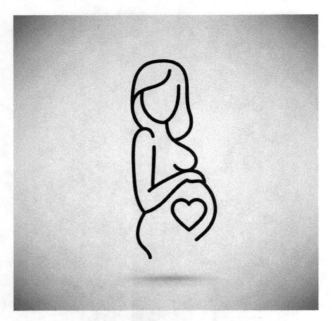

Figure 5.8 Drawing of pregnancy

So, Buss and 50 others scientists, conducted an extensive survey on the heterosexual mating preferences of men and women. Although no survey, short of questioning the entire human population, can be considered complete, their study crosses a range of geographic, cultural, political, ethnic, religious, racial and economic groups.

Their findings revealed that men everywhere preferred women whose physical features, such as youthful faces and health, suggested fertility. Women everywhere preferred men whose wealth, power, and ambition suggested resources for protecting and nurturing offspring. Also, their findings showed that everywhere men tend to marry younger women. The older the man, the greater the age difference he preferred when selecting a mate (Kenrick & Keefe, 1992).

From these findings and other cross-cultural studies evolutionary psychologists hypothesized, that there are evolutionary causes for these sexual preference differences (Schmitt, 2005). Evolutionary psychologists claim that men place high importance on youth because youthful appearances signal fertility. Because men seek to maximize their number of mates capable of passing on their genes, men place high value on fertility cues. The findings also revealed that women desire older mates. The researchers hypothesized that

Figure 5.9 Photo meant to depict a "rich man" with money flying around

older men might have higher social status that could lead to more resources for a woman and her offspring, and could therefore increase a woman's likelihood of sexual success and reproduction (Chang, Wang, Shackelford, & Buss, 2011).

Another area in which the two sexes were found to differ was in their reactions to sexual and emotional infidelity. Researchers found that women were more jealous of emotional infidelity while men were more jealous of sexual infidelity. Researchers hypothesized that women find emotional infidelity more threatening because it could lead to the woman losing the resources she had gained from that mate and having to raise children on her own, and men find sexual infidelity more threatening because they could risk spending resources on a child that may not be their own. This sex difference in the nature of jealousy has been found by different researchers—psychologically, physiologically, and cross-culturally (e.g., Buss et al., 1992; DeSteno et al., 2002; Geary et al., 1995; Harris, 2000; Pietrzak et al., 2002; Shackelford, Buss, & Bennett, 2002; Shackelford et al., 2004).

Reflecting on the findings on sexual differences and preferences, evolutionary psychologists concluded that the results indicate that human beings, like other animals, exhibit species-typical preferences when it comes to the selection of a mate. Evolutionary psychologists claim that Darwin's initial insights into sexual selection have turned out to be scientifically profound for people, even though Darwin did not stipulate the importance of relative parental investment for sex differences in mate selection (Buss, 1994, p. 249).

However, critics have pointed out that the findings from studies on sexual preferences have limitations. The findings come from samples of populations that are limited to urbanized, cash-economy cultures. Rural, noncash cultures were not studied. In addition, arranged marriages present another limitation. The studies on gender and mating preferences lack data and information on arranged marriage and its link to evolutionary adaptedness.

The percent of arranged marriages in the world is estimated to be 53.25% (http://www.statisticbrain.com/arranged-marriage-statistics). In some Eastern cultures (and some religions), marriage is regarded as a sacred institution (Marshall, 2008). Deep-seated norms and customs surround this practice, with often strict cultural sanctions against those who defy these standards (Netting, 2010). While in Western cultures it is usually left to the choice of individuals to select their own marital partner, in Eastern cultures this process usually involves the input of family members to confirm that the partner is a good fit within the family network (Myers et al., 2005).

Choosing a marital partner, within Eastern cultures, helps to reinforce family obligations, and young adults are expected to marry in order to fulfill cultural and familial commitments (Zhang & Kline, 2009). So, families are often included in the mate-selection process from the very start (MacDonald et al., 2012). Parents urge children to adopt a practical approach to marriage, giving importance to those qualities and attributes in a potential mate that are compatible with cultural and familial standards (Levine et al., 1995). Although arranged marriages occur around the globe, critics argue that studies on gender and mating preferences have failed to take into account how individual gender and mating preferences evolve or are expressed in the context of arranged marriages.

In sum, according to evolutionary psychologists human mate choice is strongly sex differentiated. Evolutionary psychologists claim that heterosexual men and women evolved powerful desires for particular characteristics in a mate. And these desires are not arbitrary, but are highly patterned and universal. The patterns correspond closely to the specific adaptive problems that men and women faced during the course of human evolutionary history.

Females were found to value cues to resource acquisition in potential mates more highly than males. Characteristics signaling reproductive capacity were valued more by males than by females. These sex differences, according to evolutionary psychologists, reflect different evolutionary selection pressures on human males and females, and provide evidence of current sex differences in reproductive strategies (Conroy-Beam, Buss, Pham, & Shackelford, 2015).

Critics, however, contend that the data from these surveys are unsupportive of evolutionary psychology's predictions when applied to mating preferences using samples from rural communities and from arranged marriages.

The Limitations of Sexual Selection Theory and Evolutionary Psychology

Unlike the theories of evolution through common descent and evolutionary change by natural selection, Darwin's theory of sexual selection has continually drawn criticism from evolutionists and evolutionary psychology's critics (e.g., Roughgarden, 2004; Roughgarden, Oishi, & Akçay, 2006).

Critics maintain that Darwin was looking to the evolution of sexual differences through the cultural and moral codes of the 19th-century Victorian society. They argue that Darwin lived in a patriarchal Victorian society in which women were instructed to behave in a passive manner, while men dominated.

These polarized gender roles, more commonly known as the "ideology of separate spheres" assumed that men possessed the capacity for reason, action, aggression, independence, and self-interest, thus belonging to the public sphere. Women inhabited a separate, private, domestic sphere, one fit for the so-called inherent qualities of femininity including emotion, passivity, submission, dependence, and selflessness, all derived, it was claimed, from women's sexual and reproductive organization. The Victorian idea that women should inhabit a separate, domestic sphere exists in Western thought as far back as the ancient Greeks (Kerber, 1988).

In Victorian society, marriage was a notable point in a woman's life. Most women were compelled to marry. Because society prevented women from working, they were dependent on men's income. To be considered a potential wife, women had to be virgins, and were expected to remain innocent of any thought of sexuality until after they had received a proposal. This requirement of chastity and absolute purity was not expected of men, as the potential husband had the freedom to participate in premarital and extramarital sexual relationships. Such an idea was one of many double standards in Victorian society that required unquestionable compliance from women.

Critics assert that Darwin was mistaken when he wrote his theory of sexual selection because his ideas about sexual identity and gender were influenced by the social mores of his community. They point, for example, to Darwin's statements that differences in sexual selection preferences exist

Figure 5.10 Victorian mother and children

because "Males of almost all animals have stronger passions than females" and "the female with the rarest of exceptions is less eager than the male . . . she is coy."

Critics contend such statements illustrate the extent to which Darwin was influenced by the attitudes about sex and gender that were current when he was writing 150 years ago. Also, critics express concern that an evolutionary and cultural explanation about sex and gender reinforces male-female stereotypes today. The Harvard Law school professor Martha Minow, for example, takes a critical look at the way gender differences are used in American law to reinforce negative stereotypes of women as being needy and dependent on men (1991).

In addition, critics argue that his elitist Victorian upper-class status influenced Darwin's theory of sexual selection. Darwin's father was a wealthy physician. His mother was the daughter of Josiah Wedgwood, one of the richest industrialists in England. Darwin married his cousin Emma Wedgwood and secured a double inheritance of the Wedgwood fortune. He

Figure 5.11 2 women imitating each other

and his wife Emma, according to Darwin's biographers, lived an aristocratic style with a full staff of servants (Desmond & Moore, 1991).

Critics maintain that Darwin's nonegalitarian lifestyle influenced his theory of sexual selection. The capitalist-industrialist class to which the Darwin-Wedgwoods belonged held the view that population growth would result in famine and widespread mortality. A proposed solution to hold the population within resource limits was to denounce charity for the poor and to discourage marriage and "breeding" among poor people. This solution was made popular by the writings of Thomas Robert Malthus, a late-18th-century economist and an ordained minister.

Malthus wrote a popular essay titled *Essay on the Principle of Population* (1798). The central theme of Malthus's essay was that population growth would always overpower food supply growth, creating perpetual states of hunger, disease, and struggle. The natural struggle for survival captured Darwin's interest, and he extended Malthus's principle to sexual selection theory.

Darwin saw poverty as an undesirable trait; therefore, he felt poor people were unfit to marry and reproduce: "The advancement of the welfare of

Figure 5.12 Drawing of 3 men

mankind is a most intricate problem: all ought to refrain from marriage who cannot avoid abject poverty for their children; for poverty is not only great evil, but tends to its own increase by leading to recklessness in marriage" (1871, p. 556). Later, Darwin softened his view and suggested there should be an open competition, and laws or customs from rearing offspring should not prevent the poor. Still, critics contend that Darwin's sexual selection theory was influenced by his elitist views.

According to his biographers, Darwin was neither saint nor Satan. Looked at in his own day, they maintain, Darwin was complex and contradictory. And, his biographers point out, unlike the modern "disinterested" scientist who is supposed to derive theories from "the facts" and only then allow the moral concerns to be drawn, Darwin was fueled by a moral passion. His passion was to show that all life, not only black and white, but all races, all sexes, all species, through all time are joined to a common ancestor (Desmond & Moore, 2009).

Darwin's biographers claim that from the very start Darwin concerned himself with the unity of humankind. "This notion of 'brotherhood' grounded his

Figure 5.13 Boys working

evolutionary enterprise. It was there in his first musings on evolution in 1837." Nevertheless, his biographers contend, "All the actors in our story—Darwin included—held derogatory views of other peoples to some extent, and used terms to match" (Desmond & Moore, 2008). However, they suggest that some terms and ideas like "Negro," "mankind," and "savages" may sound offensive to us now, but should be viewed as historically constructed respective period terms. Whether the "great evils of poverty" and "coy females" fit the list of historically respective terms remains unclear.

Critics also see problems more generally with evolutionary explanations (e.g., Bussey & Bandura, 1999; Duchaine, Cosmides, & Tooby, 2001; Ehrlich & Feldman, 2003; Tooby & Cosmides, 1992). Critics contend that evolutionary psychologists sometimes start with an effect, such as the male-female difference in mate preferences in sexual selection, and then work backward to hypothesize an explanation for it. The logic works like this: "Why do men prefer fertile women and women prefer successful men? Because it serves a reproductive strategy."

Critics argue that many hypotheses put forward to explain the adaptive nature of human behavioral traits are examples of hindsight reasoning and "just-so stories" neat adaptive explanations for the evolution of given traits that do not rest on any evidence beyond their own internal logic. As the biologists Ehrlich and Feldman (2003) have pointed out, the evolutionary theorist can hardly lose when employing hindsight.

The way to surmount the hindsight bias is to imagine things turning out differently. Imagine that women were more sexually aggressive than men. Someone might say, "Better for producing more children and passing on her genes." And if men were known to be strictly monogamous, someone might say, "Better for ensuring certainty of paternity."

When the well-known scholar Noam Chomsky was interviewed, he reportedly disparaged evolutionary psychology as "a philosophy of mind with a little bit of science thrown in." He suggested that the field is unscientific because it can account for every possible point. "In fact, just about anything you find, you can make up some story for it" (Chomsky & Trivers, 2006; Robert Trivers and Noam Chomsky [Video File]. Retrieved from https://www.youtube.com/watch?v=WJe5UmBlxdE).

Though evolutionary psychology's critics recognize that Darwin's sexual selection theory may help explain our commonalities, they contend that a common evolutionary heritage does not, by itself predict the cultural variations in mate selection and marriages (e.g., homosexual marriages, polygyny, polyandry, group marriages, and so forth) or explain the changes in cultural and behavior patterns over time.

The most significant feature of human nature is the ability to adapt, to learn, and to change. Social psychologists refer to this as culture's shaping power. Social psychologists define culture as what is shared by a group and transmitted across generations—such as norms, values, ideas, attitudes, behaviors, and traditions. And in public policy, the term "culture change" is used to emphasize the influence of cultural capital on individual and community behavior over time. People in addition to being products of biological evolution, are perhaps—more than other organisms—also products of a process of cultural evolution. Cultural evolution consists of changes in the nongenetic information stored in brains, stories, myths, songs, books, computers, memories, histories, and museums (Ehrlich & Levin, 2005).

In terms of sexual selection, in fact, researchers have noted that cultural changes have greatly influenced mate preferences over the years. Traditionally, heterosexual marriages were characterized by clearly defined gender roles: women were responsible for domestic needs, while men were the primary breadwinners. Over the years, however, marital dynamics have shifted.

Cultural influences such as later onset of marriage, increased education, women's independence, higher demand for dual-earner households, and heightened awareness of sexual harassment and other forms of sexism led to changes in gender roles and mate preferences (Barnett & Hyde, 2001; Wierda-Boer et al., 2009).

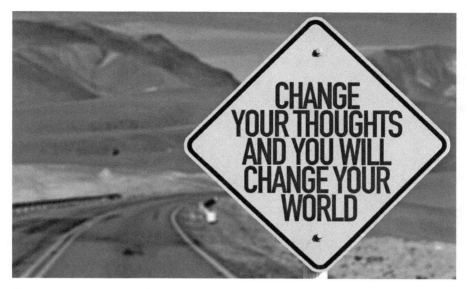

Figure 5.14 Sign saying "change your thoughts and you will change your world"

Indeed, researchers who conducted the extensive surveys on mate preferences found a notable shift in mate preferences over 57 years. For example, gender-related traits—such as cooking skills, housekeeping abilities, and chastity—became less important, and men and women increasingly converged in their preferences over time (Buss, Shackelford, Kirkpatrick, & Larsen, 2001).

According to the researchers, in the context of these cultural changes the empirical data clearly showed a link between the cultural evolution of values and mate preferences. The researchers note that it would be astonishing if mate preferences and values in human mating had remained impervious to cultural changes (Buss et al., 2001).

Relationships and the Love Factor

One of the foundation principles of evolutionary science is that what we are today is the result of evolutionary forces acting on our ancestors in the past. But, researchers have pointed out, the idea that the human brain was molded only once during one period of history is misguided. We have a long evolutionary course during which our brains and bodies adapted, and are still

Figure 5.15 Ring on finger

adapting. And the notion that our preferences about the ideal mate represent some truth that is removed from cultural influences is unlikely.

The importance that people attach to specific characteristic in a mate provides one test of the evolution of values. In a rare research opportunity, evolutionary psychologists were able to assess the cultural evolution of values in samples spanning more than half a century using six different times ranging from 1939 to 1996 (Buss, Shackelford, Kirkpatrick, & Larsen, 2001).

The researchers state that the most dramatic finding that occurred over the generations is the convergence between men and women in their mating values over the past 3 decades. The shift in values centers on the importance of love for both men and women. The data show that from 1967 on, love steadily increased in importance for both sexes, reaching second for men in 1967 and first in the two most recent assessments. For women it reached third in 1967 before it landed at first in 1977, where it remains in the two most recent assessments (Buss et al., 2011).

Figure 5.16 2 birds making a heart in the sunset

The researchers note that exactly why this merging between the sexes and shift in values occurred is unclear. It may be because marriage may be evolving from a more institutional form to a more companionate form. Or one might assume that the decline of the extended family and delay of child-birth has created an increased importance of marriage as the key source of social satisfaction.

However, the researchers point out, this guesswork does not fit with the finding that love achieved primary value nearly universally. Among 34 of the 37 cultures worldwide for which the love factor has been examined, including cultures varying widely on the nature of family and number of children, both sexes rated it as one of the most important three factors among the 18 factors examined.

Interestingly, Darwin also tried to explain why love (and the distinct emotion of sympathy or what we would term compassion today) was so important to the advancement of human beings. He concluded that love and sympathy were social instincts that provided the foundation for our moral values:

> The development of the moral qualities is a more interesting problem. The foun-
> dation lies in the social instinct, including under this term the family ties. These

instincts are highly complex, . . . but the more important elements are love, and the distinct emotion of sympathy. Animals endowed with social instincts take pleasure in one another's company, warn one another of danger, defend and aid one another in many ways. These instincts do not extend to all individuals of the species, but only to those of same community. As they are highly beneficial to the species, they have in all probability been acquired through natural selection. (Darwin, 1871, p. 549)

More recently, the Chilean evolutionary biologist Humberto Maturana and his colleague published the book *The Origin of Humanness in the Biology of Love*. They propose, similarly to Darwin, that love is part of our biological makeup. They hypothesize that human beings belong to an evolutionary history in which daily life was centered on cooperation.

Since cooperation takes place in social relations, and not in relations of domination and submission, the emotion of love was necessary. They contend that this claim is a biological claim, not a philosophical one. Humans, they contend, are love-dependent animals and suffer "in the negation of love" (Maturana & Verden-Zöller, 2008).

Recent work by a multidisciplinary international group of researchers lends support to the notion that love is related to optimal functioning. Combining studies of love and close relationships to the theories and perspectives of positive psychology, the researchers show that love, intimacy, friendship, and relationships bring out the best in people by promoting optimal functioning. When people are in love, they succeed by showing growth, resilience, and care for and connection to others; they take pleasure in being alive (Hojjat & Cramer, 2013).

It may sound logical to assert that love is a necessary emotion for cooperative and optimal functioning that one wonders if empirical confirmation is needed. But, in psychology, there was a long period in which human and animal behavior was explained by reward and punishment schemes. There was little attention to the love factor.

The most outspoken representative of the behaviorist school, B. F. Skinner, saw feelings and emotions as meaningless byproducts of conditioning. "What is love except another name for the use of positive reinforcement?" Skinner said. According to Skinner's behavioral theory, thoughts, emotions, and actions were exclusively products of the environment. His behaviorism was a deterministic theory. Strong mother–infant bonds, found in all mammals, were explained by the rewards derived from mother's milk. According to behaviorists, that was all there was to it.

Figure 5.17 Woman training dog

Behaviorists viewed infants as becoming attached to those who satisfied their needs through the mechanism of conditioning. Caregivers act as conditioned reinforcers who become associated with gratification. This generalizes into a feeling of security when the caregiver is present. Behaviorist explanations implied that attachment is a form of "cupboard love." "Cupboard love" is a British English expression referring to affection that is given just to gain a reward.

Harry Harlow (1905–1981) the American experimentalist psychologist, refuted behaviorist explanations by showing in a famous series of experiments on monkeys that the need for love and comfort was essential for cognitive and social development.

Before describing the details of Harlow's experiments, it is worth mentioning that the ethical aspects of Harlow's research have been criticized. His experiments have been seen as extremely cruel. It was evident that the monkeys in his studies suffered from emotional harm from being reared in isolation. This was clear when the experimental monkeys were placed with a normal monkey (reared by a mother); they sat hunched in a corner in a state of fear and depression.

Figure 5.18 Mother breastfeeding baby

Whatever we think of the ethics of Harlow's research, his research showed that attachment was linked to emotional care rather than physical (food). To demonstrate this, Harlow took baby monkeys from their own mothers and placed them with doll-like objects that he called "surrogate monkeys." Harlow gave the baby monkeys two such surrogate mothers. One was made of a metal wire and provided with a milk nipple. The other "mother" was without a nipple but covered with soft sponge rubber and terry cloth; it was an object the baby monkey could hug and cling to.

The baby monkeys formed a bond with the second type of surrogate, spending the day on "her" and making only brief excursions to drink from mother number one. The results suggested that something about the terry-cloth surrogate provided the baby monkey with comfort, protection, and a sense of a secure loving base. Harlow concluded, "That the control monkeys develop affection or love for the cloth mother when she is introduced into the cage at 250 days of age cannot be questioned" (Harlow, 1958, p. 23; 1961).

Harlow demonstrated that "cupboard love" could not explain the behavior of the monkeys who became attached to a cloth surrogate mother with no feeding bottle, rather than a wire one with a bottle. If attachment were merely "cupboard love," the infant monkeys would have chosen the surrogate, which supplied the food. From the monkeys' behaviors, it appeared they formed an attachment to the cloth mother. And then used her as a secure base from which to explore their environment, and ran to her when frightened by threatening stimuli.

Harlow's pioneering exploration of what he termed "the affectional system" of monkeys has been and still is highly influential, although his conclusions met with resistance. For some scientists it was hard to accept that monkeys have feelings. Harlow described what happened at a professional meeting when he used the term "love" to describe the feelings of monkeys. His colleagues at the meeting objected to the word and countered with the word "proximity." Harlow relented and used the term "affection" when he realized his colleagues objected to the idea that love is a primary drive (Harlow & Mears, 1979).

In the classic paper, "The Nature of Love," Harlow challenged his colleagues to acknowledge that the field of psychology ignored studying love:

> Because of its intimate and personal nature it is regarded by some as an improper topic for experimental research. But, whatever our personal feelings may be, our assigned mission as psychologists is to analyze all facets of human and animal behavior into their component variables. So far as love or affection is concerned, psychologists have failed in this mission . . . But of greater concern is the fact that psychologists tend to give progressively less attention to a motive which pervades our entire lives. Psychologists, at least psychologists who write textbooks, not only show no interest in the origin and development of love or affection, but they seem to be unaware of its very existence. (Harlow, 1958, p. 1)

Though Harlow's American colleagues were reluctant to accept his views, the British psychiatrist John Bowlby (mentioned in chapter 2) was in contact with Harlow and shared his view on the importance of an affectionate bond. And though Bowlby was a clinician and Harlow an experimentalist, the two had much in common. Both challenged the prevailing psychoanalytic and behaviorist views on love that dominated psychological thinking.

In developing their new theories on the nature of the bond between babies and their mothers, Bowlby benefited from Harlow's experimental work with monkeys, and Harlow benefited from Bowlby's clinical observations. Bowlby had observed that children experienced intense distress when separated from their mothers. Even when other caregivers fed such children, this did not reduce the child's anxiety. Bowlby's findings supported Harlow's research showing that the need for emotional contact is a crucial factor, perhaps more than the fundamental need for milk.

As mentioned in chapter 2, Bowlby defined attachment as a lasting psychological connectedness between human beings. Bowlby extended his theory to cover not just parent–child bonding or caregiver–child bonding, but eventually all human relationships. And researchers have demonstrated that adult bonds may exploit the existing physiological systems designed for attachment between mothers and infants (Brown & Brown, 2006; Hazan & Shaver, 1994).

Though the terms "affectionate" and "attachment" may sound cold and clinical, Harlow's and Bowlby's work helped to define a phenomenon that was long ignored in psychology, and that is the love factor (and its corollary, exclusion and emotional deprivation).

Gradually, in recent years scientists have started to investigate love—a factor once ignored in psychology and consigned to poetry and religion, and still considered "mysterious" and "unscientific" by many—using sophisticated methodologies. The most common methods used in studying love are functional magnetic resonance imaging (fMRI) and evoked response potentials (ERPs). Other methods that are used are neurobiological markers (e.g., hormones) and animal models that test relationship processes in animals such as primates and rodent mammals (e.g., Bales et al., 2007).

The results suggest that love relationships including romantic early stage love, and long-term love, and maternal love seem to share a common biological substrate (e.g., Hazan & Shaver, 1987; Fisher, 1992; Carter, 1998; Mikulincer & Shaver, 2007). This finding has been supported by neuroimaging work showing similar patterns of neural activation (e.g., Bartels & Zeki, 2004; Acevedo, Aron, Fisher, & Brown, 2011).

For example, studies using fMRI suggest that love—both in the early stages of love and long-term—is correlated with activation of the brain's dopaminergic reward system (e.g., Acevedo et al., 2011; Aron et al., 2005; Bartels & Zeki, 2000, 2004; Fisher et al., 2005; Ortigue et al., 2007; Xu et al., 2011).

Researchers in London, using one of the first fMRI methodologies to study the neural correlates of early-stage romantic love examined brain activations of 17 female and male participants in-love with an opposite-sex partner (Bartels & Zeki, 2000). Face images of romantic partners and friends matched to the partner on gender, age, and relationship length as comparisons were shown to the study participants. The results suggested activations to viewing the partner in main areas of the brain's dopaminergic reward system (the caudate nucleus and putamen) and an area commonly involved in memory (the posterior hippocampus).

Another study on early-stage romantic love was conducted by researchers in the United States (Aron et al., 2005; Fisher et al., 2005). They investigated the neural activations of 17 female and male participants while viewing face images of their beloved.

The controls included a familiar, neutral person. The results showed significant activations in key areas associated with the dopaminergic reward system (the ventral tegmental area [VTA] and several sites of the caudate), and the posterior cingulate (implicated in attention and autobiographical memory).

In another study, US researchers and Chinese researchers investigated early-stage romantic love (Xu et al.,2011). In the study, 18 females and males in relationships of about 7 months on average underwent fMRI scanning, replicating procedures used by Aron et al. (2005) where participants viewed face images of their beloved and a familiar, neutral person. Once again, the data showed activation of the VTAin response to the beloved (versus the familiar, neutral acquaintance). Additional activations were seen in the mid-orbitofrontal cortex and areas of the cerebellum in response to the beloved.

In another study at Stanford, researchers investigated the neural activations of 15 individuals in relationships of 9 months or less undergoing periods of moderate and high thermal pain while they viewed images of their partners, a familiar acquaintance, or a word task (Younger et al., 2010). Results showed that even in a situation of thermal pain, viewing images of a romantic partner

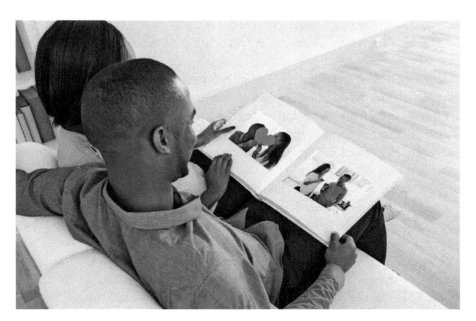

Figure 5.19 Couple looking at photo album

was associated with greater analgesic effects reflected by activation of reward systems (such as the caudate, nucleus accumbens, and orbitofrontal cortex). Additional activations were found in areas involved in emotion-processing and emotion regulation, namely the amygdala and dorsolateral prefrontal cortex.

In addition to romantic love in its early stages, for the first time researchers examined the neural correlates of long-term intense romantic love using functional magnetic resonance imaging (fMRI). Ten women and 7 men married an average of 21.4 years underwent fMRI while viewing facial images of their partner. Control images included a highly familiar acquaintance; a close, long-term friend; and a low-familiar person. Overall, the results suggested that on average the reward-value associated with a long-term partner may be sustained, similar to early-stage love, but also involves brain systems implicated in attachment and pair-bonding (Acevedo et al., 2012).

Also, researchers hypothesized that because romantic and maternal love are highly rewarding experiences, and both are linked to the perpetuation of the species they would have a closely linked biological function of key evolutionary importance (Bartel & Zeki, 2004).

So, they used fMRI to measure brain activity in mothers while they viewed pictures of their own and of acquainted children, and of their best friend and of acquainted adults as controls. The activity specific to maternal attachment was compared to that associated to romantic love tested in a previous study and to the distribution of attachment-mediating neurohormones determined by other studies.

The results showed both types of attachment activated regions specific to each as well as overlapping regions in the brain's reward system that match with areas thick in oxytocin and vasopressin receptors. Also, both types of love deactivated a common set of regions connected with negative emotions, social judgment and "mentalizing," that is, the valuation of other people's intentions and emotions. The researchers concluded that attachment uses a push–pull mechanism that overcomes social distance by deactivating networks used for social judgments and negative emotions, while it bonds individuals through the connection of the reward circuitry, explaining the power of the love factor (Bartels, & Zeki, 2004).

Last, researchers conducted correlations with neural activity and several relationship measures including a standard measure of closeness, the Inclusion of the Other in the Self Scale (IOS Scale)—a frequently used tool to measure the closeness in relationships (Aron, Aron, & Smollan, 1992). The scale consists of seven Venn diagram-like pairs of circles that vary on the level of overlap between the self and the other. Respondents are asked to select the pair of circles that best represents their current close relationship. Several studies have showed that this measurement tool is effective in getting accurate depictions of the amount of closeness and the inclusion of the other in the self.

The results suggested that the inclusion of other in the self was associated with dopaminergic reward system activity in neural regions of the VTA and regions (e.g., Acevedo et al., 2011; Craig, 2009; Kurth et al., 2010, meta-analysis; Enzi et al., 2009; Northoff et al., 2006, meta-analysis).

In sum, researchers have concluded that both romantic and maternal love share a common evolutionary purpose, specifically the preservation and perpetuation of the species. Both ensure firm bonds between persons by making the love factor a rewarding experience. But, until recently little was known of brain areas and pathways that correlate with the love factor in people (Bartel & Zeki, 2004). The data show that romantic and maternal love share a core of common neural mechanisms that suggest a tight coupling between attachment, love, and the neural systems for reward (Carter, 1998; Insel & Young, 2001; Kendrick, 2000; Pedersen & Prange, 1979).

The findings show that both romantic and maternal love activate particular regions in the reward system. In turn, this leads to stoppage of activity in the neural mechanisms associated with critical social judgments of other people and with negative emotions. As the positive reward system is turned on, the negative critical judgment system is turned off. Researchers have suggested that these findings may help explain in neurological terms why "love is blind."

According to researchers, love increases parts of the brain's reward system that produces feelings of euphoria, and shuts down other parts of the brain. The prefrontal cortex, which helps us make judgments about other people, switches off when a person is in love. When parents, for example, think about their children, areas that deal with negative emotions like aggression are deactivated. That could explain, according to the researchers, why we do not notice obvious faults in our partners and children. Love, it seems, is really blind to the negative features (Bartels & Zeki, 2004).

Researchers have speculated that the neural mechanisms associated with negative judgments that are turned off, when active might be responsible for keeping an emotional barrier toward unfamiliar people. When the negative judgmental evaluation system is turned on, it correlates with avoidance behaviors observed both in rats and in voles against pups or potential partners, which is reversed by administration of oxytocin (Insel & Young, 2001; Pedersen, 1997; Pedersen et al., 1982; Winslow et al., 1993).

So, researchers have concluded that it may be important to further study the social, psychological, and clinical consequences of the link between positive and negative emotions. The consistently activated and deactivated brain

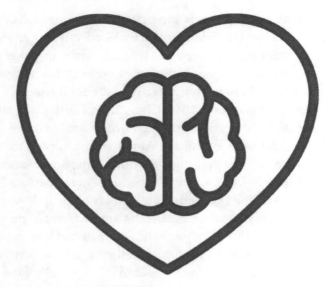

Figure 5.20 Drawing of brain inside heart

regions with maternal and romantic love suggest that a fine balance between activity states of these regions needs to be maintained to ensure healthy social interactions.

Researchers have noted that when this balance is interrupted through inheritance, lesion, upbringing, or social factors there may be interventions that could be used either to increase or suppress positive or negative feelings, as it has been successfully done in animals (Alexander, 1992; Benoit & Parker, 1994; Cassidy & Shaver, 1999; Ferguson et al., 2000; Insel & Young, 2001; Suomi et al., 1975; Winslow et al., 1993).

Overall, studies using sophisticated methodologies have elucidated the neural basis of love. The studies suggest that love has a neural mechanism that helps make relationships a deeply rewarding and pleasurable experience, and thereby ensures the survival and perpetuation of the species. It may be important to mention here that a study recently published in the Proceedings of the National Academy of Sciences revealed flaws in the software researchers use to analyze fMRI data. The glitch can cause false positives suggesting brain activity where there is none (Eklund, Nichols, & Knutsson, 2016).

But, in addition to the fMRI data, biological anthropologists have studied 166 societies using a survey methodology and found evidence of romantic, euphoric love in 147 of them. This ubiquity, researchers have concluded, suggest that there is good evidence to suspect that the pleasure of love is cross-cultural and basic to our biological nature (e.g., Fisher, Aron, & Brown, 2005; Jankowiak & Fischer, 1992).

Relationships and Cooperation

The pleasure associated with the love factor is necessary for cooperation. Love and the related feelings of empathy, sympathy, and compassion constitute the glue that holds relationships together (Weissmark, 2004). The cooperation of two parents was probably crucial to the survival of human children throughout evolutionary history.

Human babies enter the world completely dependent on caregivers to tend to their every need. Though human mating arrangements vary from culture to culture, all involve long-term cooperative relationships in which both the male and female contribute to the offspring's welfare (Daly & Wilson, 1983; Geary, 1998). So, a key adaptive problem for both sexes, involving issues beyond mate choice, is to maintain relationships with cooperative partners (Buss, 2007; Hazan & Diamond, 2000).

Drawing from fieldwork and laboratory research on chimpanzees, bonobos, and capuchins—and on dolphins and elephants—researchers show that many animals are prone to care for their children, help one another, and, sometimes, risk their lives to save others. Researchers claim that love, empathy, compassion, all of which are necessary for cooperation, have the backing of a long evolutionary history.

The neural wiring for love suggests that people are social animals with brains designed by evolutionary process to manage different kinds of relationships, and the challenges and prospects these types of relationships present. In addition to providing food, warmth, and safety for their children, parents invest many years socializing them to meet relationship challenges such as getting along with parents and siblings, starting friendships with people outside the family, maintaining those friendships, gaining respect, resources, and status from one's social group, and protecting oneself from members of other groups who might take one's resources or threaten one's life. Humans exist today because our ancestors successfully handled a set of relationship problems by cooperative methods (Kenrick, Neuberg & White, 2013).

Most relationships have to deal with the problem of selfish behaviors, the me-first attitude. The father of economics, Adam Smith, understood that the pursuit of self-interests needs to be tempered by "fellow feeling." This is how he famously opened his book *The Theory of Moral Sentiment*:

> How selfish soever man may be supposed, there are evidently some principles in
> his nature, which interest him in the fortune of others, and render their happiness
> necessary to him, though he derives nothing from it except the pleasure of seeing
> it. Of this kind is pity or compassion, the emotion which we feel for the misery of
> others, when we either see it, or are made to conceive it in a very lively manner.
> That we often derive sorrow from the sorrow of others, is a matter of fact too ob-
> vious to require any instances to prove it. (Smith, 1976)

Smith rejected the idea that selfishness alone is enough for the marketplace
or for a good human life. He argued, "to restrain our selfish, and to indulge
our benevolent affections, constitutes the perfection of human nature." Smith
proposed that it is in our own self-interest to develop our benevolent nature.
Self-interest, Smith points out, is not the same as selfishness.

For example, when Mother Teresa used her Nobel Prize award to build
more homes for the destitute, especially for the lepers, she was acting in a self-
interested way, because those resources were used to advance something she
cared about. But she did not act in a selfish manner.

Primatologists and ethnologists have pointed out that primate families and
communities have survived not by acting selfishly, eliminating each other, or

Figure 5.21 Family holding hands on the beach

keeping everything for themselves, but by acting in their own self-interest by sharing and cooperating. As one of our closest living relatives, chimpanzees have generated a lot of research interest because of the insights they provide to understanding the evolution of cooperation.

Since the pioneering research of Jane Goodall (Goodall 1979) and Toshisada Nishida (Kawanaka & Nishida, 1975; Nishida, 1983; Nishida & Kawanaka,1985), considerable field research, totaling more than 180 years at 7 sites has been undertaken. Because of this work, researchers now have much information on cooperation in chimpanzee relationships (e.g., DeWaal, 1989; Moore, 1996; Wilson & Wrangham, 2003; Wrangham, 1999; Wrangham & Pilbeam, 2001).

The research shows that chimpanzees are highly social beings, just like humans. Chimpanzee family bonds are strong, especially mother–daughter bonds. And social interactions are essential in a chimpanzee's development, learning, and general well-being. In a study done in the Ivory Coast, chimpanzees took care of group members injured by leopards. They licked their mate's blood and shooed away flies that came close to the wounds. And they protected injured companions (de Waal, 1989).

All of this is logical because chimpanzees live in groups for a reason; the same way wolves and humans are group animals too. Researchers contend

Figure 5.22 3 chimpanzees

that the human species would not be where it is today if our ancestors were socially distant and indifferent, lacking the fellow-feeling of compassion. Personally speaking, this statement applies to my family history. I would not be alive writing this book today, if it were not for the compassionate feelings of the Seebass family.

As mentioned in the preface, my father was close to death, sick with typhus, and covered in lice when he escaped from a concentration camp in Germany. With his last ounce of strength, my father managed to make his way to the nearby village of Börnecke, where he knocked and then collapsed by the front door of a house. A man of 50 or so opened the door and carried my father, still wearing his striped camp clothing into his home.

He introduced himself as Pastor Julius Seebass. In the next few months Pastor Seebass himself, his wife Hertha, and their sons and their two daughters, Ricarda and Renata, acting out of compassion, cared for my father, a half-dead fugitive. Ricarda, about 20 years old, made special efforts to nurse my father back to health. Months later, when my father recovered, he left the Seebass home to immigrate to the Unites States. He later found out that Ricarda Seebass had died of typhus a few weeks after he left their home. My father felt that Ricarda possibly caught typhus from him, and sacrificed her life to save his life, a total stranger.

In an essay titled "Compassion," Lawrence Blum writes, "Characteristically . . . compassion requires the disposition to perform beneficent actions, and to perform them because the person has had a certain sort of imaginative reconstruction of someone's condition and has a concern for his good. The steps that the person takes to ameliorate the condition are guided by and prompted by that imaginative reconstruction and concern" (Blum, 1980, p. 513).

Similarly, Darwin and Smith proposed that compassion stems from our ability to imagine and place ourselves in the situation of another person. We can conceive and understand another's pain, and this gives rise to the desire to alleviate another's suffering. The English noun "compassion"," meaning "to love together" comes from the ecclesiastical Latin *compassion* (n-), from *compati* "suffer with" (retrieved from English Oxford Living Dictionaries).

In almost all the major religious traditions and in many philosophies, compassion is considered among the greatest of virtues. For example, in Jewish tradition compassion comes from the Hebrew word *rehem*, "womb," originating in the idea of motherly love. It is considered among the highest of virtues, as its opposite, cruelty, is among the worst vice. In the Jewish text, the Zohar (iii. 92b) it says: if a person performs a deed of compassion "he crowns that day with mercy and it becomes his protector in the hour of need. And, if he performs a cruel action, he has a corresponding effect on that day and impairs it, so that subsequently it becomes cruel to him and tries to destroy him, giving him measure for measure."

Likewise, in the Catholic tradition compassion is among the highest virtues. In Catholic tradition, compassion is expressed in biblical Greek mostly through words derived from the root *ele-* (such as in the liturgical phrase "Kyrie, eleison," "Lord, have mercy"). The noun *eleos* is best translated "mercy" or "compassion"—both express positive feelings toward someone. According to Catholic tradition compassion—entering into the feelings of others—is the basis for reconciliation. Through compassion the barriers are broken down. It unites people in a bond of compassion that becomes love. For a Christian to share the suffering of another means they bring a light into the pain of that person's life.

In the Islam tradition, compassion is among the highest virtue too. The Arabic word (*ar-raHmaan*) for "compassion" is in the opening line of the Koran, the Islamic sacred book. "Compassion" is the most frequently occurring word in the Koran. Each of its 114 chapters, with the exception of the 9th, starts with the invocation, "In the name of God, the Compassionate, the Merciful." The Islamic tradition teaches one to worship Allah and to do good, and calls for good actions that include having compassion for others less fortunate. The Koran frequently speaks of God's plan for diversity, and the goodness of difference and compassion as part of this plan. "O mankind, We have indeed created you as male and female, and made you as nations and tribes that you may come to know one another" (49:13). The great mystical writers of Islam, the Sufis, wrote frequently of love and compassion as essential to the spiritual path of the Muslim. Love and compassion they described as the remedy of all ills and the alchemy of existence; love and compassion transform poverty into riches, war into peace, ignorance into knowledge and hell into heaven.

Also in Buddhist tradition compassion is among the highest virtues. The Buddha taught that, to realize enlightenment, a person must develop the two qualities of wisdom and compassion. The Sanskrit word *karuna*, usually translated as "compassion," is understood to mean active sympathy or a willingness to bear the pain of others. In practice, wisdom gives rise to compassion, and compassion gives rise to wisdom. In Buddhist tradition, you cannot have one without the other. They are both the means to realizing enlightenment. To achieve wisdom, according to Buddhist tradition, it helps to realize that the "individual me" and the "individual you" are mistaken ideas. Rather all beings are interconnected. Compassion, in Buddhist tradition, is an aspiration, a state of mind, wanting others to be free from suffering. The Dalai Lama once said that "compassion is a necessity, not a luxury" and that "it is a question of human survival."

Finally, in humanistic traditions compassion is considered a core value along with reason and hope. Humanists rate reason and science as the best way to generate accurate knowledge about the world. And both are driven by compassion, or the idea that all people—regardless of nationality, ethnicity, race, creed, sexual identity, or other characteristics—are fundamentally of equal moral worth.

In sum, the research shows love and compassion have the backing of a long evolutionary history. Human biology, researchers contend, endows people with the possibility to strive for a cooperative society, since every human is designed to get pleasure from loving and acting humane and cooperatively.

But, the fact is, human history is replete with violence. Human biology endows people with the ability to feel angry, hateful, revengeful, and murderous too. During the last century, some 250 wars killed 110 million people. Adding in genocides and human-made famines, there were approximately 182 million "deaths by mass unpleasantness" (White, 2000).

Personally speaking, this statement applies to my family history too. Apart from my parents, every family member (besides a few cousins) was murdered by the Nazis. My aunts, my uncles, my cousins, my grandparents, my great grandparents, all were murdered at concentration camps. The youngest died at about age 4 at Auschwitz, the oldest at 87 at Dachau. They were good people, underserving of their cruel and violent deaths.

Also, in terms of family violence, the US Department of Justice report on family violence shows that family violence in the United States accounted for 11% of all reported and unreported violence between 1998 and 2002. Of these roughly 3.5 million violent crimes committed against family members, 49% were crimes against spouses, 11% were sons or daughters victimized by a parent, and 41% were crimes against other family members.

Woody Allen's joke "Violence breeds more violence and it is predicted . . . kidnapping will be the dominant mode of social interaction" reminds us that aggression is real and frequent (Carroll et al., 2010).

And a Ruth Graham quip reminds us that aggressive feelings are present in healthy long-term relationships too. Ruth was the wife of the well-known evangelist Billy Graham. The Grahams were married 64 years. Barbara Bush and Ruth Graham were close friends, and shared an extensive correspondence over the years. In 2006 Barbara noted that Ruth had once been asked whether, as a Christian, she had ever contemplated divorce. Barbara explained, "Her answer, was, 'Divorce? No. Murder? Yes.'" Added Barbara, "I could understand that" (Gibbs & Duffy, 2007).

In the social sciences, aggression is defined as physical or verbal behavior intended to cause harm. Psychologists have distinguished two types of aggression, hostile aggression and instrumental aggression. The distinction between hostile and instrumental aggression is one of the oldest and most prevalent classification schemes in social psychology (Bushman & Anderson, 2001; see Buss, 1961; Feshbach, 1964; and Hartup, 1974, for early discussions).

Hostile aggression comes from anger and its intent is to injure. For example, most murders are hostile aggressions. About half result from arguments and from romantic triangles or under the influence of alcohol or narcotics (Levitt & Leonard, 2013).

Instrumental aggression aims to injure too, but only as a means to an end. Most wars and terrorist attacks are instrumental aggression. Studies conducted on suicide bombings have concluded that the goal of such attacks is to force liberal democracies to withdraw military forces (Pape, 2003; Kruglanski & Fishman, 2006).

Another common distinction made in social psychology is to classify aggressive behavior by response mode. Aggression has been classified as physical, verbal, or relational (Bushman & Huesmann, 2010). Physical aggression entails physically hurting another person (e.g., punching, kicking, stabbing, or shooting). Verbal aggression entails using words to hurt another person (e.g., insulting, cursing, or shouting).

Relational aggression, sometimes termed social aggression, entails hurting another person by damaging their social relationships or making them feel unaccepted or excluded (e.g., spreading lies or rumors, bullying, or telling others not to befriend someone). Also, some researchers have suggested that aggression can be postural in nature (e.g., mocking someone nonverbally, making threatening gestures, or invading someone's personal space (e.g., Krahé, 2013; Parrott & Giancola, 2007).

Because aggression is a complex behavior, no one specific place in the brain controls it. But researchers have discovered neural systems in both animals and humans that influence aggression. Researchers, who used brain scans to measure brain activity in convicted murderers, for example, found that the gray matter that acts like a brake on deep areas involved in aggressive behavior was less active.

The murderers' brains showed significant reduction in the prefrontal cortex, "the executive function" of the brain, compared with the control group. Advances in neuroscience suggest that such a deficiency can result in an increased probability of several behaviors, including less control over the limbic system, which generates primal emotions such as anger and rage, a greater need to risk, a lessening in self-control, and weak problem-solving skills—all behaviors that might induce a person to violence and aggression (Yang & Raine, 2009).

Other researchers have suggested that the recipe for aggressive behavior is environmental, such as childhood maltreatment. Some studies suggest that childhood maltreatment alters the gene that regulates neurotransmitters that balances aggressive behaviors (Caspi et al., 2002; Moffitt, 2003). Physically aggressive children are more likely to have had physically punitive parents, who disciplined them by showing aggression with screaming, slapping, and beating. These parents, in turn, often had parents who were physically aggressive too. Researchers have estimated that abused children are four times more likely than the general population to abuse their own children (Kaufman & Zigler, 1987; Widom, 1989).

Other researchers have suggested aggression is a learned social behavior. According to this view, people are exposed to aggressive models in the family, in one's community, and in the mass media. Consequently, people learn aggressive responses by experience and by observing aggressive models (Bandura, 1979, 2016).

Whatever the cause, research and history show that violence and aggression is part of human reality. Our good fellow-feelings are often inadequate to override our selfish and aggressive tendencies. The famous German philosopher Immanuel Kant saw little value in the good fellow-feeling of human compassion. Kant praised compassion as beautiful yet considered it irrelevant to a virtuous, cooperative social life. Social scientists concur that there are relationships where love and compassion may not be as strong a motivator for cooperation.

So, social scientists contend that cultural norms (and relational commitments) have evolved as a means to uphold the social order and cooperation by guiding behaviors.

Norms function as social constraints and are the pillars that maintain relationships and civilized societies. Cultural norms may be defined as implicit or explicit rules that are understood by members of a group. They guide and constrain behavior without the force of laws to produce proper behavior.

We turn now to consider diversity and groups.

6
Diversity and Groups

Groups in Historical and Evolutionary Perspective

Today, at almost every turn, we are linked to groups. We all typically belong, or are assigned, to many different types of groups. The earth has 230 countries and territories, roughly one billion families, millions of local communities, economic organizations, ethnic groups, and hundreds of millions of other formal and informal groups (both online and offline), and roughly 4,200 religious groups.

Worldwide, more than 8-in-10 people identify with a religious group. A comprehensive demographic study of 230 countries and territories conducted by the Pew Research Center's Forum on Religion and Public Life estimates that there are 5.8 billion religiously affiliated adults and children around the globe, representing 84% of the 2010 world population of 6.9 billion.

Why do groups exist?

Anthropological and ethnographic evidence suggests that humans lived in groups for the benefit of mutual exchange, sharing of resources, and division of labor. Humans faced a wide range of social action problems, like how to develop hunting methods to hunt large game, how to support each other during dangers and hardships, how to organize defense against predators, how to take care of children, and how to protect group resources from being stolen or kept by selfish persons.

Such group problems, according to Darwin and evolutionary psychologists, were overcome through the evolution of social psychological behaviors and emotions that promoted group cooperation and detected and punished defectors within the group.

Hunter-Gatherer Groups

Until around 12,000 years ago, according to researchers, all human beings were hunter-gatherers living in small groups in which most or all food was

The Science of Diversity. Mona Sue Weissmark, Oxford University Press (2020). © Oxford University Press.
DOI: 10.1093/oso/9780190686345.001.0001

obtained by foraging (hunting animals and gathering plants). Hunter-gatherers were often grouped together based on kinship and band membership. They lived in small nomadic groups known as band societies, often in caves.

A band society is the simplest form of human groups. The group consisted of a small number of family units who were related. It generally consisted of a small kinship group no larger than an extended family. Researchers have noted they know of no period where humans did not live with families as a basic unit in society.

Researchers maintain that hunter-gatherers did not have permanent leaders. A band group had informal leadership and nonhierarchical social structures (unlike agricultural and urban societies). The person taking the initiative at any one time depended on the task being performed. There were no written laws and no law enforcement. Norms and customs were transmitted orally (Cummings, Jordan, & Zvelebil, 2014).

According to researchers, there was social and economic equality in hunter-gatherer societies. Mutual exchange and sharing of resources (such as meat gained from hunting and plants from gathering) were important in the economic systems of hunter-gatherer societies. These societies have been

Figure 6.1 Cave drawing

described as based on a "gift economy." The earliest research on a gift economy is primarily based in anthropology and sociology.

One of the first empirical examples is Malinowski's 1922 study of gift exchange among the Trobrianders of Melanesia in the southwest Pacific. According to researchers, a gift economy reflects different underlying values from a market economy (Baker & Levine, 2013; Malinowski, 1922). A gift economy is a system where valuables are not traded or sold, but rather given without an explicit agreement for immediate or future economic rewards. Social norms and customs govern the gift exchanges. (By contrast, a market economy involves hard bargaining and purely serves economic purpose.)

According to researchers, in the typical hunter-gatherer society goods were typically distributed via gift-giving, reciprocal exchange, and sharing. Communal living conditions allowed for easy policing of hoarding and effort, and easy transmission of social norms and customs (Baker, & Swope, 2005).

Young mothers received childcare support from their own mothers, who continued living nearby. Recent archaeological research suggests that the sexual division of labor in band societies was the central organizational innovation that gave *Homo sapiens* the edge over the Neanderthals (our closest extinct human relatives) allowing our ancestors to migrate from Africa and spread across the globe (Lovgren, 2006).

Today, there are still a few hunter-gatherer groups who continue their ways of life. Though there have been some modifications (e.g., some women hunt the same kind of quarry as men, sometimes doing so alongside men). Researchers theorize that by the end of this century, the last hunting and gathering societies will vanish.

In sum, hunter-gatherer societies tended to have very low population densities. Only a limited number of people could congregate without quickly exhausting the local food supplies. People lived in direct face-to-face-groupings. So, they were familiar with each other and could easily recognize each other. The smooth operation of social life depended on kinship, which was the major force regulating interpersonal behavior.

Kinship is a system of social relationships expressed in biological phrases through terms such as "mother," "son," and so on. Everyone with whom one interacted in the normal course of life was classified and called by a kin term, and the behaviors between any two people were expected to conform to what was deemed appropriate between kin.

Kinship terms provided everyone with a ready-made guide to expected social behaviors. Everyone with whom one interacted in the normal course of life was not only classified and called by a kin term, but the behaviors between

Figure 6.2 Tents in snow

Figure 6.3 Chinese stone carving on wall

any two people were expected to conform to what was deemed appropriate between kin.

A person showed respect and deference to kin of the first ascending generation (i.e., "fathers," "mothers," "uncles," and "aunts") and claimed the same from all members of the generation below (i.e., "sons," "daughters," "nieces," and "nephews").

Kinship terms provided everyone with a clearly defined guide to norms and expected behavior, indicating, for example, the norm expectation of sexual familiarity, a casual relationship, self-control, or complete avoidance (Berndt & Tonkinson, 2018).

According to anthropologists, friendships and temperament led some people to stretch the rules, and at times of intensified emotion, as during conflicts, some people broke them. But repeated breaking of kinship norms brought disapproval, since it threatened the group social structure (Cummings, Jordan, & Zvelebil, 2014.)

Farming Groups

Gradually, humans discovered agriculture. Hunter-gatherer kin groups were displaced by farming and pastoralist groups in most parts of the world.

These settled communities permitted people to observe and experiment with growing plants to learn how they grew and developed. Archaeological data suggests the transition of prehistoric hunter-gatherers to the first farmers and first herders evolved in separate locations worldwide around 12,500 years ago. Researchers refer to this time as the Neolithic Revolution or Agricultural Revolution (Childe, 1936, 1950).

Researchers contend that the Agricultural Revolution is a central turning point in human history. It denotes the beginning of the first manipulation of the natural environment alongside critical social changes in human groups, and it lies directly at the origins of our current group relations (Cauvin, 2000).

The Agricultural Revolution was characterized by the widespread transition of human cultures from a lifestyle of hunting and gathering to agriculture and permanent settlements, making possible an increasingly larger population. The Agricultural Revolution radically transformed the small, mobile kinship groups of hunter-gatherers that had dominated human prehistory into sedentary societies based in villages and towns.

Densely populated groups of people now lived in permanent settlements. Personal land and private property ownership led to a trading economy and a hierarchical society, with an elite social class and containing a nobility, polity,

Figure 6.4 Plowing with 2 oxen

and military. The development of larger societies led to the development of different social groups and relationships. With the increase in population, and the growth in the size of communities, and the beginnings of town life, social relationships increased in complexity. The smooth operation of social life now required a corresponding increase in social complexity.

People no longer recognized or knew each other. The change from face-to-face societies into larger societies in which interactions with strangers were commonplace required stronger methods of regulating expected social

Figure 6.5 Ordinary village life

behaviors, enforcing norms, managing the economy, and governing social interactions.

Kin mechanisms worked well in hunter-gatherer groups because such groups were small enough that each individual could keep track of group membership and the behavior of other group members. In hunter-gatherer societies, people could easily report on the socially harmful actions of a person who free rode, cheated, or defected. By contrast, in large agricultural societies, people did not recognize or know each other. Many social interactions happened between strangers, under the cover of anonymity. Under such conditions, there was a greater chance a person could transgress while eluding detection or a person's wrongdoings could go unreported.

To handle these changes new psychosocial mechanisms emerged. Recent research has proposed that additional behaviors and emotions that promoted group cooperation and detected and punished defectors developed during the Agricultural Revolution. These new psychosocial mechanisms developed over and above those provided by our ancient hunter-gatherer kin norms so that large-scale societies could persist.

For example, during the Agricultural Revolution there emerged new kinds of religions in which gods were attributed the power to detect and punish transgressions (Shariff & Norenzayan, 2011; Gervais and Norenzayan, 2012; Norenzayan and Gervais, 2012). Belief in such gods is thought to have restored the effects of surveillance even in anonymous social relations.

These new religions produced standardized norms and practices by preaching and through rituals (Whitehouse, 2000). Researchers contend that "credibility enhancing displays" such as rituals and architecture served to demonstrate the conviction of believers and the transmission of their religious beliefs and social memberships (Henrich, 2009; Henrich & Gil-White, 2001; Whitehouse, 2000).

Researchers maintain that organized religion began as a way to ease group conflicts that inevitably arose when hunter-gatherers settled down, became farmers, and developed large societies.

Compared to a nomadic band, the society of a village had longer-term, more complex collective aims, such as storing grain and sustaining permanent homes. Villages would be more likely to accomplish those aims if their members were committed to a group enterprise. Though primitive religious practices such as burying the dead and creating cave art and figurines emerged tens of thousands of years earlier, organized religion arose, according to researchers, when a common vision of a celestial order was needed to bind together these new large, fragile groups of people.

Figure 6.6 Cave drawing

Also, researchers maintain a crucial role of religion was to mark out those whom one could trust and expect to provide mutual support. Simple emblems (such as religious symbols or styles of dress or body markings) were used to convey socially strategic information about a stranger's beliefs and habits, acting as a kind of movable reputation in an anonymous marketplace (Whitehouse, 2004). Because kin detection recognition systems were no longer sufficient, people became highly attuned to group membership and signals of group identity as a way of recognizing and determining how far to extend trust and cooperation (Billing & Tajel, 1973; LeVine & Campbell, 1972; Sumner, 1906).

In addition, according to researchers, the new religious groups helped to justify the social hierarchy that emerged in a more complex society. Those who rose to leadership roles were seen as having a special link to the gods. Communities of the faithful, united in a common view of the world and their place in it, were more cohesive than clusters of combative people.

In sum, the invention of farming, referred to as the Agricultural Revolution, led to a marked rise in population, to a growth in the size of communities, and to the beginnings of town life. The invention of farming equipment allowed societies to become focused on agricultural practices to produce large amounts of food. Because the speed of technological innovation increased so greatly, human social structures underwent a corresponding increase in complexity.

The social problems that appeared in these new, complex farming communities were many and varied. They included dramatic increases in population with pressing demands on housing and food supply and disputes flaring up because families lived near each other. Crime and threats from within and without the community made leadership and social organizational skills necessary to the survival of farming communities.

A new political class emerged, specializing in the skills of governance. These people were in a position to enforce laws, punish lawbreakers, rule over internal disputes, fight wars, and commission public works. They surrounded themselves with close groups of advisors and experts to help maintain their position of privilege.

The ability to harvest large amounts of food through agricultural processes also brought about key numerous social-economic changes. Farming tools allowed for surplus amounts of food to be gathered and stored. Those who controlled large amounts of resources and had the means to protect them were considered socially elite. This brought about social stratification and class differences in human societies, as the elite attempted to solidify their social positions of wealth while the lower class worked for or bought food from them.

Figure 6.7 Ancient Greek pottery featuring Spartan warriors

Urban Groups

After the agricultural revolution, approximately 5,000 years ago, another cultural transition took place. This change, which occurred independently in several parts of the world, is recognized as a crucial turning point in human history too. Researchers refer to this transition period as the Urban Revolution. The archaeologist C. Gordon Childe introduced the term "Urban Revolution" (as well as the term "Agricultural Revolution") to refer to the processes by which agricultural village societies developed into socially, economically, and politically complex urban societies (Childe, 1936, 1950).

Childe identified ten formal criteria that, according to his system, indicate the development of urban civilization: increased settlement size, concentration of wealth, large-scale public works, writing, representational art, knowledge of science and engineering, foreign trade, full-time specialists in nonsubsistence activities, class-stratified society, and political organization based on residence rather than kinship (Childe, 1950).

Childe used the term "Urban Revolution" to refer to this interconnected series of changes. He did not limit the term to the development of cities. For Childe, cities were just one aspect of the overall process by which complex, state-level societies came into being. Childe was among the first to apply a cultural evolution framework to archaeological data.

Whereas previous archaeologists had concentrated on chronology and technology, Childe was the first to synthesize the large volume of new

Figure 6.8 Ink drawing of port

archaeological data in the early 20th century and apply concepts and theories from the social sciences to interpret archaeological findings in social terms. He turned to theory and synthesis and applied social models to archaeological data to describe the major transformations in the evolution of human society.

Although current models for the origins of complex urban societies have progressed beyond Childe's original work, there is general agreement that he correctly identified a major social transformation prior to the Industrial Revolution, as well as the key processes involved in the change. Researchers agree that the Urban Revolution led to fundamental changes in society and people's lives and was even more drastic and fundamental in terms of social changes than the Agricultural Revolution.

It brought in a new era of population growth, urban development, and the development of institutions such as the bureaucratic state, warfare, architecture, and writing. Childe chose the phrase "revolution" deliberately in order to compare these major social transformations of prehistory to the Industrial Revolution.

According to researchers, the Urban Revolution depicts the emergence of urban life and the related transformation of human settlements from simple agrarian-based systems to complex and hierarchical systems of manufacturing and trade. Researchers contend that the word "revolution" should not be taken as meaning a sudden violent catastrophe.

Rather, Childe meant it to be used for the culmination of a progressive change in the economic structure and social organization of communities that was accompanied by dramatic increases in the population sizes. The first cities represent settlement units of up until then unparalleled population size. There was a dramatic increase in the size of settlements and the density of population. The increase was mainly accounted for by the multiplication of the numbers of persons living together in a single built-up area.

But it was not just their size that created their distinct character. The Urban Revolution brought about new ways of life and new forms of society. With the Urban Revolution, former freedoms and independence of individuals, households, and communities were replaced by servitude, taxes, rules, and regulations. Society and human life was forever altered.

If urbanization were only about large numbers of people living in dense residential settlements, it would be rather jejune for researchers. But urbanization holds great interest for researchers because it reveals the processes related to social evolution. The first of the major sociological theorists to write about urbanization and its connections to social life was the German social theorist, Georg Simmel (1858–1918). Much of modern philosophical foundations of modern urban sociology originate from his work.

Figure 6.9 Greek drawings

Simmel saw in the nature of urbanization and the growth of the modern metropolis elements that were typical not just of cities but also of the broader development and change unfolding in the modern world. Simmel maintained that the modern city induced people to treat one another in an indifferent and detached manner. Instead of relating to one another as intimates, people related to one another in an instrumental and calculating mode. Relations were defined by questions such as, What can you do for me? or What can I get out of this relationship?, rather than statements like, Let us get to know one another better.

Figure 6.10 Drawing of village

According to Simmel, this mode of rational calculation and its effects on the lives of people in large urban areas were inescapable throughout city life. The rise of these major centers of population shaped the character of society and interpersonal relations. Urban societal groups required people to adjust to its dictates and constraints. Life was rushed in the city, relations were transitory, and people were compelled to adapt new mental attitudes and social relations.

Urbanization and Social Alienation

Several classical and contemporary theorists developed the concept of "social alienation" to describe the influence urbanization had on mental attitudes and social relations (e.g., Durkheim, 1951, 1984; Fromm, 1941, 1955; Marx, 1846, 1867; Rousseau, 1762; Seeman, 1959; Simmel, 1950, 1971; Wirth, 1938). The concept of alienation has a long history and has many discipline-specific uses. It can refer to a personal, subjective psychological state and to a type of social, objective relationship.

Jean-Jacques Rousseau (1712–1778), a Geneva-born philosopher, was one of the first modern writers to develop the concept of alienation in political philosophy and moral psychology. From Rousseau came the idea of how people went from a state of autonomy to a state of dependence and alienation.

"Man is born free; and everywhere he is in chains." This is the opening sentence of chapter one in Rousseau's *The Social Contract* (1762, p. 5) and it summarizes Rousseau's view. The concern that dominated Rousseau's work was to find a way of preserving human freedom in a world where human beings were increasingly dependent on one another for the satisfaction of their needs.

This concern has two aspects—the material and psychological, of which the latter was of greater importance according to Rousseau. Rousseau published several influential works on the topic, and popularized a more social-psychological concept relating to social alienation.

Rousseau regarded economic inequality as a psychological problem by which people became alienated. According to Rousseau urban society led people to resent one another to the extent that their economic interests were in conflict, and the best they could do is hide their resentment behind a mask of civility. Civil society, as Rousseau described it, came into being to serve two purposes: to provide peace for everyone and to ensure the right to property.

According to Rousseau, it is mostly to the advantage of the rich, since it changes their de facto ownership into rightful ownership and keeps the poor deprived. So, according to Rousseau, the social contract that introduced government was deceptive, since the poor get less out of it than do the rich. Even so, Rousseau maintained, the rich are no happier in civil society than are the poor because people in society are never satisfied.

Figure 6.11 Social disparity drawing

Rousseau maintained that primitive societies (e.g., hunter-gatherer societies) were good while they lasted; they were the idyllic age of human history. Only they did not last. Neighbors started to compare their abilities and achievements with one another, and that marked the first step to jealousy, inequality, and vice.

Rousseau maintained that the introduction of property marked a further step toward inequality, since it made law and government necessary as a means of protecting it. Rousseau lamented the concept of property describing the horrors that resulted from leaving the condition in which the earth belonged to no one.

Throughout his writings, Rousseau returned to the thought idea that people are good by nature but have been corrupted by society and civilization. Rousseau's ideas interested later theorists such as Karl Marx, but Rousseau did not think that the past could be reversed in any way. There was no point in imagining a return to the idyllic age, according to Rousseau.

Karl Marx (1818–1883), the German-born sociologist, historian, and economist, addressed the same issue as Rousseau, but Marx believed that alienation resulted from a capitalistic market. Marx's theory of alienation was based on his observation that under capitalism, workers inevitably lost control of their lives and selves by not having any control of their work.

Essentially, according to Marx, there was an "exploitation of men by men," where the division of labor created an economic hierarchy of stratified social classes. Under the economic system of stratified social classes, society divided itself into two main classes: the property owners and the propertyless workers. In such an economic system, workers not only suffer impoverishment but also experience alienation.

Briefly, Marx describes four main types of alienation. The first type of alienation is the alienation of workers from the product of their work. Because workers do not own the fruits of their labor, that capitalism appropriated from them, workers becomes alienated from what they produce.

The second type of alienation is the estrangement of workers from the activity of production. The work that workers perform does not belong to the workers. They work for survival and are forced to do it for someone else. So, their working activity does not derive from within them as natural act of creativity but instead exists outside of them and suggests a loss of their selves.

The third type of alienation is the worker's alienation from what Marx calls their "species-being," or human identity. According to Marx, for human beings work amounts to a life purpose. The process of creating things is at the core identity of the human being. But in the capitalistic system of private ownership and the division of labor, workers are estranged from this essential source of identity and life purpose.

The fourth and final form of alienation is the estrangement of person to person. Since someone else owns the worker's product, the worker considers this person, the capitalist, as unfamiliar and hostile. The worker feels alienated from and aggressive toward the entire system by which capitalists take both the objects of production for their own enrichment at the expense of workers and the worker's sense of identity and wholeness as a human being.

Georg Simmel, the German cultural sociologist previously mentioned, further expanded on Marx's concept of alienation in relation to its social effects. In his book *The Philosophy of Money* (1900) Simmel examined the wider social implications of urbanization and economic exchanges. Economic exchange, Simmel argued, can best be understood as a form of social interaction. When monetary transactions replace earlier forms of barter, significant changes occur in the forms of social interaction between people (Simmel & Frisby, 2004).

Figure 6.12 Exploitation of workers cartoon

Money is subject to division and manipulation and permits exact measurement of equivalents. It is impersonal unlike objects of barter, like crafted gongs and collected shells. So, exchange of money promoted objectivation, rational calculation, and impersonality in human interactions that is characteristic of modern society. When money became the prevalent link between people, it replaced kinship exchanges that were based on personal exchanges.

According to Simmel, money displaced "natural" groupings by voluntary associations that are set up for specific rational material purposes. Wherever the cash nexus entered, it dissolved bonds based on the ties of blood or kinship or loyalty. Money in the modern world is more than a standard of value and a means of exchange. Over and above its economic functions, it symbolizes and embodies the modern consciousness of rationality, of calculability, of impersonality.

According to Simmel, money was the major mechanism that paved the way from "Gemeinshcaft" to "Gesellschaft," generally translated into English as from "community" to "society." (The terms were originally coined by the German social and political theorist Ferdinand Tönnies [1855–1936]). The dichotomy labels social group ties, on one hand, as belonging to personal, social interactions and the roles, values, and beliefs based on such interactions or on the other hand as belonging to impersonal, social interactions and the roles values, and beliefs based on such interactions.

According to Simmel, money and city life changed human consciousness itself. "The modern mind has become more and more a calculating one" (Simmel, 1903, p. 13).

In his widely read essay, "The Metropolis and Mental Life" (1903) Simmel concluded,

All emotional relationships between persons rest on their individuality, whereas intellectual relationships deal with persons as with numbers, that is, as with elements which, in themselves, are indifferent, but which are of interest only insofar as they offer something objectively perceivable. It is in this very manner that the inhabitant of the metropolis reckons with his merchant, his customer and with his servant, and frequently with the persons with whom he is thrown into obligatory association. These relationships stand in distinct contrast with the nature of the smaller circle in which the inevitable knowledge of individual characteristics produces, with an equal inevitability, an emotional tone in conduct, a sphere which is beyond the mere objective weighting of tasks performed and payments made. (Simmel, 1903, p. 12)

Wright Mills (1916–1962), an American sociologist, expanded on Simmel's work. Mills conducted a major study on alienation in modern society. In his book *White Collar: The American Middle Classes* (1951), Mills describes how modern consumption-capitalism has shaped a society where you have to sell your personality in addition to your work. Mill's work has been described as a major study of social alienation in the modern world of advanced capitalism where cities are dominated by the "salesmanship mentality."

Mill describes the forming of a "new class" that he refers to as white-collar workers.

The issues in the book were reported to be close to Mills' own background. His father was an insurance agent and Mills worked as a white-collar research worker for the Bureau for Social Research. So, Mills was familiar with white-collar work.

Mills argued that in a society of employees dominated by the marketing mentality, it is inevitable that a personality market should arise. For in the shift from manual skills to the art of handling, selling, and servicing people, employees are drawn into the sphere of impersonal exchange and become commodities in the labor market.

Figure 6.13 Blacksmith forging

Kindness and friendliness become aspects of personalized service or of public relations of big firms, rationalized to further the sale of something. With anonymous insincerity, successful salespeople make an instrument of their own appearances and personalities to close the deal or make the sale. According to Mills, the personality market and sales mentality underlie the all-pervasive distrust and self-alienation characteristic of metropolitan people.

Without common values and mutual trust, the cash nexus that links one person to another in transient contact seeped into all areas of urban life and relations. People are required by the salesperson ethic and convention to pretend interest in others in order to manipulate them.

Later, other scholars further expanded the psychosocial research on alienation. Building on the work of his predecessors, Eric Fromm (1900–1980) the well-known German-born social psychologist and psychoanalyst employed the concept of social alienation to explain why people give up their freedom and are willing to accept an authoritarian government.

His special emphasis was on the psychosocial conditions that facilitated the rise of Nazism. Beginning with his book *Escape from Freedom* (1941),

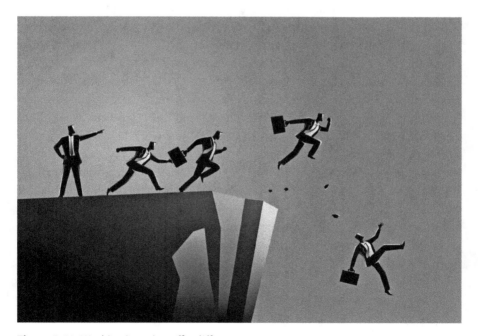

Figure 6.14 Working jumping off a cliff

Fromm's writings are known for both their social and political commentary and their philosophical and psychological underpinnings. *Escape from Freedom* is viewed as one of the founding works of political psychology.

According to Fromm, urbanization led to the weakening of kinship bonds, the declining social significance of the family, the disappearance of neighborhoods, and the undermining of the traditional basis of social solidarity. Fromm maintained that alienation led to the perversion of all values. By making economy and its values the supreme aim of life, people failed to develop truly moral values such as the riches of a good conscience, of virtue, and so forth.

In *Escape from Freedom*, Fromm focused on the social conditions that developed in Europe between the Middle Ages and the 20th century that ended with Adolf Hitler and the Nazi Party in Germany. Fromm identified basic psychological needs that led to the support for the Nazis in Germany and ended by warning that these needs are not automatically filled in a democracy.

Fromm's core question focused on why the German people would willingly and with fervent support allow Hitler's totalitarian regime to gain power? Another question Fromm explored concerned is whether democracy like that found outside of Germany makes people safe from similar developments.

Fromm maintained that the social character of the German people after World War I made them especially susceptible to the message of the Nazi Party. Fromm traced the social character to the individual psychological characteristics of the people in the German lower middle class. According to Fromm, the middle-class people became especially alienated from their work and their society owing to the rise of capitalism. They became economically "free" as employees of the capital holders, but this freedom was really a burden, as they tried to reconnect the ties to their work that earlier generations experienced.

According to Fromm, the origins of this alienation were further exacerbated by the Protestant doctrine. The Protestant doctrine taught that people stand alone before God, not with the Catholic Church as their authority and an intermediary. People were free from Church authority, but were now responsible for themselves before a vengeful God. So, people sought to escape from the isolation and alienation that accompanied this growing "freedom," Fromm maintained.

By applying psychosocial concepts, Fromm concluded that one primary way by which individuals escaped was by making themselves dependent on others. Tied directly to this way was the parallel inclination for individuals to be aggressive and to dominate others. Adolf Hitler and the Nazi Party exploited these psychological needs, Fromm explained, by promising their followers a kind of freedom that appealed to their desire to submit and conform to a powerful leader and to belong to party that would lead them into victory over others.

Fromm concluded with the warning that this kind of psychological need is largely a function of capitalism that tends to isolate people from their work and from each other. So, according to Fromm, a totalitarian regime could theoretically gain power under a democracy. "Alienation as we find it in modern society is almost total; it pervades the relationship of man to his work, to the things he consumes, to the state, to his fellow man, and to himself" (Fromm, 1955, p. 124).

Melvin Seeman, an American sociologist, was part of a surge in alienation research during the mid-20th century, when he published his paper "On the Meaning of Alienation" in 1959. Seeman described five logically distinct psychological states that cover alienation: powerlessness, meaninglessness, normlessness, isolation, and self-estrangement (Seeman, 1959, 1975, 2001). Seeman later added a sixth state (cultural estrangement), although this state is not included in later discussions of his work.

Social science researchers have debated the validity of the existence of six separate dimensions. For example, Dean (1961), drawing from Seeman's work, redefined alienation as consisting of only three dimensions: social isolation, normlessness, and powerlessness.

Psychologists have extensively studied the dimension of powerlessness (sometimes referred to as helplessness) and have developed scales to measure the construct. For example, Rotter's (1966) Internal External Scale measures a person's generalized expectancy for Internal-versus-External control and is one of the most popular measures in the social sciences.

Locus of control (LOC) is the degree to which people believe that they have control (the opposite of powerlessness or helplessness) over the outcome of events in their lives, as opposed to external forces beyond their control. It reflects the degree to which an individual sees outcomes as being related to personal behaviors and characteristics versus external factors.

Existing along a continuum, individuals considered to have a more "internal" LOC tend to see outcomes as being contingent on their own actions, whereas those considered to be more "external" tend to believe that outcomes are a result of external forces, such as luck, fate, chance, or powerful others. Locus of control has generated much research in a variety of areas in psychology in such fields as educational psychology, health psychology, clinical psychology, political psychology, and organizational psychology.

The importance of perceived control versus feeling powerless or helpless to psychological functioning has been well discussed in psychological theories.

Figure 6.15 Businessman chained to a bomb

For instance, the self-determination theory (Deci & Ryan, 2000) puts forward the benefits of internal control in motivating people to gratify their need for competence by actively engaging in strategic coping behavior.

The learned helplessness theory (Seligman, 1972, 1975) purports the maladaptiveness of external control, which reduces people's tendency to engage in problem-solving activities and causes depressive symptoms. Consistent with Seligman's hypotheses, many studies have documented a link between LOC and depression (e.g., Akande & Lester, 1994; Holder & Levi, 1988; Tobin & Raymundo, 2010; Wang, Wang, & Zhang, 1992). To merge and summarize the significant number of studies, Benassi, Sweeney, and Dufour (1988) conducted a meta-analytic review and found a moderately strong relationship between external LOC and depression. These findings suggest that psychological distress is linked to a generalized belief of a lack of control over events and outcomes. Despite being the subject of thousands of research studies, much remains to be learned about LOC, including whether it is causally linked to its many correlates, whether it can be changed and whether there are cultural variations (Cheng, Cheung, Chio, & Chan, 2013).

For over 60 years, alienation has been a topic of interest in organizational psychology too. So, researchers in that field conducted a meta-analytic study as well. They examined data from 45 primary studies and 227 statistically independent relationships to provide a meta-analysis. Based on their results, the researchers concluded that the cumulative evidence across multiple settings and respondents suggests that alienation is an important construct that has a strong association with a number of worker attitudes and work outcomes (Chiaburu, Thundiyil, & Wang, 2014).

After the boom in alienation research that characterized the 1950s and 1960s, interest in the concept of alienation per se decreased. But, in the 1990s and 2000s, there was again an increased interest in the concept of alienation prompted by globalization, megacities, and migration.

Urbanization, Alienation, and Migration

Some scholars contend that since approximately 1950, another urban evolution has been taking place around the globe. The increasing number of megacities of more than 8 million people demonstrates profound demographic, population, and social changes. In 1950, only two cities, London and New York, were that size. In 1975, there were 11 megacities, including 6 in the industrialized countries. In 1995, there were 23 total with 17 in the developing countries. In 2015, there were 36 megacities. The largest of these are the megacities of Tokyo and Shanghai. Both have populations of over 30 million people. In short, the urban revolution is now a global trend that is taking place at different speeds on different continents.

Migration is the demographic process that spurs the population growth of cities. Ever larger numbers of people are migrating to establish residence in relatively dense areas of population. A phenomenon has existed throughout the ages from ancient times to the present. Large numbers of people have gathered and created urban sites in places like ancient Rome and Cairo as well as in ancient Peking in China. Yet in recent times, the process of urbanization has gained increasing momentum and with it greater attention as well. Today, more than half of the world's population lives in what are considered urban places, and demographers project that by the year 2050 much of the world's population will reside in them.

The United Nations has predicted that by 2050 about 64% of the developing world and 86% of the developed world will be urbanized. That is equivalent to approximately 3 billion urbanites by 2050, much of which will occur in Africa and Asia. Notably, the United Nations has also recently projected that nearly

Figure 6.16 Cityscape

all global population growth from 2017 to 2030 will be absorbed by cities, about 1.1 billion new urbanites over the next 13 years (United Nations World Urbanization Prospects, 2014).

Between 1980 and 2015, the worldwide population of migrants more than doubled (Migration Policy Institute, 2014). The process of migration has

Figure 6.17 Mumbai metro train

generated a series of concerns, including concerns about economic, environmental, and political tensions and concerns about the social adaptation of the migrants themselves. A survey conducted by the European Commission in 2015 showed that migration is the major challenge facing the European Union (European Union, 2015).

For example, since the fall of the Soviet Union and the end of the Cold War migrants from eastern Europe and the developing countries have migrated to developed countries in search of a better living standard. This has led to entire social communities becoming uprooted, no longer inhabiting their homelands, but neither integrated into their adopted communities.

Researchers have suggested that migrants from low-income communities or religious minorities feel alienated from mainstream society, leading to backlashes such as the civil unrest that occurred in French cities in October 2005. The fact that the violent riots later spread to Spain, Greece, Belgium, Denmark, Germany, Switzerland, and the Netherlands suggests that not only did these communities feel segregated from mainstream society but also they identified in their isolated communities with other people they regarded as kindred (Senekal, 2019).

In one of the first empirical psychology studies on violent extremism in the United States, researchers revealed similar findings (Lyons-Padilla, Gelfand, Mirahmadi, Farooq, & van Egmond, 2015). The researchers underscore that violent extremism is not limited to any single faith community. Rather it is a broad term that applies to threats coming from different organizations that use violence to pursue ideological, social, or political goals (e.g., White supremacist movements, anarchist militias, eco-terrorists, and Muslim militants associated with terrorist organizations such as Islamic State of Iraq [ISIS] and al-Qaeda all fit this category.)

The researchers surveyed 198 Muslims in the United States about their sense of isolation and attitudes toward extremism. The findings suggested that a person's sense of isolation and cultural identity played a key role in radicalization. The data suggested that immigrants who did not identify with the culture they were living in felt alienated, marginalized, and insignificant. According to the researchers, radicalism promised a sense of kindred identity, meaning, and life purpose (Lyons-Padilla et al., 2015).

Recruitment material made by al-Qaeda and associates, for example, often mention the humiliation and suffering of Muslims throughout the world, which can resonate with people who relate to a collective experience. In propaganda videos and other recruitment materials, committing to a violent extremist organization's definition of *jihad* is presented as a way to regain a clear identity, purpose, meaning, and connection.

Figure 6.18 3 figures vs. one figure

Terrorist organizations, in other words, offer a sense of belonging, purpose, and the guarantee of a restored identity. According to researchers, this is similar to the sense of community that street gangs promise to American youth who feel alienated and lack belongingness in their lives (Lyons-Padilla et al., 2015).

In sum, the evolution of groups is not only the story of how people learned to come together in ever greater numbers—from hunter-gatherer bands to tribes to farms to cities to nations, but at each step humans learned a new way of being, thinking, and feeling (Lefebvre, 2003). Urbanization is as much a psychological process as it is an economic and a territorial and social process. As a result of changes in the economic and social structures from nomadic, small, kinship, gift-giving communities to sedentary, large, anonymous, market economic systems human psychology changed. People became more competitive and individualistic, and human relations became more impersonal.

Alienation and Identity

As mentioned previously, researchers have studied the economic and social changes that resulted from urbanization and concluded they produced alienating effects. However, some researchers contend that economic and social factors alone cannot adequately explain alienation. Socioeconomic explanations fail to explain the fact that persons in the same social class express and experience their alienation in different ways. For example, not all migrants from low-income communities or religious minorities feel alienated from mainstream society.

Also, some researchers contend that Fromm's psychosocial theory is limited because it does not provide a framework for understanding the internal, psychological factors of alienation. They contend that the conditions or mechanisms of alienation are not only outside a person but are part of a person's psychological developmental process too (Shin, 2012).

In addition to external factors that create environments of alienation, researchers contend that alienation is also determined by psychological or inner factors. These inner psychological factors either weaken or strengthen an individual's resilience, inner competence, and self-esteem to withstand alienating forces. Therefore, researchers maintain, a more holistic approach is required to better understand alienation. More specifically, they suggest that alienation can best be understood by considering the psychological developmental process of identity formation and its link to resilience (e.g., Luthar, 1991, 2006; Luthar & Goldstein, 2004; Luthar & Zelazo, 2003; Masten, 2007).

Erik Erikson (1902–1994), the German-born American developmental psychologist, studied the psychosocial factors related to a person's identity formation and was the originator of the term "identity crisis." Erikson knew much about the experience firsthand. He wrote about himself in a *Daedalus* piece titled, "Autobiographic Notes on the Identity Crisis" (1970), and used a first-person narrative in his books, revealing much about his identity struggles as a young adult and later as an immigrant (Erikson, 1964).

As a young adult, Erikson experienced what he described as an identity crisis related to his ethnic, religious, and personal identity. Erikson's mother was a Danish Jew and was married to a Danish Jewish man, Valdemar Salomonsen, but had been estranged from him at the time Erik was conceived. Little is known about Erik's biological father except that he was a Danish gentile. On discovering her pregnancy, his mother fled to Germany and Erik was given the surname Salomonsen.

Some years later, his mother married a German Jewish pediatrician, Theodor Homberger. Erik was officially adopted by his stepfather, and Erik Salomonsen's name was changed to Erik Homberger. During his childhood and early adulthood, Erik was known as Erik Homberger, and his parents kept the details of his birth a secret.

As he grew up in Karlsruhe, Germany, Erikson also experienced some of the confusion related to religious and ethnic identity. He was raised in the Jewish religion, but friends at the temple came to refer to the blond-haired and blue-eyed Erik as "the goy." Meanwhile, in his school, he was known as a "Jew" (Hopkins, 1995). After graduation from high school, Erikson decided he would be an artist. Erikson became alienated from his family and from the conservative context in which he grew up. He wandered for a year or so around Europe.

In 1930, Erikson married a Canadian dancer and artist and converted to Christianity. In 1933 with Hitler's rise to power in Germany Erik and his wife and children left German and emigrated to Copenhagen and then to the United States.

Erikson stated, "I think I have now said enough about myself to come to the question of how the concepts of "identity" and "identity crisis" emerged from my personal, clinical, and anthropological observations in the thirties and forties. I do not remember when I started to use these terms; they seemed naturally grounded in the experience of immigration and Americanization" (Erikson, 1970, p. 747).

Erikson referred to his uprootedness and forced migration to the United States as traumatic. "Transmigrations, like all catastrophes and collective crises produce new traumatic world images, and seems to demand the sudden assumption of new and often transitory identities" (Erikson, 1964, pp. 85–86). Erikson goes on to describe the external situational factors that makes forced migration such a traumatic experience and then concludes by stating that the inner mental mechanism of an identity is central to coping with the trauma of forced migration.

> What motivates and moves the transmigrant; how he has been excluded or has excluded himself from his previous home; how he has been transported or has chosen to traverse to distance between home and destination; and how he has been kept or has been kept separate, or has been absorbed and has involved himself in his new setting—these are the situational determinants. They do not account in themselves, however for the second set of determinants, . . . a mental mechanism of "turning passive into active," a mechanism central to the maintenance of man's individuality, for it enables him to maintain and regain in this world of contending forces an individual position marked by *centrality*, *wholeness*, and *initiative*. You may suspect that these are the attributes of what we call identity. (Erikson, 1964, p. 86)

Erikson (1950, 1963) is known for his theory of how a person develops an identity. His theory produced insights into the psychosocial aspects of identity

Figure 6.19 Magazine of Brexit

development, and has been the basis for research for half a century. Its influence continues, and the case could be made that research on Erikson's theory is accelerating. The issue of identity has gained importance with globalization, megacities, migration, and technological advances (e.g., Haggbloom et al., 2002; Subrahmanyam et al., 2006).

Erikson's Stages of Psychosocial Identity Development

Briefly, Erikson's theory of identity development posits eight distinct stages. Erikson assumes that a crisis occurs at each stage of development. For Erikson (1963), these crises are of a psychosocial nature because they involve psychological needs of the individual (psycho) conflicting with the needs of society (social).

According to Erikson's theory, successful completion of each stage results in a healthy ego identity and the acquisition of basic virtues (sometimes referred to as psychological strengths).

Basic virtues are psychological strengths that the ego identity can use to resolve later crises. Failure to successfully complete a stage can result in a reduced ability to complete further stages and therefore can result in an unhealthier ego identity and sense of self. These stages, however, can be resolved successfully later.

Erikson proposed a series of eight stages, in which a healthy developing individual should pass through from infancy to adulthood. All stages are present at birth but only begin to unfold according to both a natural scheme and one's situational and cultural upbringing. In each stage, the person confronts, and hopefully masters, new challenges. Each stage builds on the successful completion of earlier stages.

As mentioned, Erikson emphasized that the development of an identity was both psychological and social. In terms of the psychological aspects, Erikson described the process of developing an identity as partially conscious and unconscious, involving inner conflicts, and occurring at certain stages in life. And in terms of the social aspects, according to Erikson, a person's ego identity develops as it successfully resolves crises that are distinctly social or interpersonal in nature.

Here is a list of the approximate period in life and the corresponding Eriksonian crisis and strength.

Figure 6.20 Boy looking in mirror

Period in Life	Crisis	Psychosocial Strength
Infancy	Trust versus mistrust	Hope
Toddlerhood	Autonomy versus shame	Will
Preschool	Initiative versus guilt	Purpose
Childhood	Industry versus inferiority	Competence
Adolescence	Identity versus role confusion	Fidelity
Young adulthood	Intimacy versus isolation	Love
Middle adulthood	Generativity versus stagnation	Care
Late adulthood	Integrity versus despair	Wisdom

Among the eight stages in Erikson's theoretical framework of ego development, the first five contribute the most to identity development and are briefly reviewed here.

Stage One: Trust Versus Mistrust

Is the world a safe place or is it full of unpredictable events waiting to happen? Erikson's first psychosocial crisis occurs during the first year of life. The crisis is one of trust versus mistrust. During this stage, the infant is uncertain about the world in which they live. To resolve these feelings of uncertainty, the infant looks to their primary caregiver for stability and consistency of care. If the care the infant receives is consistent, predictable, and reliable the infant will develop a sense of trust that will carry over to other relationships, and will be able to feel secure even when threatened.

Success in this stage will lead to the virtue of hope. By developing a sense of trust, the infant can have hope that as new crises arise, there is a good possibility that other people will be there as a source of support. Failing to acquire the virtue of hope will lead to the development of fear.

Stage Two: Autonomy Versus Shame

The child is developing physically and becoming more mobile. Between the ages of 18 months and 3 years, children begin to assert their independence, by walking away from their caregiver, picking which toy to play with, and making choices about what they like to wear, to eat, and so forth.

The child is discovering that he or she has many skills and abilities, such as putting on clothes and shoes, playing with toys, and so forth. Such skills demonstrate the child's growing sense of independence and autonomy. Erikson

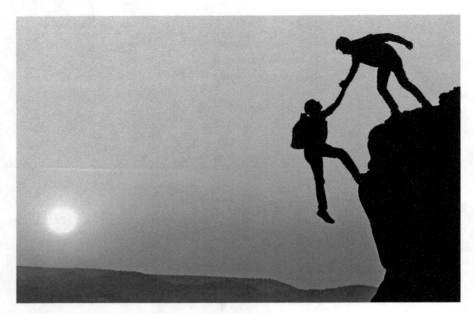

Figure 6.21 Person helping another reach top of mountain

states it is critical that parents allow their children to explore the limits of their abilities within an encouraging environment that is tolerant of failure. The aim should be "self control without a loss of self-esteem." Success in this stage will lead to the virtue of will.

If children in this stage are encouraged and supported in their increased independence, they become more confident and secure in their own ability to survive in the world. If children are criticized, overly controlled, or not given the chance to assert themselves, they begin to feel inadequate in their ability to survive, and may then become overly dependent on others, lack self-esteem, and feel a sense of shame or doubt in their abilities.

Stage Three: Initiative Versus Guilt

Around age 3 and continuing to age 5, children assert themselves more frequently. These are particularly active, rapid-developing years in a child's life. It is a "time of vigor" of action and of behaviors that the parents may see as aggressive.

During this period, the primary feature involves the child regularly interacting with other children at school. Central to this stage is play, as it provides children with the chance to explore their interpersonal skills through initiating activities. A healthy balance between initiative and guilt is important. Success in this stage will lead to the virtue of purpose.

Stage Four: Industry (Competence) Versus Inferiority

Industry versus inferiority is the fourth stage of Erik Erikson's theory of psychosocial development. The stage occurs during childhood between the ages of 5 and 12. Children are at the stage where they will be learning to read and write and to do things on their own. Teachers begin to take an important role in the child's life as they teach the child specific skills.

It is at this stage that the child's peer group will gain greater significance and will become a main source of the child's self-esteem. The child now feels the need to win approval by demonstrating specific competencies that are valued by society and begin to develop a sense of pride in their accomplishments. If the child cannot develop the specific skill, they feel society is demanding then they may develop a sense of inferiority.

Success in this stage will lead to the virtue of competence.

Stage Five: Identity Versus Role Confusion

The fifth stage is identity versus role confusion, and it occurs during adolescence, from about 12 to 18 years. During this stage, adolescents search for a sense of self and personal identity, through an intense exploration of personal values, beliefs, and goals. The adolescent mind is essentially a mind suspended between childhood and adulthood, and between the morality learned by the child and the ethics to be developed by the adult (Erikson, 1963, p. 245).

During adolescence, the transition from childhood to adulthood is most important. Children are becoming more independent, and begin to look at the future in terms of career, relationships, families, and so forth. The adolescent wants to belong to a society and fit in.

This is a major stage of development where the adolescent has to learn the roles he or she will occupy as an adult. It is during this stage that the adolescent will reexamine his or her identity and try to find out exactly who he or she is.

Figure 6.22 Girl crying in mom's arms

According to Erikson, what needs to happen at this stage is a reintegrated sense of self, of what one wants to do or to be. Success in this stage will lead to the virtue of fidelity. Fidelity involves being able to commit one's self to others based on accepting others, even when there may be ideological differences.

During this period, adolescents explore possibilities and begin to form their own identity based on the outcome of their explorations. Failure to establish a sense of identity within society can lead to role confusion. Role confusion involves the individual not being sure about themselves or their place in society. In response to role confusion or identity crisis an adolescent may begin to experiment with different lifestyles. Also, pressuring an adolescent into an identity can result in rebellion in the form of establishing a negative identity, and in addition to this a feeling of unhappiness.

In conclusion, according to Erikson, a person who successfully passes through each psychosocial crisis at a specific developmental stage will then develop the particular ego identity strength indispensable to that stage. In turn, this will influence the formation of an individual's identity in succeeding developmental stages.

According to Erikson, alienation is the estrangement stemming from an interruption in the formation of the appropriate identity elements and ego strengths. If an individual does not successfully integrate identity elements developed in the earlier stages into a meaningful inner frame of reference in a succeeding stage, he or she will suffer from identity confusion and feel alienated.

So, according to Erikson, a healthy identity means having the consciousness of being a coherent, whole self, whereas alienation for Erikson connotes an unhealthy identity in which an individual's self is fragmented, unstable, and incoherent, lacking a consistent frame of reference for interpreting, explaining, and understanding self, others, and the world (Erikson, 1968). At the same time, in a narrower sense, alienation refers to the state of an individual's identity confusion during adolescence. It occurs in a situation where an individual did not cope well with identity crises in earlier stages and failed to build the necessary stable ego strengths.

Erikson postulated that adverse socioeconomic conditions could influence identity formation. Living in poverty, for example, can influence a series of psychosocial crises in the course of an individual's identity formation. Adverse socioeconomic conditions can influence parents' own functioning

Figure 6.23 2 male silhouette, orange and blue

and parenting behaviors. And an inadequate childcare environment can negatively influence the formation of children's sense of basic trust, the key foundation for personal identity. Also, living in poverty can lead to what Erikson describes as a feeling of "shame," the sense an individual is completely exposed and conscious of being looked at—in a word, self-conscious. Shame as a core element of identity is also closely related to a sense of inferiority.

The division between economically vulnerable and economically stable children, established early on in the school age can continue during adolescence. Erikson points out that young people can become clannish, intolerant, and cruel in their exclusion of others who are "different," in skin color or cultural background, in tastes and gifts, and often in entirely trivial aspects of dress and gesture arbitrarily selected as the signs of an in-grouper or out-grouper. These circumstances of separation can undermine an individual's sense of self-continuity and self-sameness, the bases for sound ego identity. Adverse socioeconomic conditions can promote environments in which individuals become conscious of their identity as a member of marginalized group.

Erikson defines alienation not as a phenomenon that occurs because of a few key events over a limited period, but instead occurs through accumulating problems in each developmental stage. Adverse socioeconomic conditions can influence the particular tasks of each developmental stage. This suggests that the transformation of structural conditions alone cannot reverse alienation. Rather, according to Erikson, vulnerable individuals need to be assisted in developing a more stable sense of personal identity and inner resilience. From a psychosocial perspective, the vulnerable individual needs help to recognize, restore, or improve their inherent inner competence and resilience.

Recently, researchers have suggested that in addition to resilience, flexibility is necessary among immigrant adolescents in the age of globalization. Researchers have hypothesized that the experiences of youth from immigrant families offer a window into how globalization may eventually shape the identity and autonomy development of adolescents more broadly. According to researchers, immigrant teens encounter rapid social and economic change. They have to prepare themselves for societies that can differ dramatically from those of their parents' generation (Stathi & Roscini, 2016).

Cultural diversity and the potential conflict between their cultural background and that of the new society challenge them to find novel ways to express their identity and independence while maintaining connectedness to their family and native culture. The researchers suggest that immigrant adolescents do this by maintaining a degree of flexibility in their identity and

Figure 6.24 Mini people figures

autonomy development that allows them to incorporate features of both the old and the new cultures (Stathi & Roscini, 2016).

Similarly, in multicultural societies, researchers contend that it is crucial to understand the dynamics of distinct majority and minority identities and how they can be integrated successfully, with minimal or no conflict. During the process of acculturation that inevitably takes place when majority and minority groups coexist, the transformation of identities can be challenging for groups in general as well as for individuals. A close examination of the role of identity and its changes in the acculturation process is needed to understand the factors that can enhance intergroup relations and reduce intergroup conflicts (Stathi & Roscini, 2016).

Critics of Erikson's theory have pointed out that Erikson was vague about the kinds of experiences people must have to develop a healthy, flexible identity. His theory does not provide a universal mechanism for identity crisis resolution. Erikson (1964) acknowledged that his theory was more of a descriptive overview of identity development. He emphasized his work was intended to provide a framework within which identity development could be considered.

In conclusion, Erikson proposed a theory of psychosocial identity development containing eight stages from infancy to adulthood. During each stage, the person experiences a psychosocial crisis that can have a positive or negative outcome for identity development.

The construction of an identity, however, develops not only through resolving developmental crises at various stages but also through the transmission of memories and histories. Identities are anchored in stories transmitted from one generation to the next. Imbued in people's identities are the stored injustices of the past, handed down from generation to generation. This is especially true when the stories contain traumas of unresolved injustices.

So, we turn now to consider diversity and social justice.

7

Diversity and Social Justice

The Origins of Justice

There is a key difference between the Old Testament on the one hand, and the New Testament, the Buddhist texts, and the Koran, on the other. Broadly speaking, the lessons to be learned from the lives of Jesus, and the Buddha, and Mohammed are exemplary. The parables and teachings may need some clarification, but in general, they teach you how to live a just and moral life.

According to his Holiness the Dalai Lama there is "a striking similarity between the narrative of the founding masters, the founding teachers, the essence of the teachings are demonstrated" (Kiely, 1996, p. 58). His Holiness explains that if you examine the lives of Jesus Christ and the Buddha, you will see all the essential practices and teachings of Christianity and Buddhism exemplified.

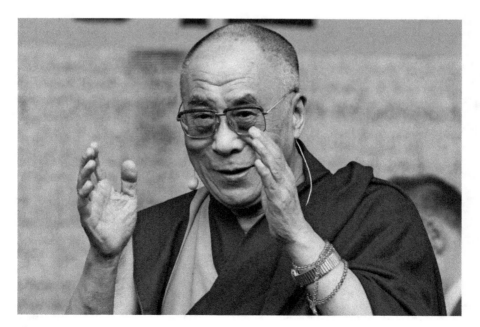

Figure 7.1 Dalai Lama (monk) speaking

The Science of Diversity. Mona Sue Weissmark, Oxford University Press (2020). © Oxford University Press.
DOI: 10.1093/oso/9780190686345.001.0001

The lives of both Christ and Buddha, according to His Holiness the Dalai Lama, demonstrate that it is only through hardship, commitment, and by standing firm on one's morals and just principles that one can grow spiritually and attain liberation. That seems to be the common and central message to Christianity and Buddhism. Likewise, the Koran teaches about justice mainly through examples of the perfection of Mohammed. Mohammed is an example of a great moral character. If you model you behavior after Jesus or the Buddha or Mohammed you will be a just person.

By contrast, the Old Testament, especially the first book, Genesis, teaches about justice mainly through examples of injustice and imperfections. The characters in the Old Testament are flawed people who sometimes do unjust things. Even God can be viewed as unjust and imperfect. The Old Testament challenges readers to react, to criticize, and to evaluate for themselves. It raises profound questions about justice and invites dialogue and disagreement. The stories provoke readers to ponder the eternal issues of what is just and what is unjust. How are we to understand the stories of injustice and an unjust God who makes mistakes and repents?

Was God unfair when he punished Adam and Eve for disobeying his commandment not to eat from the "Tree of Knowing of Good andEvil?" After all, they had no knowledge of good and evil before they ate the apple. So how

Figure 7.2 Buddha sculpture

Figure 7.3 Stained glass window

could they have made the right decision before having any knowledge or experience?

Was God responsible for the first genocide? God destroyed innocent beings, including innocent babies, during the flood. "And the Lord said, I will destroy many whom I have created from the face of the earth; both man, and beast, and the creeping things, and the fowls of the air; for it repennteth me that I have made them" (Genesis: 6:7). "And, behold, I, even I, do bring a flood of waters upon the earth, to destroy all flesh; wherein is the breath of life, from under heaven; and every thing that is in the earth shall die," God declares (Genesis: 6:17).

Later, God evaluates his own actions. Though God blames man for having an evil heart, God repents and promises not to flood the world again. "And the Lord smelled a sweet savour; and the Lord said in his heart, I will not again curse the ground any more for man's sake; for the imagination of man's heart is evil from his youth; neither will I again smite any more every thing living, as I have done" (Genesis 8:21).

But, God ends up destroying innocent babies in the fire and brimstone of Sodom and Gomorrah. God says he will go down to see and if the people are sinful and if so he will destroy the cities. And the Lord said, "Because the

Figure 7.4 Black and white biblical scene

cry of Sodom and Gomorah is great, and because their sin is very grievous" (Genesis 18:20), "I will go down now, and see whether they have done altogether according to the cry of it, which is come unto me; and if not, I will know" (Genesis 18:21).

Abraham is disturbed by God's unjust decision to destroy the cities. So, Abraham confronts God. And God lets Abraham lecture him about injustice. "And Abraham drew near, and said, Wilt thou also destroy the righteous with the wicked? Peradventure there be fifty righteous within the city: wilt thou

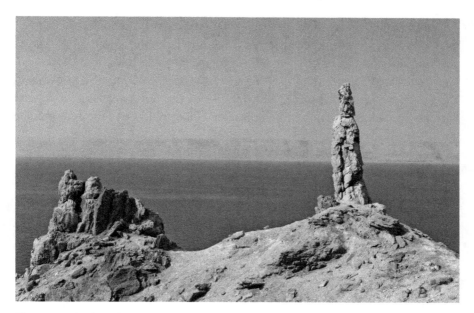

Figure 7.5 Rock sculpture

also destroy and not spare the place for the fifty righteous that are therein?" (Genesis 18:23, 24).

Abraham challenges God, saying that, as he is the judge of the earth, he is expected to be just. "That be far from thee to do after this manner, so to slay the righteous with the wicked: and that the righteous should be as wicked, that be far from thee: Shall not the judge of all earth do right?" (Genesis: 18:25).

Abraham attempts to reason and negotiate with God, asking him if, were there just 40, 30, 20, or 10 righteous people, he would reconsider his decision to destroy the cities. God promises Abraham that he will not destroy the city if there are 10 righteous people living there. Still, the divine judgments by God were passed on Sodom and Gomorrah and two neighboring cities, and are destroyed by fire and brimstone. Why would God call for the massacre of innocent citizens? There are other examples of God's unjust actions for the reader to consider.

Was God unjust when he praised Abraham for his willingness to offer his beloved son Isaac as a burnt offering? Why would God demand that a father kill his own son?

Why did God reward Jacob for cheating his older twin out of his birthright, his inheritance, and his father's blessings?

Why did God allow Sarah to expel Hagar and her son Ishmael (Abraham's first son) out of their home without food or water? When Abraham despaired over the situation, God told him not to worry, he would make his second son, Isaac, into a nation: "And God said unto Abraham, Let it not be grievous in they sight because of the lad, and because of thy bondswoman; in all that Sarah hath said unto thee; hearken unto her voice; for in Isaac shall thy seed be called" (Genesis 21:12).

And when Hagar despaired over the situation because she was afraid her son would die without food and water, God told Hagar not to worry because he would make her son Ishmael into a nation too: "Whataileth thee Hagar? Fear not; for God hath the voice of the lad where he is. Arise, lift up the lad, and hold him in thine hand; for I will make him a great nation" (Genesis 21:17, 18).

How are we to understand God's actions? Did God think his two-nation solution would remedy the original injustice? And what about the relationship between Isaac and Ishmael and their descendants? Was God concerned at all about the possibility of lingering resentments created by the injustice of expelling Hagar and Ishmael? Or did God assume Hagar and Ishmael would forgive and forget what happened? Did God think Hagar and Ishmael would develop a good relationship with Abraham and Isaac because the solution was a fair one (a nation for each)? Did God assume a just solution to an original injustice would result in an attitude of let bygones be bygones?

As the reader probably knows, these are not just historical biblical questions, but may have relevance for ethnic conflicts, current events, and relationships today. In Islamic tradition, Muslims recognize Ishmael as the ancestor of several prominent Arab tribes and the forefather of Muhammad. So, Ishmael is considered the ancestor of the Arab people. And Muhammad is considered a descendant of Abraham through Ishmael. In Islamic tradition, Muhammad is recognized as an important prophet and the patriarch of Islam. Muslims believe Muhammad was the descendant of Ishmael who would establish a great nation, as promised by God in the Old Testament.

In Jewish tradition, Abraham is called *Avraham Avinu*, meaning "our father." Abraham is considered the first Jew and biological progenitor of the Jews and the father of Judaism. In Jewish tradition, Abraham and his son Isaac and his grandson Jacob are referred to as the three patriarchs of the people of Israel. Jews believe that Abraham and his son Isaac and all his descendants were circumcised as a symbol of the "special nation" (covenant) that God promised Abraham. So, Jews believe it was through Abraham's son Isaac that the covenant was fulfilled.

Figure 7.6 Abraham/Hagar/Ishmael scene

What lessons about injustice are we to learn from the unequal treatment of Isaac and Ishmael? (Does this past injustice have any relevance for ethnic conflicts between their descendants today?) What lessons about injustice are we to learn from God's genocide against Noah's peers? Or from God's massacre of the citizens of Sodom and Gomorrah?.

And, turning to some of the main characters in the Old Testament, what lessons about injustice are we to learn from a brother cheating his twin brother out of his inheritance? Or from a father who is willing to murder his own son?

Or from Cain murdering his younger brother Abel because Cain is jealous that God respected Abel's offerings more than his offerings (Genesis 4:3–7)?

These are just a few examples of the unjust things that happen in Genesis. When we read these narratives, they challenge us to ponder the question: What is justice?

It is, perhaps, the most profound question, embracing as it does not only those essential questions about what is fair and how we should punish those who act unjustly, but also how we should feel when other people harm us or

Figure 7.7 cain and abel

others. Should we feel vengeful or should we forgive wrongdoers? Should we feel envious because some people with less skill and talent prosper more than we do? Should we feel resentful because of social and economic disparities? Should we feel angry if we think some people are cutting ahead unfairly (to borrow an image from Hochschild's 2016 study of working-class Republicans)? Should we feel guilty because others have so little, not even enough to eat or a place to live?

Should we think of life as a zero-sum game or as a cooperative venture?

Our answers to such questions will differ because we as human beings differ, and different societies may have different ideas of what is fair and what is not. What we call justice would not have been recognized as justice in Athens during Plato's or Aristotle's time, when slavery, for example, was considered natural, and women had few rights.

It is different from the justice that one would find in England during Darwin's time, when people reasoned that poor people were "naturally" weak and unfit and it would be an error to allow the weak of the species to continue to breed. Or from the 18th and 19th centuries in the United States and England, when slavery was considered necessary for the foundation of their economies.

It is different from the justice one would find in Germany during the Holocaust, when people promoted the idea that some races were biologically superior to others. And it is different from the justice one finds in contemporary Iran or Sweden and may well differ from Cambridge, Massachusetts, to the Appalachian region.

Ideas of justice may differ, but the psychological concept of injustice seems to be singular.

According to Darwin, people have an inborn sense of what "ought" to be. Darwin argued that our feeling of right or wrong is the most important of all feelings. He compared our sense of injustice to our sense of beauty. People may have differing views of what is beautiful or what is just, but the underlying mechanisms (of judging and evaluating) are the same.

In the same manner as various animals have some sense of beauty, though they admire widely-different objects, so they might have a sense of right and wrong, though led by it to follow widely different lines of conduct. If, for instance, to take an extreme case, men were reared under precisely the same conditions as hive-bees, there can hardly be a doubt that our unmarried females would, like the worker-bees, think it a sacred duty to kill their brothers, and mothers would strive to kill their fertile daughters; and no one would think of interfering. Nevertheless, the bee, or any other social animal, would gain in our supposed case, as it appears to me, some feeling of right or wrong, or a conscience. For each individual would have an inward sense of possessing certain stronger or more enduring instincts, and others less strong or enduring; so that there would often be a struggle as to which impulse should be followed; and satisfaction, dissatisfaction, or even misery would be felt, as past impressions were compared during their incessant passage through the mind. In this case an inward monitor would tell the animal that it would have been better to have followed the one impulse rather than the other. The one course ought to have been followed, and the other ought not; the one would have been right and the other wrong. (Darwin, 1871, p. 81)

The Psychological Sense of Ought

Fritz Heider (1896–1988), the Austrian-born psychologist and pioneer of the modern field of social cognition and attribution theory, borrowed Darwin's idea of ought and applied it to social psychology. In his book *The Psychology of Interpersonal Relations* (1958), Heider included a chapter titled "Ought and Value." Although Heider's attribution theory received a lot of attention, his chapter "Ought and Value" did not receive much attention in the scientific psychological literature until recently (Weissmark, 2004; Gollan & Witte, 2008).

Heider contended that people

often have the feeling that someone ought to get a reward or a punishment, that we or other people should do something, that someone does not deserve his bad or good luck, or that he has a right to act in a certain way. These oughts or obligations play a major role not only in the evaluation and determination of behavior and its consequences, but also in the fashioning of the content and the emotional quality of experience. (Heider, 1958, p. 218)

Heider argued that our sense of ought is similar to visual (perceptual) organization that follows the rule of cognitive consistency and balance. Heider took the idea of cognitive consistency and balance from research in Gestalt psychology. In the 1930s and 1940s, the researchers Max Wertheimer, Wolfgang Köhler, Kurt Koffka, and Kurt Lewin applied Gestalt theory to the study of visual perception.

The word "Gestalt" is used in German to mean the way a thing has been "put together." There is no exact word in English. In psychology the word is often defined as "pattern" or "configuration." Gestalt theory postulated that the whole of anything is more than its parts. And that the attributes of the whole are not deducible from analysis of the parts in isolation.

Gestalt researchers argued that perceptions are the products of complex interactions among various stimuli. (Contrary to the behaviorist approach to focusing on just stimulus and response, Gestalt psychologists tried to understand the underlying organization of perceptual processes.) Researchers postulated that there is a Gestalt effect, which is the tendency of our brains to generate whole forms with self-organizing tendencies of consistency and balance.

Wertheimer and other Gestalt researchers maintained that perception is an emergent experience, not present in the stimuli in isolation but dependent on the relational characteristics of the stimuli. As something is perceived, a person's nervous system does not passively register the physical input in a piecemeal way. Rather, the neural organization as well as the perceptual experience springs immediately into existence as an entire field to form a good, whole Gestalt.

Gestalt researchers demonstrated people tend to perceive global figures instead of just collections of simpler and unrelated elements (e.g., points, lines, curves, and so on). The main principle of gestalt perception is the law

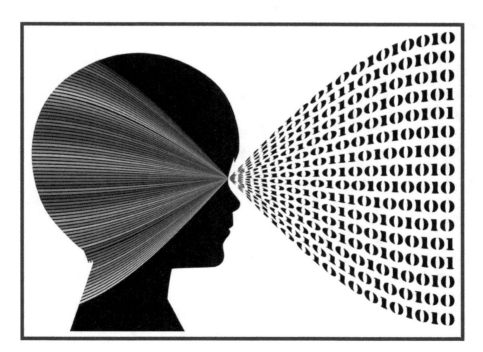

Figure 7.8 Visual perception of 0s and 1s

of *prägnanz*. According to this law, people tend to order their experiences in a regular, consistent, balanced, and simple way. Gestalt psychologists tried to discover the specifics of the law of *prägnanz*. This involved defining explicit grouping of laws that predict how the mind understands external stimuli as a whole rather than the sum of their parts (Carlson & Heth, 2010).

Wertheimer (1923/1938), in a seminal paper, introduced the visual Gestalt grouping laws, and Köhler (1929), Koffka (1935), and Metzger (1936/2006) further developed them (see review by Todorović, 2008; see textbook demonstration Palmer, 1999). Gestalt psychologists argued that these laws exist because the mind has an innate disposition to perceive whole, balanced, and consistent patterns. Gestalt researchers organized the laws into several categories including two termed closure and symmetry (balanced).

Readers might find it interesting to actually experience these innate dispositions of the mind by first looking at the following examples and then reading about them.

First example:

https://commons.wikimedia.org/wiki/File:Gestalt_closure.svg#/media/ File:Gestalt_closure.svg

In this example, the law of closure states that when parts of a whole picture (or shapes or letters, and so forth) are missing our perception fills in the visual gap. The law of closure posits that we perceptually close up, or complete, objects that are not, in fact, complete. In this example, the figure that depicts the law of closure reveals what we perceive as a circle on the left side of the image and a rectangle on the right side of the image. But gaps are present in the shapes. If the law of closure did not exist, the image would reveal a collection of different lines with different lengths, rotations, and curvatures— however, because of the law of closure, our minds perceptually combine the lines into whole shapes.

Second example:

https://en.wikipedia.org/wiki/File:Law_of_Symmetry.jpg#/media/ File:Law_of_Symmetry.jpg

In the second example, the law of symmetry states that the mind perceives objects as being symmetrical. The law of symmetry posits that when two symmetrical elements are unconnected the mind perceptually connects them to form a coherent shape. A typical textbook example of the law of symmetry consists of a configuration of a number of brackets. The figure here depicting the law of symmetry shows a configuration of square and curled brackets. In this example, when perceiving the configuration, we tend to see three pairs of symmetrical brackets as opposed to six individual brackets, or two pairs, and two singles. The law of symmetry posits that we perceptually close up, or complete, objects that are not, in fact, complete. The more alike objects are, they more they tend to be grouped. According to Gestalt theory, it is perceptually pleasing to divide objects into an even number of symmetrical parts. Therefore, when two symmetrical elements are unconnected the mind perceptually connects them to form a coherent shape.

According to Heider, our psychological sense of ought also follows Gestalt perceptual laws. As mentioned previously, Heider defined our sense of ought as a cognitive consistency motive or drive toward psychological balance. Heider argued that social perception (including the psychological sense of

Figure 7.9 Building shot, bottom looking up

ought) is similar to Gestalt perception in the sense that people have an innate cognitive tendency to seek balance, wholeness, and consistency.

Building on the work of Solomon Asch (1907–1996), the Polish-born American Gestalt social psychologist, Heider defined the sense of ought as beliefs about the "requiredness" of acting in a particular way. Heider used the concept of "requiredness" to describe situations in which people feel that something "ought to happen." To illustrate the idea, Heider referred to Asch's research on situations in which the experience of ought is produced.

According to Asch, (1952, p. 357), all situations of requiredness describe a situation in which we feel something "ought to happen." Asch argues that all of them

> contain a gap or disjunction; the person was in need of help, or action was called for in a given case. The situation was in some sense incomplete; our apprehension of the facts and their relations, or the need of the situation, laid a claim upon us to improve or to remedy it, to act in a manner fitting to it. Action that fits the requirements we judge to be appropriate or right; to fail to act appropriately we experience as violating a demand, or being unjust. (Asch, 1952, p. 357)

So, according to Heider, requiredness to act is rooted in the gap or incompleteness or injustice of a situation. Acting in a way that brings about the necessary closure, then, becomes identified with the just and right. Heider contended that happiness and goodness are often thought of as belonging together for intrinsic reasons. They are in harmony as two positive states that reflect the requirements of justice, according to Heider (1958, p. 219).

> When they coexist, we feel that the situation is as it should be, that justice reigns. On the other hand, the coexistence of happiness and wickedness is discordant no matter how much the person likes his wickedness. Happiness, reward, fortune are far more befitting to virtue than to evil. (p. 235).
>
> Common-sense psychology tends to hold that any imbalance represent a temporary state of affairs, that the wicked may have their field day now, but that they will eventually be punished and the good rewarded. (p. 235)

"The relationship between goodness and happiness, between wickedness and punishment is so strong, that given one of these conditions the other is frequently assumed." Aligning goodness and happiness, wickedness and unhappiness, can also be a tendency toward balance between the realms of ought and existing reality. When we think that the wicked will be punished, our idea

Figure 7.10 Hand in hand

of "what is" is influenced by our idea of "what ought to be" (Heider, 1958, p. 235).

Heider goes on to say that we often justify what "is" because of tradition, and then accept the is as just and what "ought" to be.

"Coordinating the "ought" and the "is" applies to other areas as well, and is probably one reason tradition is so potent in preventing change. Tradition represents the existing reality made solid by a long history in which it becomes identified with the just, the ethical, and the "should be." It is also one reason we often fail to perceive abuses in the world around us or why we become apathetic to them. The "is" takes on the character of the "ought" or the deviation from the ought becomes less obvious" (Heider, 1958, p. 235).

At approximately the same time Heider published his theory on the ought as a motivating factor in interpersonal relations, the American social psychologist Leon Festinger (1919–1989) published a seminal paper on cognitive dissonance (1957). Cognitive dissonance is one of the most studied concepts in psychology.

Psychologists have long been interested in the nature of cognitive dissonance, as this concept has implications for many areas of psychology, including justice, prejudice, attitudes, and social relations. The theory is simple, but its application is wide-reaching, making "cognitive dissonance" a popular concept. It assumes that people feel tension or a lack of harmony (dissonance) when two thoughts, beliefs, or attitudes are inconsistent. To reduce the unpleasant tension people are motivated to restore harmony by making some kind of adjustment. They may revert to defensive adjustments—justify, rationalize, reject, explain away, or avoid new information—or persuade themselves that no conflict exists, or reconcile the differences, or use any other defensive method of maintaining balance, harmony, and consistency.

Nearly five decades after Festinger proposed his theory, social psychologists continue to study and debate alternative views of what causes dissonance and the kinds of adjustments people make to maintain cognitive consistency (e.g., Lieberman, Ochsner, Gilbert, & Schacter, 2001). Although agreement has not been reached, the simple concept of cognitive dissonance and the predictions derived from it have produced more than 2,000 studies (Cooper, 1999, 2007).

An early and classic empirical test of the cognitive dissonance theory published by Festinger and Carlsmith (1959) found that after performing an unpleasant behavior, individuals who received smaller (compared to larger) incentives changed their attitudes to favor the behavior. Other early studies testing cognitive dissonance theory also provided evidence that people will change their attitudes to maintain cognitive consistency. For example, Aronson and Mills's (1959) classic study provided evidence that extreme socialization such as hazing leads to increased organizational commitment for members who stay with the organization, as this increased commitment justified the unpleasant behaviors they engaged in to join the organization.

The classic assumption in cognitive dissonance theory is that people are motivated to defend their attitudes, beliefs, and behaviors from challenges (e.g., Festinger, 1957; Olson & Stone, 2005). A recent meta-analysis tested this assumption by assessing whether exposure to information is guided by defense or accuracy motives (Hart et al., 2009). The studies included examined information preferences in relation to attitudes, beliefs, and behaviors in situations that provided choices between congenial information, which supported participants' preexisting attitudes, beliefs, or behaviors, and uncongenial information, which challenged these tendencies.

The meta-analytic results showed that people prefer to receive information that supports their positions and conclude that their views are correct. Rather than receive information that contradicts their views on an issue that makes them feel misled or ignorant but may allow access to a valid representation of reality (Hart et al., 2009).

Other researchers (Davis & Jones, 1960; Glass, 1964; Milgram, 1963, 1964) have found that when people harmed someone, they would devalue the victims. Apparently, the persecutors justified their unjust behavior by persuading themselves that the victims deserved what happened to them. This justification reduced their cognitive dissonance by coming to believe that their innocent victims were guilty.

Though the cognitive consistency motive as a drive toward psychological balance has been an influential theory in psychology, until recently little was known about how cognitive dissonance is represented in the brain. So, using functional MRI (fMRI), Van Veen and colleagues (2009) investigated the neural basis of cognitive dissonance. They scanned participants with fMRI while they claimed that the uncomfortable scanner environment was a "pleasant experience."

The researchers found that cognitive dissonance involved the dorsal anterior cingulate cortex and anterior insula. Also, the researchers found that the activation of these regions predicted participants' later attitude change. The data showed that the more the anterior cingulate cortex signals conflicted the more dissonance a person experienced and the more their attitudes changed. These effects were not observed in a control group. The findings demonstrated

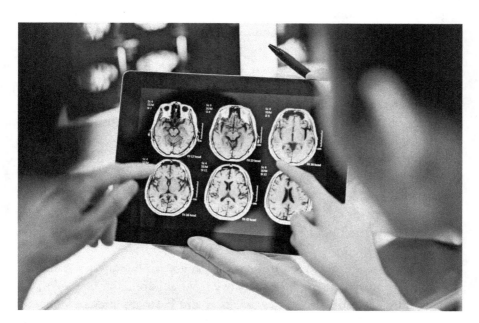

Figure 7.11 Brain scan

the neural representation of cognitive dissonance, and supported the role of the anterior cingulate cortex in perceiving cognitive conflict and the neural prediction of attitude change.

Later fMRI studies also examined the decision-making processes in the brain where participants were trying to reduce dissonance (Jarcho, Berkman, & Lieberman, 2011). The data showed that brain activity increased in the right inferior frontal gyrus, medial frontoparietal region, and ventral striatum, whereas activity decreased in the anterior insula. The researchers concluded that rationalization activity might take place quickly (within seconds) without conscious deliberation.

The researchers concluded that the brain might engage emotional responses in the decision-making process. According to the researchers, the findings suggested, "The fact that neuro-cognitive processes engaged during a few seconds of decision making are associated with attitude change suggests that, though attitude change may appear like disingenuous rationalization from the outside, the processes driving it may in fact be engaged quite quickly, and without the individual's explicit intention" (Jarcho, Berkman, & Lieberman, 2011, p. 466).

In addition to these recent neuroscience findings, studies have investigated cognitive dissonance reduction in children and other species (monkeys) (Egan, Santos, & Bloom, 2007). The results provided the first evidence of decision rationalization in children and nonhuman primates. Like adult humans tested in similar studies, the results showed that children and monkeys devalue alternatives they have chosen against, and change their attitudes and preferences to match the choices they made.

The researchers concluded that the mechanisms underlying cognitive dissonance reduction in human adults might have originated both developmentally and evolutionarily earlier than previously thought. Also, the researchers note that the mechanisms that drive cognitive-dissonance-reduction processes in human adults may emerge because of developmentally and evolutionarily constrained systems that are consistent across cultures, ages, and species. They point out that cognitive-dissonance reduction, therefore, may be more automatic than has been previously suspected (for support of this view, see Lieberman, Ochsner, Gilbert, & Schacter, 2001).

In short, the neuroimaging evidence on cognitive dissonance reduction during decision-making and the evidence from children and monkeys suggest that the need for consistency, balance, and harmony may be innate in both humans and animals. The data suggest that dissonance produces a negative biological state. This in turn drives people to change their attitudes in an effort to reduce the negative affect and restore consonance.

Figure 7.12 Mechanism icon

The Justice Motive

Some social psychologists argue that cognitive dissonance theory cannot fully explain the tendency of people to blame victims for their suffering and other phenomena. In a series of experiments the American social psychologist Melvin Lerner and his colleagues (Lerner, 1980, 2003; Lerner & Miller, 1978) demonstrated that just observing an innocent person being victimized is sufficient to make the victim seem unworthy. And, in a study on rewards, Lerner observed that when one of two men was chosen at random to receive a reward for a task, this caused him to be more favorably evaluated by observers, though the observers had been informed that the recipient of the reward was chosen at random (Lerner, 1965).

According to Lerner, existing social psychological theories, including cognitive dissonance, cannot fully explain these phenomena. To explain these studies' findings, Lerner argues that people are motivated by a belief in a just world. Lerner contends that the evidence points to a "justice motive" as a distinct source of motivation and influence in people's lives.

Lerner theorizes that from early childhood people are taught to believe that good is rewarded and evil is punished.

According to Lerner, people assume that those who succeed must be good and those who suffer must deserve their fate. Lerner argues that the belittling of innocent victims results from the need to believe that "I am a just person living in a just world. A world where people get what they deserve." So blaming victims, according to Lerner and colleagues stems from the common belief that this is a just world and people get what they deserve.

Many studies have confirmed this justice-world belief (Hafer & Begue, 2005). Researchers have reported that the just-world belief influences our impressions of rape victims (e.g., Carli et al., 1989, 1999; Bieneck & Krahe, 2011). Those who assume a just world believe that rape victims must have behaved seductively (Borgdia & Brekke, 1985), that battered spouses must have caused their beatings (Summers & Feldman, 1984), that poor people do not deserve better (Furnham, 2003; Furnham & Gunter, 1984; Furnham & Procter, 1989; Maes, 1998). Blaming the victim results from the presumption that because this is a just world, people get what they deserve.

Though the justice motive has been an influential theory in psychology, until recently little was known about how it might be represented in the brain. So, researchers investigated whether a person's inclination to believe the world as being just is related to neural responses to unfairness and moral evaluations.

To test this they used an fMRI approach to examine neural correlates for the perception of norm violations. They presented short scenarios to the participants describing norm-violation or norm-following behavior, followed by questions in which the participants were asked to judge the protagonist's behavior. They hypothesized that the belief in a fair world would interact with the neural network elicited by the perception of unfair and immoral behavior. More specifically, they assumed that in particular the insula, as a brain region known to reflect social norm violations, is linked with the belief in a just world (Denke, Rotte, Heinze, & Schaefer, 2014). The results suggested that peoples' beliefs in a just world are associated with neural responses of the insula and somatosensory cortices when witnessing unfairness or norm-violating behavior.

In addition, many behavioral and self-report studies using economic exchange games have established that people dislike unfair treatment to the extent that they will forego monetary rewards. Studies show that people do not maximize monetary payments by accepting every offer; rather, they usually reject unfair offers. Unfair offers that are rejected tend to elicit activity in the anterior insula, and the more likely a person is to reject unfair offers, the more activity this insula region exhibits (Tabibnia & Lieberman, 2007).

Also, a number of behavioral and self-report studies have examined the separate impact of fairness on positive emotions and have found substantial increases in self-rated positive emotions associated with fair treatment, even after controlling for material outcomes (Gächter & Fehr, 2001; Haselhuhn & Mellers, 2005). Fair offers that led to higher happiness ratings tend to elicit increased activity in several reward regions of the brain compared with unfair offers of equal monetary value (Tabibnia & Lieberman, 2007).

In sum, as Darwin, Heider Asch, Festinger, Lerner, and other social psychology and neuroscience researchers have proposed, the sense of justice is deeply rooted. Research suggests that the tendency for people to prefer harmony, balance, and consistency is part of human perceptual, cognitive, and emotional makeup. Altogether, the research shows that human behavior is not only driven by material results; fairness and justice matter as well.

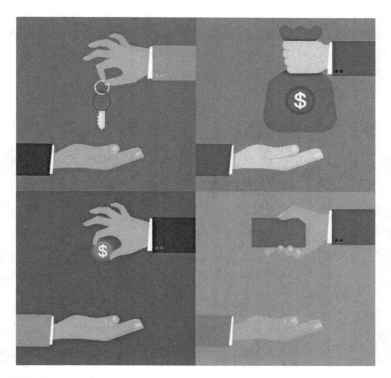

Figure 7.13 Money exchange

The tendency for people to prefer justice and resist unfair outcomes is engrained in human nature. This "injustice dislike" is so strong that people are willing to sacrifice personal gain to prevent another person from receiving an unfair better outcome. Perceived injustice can produce negative emotional states. Conversely, perceived justice may have the opposite effect and produce positive emotional states.

The human need to restore moral balance popularly appears in the English language in sayings that imply balance and consistency, such as "What goes around comes around," "You got what was coming to you," "Chickens come home to roost," or "As you sow, So shall you reap." These expressions imply the existence of some cosmic justice, order, balance, harmony, and consistency.

Indeed, the symbol of the judicial system, seen in courtrooms throughout the United States, is the figure of Lady Justice. An allegorical personification of the moral balance in judicial systems, Lady Justice is most often depicted with a set of scales typically suspended from her left hand, suggesting justice is equated with a balanced measure.

So, if people are built to be sensitive to fairness and to restoring justice, what are the real-world consequences of injustices that cannot be rebalanced? The injustices of slavery and the Holocaust, for example, were of such magnitude that the agencies of law were inadequate to address the wrongdoing, as were individual attempts to restore justice.

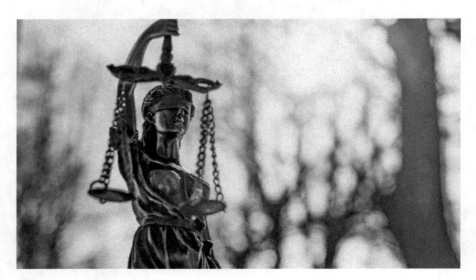

Figure 7.14 Lady justice

Although legal justice was served, research suggests that the negative feelings of the injustices did not go away. Victims of the Holocaust were indignant at the immoral, unjust, wrong, bad, heinous acts of the Nazis (Weissmark, 2004). Their indignation was caused by how they were treated. They were abused, degraded, and humiliated. They were not just victims of some disaster; they were subject to extreme disrespect. The degrading treatment they received at the hands of another broke all social norms under which people of a moral community are expected to live. All people are entitled, by benefit of their humanity, to be treated in a way that promotes positive self-regard (Rawls, 1971).

The disregard of how they ought to have been treated was an insult to their integrity. And it triggered in them both indignation and the urge to punish the wrongdoers. The judicial proceedings did not satisfy that urge entirely. Legal punishment gave the victims a brief satisfaction, but in the end, their sense of injustice was not fully settled. Legal justice could not wipe away the stain of injustice as they experienced it, because more than legal or material abuses were involved. The injustices of the Holocaust were of such enormity and scale that the impersonal courts of law were inadequate to address the wrongdoing (Weissmark, 2004).

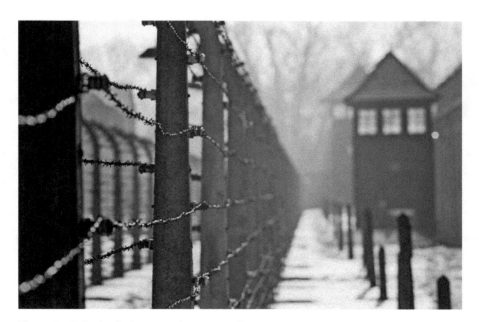

Figure 7.15 Barbed wire around concentration camp

This is not to comment on the law but to show how psychologically complex the notion of injustice is. From a psychological perspective, injustice is a personal issue—that is, it refers to how people experience injustice and the ways in which they respond to it. Victims' responses to the injustices that they suffered were not just a call for legal procedures, but for revenge (Lickel, 2012).

Research shows that victims of injustices are enraged by the degrading treatment they suffer. And victims may feel the need to "get even." Getting even for victims is often a personal matter. Recent neuroimaging studies show that when men (but not women) watch *unfair* partners receive pain, activity increased in reward regions such as the ventral striatum. This finding suggests that the establishment of justice, through punishment of unfair behavior, may elicit positive feelings. This effect was accompanied by increased activation in reward-related areas, correlated with an expressed desire for revenge.

The results suggest a neural foundation for the need for revenge and retribution. The results suggest that people like punishing unfair opponents. Although the neurobiological observations were more prominent in men, according to the researchers, further experiments are needed to confirm the

Figure 7.16 Pushing a man off the edge

gender specificity of the effect. It is possible that their experimental design favored men because the modality of punishment was related to physical threat. In any case, the findings suggest a predominant role for revenge and retribution in the maintenance of justice and punishment of norm violation in human societies (Singer et al., 2006).

What happens, however, when people cannot rebalance an injustice by means of punishment, revenge, retribution, or forgiveness? For example, historical data show that Holocaust survivors did not engage in retributive actions because they felt that no level of compensation would be adequate, they avoided contact with former Nazis, the majority of survivors left Germany at the end of the war, and they found other ways of reducing the distress caused to them. Also, former Nazis did not seek out survivors of the Holocaust asking for forgiveness. The reconstruction of Germany after World War II was a long process, and former Nazis worked to rebuild the country's cities and their economic recovery. So, if Holocaust survivors and former Nazis could not rebalance the injustice what then?

Justice as Intergenerational

I was teaching a course at Harvard when the idea struck me: injustice is an intergenerational matter. Anthropological and historical data suggest that if an injustice is not rebalanced between people, the imbalance does not disappear with the death of the original people but is extended to their descendants (Weissmark, 2004; Weissmark, Giacomo, & Kuphal, 1993). The need for justice, in other words, is intergenerational. (I have described this research in detail in my book *Justice Matters: Legacies of the Holocaust and World II*. Portions of this chapter and the next chapter were adapted from *Justice Matters*.)

Viewpoints and feelings about injustice, including those about the "other side," are passed from one generation to the next. With this hypothesis in mind, my first task was to search the literature. I found many books had studied the psychological effects of the Holocaust on the descendants of the survivors. And several books had studied the psychological effects of the Holocaust on the descendants of Nazis, but at the time, there were no endeavors to study the intergenerational impact of injustice and compare the two groups. Besides, the research was mainly individuocentric, psychoanalytic, and pathological in focus, unconcerned with how historic injustices thread together the two sets of descendants as they adapt to an unjust historic event.

Previous psychological studies ignored how stories about past injustices are transmitted from former Nazi parent or survivor parent to child, how the offspring of both sides make sense of the stories, the way the stories influence their identities and rebalance an injustice in their lives. There were no studies relating to the actual experiences of offspring whose parents perpetrated injustice or of those whose parents suffered injustice. In brief, there was no research on the quality of emotions or cognitive processes that follow perception of a past injustice.

To advance the research in this area, I undertook with my colleagues and a team of students at Harvard to study the different ways in which thoughts, feelings, and behavior of injustice manifest themselves in the lives of descendants of Nazis and survivors. To this end, I conducted a groundbreaking study, bringing children of Holocaust survivors face-to-face with children of Nazis (and later, great-grandchildren of African American slaves with slave owners, which will be discussed in the next chapter.)

The notion that descendants will be burdened by the evil acts of the fathers is as ancient as the Greek classics and the Bible. According to Plato, the evil acts of a wrongdoer influence the community and the next generation. Plato tells us that the temple robber and murderer are in danger of polluting those near them and of bringing divine anger upon all. Not only one's community but also one's offspring are endangered, for guilt will be inherited by them (Plato, 1980).

Likewise, according to the Bible, evil acts of a wrongdoer influence the next generation. In the Ten Commandments God portends to punish "the iniquity of fathers on children, to the third and fourth generation." And throughout the Bible there are many stories of descendants who receive payback for the evil acts of their ancestors. For example, God orders the destruction of Amalek throughout the generations for the crimes of one generation. The flood, the destruction of Sodom and Gomorrah, and the killing of the entire clan of Shechem are other examples of collective or familial punishment. "Sometimes the collective punishment is vertical (down through the generations), other times it is horizontal (within one generation, but extending to the entire family, clan, or city)" (Dershowitz, 2000, p. 233).

The Bible also says that it is wrong to punish anyone for the sins of another; punishment, if it is to be just, must be individualized. The change from collective responsibility—of the family, the tribe, the nation, the race, the religion, and so on—toward individualized responsibility is shown in the early books of the Bible. However, it has not been a linear movement in history, because the emotional pull of collective accountability and of revenge remains powerful (Dershowitz, 2000, p. 234).

A Study of Injustice in the Lives of Survivors' and Nazis' Offspring

To study the intergenerational effects of injustice, together with my colleagues I undertook to compare the generational legacy of the Holocaust for the descendants both of Nazis and of concentration camp survivors (Weissmark, Giacomo, & Kuphal, 1993).

How had these children of victims and of perpetrators dealt with their heritage, with the past injustices and their parents' involvement in those injustices? How had they found out about the past injustices? How had they made sense of the stories transmitted to them by their parents? What impact did it have on their identities? What coping responses did they use to deal with the past injustices? How had they tried to rebalance the past injustices in their present lives? Did the children of concentration camp survivors want to avenge the injustices their parents suffered? Did the children of Nazis feel their parents' roles in those injustices were justified? And how did they view the descendants of the other side?

Figure 7.17 Nazi concentration camp

We set out to ask children of Nazis and children of concentration camp survivors these questions and then compare their responses.

Our first task was locating the children. With help from colleagues in Germany, a form letter, a one-page description of the study, and biographical information about the researchers were sent to 31 people. Each was told that an interview study of children of concentration camp survivors and children of Nazis was being conducted and that a meeting with the children would be held later. We eventually chose to interview 10 children of Nazis and 10 children of concentration camp survivors.

Three criteria were used for choosing children of survivors: having at least one parent who was a survivor of either a Nazi concentration camp or slave labor camp, not having a parent who was a member of an organization that actively fought against the Nazis, and agreeing to participate in a meeting with children from the "other side" that would be televised on network television. Three criteria were used for choosing children of Nazis: having at least one parent who was an active member of the Nazi party during the Third Reich, not having a parent who was a member of an organization that actively fought against the Nazis, and agreeing to participate in the videotaped meeting.

Of the 20 interviewed, the average age was 43, ranging from 30 to 48. Fourteen were female and six were male. Ten were born in Germany, one in Israel, and the remaining nine in the United States. Their parents' background varied. For survivors' children, some came from families where both parents were survivors of death camps and a large part of the family was killed. Others came from families where only one parent was a survivor of a labor camp and a limited part of the family was killed. Still others came from families that spent some time hiding in the forest before being transported to concentration camps. Similarly, Nazis' children came from varied backgrounds. Some were the children of high-ranking Nazis like the Gestapo chief, the deputy armaments minister, and lieutenants in the Third Reich's Waffen-SS. Others were the children of lowly Wehrmacht soldiers who served on the eastern front. Obviously, this is not a random group, but those who decided to speak on the record and agree to attend a televised meeting at Harvard.

The interviews were conducted in English and German, tape-recorded, and transcribed. They usually lasted about 2 hours and took place primarily in the Boston, New York, Hamburg, and Berlin areas. A semistructured interview was designed as the chief instrument of the study. The interview was designed to generate data by focusing on broad areas. We hypothesized that these areas would yield useful data for comparing (the similarities and differences) between the two groups of descendants. The areas also determined the sequence of inquiry followed during the interviews. The areas were: (1) participants' developmental histories, with special attention to the evolution of finding out about the war, the Holocaust, and their parents' involvement; (2) participants' reports of their responses to information about the war and the Holocaust and of its influence on them; (3) participants' perspectives on justice; and (4) participants' views on descendants of the other side.

Participants were told that the interview was designed to help provide an understanding of the lives of people whose parents were survivors of concentration camps or whose parents were Nazis. They were told that the schedule of questions the interviewer kept was aimed at helping this goal. The potential risks and benefits of being interviewed and attending a joint meeting were explained to the participants. The participants were told that there were no serious risks involved except for the issue of confidentiality. All participants were cooperative and friendly toward the interviewers. The atmosphere during the interviews, however, varied. Although the interviewers had a general concern that they were intruding into a very private and difficult area of the participants' lives, this was especially acute with particular participants. At times, a few participants would cry and said they never discussed these matters.

After getting verbatim transcripts, the major task of the study was to organize the mass of data into the areas the interview was designed to investigate. In the process, themes within each area were identified. Here, I compare the responses that emerged from the recollections of the sons and daughters of Nazis and of survivors and their significance for understanding justice as intergenerational. In the next chapter, I will discuss the meeting with the sons and daughters of Nazis and of concentration camp survivors and its significance for understanding how injustice affects interpersonal behavior.

Voices from the Interviews

The responses of children of survivors and children of Nazis revealed similar threads of feelings and associations with the past running through their lives. These include several themes: ethnic identification, double victimhood, feelings of indignation, and a personal sense of justice. Each is discussed in turn.

Ethnic Identification

Although these second-generation children were uninvolved in the events of their parents, the past injustices still affected them in profound ways. The offspring of both Nazis and of survivors said they felt they inherited a dark legacy submerged into their identities, which consumed large parts of their lives.

Typical answers to the question "How did the information about the Holocaust and the war influence you?" showed that their parents' experiences influenced their identification with their ethnic group.

For example, a daughter of an Auschwitz survivor, who was 6 years old when her mother first told her stories about the camps, said,

> "My whole Jewish identity revolves around my parents' having been concentration camp survivors. I always felt, since I was a child, that I had to know more, so I could really understand why this happened to the Jews. Later it made me proud to be a Jew because we survived that, but also very hateful of Germans and mistrustful of all non-Jews. When I got older I became a Zionist because I felt Jews could only be safe if they had their own country. I remember in high school I use to have this pin that said 'Never Again.' It's hard really to describe the influence it had on me. But I guess I'd have to say my whole life has been determined by the fact that my parents were survivors. It is something that is deep in me, and I want my children to know what their grandparents went through."

A son of a Nazi, who was 9 years old when his mother told him his father was a high-ranking Nazi, said,

> "The simple fact is that even those who were born after the War have grown up in a situation in which that happened. All Germans have this historical legacy. None of us can escape it because our identity as individuals and as Germans is woven into it. Since I found about my father's role in the National Socialist German Workers' Party, I was curious to know more. In school we got very little of it, so I had to search out the information myself. It consumed a large part of my life. I think any young German person growing up in Germany after World War II felt their identity was linked to that period. There were many untrue things said of what we Germans have been told about our history. The party was trying to save Germany's rightful position, to build a unified Germany, and to stop the Western Powers from destroying Germany. My father, like millions of Germans, thought they were doing their best for Germany. This historical legacy is still with us."

Figure 7.18 Candleslit

Double Victim

One difference that emerged from the recollections is that most children of Nazis reported their parents told them stories about the *war*, whereas children of survivors reported their parents told them stories about the *Holocaust*.
   The daughter of a survivor put it like this:

> "I didn't even know there was a war until I was a teenager. I didn't even know fifty million people were killed during the war. I thought just six million Jews were killed. The stories I heard were always about taking the Jews to concentration camps. For my whole childhood I think I thought it was only the Jews who were killed. That it was just Nazis killing Jews. It wasn't until some history class that I realized this was a major war. But you know, still I think the Jews had it the worse, they suffered the most because every Jew was a victim like someone said."

The daughter of a Nazi officer put it like this:

> "I didn't know about the concentration camps until I was in my teens. First I heard about the party. Then I heard stories about the war, about bombs falling or about not having food. I would hear that my father was an officer in the army, and I remember seeing pictures of him in uniform. And I remember his black shiny boots.

And I saw a picture of him on a horse. At first I remember feeling proud to find out my father was an officer in the army."

Because children of Nazis first heard their parents talk about the war, they believed their parents were victims too. In fact, many children of Nazis recalled their parents telling them stories about how they suffered during the war.

This is described by the son of a high-ranking Nazi:

"At the end of the war, my family was forced to move from their large house to a small, cold apartment, and food was difficult to find. All our property was taken, and my mother literally had to go beg for food to feed the family. She really suffered to do this." Another son of a Nazi described it like this: "I remember my mother crying because of the bad situation they had. There were several years after the war when they did not have anywhere to live. They went from apartment to apartment. The British expropriated my father's business. I think that was unjust and wrong."

As expected, all of the children of survivors recalled their parents telling them stories about how they suffered in the concentration camps. One son of a survivor described the details of that suffering like this:

"I remember my father would tell me stories about the camps, about how he was brutally beaten and starved. He told me if you were called a *Muselmanner* (one of the walking dead) that meant you wouldn't survive much longer. In my mind I could see the grotesqueness of the scenes, the image of my father neither dead nor alive. For me the picture of him and the other Jews being victimized by brutal Nazis was very strong."

Another son of a survivor, whose father was a Jewish "kapo," a concentration camp inmate to whom the Nazis had assigned supervisory positions, recalled his father telling him how he suffered too. The kapos had authority to impose punishment and many were famous for their cruelty. The son who was interviewed admitted his father was a kapo, but he defined himself as the son of a survivor (not the son of a war criminal or a Nazi collaborator), and he described his father's suffering like this: "My father said many good Jews then did all kinds of jobs because they had no choice. That it's not so horrible. That they suffered to do it and that to survive you couldn't refuse to accept the job of a kapo."

Feelings of Indignation

Many children of survivors recalled their emotional reactions to the stories about the past injustices, which included feelings of indignation, which in turn incited the desire to seek revenge. The son of a survivor said,

> "When my mother talked to me about the camps and the torture and showed me pictures of dead relatives, she didn't have to say she's angry. You felt it. I think I have a much more powerful sense of anger and hate and wanting to get vengeance than most people do. There were times when I said I would just love to shoot a Nazi. I'm not stopped from doing an act of violence toward a war criminal on ethical grounds. I'm stopped by a practical issue. I don't want to go shoot some Nazi living in Argentina and then spend the rest of my life in jail. I know if I was going to die soon, I would love to have the option to do that."

Another child of a survivor described it like this:

> "I felt a deep sorrow and loss. They took everything from my family—they killed my family, they took all the properties, and money, everything. My parents came here with nothing. And what did the Germans get for their crimes? I wish there was more I could do. But at least I'm involved in Jewish activities, and I do lot of lecturing, writing about the Holocaust so people can't forget. And to this day I will not visit Germany or buy any German products. I don't think the Germans have paid for what they did to us. Look at how well they live now."

Many children of Nazis recalled their emotional reactions to the stories about the past injustices, which also included feelings of indignation. The son of a Nazi said,

> "I was angry when I heard what the Allies did to my family. My father said the former Allies were wrong, and I think they were. I think the former Allies were wrong. They split Germany up like in Versailles and wanted history to say that every German was a Nazi and all Nazis were evil so that all of Germans would feel guilty. But that is not the truth. And I will do my part to see the Allies are repaid for the wrong they did and that things are discussed in the proper perspective."

Another child of a Nazi described it like this:

> "I think the Americans and the Allies went too far. I think the bombing of German cities like Dresden was unfair. And I don't think it was right that the Allies tried the Nazis. It should have been done by German courts. And the other thing is, not all Germans were Nazis. The first people killed in Dachau were German people, not Jewish people. I think the Jews want to make it seem like they were the only victims but they were not. The German people suffered too, and people need to know it, but Germans are afraid to talk about it."

A Personal Sense of Justice

For both the children of Nazis and survivors, the stories of the Holocaust and the war provide visions of a perceived injustice and visions for understanding moral responsibility. In turn, those visions provide a framework for acting in the world. All the children reported that they felt their parents did not sufficiently engage in retributive actions—that is, actions aimed at restoring justice. Thus, the children both of Nazis and of survivors reported they felt the need to rebalance the past injustices in their lives.

For instance, the son of a Nazi said, "I feel I have a special obligation to let people know how unfairly Germany was treated. I think the real facts should come out."

The daughter of a survivor said, "It is important to me that my children know about the horrors of the Holocaust about how unfair and cruel Jews were treated. And I feel I have a duty to let others know too."

Summing Up

The interview data suggests that the second generation of Germans were burdened by the deeds of their Nazi parents. The recollections of Nazis' and survivors' children show the intergenerational process of ethnic identification at work. Summarizing the significance of the children's recollections, the interview data show the indelible imprint of the parents' stories on the children's ethnic identities, on their loyalties to their parents, and on their need to rebalance the past injustices.

Also the children's reports reveal the double victim phenomena. Both Nazi parents and survivor parents (and even a kapo parent) told their children stories about the injustices they suffered. These stories conveyed a sense of victimhood. Nazi parents told their children stories about how they suffered during the war, about the injustices perpetrated by the Allies, and about the injustices of the Versailles treaty. Survivor parents told their children stories about the injustices perpetrated by the Nazis in concentration camps and in the ghettos, and about anti-Semitic incidents before the War.

Although Nazi and survivor parents' descriptions and details of their experiences varied in detail and vividness, all the children reported the stories had an intense emotional impact on them. They felt a need to construct meaning out of the stories, which they thought would help to better understand themselves. Survivors' children expressed the need to redress the past injustices by educating others about the Holocaust and by seeking revenge. Also survivors' children expressed a deep loyalty to their Jewish identities and a distrust of gentiles. Nazis' children expressed loyalty to their German identities and a desire to inform others that "not all Germans are Nazis." Also some children of Nazis expressed the need to redress the past injustices by educating others about how the German people suffered during the war and about the injustices perpetrated by the Allies.

Nazis' children and survivors' children have been locked into a special relationship. Both of their identities have been shaped by World War II and the Holocaust. What the Germans call *Vergangenheitsbewältigung*, mastering the past, coming to terms with their parents' experiences, is a painful and difficult legacy for both groups.

In sum, understanding the complexities of injustice—historical and current—requires an understanding of the psychological make-up of people. As mentioned earlier, Heider viewed the "ought forces" as a deep feeling, stemming from the more general principle of cognitive balance. In Heider's terms, justice is an *ought* force that people view as inherent in their environment, conceived as a harmonious fit between happiness and goodness and between unhappiness and wickedness.

When they coexist, people feel the situation is as it should be, that justice reigns. On the other hand, the coexistence of happiness and wickedness is discordant. Common-sense psychology contends that any imbalance represents a temporary state of affairs that the wicked may have their field day now, but that they eventually will be punished and the good rewarded.

People's actions, therefore, are guided along certain standards of what ought to be. People often have the feeling that someone ought to get a punishment. These ought forces play a major role in people's lives. Viewed from this perspective, perceptions of injustice arouse strong feelings of anger and punitive impulses that call out for getting even and rebalancing an injustice. Some injustices, however, have a transcendent quality, which is one reason

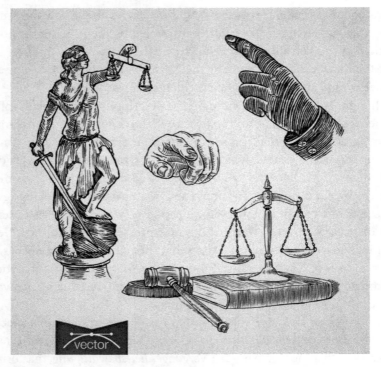

Figure 7.19 Symbols of the justice/legal system

feelings about injustices are passed on from generation to generation. There are situations, like the Holocaust, World War II, and slavery, where the evil done survives the person who has suffered and who has done it and can become a burden weighing on the memory of later generations.

We turn now to the next chapter to consider diversity and ethnic conflicts.

8
Diversity and Ethnic Conflicts

Revenge and Ethnic Conflicts

As mentioned in the previous chapter, the impulse for revenge is not just aggression but also a deep psychological sense of getting even, putting the world back in balance, supplying the retribution that will put things right and pay back the wrongdoer. "Whoever has done me harm must suffer harm; whoever has put out my eye must lose an eye; and whoever has killed must die," says Albert Camus in *Reflections on the Guillotine*, Camus, 1957).

Evolutionary biologists, psychologists, and primatologists have documented revengeful behaviors in other animals. Research shows that primates respond to conflict and perceived injustices with revenge too. For example, De Waal reports that in groups of chimpanzees a "system of revenge" grew out of transgressions of reciprocity norms that form the bases of that species' sociality. According to De Waal, chimpanzees keep negative acts in mind, repaying offenders with other negative acts—sometimes even after considerable time has passed (De Waal, 1996). De Waal reports that among Arnhem chimpanzees, individuals may go as far as to fake a friendly mood to reach exactly the opposite goal: revenge (DeWaal, 1989).

De Waal describes an adult female who was unsuccessful at catching her enemy during a previous aggressive episode. The female would approach her escaped enemy with an invitational gesture, such as an outstretched open hand, and keep her friendly posture until the other, who was attracted by it, had come within arm's reach. Then the female would suddenly grab and attack her enemy. De Waal says the attacks were much too abrupt and vicious to have resulted from hesitation and conflicting emotions. "I believe, in short, that these were premeditated moves to square an account" (De Waal, 1989, p. 240).

Planned revenge or punitive reciprocity—an eye for an eye, a tooth for a tooth—is as common in human culture as in animal behavior. Planned revenge means that there is a strategy involved in response to an injustice. The Kiwai-Papuans, for example, place a bundle of small tally sticks on the village path to show how many enemy lives they intend to take in retaliation for a previous offense. In New Guinea every death was attributed to some enemy

The Science of Diversity. Mona Sue Weissmark, Oxford University Press (2020). © Oxford University Press.
DOI: 10.1093/oso/9780190686345.001.0001

Figure 8.1 Guillotine sketch

from another family, who was then accused of witchcraft (now outlawed) and clubbed to death (Solomon, 1990).

Planned revenge can also be a culturally forced duty. For example, in Sardinia, according to the ancient code of the vendetta, an individual has a culturally imposed duty to avenge one's relatives for a previously offensive action. "An action is offensive when the event from which depends the existence of such offense is foreseen in order to damage dignity and honor" (cited in Solomon, 1990, p. 41). And in Albania revenge is a culturally sacred duty as well. The *canon* compiled by Leke Dukagjini, a 15th-century Albanian nobleman, lists every variety of offensive action that calls for revenge (cited in Blumenfeld, 2002a, p. 76). They are organized under headings:

CXXVI: Blood Is Paid for with Blood
CXXVII: A Crime May Not Be Recompensed with Blood
CXXVIII: Blood Is Not Paid for with a Fine
CXXIX: Blood for Evil Acts

Figure 8.2 Sticks and stones

Whether vengeful acts are spontaneous reactions, planned strategies, or culturally imposed duties, they stem from a sense of justice and the need to get even, to counteract in some way an interpersonal wrongdoing. The need for revenge arises from the emotion of indignation that is defined as "anger provoked by what is perceived as unfair treatment" (*The New Oxford American Dictionary*, 2001). When an offended person feels indignation, the need to seek revenge is intensified.

As the psychiatrist and Auschwitz survivor Viktor Frankl states, "there are moments when indignation can rouse even a seemingly hardened prisoner—indignation not about cruelty or pain, but about the insult connected with it" (Frankl, 1963, p. 39). An insult, and seemingly any disrespectful act, arouses a sense of injustice because it creates a social imbalance, and involves a violation of fundamental norms that guide interactions and relationships. Even minor transgressions can be viewed as violations of social exchange norms and, so, spark a strong emotional response (Leary, Diebels, Jongman-Sereno, & Fernandez, 2015; Miller, 1993).

As mentioned previously, one possible intent underlying revenge is the desire to "balance the scales," "get even," "get blood for blood" or "an eye for an eye." The expressions used for revenge show the perceived use of revenge for restoring justice and moral balance. So, revenge might be understood, at least from the vengeful persons viewpoint, as truly just.

Revenge also involves the desire to teach the wrongdoer a lesson (Cox & Wood, 2017; De Waal, 1996; Heider, 1958; Murphy & Hampton, 1988). Revenge, in this sense, is symbolic behavior intended to show the wrongdoer that the insult will not be tolerated or go unpunished. Victims frequently attribute to their wrongdoers a belief that the victim was not worthy of better treatment (Heider, 1958).

For instance, Frankl recounts the demeaning treatment he received from a concentration camp guard. The guard threw a stone at him and did not think it worth his while to even say anything. Frankl describes the demeaning treatment like this, "Strangely enough, a blow which does not even find its mark can, under certain circumstances, hurt more than one that finds its mark. Once I was standing on a railway track in a snowstorm. In spite of the weather our party had to keep on working. I worked quite hard at mending the track with gravel, since that was the only way to keep warm. For only one moment I paused to get my breath and to lean on my shovel. Unfortunately the guard turned around just then and thought I was loafing. The pain he caused me was not from insults or blows. That guard did not think it worth his while to say anything, not even a swear word, to the ragged, emaciated figure standing before him, which probably reminded him vaguely of human form. Instead, he playfully picked up a stone and threw it at me. That, to me, seemed the way to attract the attention of a beast" (Frankl, 1963, pp. 36–37).

Using Heider's language, revenge is a means for changing the belief-attitude of the wrongdoer that gave rise to the unjust act in the first place. Heider says the feeling of resentment is a wish to produce a change in the underlying belief-attitude of the wrongdoer, and revenge is the means of realizing this wish (Heider, 1958, p. 267). By reacting to the first unjust act with even more aggression, the victim tries to communicate an even stronger message to the wrongdoer about his or her self-worth. "In naive psychology this purpose is often recognized by such expression as: I will teach him; he has to learn that he can't do that; who does he think he is; I can't take this lying down—my honor is at stake, etc." (Heider, 1958, p. 267).

The concept of revenge, although not a traditional focus of psychology, is growing (e.g., for review see Lickel, 2012). In recent years, researchers have been studying the relationship between the nature of the revenge system, forgiveness, and aggressive acts. They have found that measures of attitudes regarding revenge are positively correlated with standard measures of ruminative thinking about the offense. It appears that ruminative tendencies and feelings of resentment interfere with people's abilities to forgive an

Figure 8.3 Prisoners of concentration camp

interpersonal transgression. That is to say, "vengeful people ruminate on the injustices and harm they have suffered to keep themselves focused on the goals of balancing the scales, teaching the offender a lesson" (McCullough et al., 2001, pp. 602–603).

In addition, researchers have found that vengeful people are high in negative affectivity and neuroticism and are low in agreeableness. Agreeableness reflects a prosocial orientation toward others that includes such qualities as altruism, kindness, and trust. People low in agreeableness have greater amounts of relational conflict and difficulties in relational closeness and commitment. They also have empathy deficits (Ashton, Paunonen, Helmes, & Jackson, 1998). Also, researchers have found that the desire for revenge is frequently cited as a motive for many destructive interpersonal behaviors, including homicide, rape, arson, and adultery (McCullough, 2001). Put simply, a considerable amount of human misery can be attributed to people's difficulties in modulating their revenge motivations (McCullough, 2001, pp. 107–108).

And finally, researchers have found that the desire for revenge is frequently cited as a motive in ethnopolitical conflicts and international relations (Waldman, 2003; Cox & Wood, 2017). At a societal level, there is the danger that one act of revenge can result in another insult to be righted. And when the revengeful act is perpetrated not against the same person who did the offense but another who is a descendant—part of the same tribe, nation, or family—the possibilities for escalation are endless. And in retrospect it is often hard to figure out which action represents the original injustice inflicted to a group and which the act of revenge. The extreme, as mentioned earlier, is the vendetta, a pattern of killing in revenge for some previous insult or injury that can go on for generations. "The Gilyak aborigines of Russia believed that the soul of a murdered man came back as a bird, pecking at his relatives to take revenge for up to three generations" (Blumenfeld, 2002, p. 81).

Accordingly, we can readily understand the need to limit or eliminate the escalation of revenge through a legal system designed to keep revenge under control. Speaking very generally, legal justice exists to control all forms of revenge in the interest of social peace and fairness. The legal system (among other things it does) tries to dilute feelings of indignation and even hatred that victims typically direct toward wrongdoers. Legal punishment is a civilized and efficient way in which such emotions may be directed toward their proper objects, allowing victims to get legitimate revenge with the control of public order. In the present age, some of us are uncomfortable talking about the legal system in such terms. We prefer to think that civilized people are not given to indignation so intense that it generates the desire for revenge.

If effective, the legal system may preempt, neutralize, and dilute indignation. However, it cannot abolish it, either as an emotion or as a motivation to seek revenge. The desire for revenge is not easily eliminated by any legal system. The law is impersonal, detached, and rule-bound, but the desire for revenge is personal, intense, and unruly (Jacoby, 1983). The law itself cannot eliminate the desire for revenge. In cases of genocide and other injustices legal punishment may remain a frustrating substitute for revenge, neither eliminating nor satisfying its urging.

One can readily appreciate the need to limit acts of revenge through a legal system, and yet history shows us that, if it ignores the emotional and psychological needs of individuals, it may not serve its purpose. Justice is a matter of personal concern, not just of anonymous legal institutions, systems, and governments. If there is an opportunity to get back at the wrongdoer, the temptation for the sense of injustice to express itself in personal revenge is strong. Unlike legal punishment, revenge meets the specific case directly,

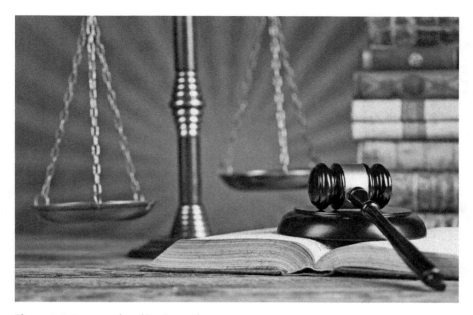

Figure 8.4 Law gavel and justice scale

indifferent to every other concern except the need to react to an unjust act or perceived wrong.

One need go no further than ethnic conflicts to see revenge at work. The word "ethnicity" is used in various ways. In the narrower way ethnic groups are racial or linguistic groups. But there is a broader meaning too. All conflicts based on birth-based group identities, real or not, such as race, language, religion, tribe, or caste can be termed ethnic. In this broader sense ethnic conflicts can range from the Protestant-Catholic conflict in Northern Ireland and the Hindu-Muslim conflict in India to the black-white conflict in the United States and South Africa and the Malay-Chinese conflict in Malaysia, the French-English conflict in Quebec, the Tamil-Sinhala conflict in Sri Lanka, and the Shia- Sunni conflict in Pakistan (Horowitz, 1984; Varshney, 2003).

Many ethnic conflicts illustrate the translation of intensely felt personal injustices into political violence. Examples can be found in Northern Ireland, Bosnia, and the Middle East. In these ethnic conflicts one sees a collapsed sense of time, where ancient grievance is current grievance. The Irish Catholics and Protestants continue in a spiral of revenge that goes back more than 300 years. The Bosnian Serbs can recall all the injustices that Muslims perpetrated during their 500 years of rule. And Palestinians can remember

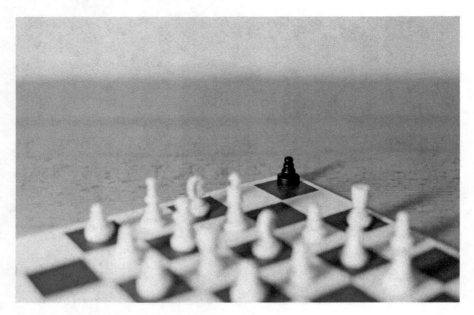

Figure 8.5 Chesspieces

all the wrongs that Israelis have committed since the establishment of Israel. Each has its list of grievances and atrocities.

Muslims have massacred Serbs; Protestants have massacred Catholics; and Israelis have massacred Palestinians. But each side has its "chosen trauma," which captures an injustice to the exclusion of any wrongs committed by themselves. The best description for that is what I call the bind of the "double victim," in which each thinks of itself as the legitimate victim. Examples of the double victim pattern abound.

Take the case of Palestinians and Israelis. Palestinians and Israelis both insist, "we" are the indigenous people here, "they" are the invaders. "We" are the victims, "they" are the aggressors. Each group brings to the conflict a deep sense of persecution not recognized by the other side, which is preoccupied with its own unjust experiences (Heradstveit, 1979; Rouhana & Bar-Tal, 1998, 2000). Or take the case of Irish Catholics and Protestants. In a classic study at the University of Ulster in Northern Ireland, the social psychologist Hunter and his colleagues (1991) showed Catholic and Protestant students videos of a Protestant attack at a Catholic funeral and a Catholic attack at a Protestant funeral. Most students attributed the other side's attack to aggressive, bloodthirsty motives but its own side's attack to virtuous self-defense.

In ethnic conflict, each side thinks of itself as the legitimate victim. Each describes the other in similar terms of wickedness and evil, with their own list of historical injustices. Like the narcissism or self-centeredness of individuals who see themselves as having been so hurt in the past that they can tend only to their own needs, each side feels no compassion for the hurt they perpetrate on others. Each side feels they have some kind of justification for what they do to the point of feeling righteous. Each has an almost mystical sense of their own victimhood.

One can see this sense of victimhood even in *Mein Kampf*, in which Adolf Hitler asserts that Germans are being victimized by "world-conquering Judaism." According to Hitler's reasoning, Judaism attempted to extricate the feeling of pride from the soul of the Aryan race, robbing Aryans of their leadership. Therefore, to give back to this noble race their former sense of superiority, the Germans are justified in destroying the Jews. Hitler also claimed that Versailles Treaty was unjustified because it was a sign of the visible subjugation of Germany and was intended to destroy Germany. Hitler considered the unification of Austria, the Saarland, the Sudetenland, and Danzig into the Third Reich to be German domestic matters because these territories had been unjustly taken away in 1919. Thus, Hitler was convinced that Germany must be restored to its rightful position.

The feeling of victimization, which is stimulated and amplified by the memories and feelings of historical injustice, often ends in the desire to seek

Figure 8.6 Hand out signaling stop

revenge. And the quest for revenge, as mentioned before, often ends in aggressive behavior (McCullough, 2001, pp. 107–108). Along with the egoism of victimization comes a tunnel vision that prevents individuals involved in the ethnic conflict from "seeing another view" or "hearing the other side." They see events through a single narrow viewpoint that blocks out context and perspective. As Mohandas Gandhi put it, "An eye for an eye makes the whole world blind." Victims avenge victims through repeated cycles that are transmitted from one generation to the other, backed by stories of atrocities and unjust acts committed by the other side and by the honorable acts carried out in revenge, in defense of one's own group and its transcendent values.

We can begin to see why claims for justice are rarely simply a matter of right or wrong but primarily a matter of ethnic identification with one's own group, whether it is on a family, religious, or national level. (As an aside, we are dealing here with claims for justice in ethnic conflicts, not in cases of criminal acts like murder, rape, and so forth.) The psychological functions served by ethnic identification are common to all human beings. Identification with one's group defines one's sense of integrity.

The philosopher Hampshire (2000) puts it like this: When "Remember 1689" is chalked on a wall in Belfast by a Roman Catholic calling to mind William III's Protestant Settlements, it would most certainly be useless to respond, "Be fair and reasonable; forget the injustices of the past, as you see them, because the past cannot now be repaired; it is more fair and reasonable to start from now and to try to build a peaceful society for the future." The response comes back: "You are asking us to forget who we are. Like everyone else, we define ourselves by what we reject. We should cease to exist as a community if we thought only of the future and of what you call reasonableness. That would be disintegration, the loss of integrity, both as individuals and as a community." Self-definition by opposition is the moral equivalent of the old logical principle *Omnis determinatio est negatio* ["I am what you are not. I am not what you are."] (Hampshire, 2000, pp. 25–26).

As mentioned in chapter 6, from an evolutionary viewpoint, we see that identification with one's group was necessary for survival. Our ancestral history prepares us to live in groups. Not surprisingly, we also define ourselves by our groups (e.g., Hogg & Williams, 2000; Turner, 1981, 1987; Turner & Hogg, 1987; Turner & Onorato, 1999). Our sense of who we are contains not just a personal identity but an ethnic identity also. Research suggests that we categorize people into groups, we identify ourselves with certain groups, and then we compare our groups with other groups, with a favorable bent toward our own group. We evaluate ourselves partly by our group memberships. Having

Figure 8.7 Stick figures singling someone out

a sense of "we-ness" strengthens our self-concept. It makes us feel good. Moreover, taking pride in our groups and seeing our groups as superior helps us feel even better (Smith & Tyler, 1997).

The notion that we have a need to belong to a group is not new, of course. The psychologist Erikson (1968) writes that human beings as a species have survived by being divided into what he has called *pseudospecies*. First each horde or tribe, class, and nation, but then also every religious association becomes *the* human species, considering all the others an odd invention of some irrelevant god. To reinforce the illusion of being chosen, every tribe recognizes a creation of its own, a mythology, and later a legacy: thus was loyalty to a particular tribe, nation, family, or religion secured (Erikson, 1968).

Like Erikson, Freud declares that ethnic identification encourages individuals to believe that their tribe, race, or religion is "naturally" superior to others. Also, according to Freud, ethnic identification can cause prejudice and conformity, and it can restrict the intellect. Freud notes that an individual's acceptance of an ethnic identity is inseparable from authority acceptance. An individual's personal quest for distinguishing good from evil, just from unjust, is cut short because ethnic teachings are assertions about facts and conditions of reality which tell one something one has not discovered for oneself and which lay claim to one's belief rather than one's intellect. The beliefs are handed down from generation to generation, and the individual is forbidden to raise questions about their authentication. The individual becomes indoctrinated with the conviction that he ought to believe because his ancestors believed (Freud, 1961).

To ensure the acceptance of the beliefs, a system of rewards and punishments is used. Excommunication, whether employed by a church, a tribe, a religious group, or a family, is a powerful punishment for bringing about individual conformity and ethnic identification. According to Freud, countless individuals have been impaired by the compromises they are forced to make because of the pressure imposed on them to accept the legacy of their ancestors. Freud says many individuals, including the ancestors who bequeathed their legacies, probably had doubts about their ethnic beliefs, but the pressure was too strong to have dared to utter them. They had to suppress their doubts, writes Freud, and thereby their intellect, because they thought it was their duty to believe; "many brilliant intellects have broken down over this conflict, and many characters have been impaired by the compromises with which they have tried to find a way out of it" (Freud, 1961, pp. 25–27). This process is in itself a remarkable psychological problem, concludes Freud.

Social identity theory and these statements by Freud and Erikson show a few dimensions of identity formation and explain why ethnic identification is so all-pervasive in our sense of justice and need for revenge—for the process of identity formation is located in the core of the individual and yet also in the core of his or her ethnic group. In psychological terms, it employs a twofold process.

The psychological development of individuals (their personalities and views of themselves) goes hand in hand with the relations they establish to

Figure 8.8 Magnifying glass on 3 people

an ethnic group. The values and beliefs underlying the ethnic group become incorporated in one's self-identity and also place one in an ethnic group. Most people carry with them tendencies that anchor their identities in some ethnic group. This process is for the most part automatic, transmitted from one generation to another by the ancient heritage of storytelling. Like material assets, legacies are handed down from generation to generation through stories about the past. Legacies transmit beliefs and feelings, conserve memory, and preserve the past.

Thus, in ethnic conflicts one often sees a collapsed sense of time where past injustice is current injustice. And whether in ethnic conflicts or in personal matters, an individual's sense of justice is never simply a matter of rationality. It is first a matter of feelings in defense of one's self and one's group, and inherent in this is the unwillingness of both sides to face the others' passions and viewpoints (Solomon, 1990). From one generation to the other, each side is told stories of unjust acts perpetrated by others, and of the loyal acts carried out in defense of one's own ethnic group and its honorable values. In view of all this, we can see that the experience of an injustice leaves a powerful imprint on both sides that continues to be transmitted through the generations.

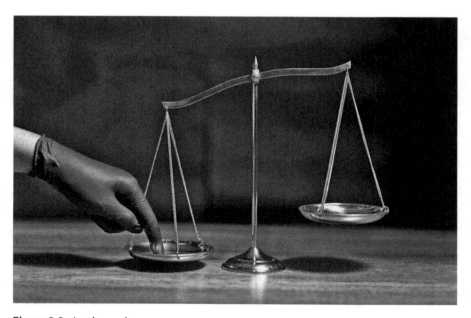

Figure 8.9 Justice scale

Justice as Interpersonal and Ethnic Conflicts

People who feel they have been treated unjustly—and who still resent the perpetrators—choose one of two coping strategies, recent research suggests (Miller, 2001). They choose either to withdraw or to even the score. And victims of severe trauma, whose psyches have been marked with anguish of the event, seek to avoid any thoughts, feelings, or reminders that could make them relive that painful experience, research also shows.

Yet, redressing such injustices often requires both parties' willingness to suspend resentment and meet and talk.

Therein lies the paradox for descendants of victims and victimizers. They seek to avoid the very thing that might ultimately resolve—or at least salve—their pain: a face-to-face encounter with each other. For to do so would give their past, as embodied in the memories of their parents' suffering, a new reality.

Indeed, even when some children of the Holocaust and Nazis' children agreed to make a historic meeting at Harvard Medical Education Center in 1992 their sense of a shared experience only took them so far. Although many

Figure 8.10 Kids playing telephone

participants from the two groups were able to relinquish some resentment and bond with the children of their parents' enemy, they could not shake their stake to the moral high ground. Survivors' children were the most intractable, feeling that there was no Nazi point of view that could justify, much less rectify, the suffering and death of their relatives in concentration camps.

The burden of confronting past injustices was transmitted to another generation. Coming to terms with their parents' dark past shaped the identities of both Nazis' children and survivors' children. The legacy of the Holocaust and World War II had a dominant influence on the children's lives and obligations.

For children of survivors, the legacy emphasized the exclusivity of the Holocaust. For children of Nazis, the legacy emphasized the general conditions of the war. The children of survivors' descriptions of how their parents suffered during the Holocaust are matched by the children of Nazis' descriptions of how their parents suffered during the war. This fact brings us to a problematic legacy of the Holocaust. Both survivors' and Nazis' accounts claim the status of victimhood. We are faced with symmetrical stories of victimhood, with the double victim phenomena.

One survivor parent told his child, "I want you to remember every Jew was a victim. Germany was a nation of murderers. They didn't have any pity for women or for children. What happened to the Jews was the greatest crime in history." A former Nazi's child recalls her father telling her, "I want you to remember. We were fighting a war. The Jews weren't the only ones who suffered.

Figure 8.11 Wall of portaits of Holocaust victims

I was in prison too. We lost the war, so the Allies wanted people to believe all Germans were guilty, but the Germans were the first to be taken to the camps."

Nazis' children and survivors' children are challenged to confront a difficult past recalled with deep-seated emotions. The deep emotions are presented not only in the survivors' stories but also in the former Nazis' stories. These stories, passed down from the generation that experienced them to the generation that now remembers, compel the children to face the uncomfortable presence of earlier unresolved roles and injustices. In each case, the demand arises to understand the injustices wrought over a generation ago, which were not settled by the previous generation.

The experience of injustice involves more than an emotional reaction to physical or economic suffering. Appealing to our everyday experience confirms that. When we are treated unfairly by others (or those close to us are treated unfairly), it affects us in profound ways. We are likely to suffer not only from the physical harm done to us, but also from the psychological injury of having been treated unfairly. The reason most people are affected by injustices done to them is not simply that they hurt in some tangible way; it is because such injuries are also messages—interpersonal communications. They are ways a wrongdoer has of saying to us, "I am superior to you" or "I have the

Figure 8.12 Adult hand in kid's palms

right to decide who should and who should not inhabit the world" or "I count and you do not" (Murphy & Hampton, 1988). When people are intentionally denied the respect to which they believe they are entitled, people feel as unjustly treated as when they are denied the material assets to which they believe they are entitled (Miller, 2001).

An intentional injustice is insulting and degrading, and thus involves an injury that is interpersonal. As Aristotle asserted, "a man can give something away if he likes, but he cannot suffer injustice if he likes—there must be somebody else to do him the injustice" (Aristotle, 1955, p. 163). Research from studies of the layperson's understanding of everyday injustices supports the notion that the experience of everyday injustice involves some form of disrespectful interpersonal treatment. For instance, when people are asked to describe unjust experiences they have experienced in daily life, the most frequently mentioned are violations of interpersonal codes of conduct like giving orders in an inappropriate tone, unjustified accusation and blaming, or ruthless use of one's status and power (Lupfer, Weeks, Doan, & Houston, 2000; Mikula, 1986; Mikula, Schere, & Athenstaedt, 1998).

People care whether their treatment is just or unjust because it suggests something critically important to them—their self-worth (Miller, 2001). The right to be treated in a way that fosters positive self-worth plays an important role in an individual's experience of injustice. According to the Harvard University philosopher John Rawls (1971), one of the entitlements individuals are due by virtue of their humanity is the right to be treated in a way that fosters positive self-worth. Research on what has been called "interactional justice" (Bies & Moag, 1986; Cropanzo & Greenberg, 1997; Skarlicki & Folger, 1997) confirms that people believe they are entitled to respectful treatment from others. "Concern for justice and respect for personhood are powerfully and inseparably linked" (Miller, 2001, p. 17).

When we (or those we love) are treated unjustly by others, it hurts us in profound ways. Our sense of dignity and self-worth is offended. So we are likely to react by feeling angry, resentful, or bitter toward those who have hurt us. These feelings function in defense of our self-esteem, of our perception of our own worth, and of what we are owed. It is a response that is chiefly concerned with our (the victim's) relationship to the wrongdoer.

The psychologist Bernard Weiner (1993) adopts the metaphor that victims are godlike, and life is a courtroom where interpersonal dramas are played out. Like God, victims regard themselves as having the right to judge others as innocent or guilty, as good or bad. These inferences then cause affective reactions that are also ascribed to God, including anger, resentment, and compassion. Weiner gives the example of a spouse failing to appear at a designated time to go to a movie. The waiting wife believes that the errant husband went somewhere else instead. The wife is angry and, upon seeing the partner, refuses to speak to him. The husband then confesses his "sin" and asks forgiveness. The wife is merciful and withdraws her sentence.

The wife's forgiveness can be an act of goodwill, but it can also be an act of arrogance (Murphy & Hampton, 1988, p. 31). Because negative emotions like anger and resentment create unequal moral relations among persons, the wife may feel her husband owes her an apology. Seeing it this way, the husband might resent the forgiveness. "Who do you think you are to forgive me?" "I don't owe you anything," the husband might respond to his well-meaning wife.

Besides creating unequal moral relations, negative emotions can stand as a fatal obstacle to the restoration of a relationship. We can see this clearly in close relationships such as marriage and friendship. Because of the nature of attachment, interpersonal injuries here are not just ordinary injustices but also betrayals (Murphy & Hampton, 1988). Because, when we relate to people toward whom we feel deeply attached, our feelings are highly susceptible to emotional extremes. When such a person does something that is contrary to our expectations it has a greater potential to hurt us. So resentment here can be deep and nearly intractable. In the previous example, the wife might have been unmoved by the pleas of her husband. She might have refused to forgive him because in her mind her husband was now untrustworthy.

In ethnic relationships too, anger and resentment can stand as an unyielding response—as revealed in this statement by a daughter of survivors: "I

Figure 8.13 2 people fighting in relationship

don't feel a need to give up my grudge. My blood is not ready to cool. The Germans cannot be redeemed. They must pay for what they did to us. And we must impress hatred of the Germans upon our children and their descendants." And we can hear the voice of resentment in this statement by a son of a former Nazi: "Every major nation has had its own Hitler period with its own atrocities. What is the Allied bombings of Hiroshima and Nagasaki? I think this talk of collective guilt has gone on for too long. I am tired of the Jewish people trying to make us Germans feel guilty. The Nazi regime forced the German people to be Nazis. If they hadn't obeyed, the Gestapo would torture them."

The law tries to redress injustices by institutionalizing and reducing feelings of anger and resentment. James Stephen, the famous Victorian judge and theorist of law, claimed that the law gives "distinct shape to the feeling of anger" and provides a "distinct satisfaction to the desire of vengeance." He wrote, "The . . . law gives definite expression and solemn ratification and justification to the hatred which is excited by the commission of the offence" (cited in Murphy & Hampton, 1988, p. 3).

Concerning the Holocaust, the Western Allies and the Federal Republic of Germany tried to institutionalize feelings of resentment by setting up a system of reparations to redress the past injustices. They established legal sanctions and a financial reparation program. The money from Germany was to be compensation for the property stolen by the Nazis and for the physical and economic damage suffered by the Holocaust survivors. The program was identified as *Wiedergutmachung*, which literally translated means "to make good again."

However, it was widely recognized that these measures had the opposite effect and were equally resented by survivors and Germans alike. The program failed to remedy feelings of hatred and resentment; in fact, it perpetuated such feelings. Many survivors resented the monetary amends of West Germany, calling them "blood money." They declared that such amends could not avenge for the suffering they endured or make up for the degradation. And some West Germans have expressed their resentment because Germany is still stigmatized although "Nazi criminals were hunted down and put on trial. Guilt was accepted, and billions were paid in restitution to survivors and heirs" (Joffe, 1998, pp. 222–223). Thus, the *Wiedergutmachung* program was unsuccessful at redressing past injustices or reducing feelings of resentment.

One can readily appreciate the desire to redress past injustices through institutionalized programs like the *Wiedergutmachung* program. But redressing an injustice sometimes demands more than establishing legal sanctions or financial reparations. An injustice is committed when rules of conduct are willfully broken. This violation, as mentioned before, results in some form of harm that violates interpersonal codes of conduct.

So, whether in policy or in close relationships, redressing an injustice is more than simply a matter of jurisprudence or economics but, first, a matter of personal concern. It is decidedly intimate, whether involving individuals, a whole family, or a whole nation of people. Redressing an injustice, therefore, may require personal involvement. It may require both parties' willingness to meet and redress the injustice (Weissmark, Giacomo, & Kuphal, 1993).

Most of us would dismiss this thought. Our response is to shun those who have wronged us or to strike back. Recent research of people's responses to being treated unfairly confirms that the most common responses to injustice fall into two broad categories: withdrawal responses or attack responses. For example, giving one's partner the "silent treatment" is a common withdrawal response; whereas "evening the score," as mentioned before, is a common attack response (Miller, 2001).

When we are treated unjustly by others, it affects us in profound and deeply threatening ways. There is an emotional response. We are affected not only by what happens to us, but also by what happens within ourselves. Since we are all, to some extent, sensitive to how others treat us, it is natural to respond

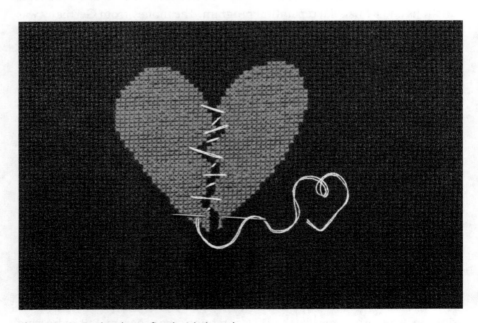

Figure 8.14 Broken heart fixed with thread

by hating and resenting those who treat us unjustly and to "want to separate ourselves from them—to harm them in turn or at least banish them from the realm of those whose well-being should be our concern" (Murphy & Hampton, 1988, p. 25). Our sense of self-worth is social in at least this sense, and it is part of human nature that we respond in these ways.

Surprisingly, during his trial, Eichmann expressed the sentiment that he would like to meet with the victims to redress the past injustices. He said he "would like to find peace with [his] former enemies"—a sentiment he shared with Himmler, who had expressed it during the last year of the war, and with the Labor Front leader Robert Ley, who, before he committed suicide in Nuremberg, had proposed the establishment of a "conciliation committee" consisting of the Nazis responsible for the massacres and the Jewish survivors (cited in Arendt, 1964, p. 53).

Arendt described Eichmann's sentiment as an "outrageous cliche," "a self-fabricated stock phrase," "devoid of reality." She thought it unbelievable that many ordinary Germans reacted in the same terms at the end of the war. And she concluded that the desire to meet with the victims was merely self-serving. Arendt wrote, "you could almost see what an 'extraordinary sense of elation' it gave to the speaker the moment it popped out of his mouth" (Arendt, 1964, p. 53).

It is impossible to know what was in Eichmann s mind or other former Nazis' minds when they uttered this sentiment. But we can, I think, understand Arendt's response. Hannah Arendt was a German Jew. She was born in 1906 in Hanover, Germany. She studied philosophy with Martin Heidegger at the University of Heidelberg, where she earned her doctorate. Her own experience with anti-Semitism forced her to leave Germany. Her former teacher and lover Martin Heidegger had joined the Nazi party. It is reasonable to assume, therefore, that Hannah Arendt herself felt betrayed and was deeply affected by the experience of injustice.

"What was decisive," Arendt recalls in 1965, "was the day we learned about Auschwitz. That was the real shock. . . . It was really as if an abyss had opened. Because we had the idea that amends could somehow be made for everything else, as amends can be made for just about everything at some point in politics. But not for this. This ought not to have happened" (cited in Kohn, 1994, pp. 13–14).

Hannah Arendt was widely attacked in the Jewish press and by Jewish organizations for her controversial interpretation of the Eichmann trial and for her description of the Jewish leadership's cooperation with the Nazis. But the Jewish press and Jewish organizations praised Arendt's response to the Holocaust—the idea that amends with the Germans could

Figure 8.15 Stamp

never be made. The Israeli newspaper *Herut* published a declaration saying that any hands raised in favor of negotiations with Germany would be "treasonous hands" (cited in Segev, 2000, p. 213). Menachem Begin, a member of the Knesset and a staunch opponent of reparations, said at an Israeli Knesset session, "There are things in life that are worse than death itself. And this is one of those things. . . . We will leave our families, bid our children farewell, and there will be no negotiations with Germany . . . We are prepared to do anything, anything to prevent this disgrace to Israel" (cited in Segev, 2000, pp. 219–220). "Twelve million Germans served in the Nazi army. There is not one German who has not murdered our fathers. Every German is a Nazi. Every German is a murderer" (cited in Segev, 2000, p. 216).

This understandable response to resent those who have treated us unjustly explains the reluctance to meet or to talk with them. Furthermore, clinical evidence shows that our reluctance to meet with those who have wronged us stems from the traumatic psychological effects of the injustice itself.

Clinical data show that victims of injustice experience intense psychological distress at exposure to external cues that symbolize or resemble an aspect of the unjust event (Figley, 1985). Exposure to reminders of the unjust event may trigger images, flashbacks, or a sense of reliving the painful experience (Yehuda, 2002; Ferry et al., 2014). Most victims, therefore, avoid thoughts, feelings, or conversations associated with the unjust event. And most victims avoid activities, places, or people that arouse recollections of the unjust event. The reluctance to meet with the wrongdoer stems from the victims' needs to protect their mental well-being. These findings may help to explain why most survivors avoided meeting or having discussions with former Nazis.

But if we accept the idea—that injustice is an interpersonal injury, that resentment can lead to bad consequences, and that resentment is a fatal obstacle to redressing an injustice—then it follows that avoidance or attack cannot always be the final response we take to those who have wronged us (Murphy & Hampton, 1988, p. 17). Redressing an injustice may sometimes require both parties' willingness to meet and discuss the injustice.

Figure 8.16 Wire shaped like a head

But getting both parties to discuss the injustice is first a matter of getting them to reason or be reasonable. And this involves "getting them to acknowledge or at least face the others' passions and points of view" (Solomon, 1990, p. 47). As Solomon says, this is why the most tragic ethnic conflicts, such as those in Northern Ireland, Bosnia, Cyprus, and the Middle East, perpetuate themselves with a refusal to acknowledge the others' points of view.

Reason has the key function of promoting mutual awareness. Whether in policy matters or in personal relationships, reason in justice involves more than proving the validity of one's point of view; instead it involves curbing one's emotions. This, in turn, can help one understand others' circumstances. Given the controversial and possibly misinterpreted implications of this idea, let me make clear that this does not imply that one should overlook or forgive an injustice. If the aim is to understand unjust behavior and the reactions and legacies resulting from this behavior rather than judge it from a moral standpoint, then one might want to consider different contexts and viewpoints. "Hearing the other side," "seeing another view," means we use thinking in an unbiased, open manner, in contrast to a biased, closed manner. It does not mean we forgive a person's unjust actions or seek to redress the injustice at all costs.

A story may make this clearer. The journalist Laura Blumenfeld (2002) chronicled her journey to meet with the Palestinian terrorist who shot her father. The attack had taken place in Jerusalem. For 12 years, Blumenfeld says she was haunted by the idea of somehow avenging the crime. "It was like a fracture that never healed," she says (Schindehette & Seaman, 2002, p. 129).

Though the bullet only grazed her father's scalp, Blumenfeld was deeply shaken. "It was my first brush with evil," she says. "It made me angry" (Schindehette & Seaman, 2002, p. 129). The idea of confronting the terrorist who shot her father never left her. "I had two impulses," she says. "One was to physically shake him and scream, Do you know what it is that you did?' The other was to reach inside him and shake up his soul" (Schindehette & Seaman, 2002, p. 130).

Blumenfeld learned that the man who shot her father was in a pro-Syria breakaway faction of the Palestine Liberation Organization. Several Palestinians had been tried and convicted in an Israeli court for the shooting of foreigners. The man who had shot her father was named Omar Khatib and was now serving 25 years in an Israeli prison.

Identifying herself simply as an American journalist interested in "hearing his story," Blumenfeld went to the West Bank to meet Khatib's family. She asked the gunman's father, "Why did he do it?" The father's response was brief. "He did his duty," he said. "Every Palestinian must do it. Then there will be justice" (Blumenfeld, 2002, p. 38). Khatib's parents showed Blumenfeld their son's report cards and high-school certificate of graduation that read, "The school administration certifies that Omar Kamel Said Al Khatib was a student. . . . His conduct was very good" (Blumenfeld, 2002, p. 38).

Only immediate relatives were allowed contact with prisoners, so Khatib's brother offered to take letters from Blumenfeld to his brother in prison. In her letters to Khatib, Blumenfeld explained that she was an American journalist and was interested about his life in an Israeli prison, about his family's history, about the events that led to his arrest, and what, in particular, had inflamed his feelings against Israel. Khatib wrote her back several times. In one letter he wrote,

> This city [Jerusalem] has shaped my identity; she planted in my mind unforgettable memories. I witnessed the Israeli aggression of the Six Day War. I was four years old then, but enough aware to understand what was going on. I remember when my mother used to hide us. . . . We were so frightened by the darkness and the sound of the guns. . . . At the end of the 60s my brother was arrested and sent to prison. . . . I saw the painful time that my family went through, searching to know the fate of my brother. I remember visiting him with my mother once or twice, but after that he was expelled to Jordan. . . . There he was sent to prison for no reason but under the pretext of crossing the borders illegally. We were such a poor family at that time, we didn't have enough money to eat. . . . I will never forget the exhaustion and pain of the journey when I accompanied my mother to visit my brother. . . . Do you know when I saw [my brother] next? It was 25 years later. This time I was the prisoner, and he was the visitor. (Blumenfeld, 2002, p. 39)

In her reply to Khatib, Blumenfeld asked him why he shot the American tourist. Khatib wrote back, "With regard to David Blumenfeld—I hope he can understand the reasons behind my act. If I were him I would. I have thought a lot about meeting him one day" (Blumenfeld, 2002, p. 40). To give Khatib a better sense of David Blumenfeld, Laura Blumenfeld replied that she had contacted David, and discovered that his grandparents had been killed in the Holocaust, and that he had come to Israel to gather material for building a Holocaust museum in New York. Blumenfeld told him that David was not hostile to the Palestinian cause, but that he was concerned about whether Khatib would ever again resort to violence against anyone, innocent or not (Blumenfeld, 2002, p. 40). When Khatib learned that David felt sympathy for the Palestinians, he wrote that he had hoped they could one day be friends.

In his next letter, Katib wrote, "Back to David, I do admire his talking to you and I appreciate his understanding, his support for my people. If these feelings are really from the depth of his heart, this may contribute a lot to our friendship. Of course my answer to his question [about committing an act of violence again] is NO" (Blumenfeld, 2002, p. 40).

In July 1999 Khatib was scheduled for a hearing on a possible medical parole. Blumenfeld returned to Israel, stood in the courtroom, and proclaimed that she was the daughter of David Blumenfeld, the man Khatib shot at. Blumenfeld says she tried to explain why she had concealed her identity for so long: "I did it for one reason. This conflict is between human beings, and not between disembodied Arabs and Jews. And we're people. Not military targets. We're people with families" (Blumenfeld, 2002, p. 40). Blumenfeld says, "I wanted them to know me as an individual, and for me to know them. I didn't want them to think of me as a Jew, or as a victim. Just Laura. And I wanted to understand who they were, without them feeling defensive or accused. I wanted to see what we had in common" (Blumenfeld, 2002, p. 362).

Blumenfeld argued for the prisoner's release. Khatib and his family stared in shock. His family wept and embraced her. The meeting, says Blumenfeld, "felt like the defining moment of my life" (Schindehette & Seaman, 2002, p. 131). Blumenfeld's story shows that her meeting with the Palestinian terrorist and his family was a transforming experience. Similar stories of transformation have been reported in journalistic accounts of families of murder victims who have had face-to-face meetings with a wrongdoer.

Still, it is true that some emotional wounds are too deep to ever really be transformed. The survivors of the death camps endured a traumatic experience of systematic injustice and cruelty. The experience of someone who lived for years merely as a thing in the feelings of others is unlikely to emerge willing to hear others' passions and points of views. But if survivors' wounds can never heal, the question remains: must they be passed on to the children of the wounded and to their children? And what about the children of Nazis, must they inherit their parents' memories too?

After the war, most former Nazis and survivors wanted to get on with rebuilding their lives. To some extent, both distanced themselves from what had happened. By distancing themselves from that dark period in their lives they could remove it from their everyday consciousness so that it did not intrude on their thinking or interfere with rebuilding their lives. Within a few years, former Nazis and survivors reconstructed themselves and their lives and became useful and productive members of a society. To do so necessitated significant changes on their part, both in terms of behavior and in their outlook.

Survivors who had been so debilitated, both physically and psychologically, could recover and immigrate to new countries, adapt to the new conditions,

Figure 8.17 Family tree with question marks

and raise a family and function on a day-to-day level (Helmreich, 1992). Also, most former Nazis, upon returning to their homes, could cast off their Nazi self and view themselves as essentially ordinary citizens (Lifton, 1986; Ryan, 1984). Both survivors and former Nazis could shed their former selves, reconstruct their lives, and form new identities. There was no reason, therefore, to contemplate meeting the other side. Indeed, the very notion of meeting the other side is an idea many survivors and former Nazis feel should not even be mentioned, an impossibility that should never be proposed.

But what about the children?

Do survivors' children and former Nazis' children want to meet the "other side"? How would children of survivors react to hearing children of Nazis tell stories about how their parents suffered during the war? How would children of Nazis react to hearing children of survivors tell stories about how their parents suffered during the Holocaust? Could they face the others' passions and points of view? Could children of survivors and Nazis talk to each other about World War II and the Holocaust and understand the anxieties of each

Figure 8.18 Doves of peace

about the other as a gateway to reestablishing a relationship? Could children of Nazis understand and acknowledge the roots of children of survivors' pain that goes back to the Holocaust? On the other hand, could children of survivors understand and acknowledge the roots of children of Nazis' fear that goes back to World War II? Or would resentment and anger stand as a fatal obstacle to restoring equal moral relations between Nazis' children and survivors' children?

A Study of Interpersonal Justice: Descendants of Survivors, Nazis Meet

I knew the answers could only be found by bringing the groups together and observing them interacting. So, as mentioned in the previous chapter, my colleagues and I and a team of Harvard students organized the first meeting between children of Nazis and children of survivors. Our aim was to study their interpersonal behavior. There was no published work in this area, so a study of children of survivors and Nazis coming to terms with the past and each other would benefit our understanding of the interpersonal aspects of injustice.

The idea to bring together children of survivors and Nazis was a simple, intuitive idea. But it was also seen as shattering a taboo. Although research aims to understand events, not change or influence them, many people feared that our research study would be interpreted as a justification of Nazism or as a challenge to the Holocaust's status as the symbol of absolute evil.

Although our research study had no intention of defending those who committed Nazi crimes or of expressing support for or identification with them, our plan was to allow the children of Nazis to express their point of view too. Since our aim was to study injustice rather than judge it from a moral point of view, we planned to allow spontaneous expressions of thoughts and feelings of any kind. We intended, in other words, to allow stories on both sides to be told, and to observe how individuals reacted to hearing the others' point of view.

We expected there might be conflicting claims advanced by individuals, including downplaying Nazism, equating Nazis' actions with the Allies' actions, comparing recruitment into the SS with being taken into concentration camp, and relating how German people suffered during the war with how Jews suffered in the concentration camps. Still whatever the subject matter, whatever the response, this "hearing the other side" was precisely the point of

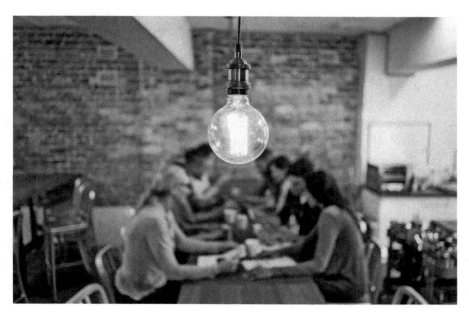

Figure 8.19 People sitting at a table

our research. Prescribing a doctrine of truth would have foiled the purpose of our study.

As mentioned in the previous chapter, in organizing the research study, we wrote to potential subjects inviting them to participate in a joint meeting. We explained that we were conducting a research study of the influence of the Holocaust and World War II in the lives of descendants of Nazis and survivors. Some individuals wrote back saying they were not interested in meeting the "other" descendants.

"I really cannot fathom why people would choose to meet with the descendants of their families' murderers," said the daughter of a survivor. "The only thing they could do for me is to bring back my grandparents, my aunts, uncles, and cousins who were all murdered. Other than that, I have no interest in helping them to work through their guilt."

"I don't feel guilty for what my father did," said the son of a high-ranking Nazi. "The title 'war criminal' for my father means nothing. In some years history will take a different perspective. It will be seen that the former Allies are anything but moral and just. As for meeting with children of KZs [shorthand for *Konzentrationslager*, concentration camp], I don't think they are ready to hear a factual examination of the truth."

Most individuals, however, wrote back saying they were interested in attending the meeting. For one son of survivors, the opportunity to interact with former Nazis' children provided him with a chance to get answers.

"The meeting will be a way for me to fill in the blacked out part of my father's life," he said. "I want to see the second generation—my contemporaries— where they were at. Did they deny the Holocaust ever happened?"

Another child of a survivor said, "I think the word I'm looking for is remorse, or something that's going to make me feel better, but I also recognize that I can't make children of Nazis feeling something just because I want them to feel it, or say something because I want them to say it."

For the daughter of a former Nazi, the opportunity to interact with survivors' children provided her with a choice: "I feel I can either choose to live with this legacy of shame or I can choose to do something useful with it," she said. "I feel a responsibility to do something with this legacy that might be helpful, to let people know not all Germans are Nazis."

Another child of a former Nazi said, "I am comfortable with my past. I want to go to the meeting because I want to recognize my heritage and to teach people that not everyone feels hatred mistrust and fear. I want to reveal the truth about what our parents had to go through too."

Locating, interviewing, and choosing participants took 17 months. Finally, in September 1992 and 1993, 22 individuals met. For four days, the group met in discussion sessions, facilitated by Daniel Giacomo, a psychiatrist from Harvard Medical School who is neither German nor Jewish. Each discussion session was videotaped and later transcribed. One discussion session was televised on the CBS program *Sunday Morning News with Charles Kuralt* and on NBC *Dateline* and Public Television.

 Readers might find it interesting to watch these meetings (and the other meeting with the descendant of slaves and slave owners) on YouTube before reading about them.

(1) "The Past Between Them" (total time around 15 minutes)
    https://youtu.be/2m_iVOwAinQ
(2) "Journey to Understanding" (Part 1 and Part 2 total time around 15 minutes)
    https://youtu.be/rbcjajTP6Ug
    https://youtu.be/IcWeufEszyo
(3) "Coming to the Table" (Part 1 and Part 2 total time approx. 15 minutes)
    Weissmark, 1995,https://youtu.be/NRB--qC7Zeo
    Weissmark, 1995,https://youtu.be/IdQnNWfrtZM

Voices from the Meeting

Betraying Their Legacies

For many of the survivors' children, the initial foray into the conference room felt like a shameful act. There was the concern that if they got close to the Germans they would be betraying their legacy. On the first day a child of a survivor asked, "I've been thinking about how this is going to impact my family. Am I betraying my parents by being here? Am I minimizing their trauma? Am I forgiving? It's certainly not in my power to forgive. And no—and it is too presumptuous even a thought about—about forgiveness."

 For many of the former Nazis' children, the initial foray into the conference room felt like a disloyal act. On the first day a child of a Nazi asked, "My *Mutter*—that's the way we call her, my mother—she never wanted us to talk about it. And I haven't even said much. It was just that my father was—an officer in the Waffen SS. But there was suddenly this feeling for me—oh my God, you know, how is my family going to react. You know, am I betraying my family. You know, what am I doing. And how are the other Germans going to react?"

Nazi Death-Camp Stories

As participants gathered in a circle, stories poured forth from all of them (except the son of the kapo, who did not talk about his father's camp experiences during the conference). The survivors' children related Nazi death-camp stories. They talked about how their parents were transported to the camps, about the brutal conditions in the camps, about liberation from the camps, and then resettlement in the United States. They talked about how their parents' death-camp experiences affected their lives. They described the anger, fear, rage, and resentment they felt when hearing about the camps.

Wartime Stories

The former Nazis' children outlined the flip side of the Nazi regime. They talked about how their parents were forced to join the Nazi party, about the brutal tactics of the Gestapo, and about a disrupted post–World War II Germany. And, they talked about how their parents' wartime experiences affected their lives. They described the fear, anger, and resentment they felt when hearing about the war.

Resentment and Rage

As participants gathered in a circle, many survivors' children spoke about their resentment and rage. "Deep down inside, I can feel all my rage," the daughter of a survivor said. "My whole life I've had the image of bad Germans. And when I look across the room now and I see all your) German faces, the blond hair and the blue eyes, I can feel my resentment bubble up. I feel the six million dead people between us. And part of me wishes to see you all suffer for what was done."

Fear of Retaliation

Many former Nazis' children spoke about their fear. At one point the daughter of a Nazi began to cry. "I was afraid that I would be subject to understandable accusations, anger, and rage," the daughter of a Nazi officer said. "I thought you children of the victims would want to kill me. But I chose to participate at any cost. The fear did not stop me. Because I am not guilty. Yes, my father's generation was. But I want to make this very clear. I've carried my father's burden. I don't want it anymore."

Looking for Retribution

The child of a survivor replied,

"I understand you did not do it. Your parents, the perpetrators are responsible, they're guilty, they should be dealt with. But the problem is my bitterness. I don't feel enough, they [the Nazis] are not enough caught, enough tried, enough convicted, and enough who paid any price. I'm looking for some kind of retribution that I don't, and I don't know what the amount is, and I don't know how much is enough because it'll never be enough, and no one can make up for my lost family, and nobody can make up for my lost childhood."

As the meeting progressed, stories poured forth from the participants about how their parents' lives had affected them.

Distrust

Weeping, a daughter of survivor said,

"I've lived with their experience. It did happen. They have numbers on their arms to prove it. It happened once. What I have to speak about here is how imprisoned I am because of it. And how imprisoned I've been all my life. How afraid I am of the—of the world, the universe. I grew up terrified. Everything frightens me, the door has to be locked, I look behind me, I'm not safe anywhere. I have a lot of claustrophobia in elevators in closed places. Any room like that reminds me of the gas chamber. I can't sit in a room without windows. I need windows and air. I grew up distrusting everyone and with a lot of rage and no place to vent it. And I need you to explain to me why it will never happen again, when I have such distrust. That I can look into the face of—of a child of German Nazis and I don't see that look anymore. I've come here to see that. I want to look into your face and believe you, that you don't hate me. And that you're not going to kill me."

"Never Said Anything Bad About Jews"

A daughter of a Nazi offered comforting words: "It would be a positive experience for me to make you feel safe. And it's almost like you have a memory stored in your head that's not yours." Then she explained,

"When my parents told me stories about their youth, they never said anything bad about Jews, and you didn't know to what degree they were involved. I also carry the—you know, the experience of my—my grandmother and, you know, a lot of other relatives who lost their home in Russia. And my father definitely transmitted that to me too, you know. The world my parents talked about, sometimes, with nostalgic feelings, it had absolutely nothing to do with those times. A lot of those things have to do with German culture. And a lot of those things are good. A lot of those things have to do with what is my heritage. It is a sense of identity that I wasn't allowed to have. More than half a century has passed since the war, and some Germans are tired of seeing their history reduced to the 12 years of the Nazi regime."

Disbelief

Unconvinced, the daughter of a survivor asked, "So you want me to believe that your parents never said anything bad about the Jews. They just joined the Nazi party, supported the killing of Jews, and then never mentioned a thing about it to their children?"

The daughter of a Nazi officer replied, "That's right, everybody would always say, 'We didn't know anything about the concentration camps,'" adding that her history books in school only covered up to the 19th-centuryPrussian chancellor Bismarck.

"When I was smaller, I would hear, 'Oh, this store belonged to a Jew,' and I didn't even know what a Jew was. The minute we tried to talk to our parents, they felt attacked and accused. . . . They would say things like you are green behind the ears, you wouldn't understand those times. When I needed to speak to someone, I felt isolated and alone. I had a friend who said, 'You Germans started the war, you lost it, I really don't give a damn what Germans are feeling right now.' I felt like I was not allowed to have any feelings about this."

Irate, a daughter of survivors replied, "You're saying that the children of Nazis endured silence, and then they endured having the identity of being a person of a culture that made others move away from them and not see them as people. You know, I look at you and the other descendants of the Nazis here, and I'm thinking now you know what it's like to be a Jew at that time, when people moved away and didn't want to associate."

"Not Just the Germans"

The most provocative hours came on the third day. A daughter of a Nazi officer said,

> "I don't think that just Germans lost their innocence; I think all humanity lost its innocence. Now we know that this is possible. I don't want to judge my father. He was only 17 years old. He disappeared after World War II. I don't know what he knew. I don't know what he did. And I honestly cannot say that if I lived in those times, that I would have been a decent person. I don't know that. I hope I would have been. But you know, it's something that I can never resolve."

"Don't Listen"

A daughter of a survivor replied,

> "You know I'm in a bind when I hear you talk. I can't ignore my feelings, which is to not deal with my anger, not to deal with my rage, because they were inappropriate in my own home because they could be destructive to my father, the victim. So I'm in a bind. I want to be true to my feelings. On the other hand, I believe there does need to be a space for something like this, for you to be heard. And when you said your father was 17 years old. I immediately said, 'He was a kid, of course.' And then I said, 'You're betraying, don't listen to her, because you're betraying your parents.' I mean at 17, I did some things I probably wouldn't do now. So I—I understand. But then I hear my mother crying, 'Don't understand.' "

Another child of a survivor said,

> "From the stories I've heard from my mother and her friends, that by the time these Jews were 17 years old, these people were no longer children. So I don't think age is the issue here. Your father had a choice. My mother told me some of the greatest *Antisemiten* [anti-Semites] were kids who were in the Hitler youth and they were just 14 years old. What you're asking me to believe is that because your father was 17 he wasn't guilty."

A daughter of a Nazi replied,

> "None of us can understand it. I came to show some compassion for a tragedy I don't think any of us will ever understand. I wasn't there. I didn't do it, but that's not the issue. I can't judge my father whether he was 17 or not. Would I have acted differently? Could I have acted differently during those times? That's not the issue. Someone has to say they're sorry. I want to help close that wound—to get a little bit of balm, not vinegar, on these wounds."

"No Restitution"

For the children of concentration camp survivors, the impassioned apologies could do little to ease the pain many still feel over the death of their relatives. One daughter of a survivor explained, "There is no restitution for the loss of our families. We carry the pain of it and the rage of it. We cannot change what happened in the past, but I don't think I can forgive it."

"We're All Victims Here"

The daughter of a Nazi replied, "But, in a way, we're all victims here. We share a legacy of pain. The German people suffered too. They were forced into the army and to join the Nazi party. Not all of them wanted this. I always saw my parents as the real victims of World War II—until I learned of the Holocaust during a history course."

"We Are Different"

The son of a kapo declared that his history and inheritance were unlike those of a Nazi child's. He said he was at the meeting so he could learn more about how his history differed from the children of Nazis. He also declared that the tendency to compare the histories was a way to obscure and diminish the memory of one's parents.

(As mentioned before, a kapo was a concentration camp inmate who collaborated with the Nazis. The kapos had authority to impose punishment, and many were notorious for their cruelty. After the war, the kapos mixed with the survivors, trying to hide their pasts. Many, however, were identified while in the DP camps, and then lynched by other Jews. Interestingly enough, the son of the kapo wanted to be identified as a child of a survivor, not as a child of a collaborator. Also, he wanted to emphasize the differences between himself and the descendants of Nazis. And finally, he was the only participant who refused to share stories about his father's concentration camp role and experiences.)

A son of a Nazi replied, "We have no choice about our inheritance. None of us. Both sides, everybody in the room. We did not ask to be born to a Jew or a Nazi. It happened to us and we have to deal with this. The question is why didn't anyone resist?"

The son of a survivor added,

"I think it's important that we make a distinction, in my mind, to make the distinction between the child of the survivor and the child of Nazi. I can't in my mind forgive and forget about the perpetrators. And I can't do it, and I haven't reached that level or whatever that is, and I don't know if you call it bigotry or hatred or whatever the hell it is, but I still got it, and I can't forgive."

Another child of survivor added,

"I find this conversation offensive. It is dangerous to talk about resistance in general because what that does is shift the blame onto the Jews. And it changes the whole way you look at it and is very convenient shorthand language for moving everything to the Jews did it themselves. And that is always convenient in a room where there are a group of Germans as well. And my reaction is, it is dangerous."

The son of a Nazi asked, "Aren't we just all asking, the Germans and Jews, why didn't our parents resist? How can we understand those times?"

Despite these provocative exchanges, the anguish of those Germans who were themselves children (or not even born) at the time of the Holocaust helped cement the two groups together in an emotional bond as strong as the legacy they both share.

The daughter of a survivor said, "I think we were able to grieve together because we all have a lot to grieve over, and to do that together is very powerful."

The daughter of a Nazi said. "In a way, we're all children of trauma here. Attending the conference has made a major difference in my life. I feel like a lot of the shame has been lifted, and because of that it's much easier for me to believe in my own sincerity."

What Was Gained

After 4 days of telling each other their personal and family histories and revealing their deepest emotions, the participants began to sense that they had accomplished something beneficial. Both the children of Nazis and survivors who chose to take part in the meeting felt they gained from it.

The daughter of a Nazi explained, "I feel an incredible sense of relief and of a new beginning. I really feel I've arrived somewhere. I've—what I've been looking for and I have a lot of hope. And I know that is—you know, cynicism will come back and fear will come back and despair will come back, but the process has started."

The daughter of a survivor explained, "There is a tremendous feeling of relief. There is a sense that I am leaving behind—metaphorically speaking—a lot of anger, a lot of resentment, a lot of fears—the burden of having carried this legacy."

The son of a Nazi said, "When we speak together about the repercussions of hatred and what it's done in our lives . . . I could not have done that a year

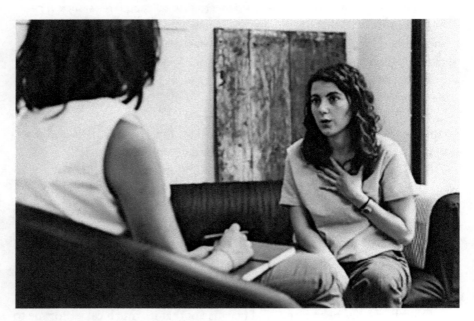

Figure 8.20 Woman talking to a therapist

ago because I could not have believed that I could be believable to children of survivors. It's a very strange process."

The son of a survivor explained, "While I was at the meeting and talking to the people, the connection and the ability to transform some of the pain and the rage that I think I carried over from my mother turned into acceptance and a desire to act from a state of tolerance and love."

For another daughter of a survivor, the fear of being "disloyal to my family who perished" was replaced by an experience she called "an exploration of my humaneness." Her experience was echoed by the daughter of a Nazi Waffen SS officer, "What better way to remember the victims than through working on something new—on people seeing each other as human beings? If we remained enemies, then we would continue Hitler's work."

Summing Up

Summarizing the significance of the conference, I would stress the children's cathartic experiences. At the end of the conference, all the participants reported feeling relieved. The participants said the conference experience brought about a satisfying release from tension. They described the experience as uplifting. Telling the "other participants" stories about their personal and family history had the effect of bringing terrible memories to consciousness, affording them expression, and then inducing relief.

A daughter of survivors said, "I felt I gained something by [their] laying eyes on us and by [our] laying eyes on them. I could not believe that there were Germans with such backgrounds who were interested in meeting us and hearing our stories."

The daughter of a Nazi said of the conference, "It was a powerful experience."

The daughter of a survivor said, "The main surprise was that we liked each other. At the end of the four days we were one happy family. I made friends."

The daughter of a Nazi officer said, "It did not take long for us to become [so] involved in each other's stories that the differences and fears faded away."

A daughter of a survivor said, "One of the participant's fathers committed suicide after the war. We were riveted by her story."

What Was Not Gained

Despite these impressive statements testifying to the participants' cathartic and bonding experiences, the participants' experiences during the

Figure 8.21 People holding hands

conference failed to modify their understanding or acknowledgment of the others' passions and points of view. This was especially true of the survivors' children. Survivors' children resisted thinking from the standpoint of Nazis' children. Instead, they insisted on proving the validity of their viewpoints. Their reluctance to acknowledge the former Nazis' children's viewpoints stemmed from their overwhelming feelings of resentment and anger. These negative emotions, in turn, had the effect of creating unequal moral relations between former Nazis' children and survivors' children.

We can see this effect occurring during the most provocative hours, which came on the third day of the conference when a daughter of a Nazi officer declared, "I can't judge my father. He was so young then. He had to join the German army. They were fighting a war." Later that day another child of a Nazi said, "The German people suffered too. Many of them did not agree with the policies, but they had not choice." And still later that day

Figure 8.22 People talking

the son of a Nazi declared, "We did not ask to be born to a Jew or a Nazi. It happened to us and we have to deal with this. The question is why didn't anyone resist?"

In each instance, the responses of the children of survivors were unyielding. "Your father's age is no excuse for what was done to the Jewish people," replied the child of a survivor. "There is no restitution for the loss of our families," explained another daughter of survivors. "We come from different pasts. And to try and blur that to me minimizes the memory of our parents," declared the son of a kapo. "I find this conversation offensive. It is dangerous to talk about resistance in general," said the daughter of a survivor. "My blood is not ready to cool. Nothing can make up for the fact that I had to grow up without grandparents, aunts, uncles. I can't forgive the Germans. And my children will learn that too," declared the child of a survivor.

The unyielding responses of the children of survivors suggest that the desire to restore justice is a double-edged sword. At one level, survivors' children exert tremendous effort to right a previous wrong. At another level, however, their desire to right a previous wrong leads not to justice but to inequity and exclusion. Of all the statements spoken by survivors' children 66% were statements that emphasized the exclusivity of their parents' suffering and victimhood. On the other hand, of all statements spoken by Nazis' children 70% were statements that stressed their parents' wartime suffering.

The significance of these conference findings is that it documents the way in which the responses of the children of Nazis and the responses of children of survivors, wittingly or not, invalidate the others' points of view. Their parents' views and feelings were passed down to them, and stand as obstacles to establishing equal moral relations. (By contrast, when discussing their *own* hurts and sufferings, which will be spelled out in more detail later, the participants did acknowledge the others' views and establish an equal moral relationship.) The depths of the offspring's emotions, especially survivors' children's emotions, in discussions about their parents' hurts and sufferings, overrule their mental abilities to see justice as two-sided, to keep an open mind.

The next section of this chapter will look at the way a person's existing views affects the way they see and interpret information. Once people adopt a view, they become more closed to information that challenges their views, research suggests. A major effect of this constraint is that people tend to become entrenched in their own one-sided views on history and justice, which makes it more difficult to acknowledge and access the view of the other.

Justice Has Two Sides

Hearing the other side requires more than anecdotal exchanges between children of Holocaust survivors and children of Nazis; it calls for a willingness—and an ability—to suspend—and perhaps even discard—ideas that have shaped their respective worldviews for a lifetime.

The demand is daunting for anyone because it militates against the human tendency to cling to one's inbred belief system, a phenomenon known as belief perseverance. In other words, new facts can be "heard" and merely interpreted in ways that reinforce an individual's original mindset.

In clinging to the known there is comfort and perhaps even pride, while altering a fundamental view could require admitting that past beliefs were mistaken.

For the intractable, psychologists suggest "hypothetical reasoning" could be a useful tool. For example, survivors' children could be asked to

Figure 8.23 Abstract image of dialogue

"make-believe" that Nazis weren't all evil and spin out the possibilities that might stem from that leap. That is, they could be asked to use the new premise to develop "the other side of the story."

For survivors' children and Nazis' children the shackles of past thinking seem not to be so easily lifted. Not only is their worldview at stake, but also their very group identity, an identity forged through visceral stories handed down directly from parents, brothers and sisters, aunts and uncles.

Thus, for many, truly hearing the other side means to deny more than closely held ideas and passionately told tales; it means to deny their ancestors, their history, and themselves.

The Power of Existing Views

The depths of the descendants' feelings of family loyalty compelled them to keep their existing view. "There is the fear that if Jews get close to Germans," said the daughter of a survivor, "we will be forgetting the past." "And there is the fear that if we get close to the Jews," said the daughter of a Nazi, "we are incriminating and blaming our parents." When discussing their parents' feelings and points of view, the participants at the conference were unlikely to revise their existing views even when new information dictated such a change.

Social psychologists have conducted striking experiments that reveal the extent to which existing views can bias the way we see and interpret information. Given the same information, opposing groups of people each assimilate it to their existing views and find their views strengthened.

For example, a classic experiment by the psychologists Robert Vallone, Lee Ross, and Mark Lepper (1985) showed how powerful existing views can be. They showed pro-Arab and pro-Israeli students identical news segments describing the 1982 massacre of civilians in refugee camps in Lebanon. Participants from the two opposing groups interpreted the media's sample of facts and arguments differently: in light of their own existing views. Each group perceived the network news as hostile to its side and believed the news coverage was against their point of view.

Another classic experiment by Lord, Ross, and Lepper (1979) asked students to evaluate the results of two supposedly new research studies. Half the students believed that capital punishment was good and half opposed it. One new research study confirmed and the other disconfirmed the students' views about the deterrent effect of the death penalty. The results showed that both proponents and opponents of capital punishment readily accepted

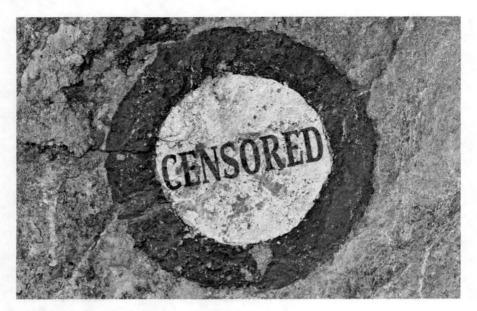

Figure 8.24 Censored painted on a wall

information that confirmed their view but were critical of disconfirming information. Showing the two sides mixed information had, therefore, not changed their views or lessened their disagreement but, rather, preserved their views and increased polarization through the mechanism of biased assimilation: that is, each group quickly assimilated or accepted at face value the evidence that seemed to support its view but subjected to critical scrutiny the evidence that threatened or undermined its view. And in follow-up studies, people exposed to mixed information have been discomfited by the challenging evidence and incited to refute the contrary information. Each side ends up perceiving the information as supporting its existing view and believes even more strongly (Edwards & Smith, 1996; Kuhn & Lao, 1996; Munro & Ditto, 1997).

Other experiments have revealed that it is difficult to change an existing view, once the person invokes an explanation for it. For instance, psychologists C. Anderson, Lepper, and Ross (1980) asked people to decide whether people who take risks are better firefighters than those who do not take risks. One group of subjects was given concrete cases to review showing that a risk-prone person was a successful firefighter and a cautious person was an unsuccessful firefighter. The other group of subjects reviewed cases considering the opposite conclusion.

After forming their view that risk-prone people make better or worse firefighters, the subjects wrote explanations for their views—for example, that risk-prone people are brave or that cautious people are careful. When information was presented that discredited their explanations, the people still held their views and therefore continued to believe that risk-prone people really do make better or worse fire fighters. The experiment showed that the more people examined their explanations and how they might be true, the more closed they became to information that challenged their views.

Thus, taken together, these studies suggest that our existing views affect how we see and interpret information. The studies suggest that our existing views, or what some social psychologists call *prejudgments*, endure despite challenging evidence to the contrary (Davies, 1997). The studies reveal that it is surprisingly difficult to revise an existing view, once a person conjures up a rationale for it. This phenomenon, named *belief perseverance*, shows that existing views can take on lives of their own and outlast the discrediting of the information that produced them (Myers, 2002).

Figure 8.25 Muscles

Assimilation and Accommodation

The notion that existing views can bias the way we see and interpret information is not new, of course. As mentioned before, Piaget spent a half-century studying the relationship between how people interpret new information and mental development. Piaget's observations have greatly influenced psychology's current position on how we think, reason, and use our intelligence to cope with new information. Piaget discovered that our mental growth—which he defined as an increased ability to adapt to new information—takes place because of two key processes that he calls *assimilation* and *accommodation*. Assimilation is the process of incorporating new information into one's existing view of the world. Accommodation is the process of changing one's view of the world when new information dictates such a change. To develop a view of the world that is realistic we must occasionally revise our worldview and extend our understanding to include new information. The process of accommodation, that is to say, revising our worldview is essential for mental growth (Piaget, 1952, 1971).

Sometimes, however, our emotional reactions block our mental growth. In such instances, we avoid accommodating altogether. Instead of changing our worldview when new information dictates such a change, we cling to our existing view through the process of assimilation. When we cling to our existing view, usually unknowingly, we ignore, deny, or downplay new information and disregard inconsistencies or dismiss them as oddities.

For both Nazis' children and survivors' children, the tension between assimilation and accommodation stems from the same demand: to change their clear-cut views and to acknowledge another viewpoint. This creates tension, because there is the fear that in acknowledging another viewpoint, their own view becomes discredited. It is precisely when they are most likely to ignore, to deny, or to downplay new information to maintain their existing worldview. There is the threat that what they have deeply believed over many years might be invalidated.

The tendency, therefore, is for Nazis' children and survivors' children to defend the beliefs of their group with all their might. Otherwise, if their own view becomes discredited—and indeed, the threat to it is great enough—then their identity collapses. So it is often a matter of trying to maintain their secure one-sided view of reality against the uncertain possibilities of revising their worldview. We might call this way of being "seeking self-protection" or "acting in defense of self" or "preserving one's identity."

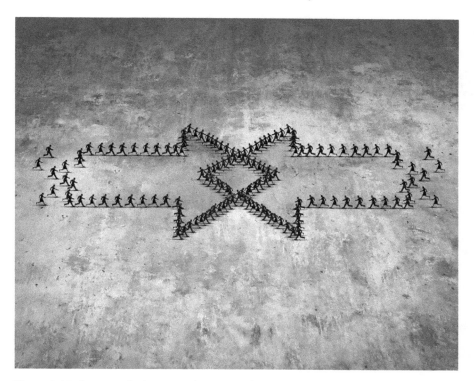

Figure 8.26 Arrows pointing towards one another

One-Dimensional Views and the Need to Belong

Also, the need to belong impels Nazis' children and survivors' children to defend their group's worldview. As noted earlier, the device of excommunication, whether used by a religious group, an ethnic group, or a family, is a powerful device for maintaining loyalty to a worldview. Baumeister and Leary note that "[a] general pattern may well be that cultures use social inclusion to reward, and exclusion to punish, their members as a way of enforcing their values" (Baumeister & Leary, 1995, p. 521). This was apparent in the conference. The participants raised questions about how their groups would judge them. Many Nazis' children were concerned about "betraying their families," and many survivors' children were concerned about "diminishing the pain of their parents' suffering." These concerns, in turn, may have limited their abilities to revise their worldview. Abundant research demonstrates that the need to belong shapes emotion and cognition.

Figure 8.27 People covering their ears

In defending a worldview, the usual cases are individuals who, from the beginning of their lives, find themselves loyal to a group, whether it is an ethnic group, a religious group, or a family. Loyalty and the need to belong to a group, as mentioned earlier, are part of our social and biological evolution. By telling stories, people pass the legacy from one generation to the next and secure each individual's loyalty. Individuals are expected to accept uncritically all the teachings and assertions that the legacy put before them and even to overlook inconsistencies.

They become indoctrinated with the conviction that they ought to believe the teachings and assertions because their ancestors believed. Their personal quests for distinguishing good from evil, for allowing different points of view to be heard, are cut short because the legacies are teachings and assertions about facts of reality that tell individuals something they have not discovered for themselves that lay claim to their beliefs and feelings rather than their intellects.

When individuals accept uncritically the teachings that the legacy puts before them and overlook the inconsistencies between them, we need not be surprised, then, at the weakness of their intellect and ability to accommodate to new information. Feelings of loyalty make no demands on individuals' intellectual capacities. Instead, loyalty demands the process of incorporating new information into one's existing view of the world. Thus, loyalty to a legacy

Figure 8.28 Kids crowding around for storytime

blocks the full mental development of individuals because feelings of loyalty are outside the control of critical reasoning.

But although this is one aspect, there is another one too. Acceptance of a legacy spares individuals the task of challenging the validity of cherished views. Also, loyalty to a group legacy gives individuals a feeling of security and of owning a valued tradition. They feel they belong to, they are rooted in, a structuralized heritage in which they have an unquestionable place. "It seems that nothing is more difficult for the average person to bear than the feeling of not being identified with a family or group" (Fromm, 1941, p. 234). They may suffer from hunger or suppression, but they do not suffer from the worst of all pains—aloneness, doubt, and anxiety (Fromm, 1941).

Thus, it is reasonable to conclude that children of Nazis and of survivors, like most people, have a deep need to feel connected to their family and group. As mentioned in a previous chapter, the need to belong is so compelling because it is biological. Human babies are born with a tendency to become attached to the adults who take care of them. It is a deeply emotional process anchored in the very core of a person's being. Mental growth and

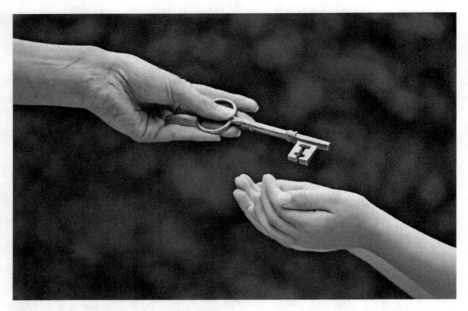

Figure 8.29 Giving key to kid

independence is influenced by attachment needs and by parental, or more broadly speaking, social pressures.

Social pressures do not end in childhood. As Freud points out, countless adults have been impaired by the compromises they are forced to make because of the pressures imposed on them to accept the legacy of their ancestors. They have had to suppress their doubts, writes Freud, and by that, their intellect and abilities to accommodate their worldview, because they thought it was their duty to believe; "many brilliant intellects have broken down over this conflict" (Freud, 1961, pp. 25–27).

If every step in the direction of mental growth and independence were matched by social approval, then the process of accommodation would be harmonious. This does not occur, however, as the meeting illustrates. There are social pressures imposed on people to accept assertions about conditions of reality that lay claim to their beliefs rather than their intellect. People are expected to conform to a one-sided view of reality. This, in turn, compels people to ignore new facts, to deny them, or to treat them as oddities. Otherwise, they may risk the threat of isolation, punishment, the loss of identity. The psychic cost of changing one's view of reality is considerable, as the data from the meeting makes clear.

In this chapter, I have noted that the children of survivors and children of Nazis tend to view reality as one-sided. Similarly, in most ethnic conflicts and even in intimate conflicts, there comes a tunnel-vision that prevents individuals involved in the conflict from "seeing another view" or "hearing the other side." Individuals become indoctrinated with the belief that their side is "right." Attachment to a family loyalty, social obligations, and pressures make it difficult for individuals to develop a broader vision. (On the positive side, however, there are many beneficial parts of belonging to a group like safety, comfort, order, and so forth. There are reasons we follow social norms, other than to exclude the other.)

In growing up, most of us have learned to inhibit behaviors that go against social expectations. But the culture has failed in teaching us internal controls on destructive behaviors that have their origins in social obligations, group values, and familial legacies. Therefore, such actions can be far more dangerous to society (Milgram, 1974). Consider Riley, an Irish Protestant person living in Belfast who, in everyday life, is gentle and kind and a loving father, yet becomes a militant and feels justified in throwing bombs that target schoolchildren only because they are Catholic.

"I never was a militant, but see me now," says Riley. "I'm not only a militant, I'm a bigot." Then, according to *Chicago Tribune* correspondent Liz Sly, "Out poured a litany of grievances, great and small, old and new: the murders of his loved ones by Catholics who will never be punished," the stones thrown at his windows by Catholic youths living across the street, and perhaps above all, the steady encroachment of Catholic households into his shrinking Protestant enclave (*Chicago Tribune*, September 9, 2001). Riley sees the act of throwing bombs at Catholic schoolchildren as fulfilling a social duty to his Protestant enclave. Thus, he does not care that his actions caused others to suffer. He does not feel compassion for the other side's hurts.

Are there ways of teaching internal controls on destructive actions that have their origins in social obligations, group values, and familial legacies? In other words, is there a remedy for belief perseverance? Are there tools to make it easier to acknowledge and hear the view of the other?

Rationality is a tool for revising one's view, for thinking logically, for opening one's mind to possibilities contrary to what was regarded as obvious. Hypothetical thinking encourages individuals to accommodate to new information. The use of the intellect and adherence to a legacy are very different.

The conference showed us that adherence to a legacy requires individuals to maintain a narrow frame of reference. (Obviously, this does not imply that the legacy of the Holocaust is just a myth or that survivors' children are irrational for having anger or saying that the Holocaust is wrong.) Unconditional

Figure 8.30 Thread connecting nails

adherence to a legacy encourages the mental process of assimilation—of ignoring or denying that which does not fit with a one-sided view of reality. The key words are "incapable of correction," "belief," "preserve," and "old." Individuals are discouraged from revising and extending their knowledge to include new information, to enlarge their frame of reference. In this sense adherence to a legacy or worldview compels individuals to be biased, close-minded, and dogmatic in their thinking.

By contrast, the rational operation of the intellect is an activity of skepticism. It encourages the mental process of accommodation and the expansion of knowledge. *Webster's Third New International Dictionary of the English Language Unabridged* (1981) tells us that intellectual activity consists of "Studious inquiry; usually critical and exhaustive investigation . . . having for its aim the revision of accepted conclusions in the light of newly discovered facts." The key words are "examination," "knowledge," "distrust," "revise," and "new." In this sense, the rational operation of the intellect compels individuals to be unbiased, open-minded, and rational in their thinking. It encourages them to continually expand their realm of knowledge through the digestion and incorporation of new information. Kant's answer to what was the activity of the Enlightenment is still valid for intellectual activity: *sapere aude*, dare to know (cited in Maier, 1988, p. 12).

The drive that leads individuals to adopt an intellectual or rational attitude includes the notion that new things can be discovered and that greater depth of understanding is achievable. Intellectual activity, then, is a form of optimism about the human condition. It is an activity that assumes individuals can

Figure 8.31 Lightbulb

transcend their personal experiences into a more inclusive view of the human condition (Katsenelinboigen, 1984). Individuals might begin by distrusting what they already believe, by actively seeking the unfamiliar, by intentionally challenging the validity of what they have previously been taught and perhaps hold dear. The path to rational thinking lies through questioning old views and beliefs.

Hypothetical Reasoning

At first, most individuals are uncomfortable questioning their old views— they prefer to stay where they are, to avoid revising their beliefs and to avoid the threat of uncertainty. But there are ways of helping individuals pass the crisis of threat. There are ways of helping them keep their minds open to possibilities contrary to what was regarded as obvious or true. The psychologist George Kelly (1969) calls it the way of "make-believe," "the invitational mood," or "hypothetical reasoning." Nothing has contributed so much to the adventuresome development of intellectual thinking as hypothetical reasoning (Kelly, 1969, p. 152).

Hypothetical reasoning invites us to make believe *as* if something is true. Instead of insisting that old truths are about to give way to new truths, we can say that we are shifting from one possibility to another. Suppose we assume we *cannot place* Nazis in a category labeled EVIL, but also, more importantly, one labeled NOT US. That is to say, suppose we assume most people will do what they are told to do. They will obey orders irrespective of the content of the order and without limitations of conscience, if they perceive that the command comes from a legitimate authority. We approach the truth, by forward steps, through the door of make-believe, writes Kelly (1969).

The point is that hypothetical reasoning serves to make an unrealistic possibility tenable for a sufficient time for the person to pursue its implication *as if it* were true (Kelly, 1969). The fact that it is regarded as a possibility, and as a possibility only, has a great psychological importance, for it enables us to break through the moment of threat. It is, after all, only make-believe, just a possible guess. Hypothetical reasoning invites us to get on with understanding the human condition. It bids us to test, to calculate new experiences and information, to profit from mistakes, rather than to be overwhelmed with guilt or fear for trying to accommodate to another viewpoint (Kelly, 1969).

Figure 8.32 Face covered with clouds

There is something in stating a new outlook as a hypothetical possibility that leaves one free to explore new viewpoints. It implies we approach knowledge, whether it is a viewpoint about the external world, the Holocaust, World War II, or about ourselves, by successive approximations, each of which is subject to further examination. Truth, then, is regarded as something to be adventured and tested, not something passed down to us by a legacy (Kelly, 1969, p. 156).

Hypothetical reasoning assumes nothing is ever confirmed. The moment we find evidence to conclude, for instance, that many ordinary persons, just like us, will act like a Nazi if they perceive that the command comes from a legitimate authority, we don't conclude we proved the truth. Instead, we always post a little note on it that says "But maybe it's something else too"—or instead, "I'll be back later to test another possibility" (Kelly, 1969, p. 159).

Thus, hypothetical reasoning is a process of learning to live with doubt and uncertainty, with a plurality of truths, and with a willingness to revise some or add some. Hypothetical reasoning demands that we be open-minded and willing to construe knowledge and values from multiple perspectives. It compels that we be as conscious as we can be about the values that lead us to our perspectives. It asks that we be responsible for how and what we know.

According to the philosopher Stuart Hampshire, the study of how the human mind works shows that we all can think alternatively, come up with different perspectives, imagine possibilities. In his book *Justice Is Conflict*, Hampshire writes that the idea of individuals considering different perspectives has sense for us, because we know what it is for a legal procedure or public discussion to consider different perspectives. We imagine ourselves hearing two or more contrary cases presented and we listen to them, allowing the evidence on both sides to be heard; then, and only then, we are to reach a conclusion. This is the process of reflecting on different possibilities (Hampshire, 2000).

"Hear the Other Side"

The weighing of evidence for and against an inner conflict; the weighing of evidence for and against a theory in a social science; the weighing of evidence in a historical or criminal investigation all demand this process of reflecting on different possibilities. This is a list of some activities that all involve the weighing and balancing of contrary possibilities bearing on a disputable issue (Hampshire, 2000). (I want to emphasize, however, that I am not implying that the facts of the Holocaust are disputable, but rather that the notion that all Germans are evil is disputable. And, that some facts are focused on more than others.)

In all these activities the individual acquires the habit of balanced, two-sided thinking. Different skills are required in each of these activities, but they can be grouped together as hypothetical reasoning in conditions of uncertainty. They are all subject to the single prescription *auid alteram partem*—"hear the other side" (cited in Hampshire, 2000, p. 8). This "hearing the other side" is precisely what identifies thinking with the exercise of the intellect, in contrast to dogmatic, biased thinking. "Hearing" becomes a metaphor. Most of the verbs, writes Hampshire, that denote reasoned thinking are also pictured with these metaphors: seeing, weighing, reviewing evidence, judging, deliberating, adjudicating, examining, evaluating, and many more. They all denote a rational process of reflecting on two-sided views of reality, on hypothetical possibilities (Hampshire, 2000).

Experimental research attests that reflecting on hypothetical possibilities is an effective strategy for debiasing one-sided views of reality. Social psychologists have been interested in studying ways to inhibit an uncritical biased assimilation of new information to existing views and attitudes. So, Lord, Lepper, and Preston (1984) repeated the capital punishment study described

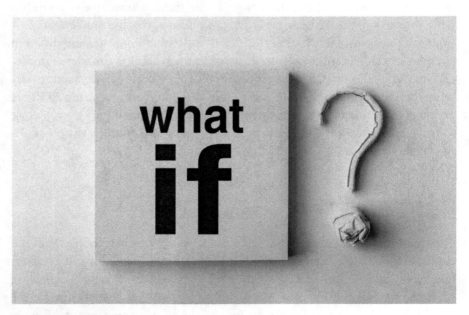

Figure 8.33 "What if?" sign

earlier and added two variations. First, they asked some of their subjects when evaluating the evidence to be "as objective and unbiased as possible." This instruction had no impact on their views. Those who received this instruction made evaluations as biased as those who did not. Next, the researchers asked another group of subjects to consider opposite possibilities. Specifically, they described the process by which biased assimilation is thought to occur and reminded subjects "to consider the other side of the coin" (Lord, Lepper, & Preston, 1984, p. 1240). After imagining an opposite finding, these people were much less biased in their evaluation of the information for and against their views.

Likewise, the psychologists C. Anderson (1982) and C. Anderson and Sechler (1986) found that explaining why an opposite view might be true—why a cautious rather than a risk-taking person might be a better firefighter—reduces or eliminates biased assimilation and one-sided thinking. And more recently, the psychologists Hirt and Markman (1995) found that considering any plausible alternative outcome, not just the opposite, reduces biased thinking.

Thus, taken together the research suggests that hypothetical reasoning is an effective remedy for reducing or eliminating belief perseverance. Hypothetical reasoning drives people to ponder various possibilities. This, in turn, promotes acknowledging and accessing the views of others. Thus, it stimulates accommodating one's beliefs and views to include new information.

Real-World Issues

However, the applicability of these results to real-world contexts is questionable. The applicability of these results to real-world contexts depends on many factors and conditions. One issue, for instance, is whether hypothetical reasoning is effective when the views involved have a strong emotional component, such as beliefs concerning the injustices of the Holocaust. Such emotional commitment may prevent one from considering other views even when presented with another perspective. Simply requiring that one hear the other side does not guarantee that all points of view will be considered. The findings from the conference, as mentioned earlier, suggested that the participants' emotional commitment to their legacies may have prevented them from considering other views.

A second issue concerns the relational component. Hypothetical reasoning may be an effective remedy for belief perseverance in an individual. But it may not be a very powerful remedy between persons, and may fail as a remedy when there are strong passions on two sides of the victimizing barricade, so to speak. The findings from the conference, as mentioned earlier, suggest that the participants' view of the other as an "enemy" made it difficult for them to consider and access the view of the other.

A third issue concerns the situational demands. Certain situations are likely to elicit one-sided thinking. In group settings, there may be strong pressure on participants to think and act in the same way, preserving the group identity. The findings from the conference, as mentioned earlier, suggest that the participants were concerned about appearing loyal to their group.

And a final issue concerns the time frame in which the views are acquired. We might expect little influence of hypothetical reasoning on a view transmitted from generation to generation. If the view has been acquired years ago and has been assimilated with other knowledge structures and the identity of the individual, it is reasonable to assume that this may prevent one from considering other points of view. The findings from the conference, as mentioned earlier, suggest that the participants' views were deep-seated and rooted in their sense of justice.

So, the question remains: what sentiment can reinforce hearing the other side when there are strong passions and views on both sides? What could possibly override the pressures and loyalties to a legacy? The next section will look at what is involved in relinquishing some resentments.

Summing Up

The rational operation of the intellect encourages us to revise their outdated views. Hypothetical reasoning is a helpful tool that was unavailable to our ancient ancestors. It was not until the past century or so that hypothetical reasoning became systematized. It can help us take the step forward to develop our intellect and expand our knowledge. Hypothetical reasoning causes a spirit of "make-believe." It causes a particular attitude toward knowledge and truth. It invites us to explore possibilities even when examining horrific events like the Holocaust and World War II. Hypothetical reasoning encourages us to be unbiased, open-minded, and rational in our thinking.

Hypothetical reasoning alone, however, is apt to fail when we have inherited a one-dimensional view. The next section will examine the way the descendants of an injustice have remembered the past. It will look at how their one-dimensional views of the past affect the way they interact with the descendants of the other group. Then, it will show that despite the tendencies toward one-sided thinking, when people experience a measure of compassion for another person's well-being a transformation occurs.

Justice as Compassion

The survivors' children and the Nazis' children who met face-to-face at the Harvard conference confronted much more than each other, their parents' past, or even their own prejudice and fear.

They confronted their ability to understand another's suffering, even that of a perceived enemy, and found that they could offer not only clemency, but also compassion. They told their stories—their histories, and in releasing anger and sorrow over the past, they captured something that had long eluded them—compassion.

To be sure, the participants' transformation of thought took time, with their ideas evolving through discernible stages during the conference.

In stage one, the "generalizing" stage, survivors' children expressed the view that Nazis' children were merely part of a blanket group—"anti-Semitic Germans"—not individuals who might be good or kind or otherwise distinguishable from each other.

In stage two, the survivors' children began listening to the Nazis' children, realizing that the descendants of the Nazis were not the malefactors. What's more, many of the Nazis' children expressed regret, sorrow, and shame over their elders' misdeeds. Suddenly, the survivors' children found that it was not so easy to continue blaming the Nazis' children for the sins for their fathers.

By stage three, the survivors' children were bewildered, for if the Nazis' children were not to blame, if they could be distinguished from their parents, who then could be held accountable for the atrocities committed against the Jewish people? The survivors' children still felt justifiable anger, but now, with the Nazis' children exculpated, against whom could their rage be directed?

During the final three stages, both sides were able to overcome long-held negative impressions, with survivors' children, in particular, recognizing that the Nazis' children had been imprisoned by their own parents' past as much as survivors' children had been locked in their parents' past.

Finally, the two groups were able to build a new relationship based on compassion, bred of their common humanity.

As discussed previously, memories about the past are kept alive generation after generation through storytelling. Stories are an ancient means of communicating, of carrying on legacies. Stories or "legacies" transmit values, beliefs, and emotions and preserve the past. One way we preserve and simplify the past is to categorize—to organize the past by classifying events and people. Social identity theory suggests that those who feel their ethnic identity strongly will concern themselves with classifying people into groups. Once we classify people into groups—Jews, Germans—then we are likely to exaggerate the similarities within groups and to understate the variety within groups.

There is a strong tendency to see individuals within a group as more uniform than they really are (Taylor, 1981; Wilder, 1981). Mere divisions into groups can create generalizations—"all Germans were anti-Semitic Nazis," "all Jews were victims." Generalizations assume a correlation between group membership and individuals' characteristics. Research on how we think suggests that we find it easy and efficient to rely on such generalizations when we are emotionally aroused and unable to cope with variety (Esses, Haddock, & Zanna, 1993; Stroessner & Mackie, 1993). Generalizations reduce ambiguities and inconsistencies.

Transformations from One-Dimensional Views to Compassion

Voices from the interviews suggested that survivors' children and Nazis' children inherited a one-dimensional view containing generalizations that influenced their way of seeing and responding to the world. Stories about the past left a powerful imprint on their minds and strongly affected the images and expectations they had about the individuals from the opposite group. Before attending the conference, several participants reported having nightmares.

For example, a daughter of a survivor reported, "I dreamed a car was waiting to take me to the conference. But when I got into the car, I realized I was being tricked. It was taking me to a concentration camp." Another child of a survivor said, "Since I've never been face to face with children of Nazis, I don't know if I can handle being in the same room with them in a conference." The daughter of a Nazi reported, "I dreamed I was being attacked by, not physically attacked, I mean, like—you know, people [other Germans and her family] were really angry at me for going to the conference."

Sitting face to face with descendants from the opposite group was an emotionally arousing experience for the participants. During the meeting one could observe many signs of stress in the participants' behavior: crying, trembling, raised voices, and sometimes anxious laughter. The children of survivors and Nazis were stressed because the presence of the other side evoked strong feelings. The central stressor, for many survivors' children, had to do with the essentially friendly context and their notably less than friendly feelings toward the participants on the opposite side. They were confronted with two incompatible prescriptions for action. Loyalty to their one-dimensional views conflicted with befriending the participants from the opposite group.

I suspect most readers have experienced being in a situation where just the presence of some person evoked strong feelings such as hatred, resentment, or anger. To gain a greater understanding of the feelings experienced by the conference participants, imagine someone has murdered your child. Now for the first time you meet the killer's child. More than likely the occasion will produce strong feelings. In such a situation you may respond not so much to the person, but based on what that person represents. The killer's child wants to be accepted as an individual without the taint of suspicion that, because his father killed your child, he is somehow a murderer. The killer's child may be a genuinely moral human being. However, in your mind's eye the killer's child symbolizes evil. Just the presence of the killer's child hurts your sense of fairness, and you want to strike out. The killer's child senses that, resents you, and withdraws from the situation.

Stage One: Generalizing

Initially, during what we might call stage one of the conference, survivors' children related to Nazis' children not as individuals, but as symbols of the generalized group—"anti-Semitic Germans." Their one-dimensional views colored their beliefs about the participants from the opposite group. They related to Nazis' children as an abstract, impersonal entity. They assumed a correlation between group membership and the participants' characteristics. The emotions and generalizations contained in their one-dimensional view were obvious in their discussions. For example, a daughter of a survivor said, "I don't want to show that rage toward these people, but it's right there; I can't do anything about it, the hate and distrust of all Germans. I see them all as killers of my family."

Nazis' children responded to such statements by emphasizing the variety of attitudes and behavior that existed among the Germans. For instance, a daughter of a Nazi said, "My parents never said anything bad about the Jews. In fact, my father always spoke about how the Jews were helpful to him in his business. He was just a teenager when they drafted him into the army. He was not an enthusiastic member of the Nazi party."

Survivors' children reacted with indignation to such statements. They refused to acknowledge the Nazi parents' view. There were moments when they not only refused, but confronted—indeed in some ways accused the Nazis' children sitting opposite them. For example, a son of a survivor said,

> "I don't believe your father didn't have a choice or that he liked Jews. From the stories that I heard from my parents the Germans were only too glad to destroy the Jews, take away their possessions. It wasn't just the Nazis. I was told young German children were anti-Semites who saw Jews as rats to be killed. So when I hear you say your father was just a teenager and that he liked Jews, I feel my rage. And I can't ignore those feelings, which is not to deal with my anger."

Stage Two: Revealing

During what we might call stage two of the conference, there was a gradual shift in the discussion. Nazis' children revealed their personal views and feelings rather than their parents' views. The Nazis' children condemned the perpetrators' actions, ideology, moral values, and conception of the victims. They said they felt enraged, guilty, ashamed, and disgraced because of the perpetrators' horrific actions. For example a daughter of a Nazi said,

> "My rage, I think, is against the same people that you [pointing to a son of a survivor] are raging against. We—it's the same, because I am enraged about the people who have done this to other people. You know, I'm enraged . . . at the inhumanity that people let themselves go into. I mean I'm enraged at these people who did this. I'm enraged that . . . my generation, we have to carry this burden of this. . . . I was enraged at my father for years, you know, I didn't know what to do with it I blamed him very much although . . . it's not just him. I mean it's just . . . I think we have the same, the same targets, in a way. That's—I'm enraged at this. I'm enraged that this could have happened. I'm enraged at the people who let it happen, who didn't say anything, you know, who just went with it, who just said yes, *Jawohl*, you know. I'm enraged at the people who did the actions, but I'm enraged also at the people who did not do anything . . . who just kind of turned away. . . . I mean I don't know—how I would have acted, but now I want to learn from this, that I do act. . . . It is my rage and I want to say . . . it made me into something. I mean I'm German, so it's like . . . I don't know how to say it, but it's guilt or this thing. I was put into this by these actions of other people."

Many Nazis' children said they were frustrated because their parents' generation would not acknowledge their guilt. Thus, they felt compelled to do penance for actions they never committed. Many Nazis' children said they felt called on to find honest answers to old questions. For example, a daughter of a Nazi said,

> "I have, in all my years in this country, have really not met a single German who was—said, you know, I did it, and, you know, who said I did all these horrible things, but, you know, when somebody asks you would you have done the same, you say, I don't know. I mean this is the kind of honesty I've always looked for in my parents and my relatives—and never found it."

Many Nazis' children at the conference said they felt a responsibility to keep the memories of the past alive. For example, a son of a Nazi said,

> "There is no way we can heal the past. Because what happened will never be undone, and it shouldn't be undone, and it shouldn't be, and the memory should be kept alive because it is really, it's like a hole that has been burned into the soul of humanity."

Statements like the above confronted survivors' children with information that was strikingly inconsistent with the generalization "Germans are anti-Semitic." Clearly, Nazis' children's beliefs and attitudes suggested that they, as individuals, did not fit the category. In turn, this caused survivors' children to question their feelings of rage and resentment. As mentioned in chapter 3, in Fritz Heider's terms, the feeling of resentment is a wish to produce a change in the belief-attitude of the wrongdoer that produced the unjust act. And revenge is the means of realizing this wish. Since the Nazis' children at the meeting held beliefs similar to survivors' children, this caused survivors' children to question their feelings of resentment toward the Nazis' children.

Stage Three: Distinguishing

During what we might call stage three of the conference, survivors' children spoke about the impact distinguishing Nazis' children from the "other Germans" had on them. Many survivors' children said it produced a conflict and was confusing. On the one hand, they wanted to punish all Germans, or at the least to vent their rage, and on the other, they felt that the Germans attending the conference were "good" people. For example, a daughter of a survivor described the confusion and conflict like this:

> "Just yesterday, before coming here, my father said, "If you ask me what I want from those German children, I would say, give me my family back. My heart would

be at peace only if I knew that there would be six million German dead to equal the six million Jews. If we can't do that, then at least we should hurt them—to spit in all their faces." So, I'm just right now sitting here, you know, like I can't control it—and I feel like being physical almost, you know, it's like that kind of rage. I feel like I want to have a [PAUSE] somebody I can just like—I don't know do what with, you know—punch or something, or do something [PAUSE] and I you know, you don't dare do it here because all these people are nice, and I think there was a confusion that, that if I show, I don't want to show it that rage towards these people, but it's right there I can't do anything about it, the hate and distrust of all Germans. I see them all as killers of my family."

A son of a survivor described the conflict like this:

"I've never met children of Nazis before. I have a golden opportunity to meet you all. But that doesn't rob me of my desire and need to be very angry. I feel a great deal of rage when I look at all of you. And I'm confused."

And a daughter of a survivor described the conflict like this:

"I can sit in this room, and I don't deal with anger and rage very well—'cause it's there inside me, and I don't want to hurt anybody with my rage, but I can separate that I have rage and anger inside me for what happened to my family and how it impacted me—and I can separate that from who, who's to blame for it. I can have rage in this room but not have to blame anybody in this room. But it is, I still worry about what my rage will do to these nice people that I, that I like, and what will they—Oh God."

Stage Four: Discussing the Here and Now

As the meeting progressed, the participants wavered between discussing their personal conflicts, feelings, and views, and their parents' views. At one point, the daughter of a survivor while discussing her feelings about Germans in general pointed to a daughter of a Nazi and said, "you look like an SS woman to me." For the participants, this statement became a springboard for exploring their interactions in the "here and now." During what we might call stage four of the conference, there was a shift in the discussion.

The participants shifted the focus of the discussion to the "here and now." That is to say, they focused the discussion on their personal, immediate experiences and the way one participant's words or actions affected the other.

Whereas before, Nazis' children did not react personally to generalizations about "the Germans," in this instance some children of Nazis focused the discussion on themselves, on their responses to being categorized and labeled. Through such exploration, each side gained some insight into the issues and concerns of the other, and the way these are affected by its own actions in the here and now. For instance, a daughter of a Nazi described her response when the daughter of a survivor said she looked like an SS woman. She interpreted the statement as an insult. With considerable personal pain, she described her response like this:

"It hurts when somebody says that. I have so many feelings about it. I mean it's like no I cannot—I mean a lot of times, I mean I'm trying, I try to kind of say OK this is I'm a symbol for that, but no, it—it also goes through me. It happened once before when somebody did that, and [PAUSE] it's like in that moment [PAUSE] I mean I'm not seen, you know, as a person, and I think that's what hurts very much, and being put into the same [PAUSE] and it's not just being, being not seen. I think it's also it's almost, being, being called a real bad name, I mean put into—do you understand what I mean? The same category of, as some thing that, that we all know we hate. But there is nothing I can do about it. I just shut up. You know to defend myself, I put a wall around myself like a—a tank. I guess it's my own protection. But I feel attacked. It took me a long time to kind of sort that out and say OK they're—[PAUSE]—it's like their pain. But it hurts. It's not like I can just say oh OK it's just that pain and I'm just a symbol, being being a symbol for Germany it sometimes, you know, it's like you put some defense up, but then it goes through too. But nothing can be done. I put a wall around myself, you know, like a tank. It's like that—you know, and I shut up. I was hurt. That I mean I was surprised, how can—you know, this nice person, how can anybody see me this way?"

Stage Five: Sharing Their Hurts

Immediately following this Nazis' daughter's statement, the other participants were quiet. No one acknowledged that a participant's words had a negative emotional impact on a participant from the opposite group. But the following day, during what we might call stage five of the conference, some survivors' children gave the impression that they were willing to understand the Nazis' children's view, rather than to accuse or to assign blame to the other side. Or justify their stake to the moral high ground.

That is to say, and I wish to stress this distinction here, when Nazis' children discussed their *own hurts* and sufferings, rather than their parents' sufferings, some survivors' children accepted the view that Nazis' children felt like victims. Some survivors' children gave the impression that they were willing to accept and give meaning to Nazis' children's hurts. The participants' here-and-now experience of seeing a daughter of a Nazi feel hurt and insulted created a new atmosphere conducive to the participants sharing their inner feelings. Participants listened to each other and tried to understand each other's hurts and sufferings. In turn, this open discussion helped the participants penetrate each other's perspective and show compassion for the other's feelings.

Survivors' children spoke about how hurt they felt by their Holocaust legacy, while Nazis' children listened attentively to survivors' children's stories, and often tried to comfort and reassure survivors' children. A daughter of a survivor described her pain to Nazis' children like this:

"The way I was brought up, everything that has happened to me has to do with the Holocaust. It's like swallowing pain, feeling pain all the time. I feel the Holocaust differently from someone who, say, watches a movie about it. It's in me. I don't trust the world. I always have the fear that I will be trampled. And then the truth is, even though it's not my experience, I've never been in the Holocaust, no one ever persecuted me directly. That's what makes it so difficult."

Another daughter of a survivor explained it like this:

"There are images, the worst images you can imagine stored in my head that can not be eliminated. I spent the first half of my life with it. Images of Germans in black boots with dogs coming to take me away, SS guards beating me, trying to kill me. And I'm trying to figure out how to escape. Images of suffocating to death, of not having enough air. I can remember when I went to the movies, I would ask my friends to sit next to the exit sign. I never told them why, but it was because I always had to sit in a room near a door or window. But, the worst image, I guess, was the one I had when my own daughter was born. I imagined she would suffocate to death in her sleep. And [participants crying the background] once I dreamed they took my daughter and me to concentration camp and I pleaded to be sent to the gas chambers, so my daughter could be saved. These are the nightmares I carry in my head."

And a son of a survivor explained it like this:

"Since the age of eight or nine I can't remember a time when the Holocaust wasn't on my mind. At times it completely consumed me. I felt I had to make up for my parents' losses. I felt an obligation to my family who was murdered and to my parents who survived. I always felt as though my life wasn't really my own, as though I was living my life for all those who were murdered too. I didn't want to disappoint my parents, to make them suffer at all. I wanted them to be proud of me. I always thought my parents had more than their share of suffering, and I was careful not to hurt them in any way. I was always aware of their experience. It's like my life's mission was to bring them happiness to make up for their suffering."

Nazis' children spoke about their pain too. They told survivors' children how the Nazi past affected their lives. For instance, a daughter of a former Nazi described it like this:

"I feel I carry this stuff that isn't mine, and I can't move any, you know, I'm sort of buried under it. I'm paralyzed by it. I don't want to deny it but I would like to take responsibility for my own time, which I haven't been able to do because I never lived in my own time, I lived in my parents' time all my life. I'm a German, so it's like [PAUSE] it's like with that I have this, this—I don't know how to say it, but it's guilt or this thing."

Another daughter of a former Nazi explained it like this:

"I've run from this for a long time, but one of the things for me—how to build a sense of self. That you have a sense of continuity. I always felt disconnected from the good things of German culture. I couldn't own it, because if I owned that I owned every-thing else too. . . . It's a sense of pride in my identity that I never really had. And that I've been looking for. And I have not been able to find that by reading Goethe and Schiller, you know, because this is not—it's not the same anymore. It's like there—there is a break, there is a bank space that I have to fill in . . . [SNIFFS]. One of the things I feel I carried was this self-hatred."

And another daughter of a former Nazi explained it like this:

"I have the impulse to accuse my father all the time. Accuse, accuse, accuse. Why did you do that? And I think I talked to my father when I was 14 or 15. And he kept his mouth shut. And since that time he never spoke. So this is my part of bringing him into silence in a way because of this impulse of accusing, accusing.

You know that's what it was like for us to grow up with the grownups around us, because you know, when you're a child, and then you find something horrible happened, and you know that some of these people might have been involved in it, and you don't know to what degree. I've wanted all my life to hear my father's story, to hear something about the why and the how. I've grown up so much feeling that my father was an animal and that I come from a people of monsters, and it's not true. German people are human beings. I was thinking how hunted I also feel, and how very frightened, how much I lived in fear my entire life."

Weeping, another daughter of a former Nazi said,

"I have lived in fear too. I've been afraid that the children of the victims would come search for me and kill me because of my guilt. When I found out about the horrible things that were done, I fell into a deep depression. I wanted to commit suicide. No one in the family wanted to talk to me about the past. There was this silence about it."

At this point, a child of a survivor reached out to embrace the daughter of a Nazi and said, "I understand you, and I believe you're a victim too. Ultimately, I believe that you have the right to speak about your childhood, as we do. You're a victim, in my opinion, you are a victim also." Another child of a survivor said, "When I look in your eyes, I don't see hate and I don't see a murderer. I see a victim."

A daughter of a Nazi responded, "And I know I'm—I must not—I must not be afraid of you."

Another daughter of a Nazi said, "When we speak together about the repercussions of hatred and what it's done in our lives . . . I could not have done that before because I could not have believed that I could be believable to children of survivors. But by hearing your stories and really taking them in, I can bring my own story out too."

A son of a survivor said, "I thank you, and I can't thank you enough, and it's so important. And the burden that we as children carried—and feelings that I have carried—it's important to know that you [Nazis' children] carry a heavy burden as well. And to be able to speak about it, recognize it, and to tell me about that is incredible."

In the relationship between Nazis' children and survivors' children, a new interaction was evident when Nazis' children and survivors' children discussed their own hurts. As they talked about their own hurts, rather than their parents' hurts, Nazis' children and survivors' children showed *compassion* for the other and tentatively restored equal moral relations. As the etymology of the word suggests, "compassion" involves "feeling with" the other person, sharing his or her feelings. Because compassion involves a sense of shared humanity, it promotes the experience of equality (Blum, 1980).

Compassion, this ability to feel for and understand another person's suffering is the cornerstone passion of our sense of justice. Without compassion there can be no justice, writes Solomon (1990). Compassion opposes and impedes causing others to suffer. To have compassion is to have some concern for the other's welfare (Nussbaum, 2001; Solomon, 1990). According to the philosopher Lawrence Blum and the psychologist Ervin Staub, compassion is an emotion that can be called "altruistic" in that it involves a regard for the good of the other person (Blum, 1980; Staub, 2002).

It is worth remembering that the human mind knows no neat dividing line between emotion and thought. To feel compassion is to have some thought for the other's good, to wish their suffering would end, and to do what will bring this end about. Compassion requires the attitude to do helpful actions, and to do them because we have an understanding of someone's suffering and a concern for the person's good (Blum, 1980). Compassion, above all else, moves us to act in constructive ways.

Having compassion, therefore, for someone's suffering is a motivational *transformation* that inclines us to inhibit relationship-destructive responses (such as the desire for vengeance) and to behave constructively toward others. In other words, compassion is a sedative to negative feelings such as anger, vengefulness, resentment, and indignation. As the philosopher Arthur Schopenhauer (1995, p. 175) put it, "For rain is to fire what compassion is to anger."

Compassion is the true antidote against anger, vengefulness, resentment, and indignation. Nothing removes our negative feelings toward others so easily as acquiring a measure of compassion for another person's welfare (Lama, 1999, 2000, 2002). The participants' cathartic experiences, may have been related to the emergence of compassion for the other's hurts and sufferings. Stating the obvious, letting go of negative feelings and acknowledging the position and feelings of someone else takes away much tension.

Stage Six: Transformation

During what we might call stage six of the conference, many participants spoke about how attending the conference made a major difference in their lives. Their statements typify the type of transformation that can occur with the emergence of compassion for the other side's hurts. The first type of transformation is about the participants' feelings. And the second type of transformation is about the participants' differentiated images or categorizations. Often their statements intertwined both changes.

For example, a daughter of a survivor describes her transformation like this:

"I think what it was, was I erased—the image of the bad Germans and I think I was able to—just—having gotten to know children of Nazis [names two specific participants] and—and having been in the conference, I just got that—negative image of Germany out of my system. I just erased it. I didn't like what it did to me before. It always made me feel uncomfortable. And I think I—deep down inside—I just knew that it was time to [get] rid of that feeling 'cause I didn't want to spend the rest of my life with it. I'd spent the first half of my life with it, and it—it—you know, cause a lot of problems. [CHILDREN CRYING IN BACKGROUND] So once I could erase—and, and get rid of those—the negative connotation of the German people, Germany, the bloodied soil, I could go forward with my life and just prove to others that you can do it too. You know, that the worst image in the world can be eliminated. You might shelve it. It'll always be part of you. But it doesn't have to gnaw away at you. And it doesn't have to haunt you the rest of your life. And for me the Holocaust, up until this meeting of coming together with Germans, really has haunted me. . . . I feel exorcized of that bad image. It feels good."

A son of a survivor describes his transformation like this:

"And I mean a real lot of things. . . . I think the important thing I'm leaving with is the distinction that I've made in my mind—to separate the children from the parents. The fear and hatred, which is diminished. I leave here grateful to all of you to allow that transformation to help happen to me. Uhhh, when I look at you I don't see Nazis, I see people. That distinction in my mind has, that generation [of] people who were Nazis were persecutors, they should be judged and tried and dealt with appropriately. There's no question in my mind, but you did not do that."

Another daughter of a survivor describes her transformation like this:

"I've been looking for release all my life. . . . And that's what I, that's what I have found here, that's what I take away from here. . . . To get through my prejudice of fear about Germany and German people, my stereotypes, to like totally defuse that crap, here, by acknowledging it and addressing it and then getting through it and over it. . . . Thank you for being a person, just an individual and not a whole phenomenon. You are not the Nazi nation, by yourself."

Another daughter of a survivor describes her transformation like this:

"Before coming here [to the conference], I thought if my mother had a gun, you know, I was just seeing this violent possibility you know, of course played out in my mind. I thought how am I going to deal with this? . . . And I think when I first wanted to come here I thought, this is fantastic; of course we should meet, of course—we're in a cycle, victim and perpetrator is in a circle; we find out the victim was a perpetrator and also a victim. It's, it's a cycle; so what's the difference? And we have to stop it. We have to stop it! And maybe the message from this place is a little light that shines and says it's possible to stop from one generation to the next. We don't have to carry the hatred; we don't have to kill each other; we don't have to live this way."

And another daughter of a survivor describes her transformation like this:

"I can't put into words what I've experience here. It's, it's just so deep. . . . If we allow ourselves to get to know each other as individuals and then take it from there! And that's what happened to me. . . . And it worked. And—one—and there's just a great sense of relief that I didn't want to attack you or [talking to a son of a Nazi]—you know—revenge. So I want to thank you for, for doing that for me and—cause it just feels like there's a big load off my shoulder too."

A daughter of a Nazi describes her transformation like this:

"I think the German people are experiencing trauma. . . . I feel after this meeting released from something—I don't know how to say this. I, I think I've tried to destroy myself you know, most of my life. I, I've wanted to be able—not knowing what to do about my heritage. I, I've been self-destructive and I've—not felt that I had a right to exist, and I've not felt that there was a place for me in the world. And coming here [the conference], really have the—I feel that I've gotten the permission to let go. And all of a sudden I realize that it's stupid! It doesn't make any sense for me to beat myself up my entire life, because it doesn't bring back your, your family. And I might as well use my pain and my legacy and do something meaningful with it."

Another daughter of a Nazi describes her transformation like this:

[SNIFFS] "I didn't even want to speak German. [SNIFFS] I just stayed away from it. . . . And I realized that I am German. I mean, you know, I can try to get—run away from it, but I am. There's no question. [SNIFFS] And I started to appreciate Germany, you know in a different way. I started to—want to speak again. I started to kind of come back in a way. And—I also would see a, I felt like I would see the, the world a little clearer about what was good that I didn't—like being German, I don't have to—it's like there are some things that are not good, but there are also good things. I started to kind of sort that; that there is a lot of good there. And—that it wasn't all bad; that there was, that I did not have to be ashamed to be German. That I am—that, that I could be, you know, it seems like I'm proud to be German. That sounds so bad."

A son of a Nazi describes his transformation like this:

> "One of the things I've learned here is that truth heals, and that lies make you sick, and—sick in your mind, and in your heart. And I think what has subsided for me is the fear. I'm not as afraid any more to ask for the truth and to speak the truth, because I know I'm not alone any more. And that happened because we all were willing to make ourselves vulnerable to each other. . . . And so I hope that maybe other people will be encouraged to do, to join, the same kind of experiment in the future."

Another daughter of a Nazi describes her transformation like this:

> "I feel I have hope, and I feel that—I feel the paralysis and the fear is gone. I feel now much more capable of going to my parents and asking them questions I didn't have the courage to ask before, because the defensive that I felt within myself, or the anger that would come up, sort of got released here, and I know that if I don't come from such a place of accusation, but when I, when I'm able to also come—they, the willingness to listen, that maybe they will be more able to talk to me!"

Another daughter of a Nazi describes her transformation like this:

> "I'm a German, so I must say something philosophical thing [Laughter]. But just help me with the translation. [Speaks In German] Differentiate. Differentiate. Okay. What I'm not very good but I try to become able to this ability to differentiate. Between first—between the parents and the children of Nazis or Third Reich, but also to—survivors, I mean, the background of being raised in a family of survivors and the other side. I mean, being raised in a family of you know, the other side. And also to differentiate between the people, I mean who do—who did bad, I say, and the conditions whom make them to these peoples. To differentiate—and it's important for me to see both my background and your background and my pains, I mean, not my, the pain of the group so to say, and your pain because it's not the same pain okay, but it's, it's another one."

And another daughter of a Nazi describes her transformation like this:

> "I've already talked a lot about feeling personally freed of this belief that I had to somehow harm myself to make up for the deeds of my father, but I felt I really got the permission here to really fully include myself in the human race [Laughs]. And I also feel like this has been a homecoming for me; I've never been able to really fully be German or even know what that means, and I have wanted to. I've really wanted to be German and to be able to be proud to be German. And by that I don't

mean to ever forget the—the pain and the memory, and I want to witness always the pain that results from the legacy that we share here. But I want to use that pain to do something useful in the world and not to just keep beating myself up with it and to distance myself from people because of the shame."

A New Relationship Based on Compassion

These statements suggest that despite past injustices and the tendencies toward revenge and one-dimensional views, when people experience a measure of compassion for another person's well-being, a transformation occurs. Transformation is not, as some people may believe, a mysterious and sublime process.

The fact that some participants described a set of changes in their feelings and attitudes tell us that descendants of victims when sitting face to face with descendants of victimizers can establish a new relationship. Establishing a new relationship does not mean that two truths are now equal in validity. Obviously, each side may hold the opinion that their view is the more valid one. From the standpoint of the child of a survivor, their parents' suffering was incomparable to what any German suffered. Establishing a new relationship means there is a willingness to discuss differences in legacies without loss of commitment to one's own legacy. It does not mean that every legacy is equal in validity.

And establishing a new relationship does not mean there should be no assessment of guilt or responsibility. It does not mean to bury the past or to forgive. Children of survivors, in my opinion, do not have the proper standing to forgive what was done to their families. And since Nazis' children have not done anything wrong and are not responsible for the injustices done, there is nothing to forgive, though perhaps much to be sad about. But because we cannot alter the injustices of the past, we can start now to strive for a better future. The conference results suggest that between the sons and daughters of the Holocaust and the children of the Nazis it is possible to create a new relationship based on compassion.

Limitations and Concluding Remarks

Social psychologists have been more successful in explaining belief perseverance in the laboratory than in discovering possibilities for overcoming it in real-world contexts. Identifying conditions for change requires a shift in empirical and theoretical attention—a shift away from speculating on the origins of sociopathology, aggression, violence, or posttraumatic symptoms, to a concern with how perceptions of injustice manifest themselves in the actual lives of people whose ancestors inflicted injustice or suffered injustice.

In these two chapters, I have provided a new framework for understanding how emotions and cognitions follow perception of an injustice. Injustices, I have pointed out, have a transcendent quality, which is one reason feelings about injustices are passed on from generation to generation. There are situations, like the Holocaust and World War II, where the evil done survives the person who has done it and can become a burden weighing on the memory of later generations.

I have presented empirical evidence suggesting that survivors' children and Nazis' children having internalized the parables of their parents, each group of children also is seeking their own justice fueled by anger, resentment, and shame. Seeking justice can turn into an escalatory, self-perpetuating dynamic. The needs and fears of individuals whose parents were involved in an injustice impose emotional and cognitive constraints on their abilities to cope with new information. A result of these constraints is that individuals may adopt a rigid belief and an unwillingness to hear the other side. And they may underestimate the possibility of change and avoid discussions altogether.

Turning from the laboratory to real-world situations has shown us the relevant points of entry at which the cognitions and emotions of individuals and the interactions between individuals can play a specific role in deciding outcomes. Thus, I have identified certain actions central to overcoming belief perseverance—including seeing justice as intergenerational, seeing justice as interpersonal, seeing justice has two sides, and seeing justice as compassion—that of necessity take place at the level of individuals and interactions between individuals.

The meeting between Nazis' children and survivors' children provided a setting in which these actions might have occurred. What would have been involved, we may ask, in carrying out these actions while overcoming belief perseverance? Specifically, what would have been involved in seeing justice as intergenerational, seeing justice as interpersonal, and seeing justice has two sides? Let me simply list some of the major conditions, desires, and attitudes that would need to be given up for these actions to occur.

- Unidimensional views
- Collective accountability
- Adherence to one's legacy
- Sense of dignity and self-worth
- Moral indignation

- The desire for vengeance
- Resentment
- Ethnic identification
- Loyalty to one's ancestors
- Unequal moral relations
- Victimization status
- And, ultimately, one's history and identity

What does this mean? Does it mean we should have expected the descendants of those who inflicted injustices and those who suffered injustices to carry out these actions while overcoming their beliefs? Hardly. We would, I think, be expecting too much. The demand is daunting for anyone.

The apology dynamic, offering and accepting forgiveness, is today's model for reconciliation. It, too, demands that individuals give up some of these conditions, desires, and attitudes. For example, studies on the promotion of forgiveness have hypothesized that people have to give up feelings of righteous indignation, the desire to seek revenge, and resentment to become more forgiving toward their offenders (McCullough et al., 2001). And it has been hypothesized that people have to give up ruminative thoughts about the injustices to become more forgiving too.

As noted before, McCullough and colleagues hypothesized that "Vengeful people ruminate on the injustices and harm they have suffered to keep themselves focused on the goals of balancing the scales, teaching the offender a lesson" (McCullough et al., 2001, pp. 602–603). The more people ruminate about an injustice, the more difficulty they have in forgiving the injustice, according to McCullough (2000). Thus, according to this line of reasoning, people should give up ruminative thoughts and feelings about the injustice to become more forgiving. The inability to do so is viewed as a lack of control to suppress feelings and thoughts about the injustices.

Despite its long history in religion and philosophy, empirical research on the promotion of forgiveness has been conducted only recently. A variety of group, individual, and psychoeducational interventions for encouraging people to forgive has been developed and tested in recent years. Worthington, Sandage, and Berry (2000) conducted a meta-analysis of data from 12 group intervention studies. They concluded that interventions were generally effective for helping people to forgive specific individuals who have harmed them.

Most of the studies analyzed involved interventions with ad hoc groups of participants. People who might or might not have a common problem were brought together or were treated individually, and an attempt was made to teach them how better to forgive someone who hurt them. For example, in one intervention study, the participants were introductory psychology students. They were asked whether they would like to learn information and skills that might help them to forgive a specific person. Participants wrote short descriptions of the unjust actions that they wanted to forgive. "The following are some examples: My ex got me pregnant on purpose, and then decided that it was too much responsibility. My father abuses drugs. He abandoned me and my mother when I was a child. When my father died, my 'best friend' was not there at all for me. She was very selfish and betrayed my trust in her when I needed her. My mother told me that I was not wanted in the family, and that I was an evil person" (McCullough, Worthington, & Rachal, 1997, p. 12).

Researchers have raised questions about the applicability of studies like these to real-world contexts (Paluck, 2012). They have questioned the generalizability of the results, since many studies on the promotion of forgiveness have targeted college students. And they have questioned the applicability of the results to severe injustices. For example, researchers Worthington et al. write,

> Severe and long-lasting harms have not been addressed via group interventions.... We recommend that the boundaries within which forgiveness interventions can be helpfully applied be investigated scientifically. Severity of hurts and offenses seems to greatly influence the ease with which people are able to forgive. There might be some evidence that hurts and offenses that are extremely severe result in revision of people's cognitive framework for understanding existence. Such cognitive reorganizations would undoubtedly require either a long time to repair or an extremely powerful intervention—probably beyond the capability of most interventions developed to date. (Worthington et al., 2000, pp. 236–237)

And Worthington et al. go on to note that "People from cultures such as Northern Ireland, South Africa, or Rwanda have many factors beyond the individual hurts that make extending forgiveness difficult for them. . . . Those culturally loaded issues often must be addressed" (Worthington et al., 2000, p. 242).

Finally, some researchers have noted the possibility that, in certain interpersonal situations, people who cope by forgiving might put themselves at risk for serious problems. Some research has suggested that forgiveness might be a sign of relational disturbance, as in relationships characterized by physical abuse. For example, the psychologists Katz, Street, and Arias found (1997) evidence that staying in an abusive relationship was mediated by the women's willingness to forgive the violent partners. It is reasonable to ask, therefore, whether the promotion of forgiveness is really a good thing for all people in all situations.

Our study was not set up to promote forgiveness, but rather to study the face-to-face interactions between descendants of victims and victimizers. However, the data suggested that forgiveness might be an inappropriate intervention model. During the conference, most survivors' children spoke against the notion of forgiveness. For example, a child of a survivor said, "Am I minimizing the trauma? Am I forgiving? It's certainly not in my power to forgive. And no—and it is too presumptuous even a thought about—about forgiveness." And another child of a survivor said, "I could never forgive what was done to my family. My entire extended family tree was forever eradicated. Can anyone forgive that?"

An important variable, according to research, that seems to have great import for forgiveness is the extent to which the wrongdoer makes sincere apologies or expressions of remorse. It is well established that offering an apology encourages forgiving, particularly when apologies are elaborate and include admissions of guilt (Darby & Schlenker, 1982; McCullough et al., 2000; Ohbuchi, Kameda, & Agarie, 1989). Thus, today's model for the promotion of forgiveness and reconciliation often includes encouraging perpetrators to offer an apology. In some instances, entire governments, as in Rwanda, Argentina, and South Africa, have encouraged perpetrators to come forth and apologize for their unjust acts (Minlow, 1998).

An apology may offer a great deal of comfort to victims. And it may, in fact, be an effective strategy for healing and for promoting forgiveness between perpetrators and victims. But to my understanding, an apology is an acknowledgment of guilt. All of this points to a fundamental question: Should we expect the descendant of a perpetrator to offer an apology for an unjust act that he or she did not commit?

During the conference, most Nazis' children spoke against the notion of inherited guilt. For example, a child of a Nazi officer said, "All my life, ever since 1945, when I was 14, have I felt guilty because there was lot of talk of collective guilt. Finally now, I am not guilty. Yes, but my father's generation sure was. And I want to make that very clear. I've carried this burden. I don't want it anymore. Because I need to live my own life." And another child of a Nazi said, "I think my generation was brought up to feel guilty for our parents because there was so much silence about it. We took on their guilt. But, of course, we ourselves did not do anything wrong, so we have no reason to be guilty."

Thus, many Nazis' children and survivors' children directly said that offering an apology or granting forgiveness was an inappropriate action. Their statements suggested they did not feel they had the proper standing to apologize for harms they did not inflict or to forgive harms that were not done to them. And survivors' children's statements suggested that their unwillingness to forgive had less to do with lack of control over ruminative thoughts than with principled moral action. For example, a child of a survivor said, "I think it is my duty as a human being to remind the world about the injustices that were done to my family." Similarly, a child of a Nazi said, "I think Germany, on the whole, has, even after 45 years, enormous responsibility to watch the development and to see in the country and outside the country all things similar to the beginnings of the murders of the Jews in the Third Reich."

So, it is reasonable to argue, as the philosopher Jeffrie Murphy (1988) has, that in some situations the unwillingness to forgive is a morally correct response. Murphy points out that the unwillingness to forgive may properly be regarded, in some situations, as respect for human dignity, for the demands of morality. It conveys emotionally the attitude for concern for the rules of morality. By contrast, forgiveness can convey the attitude of excusing the wrongdoing. Taken to its extreme, it can convey the attitude of moral relativism. Or it can convey the attitude of forgetting the harms that were inflicted on a victim.

The unwillingness to forgive and rumination may be pathological, as some psychologists have suggested, but in some situations they may be positive responses. Rumination and the unwillingness to forgive may have general social utility. In other words, ruminative thoughts may play an important role in the development of moral life. To ruminate means to ponder, to reflect, to engage in contemplation. By ruminating about an injustice one remembers, bears witness, and memorializes past wrongs. Rumination also can play the role of helping to establish taboos.

"Wundt describes taboo as the oldest human unwritten code of laws. It is generally supposed that taboo is older than gods and dates back to a period before any kind of religion existed" (cited in Freud, 1950, pp. 8–9). We tend to think taboos are practices that primitive savages had, and that we civilized people have outgrown this sort of thing. But let me suggest that establishing a taboo against genocidal acts might serve a purpose in today's world, where the deliberate and systematic aggression against ethnic groups still occurs.

Social scientists have demonstrated that aggression, the desire to gain power, and the need to survive, to reproduce, and to protect are basic human instincts, which may lead to immoral acts. Sigmund Freud in his book *Totem and Taboo* writes that taboos help to inhibit immoral acts which we nevertheless desire to commit. Freud applied this viewpoint to the most universal of all taboos: the taboo that prohibits sexual relations between close blood relatives and the taboo that prohibits the practice of cannibalism. The horrors of incest and cannibalism might seem obvious to us today, but it took a long time for human beings to prohibit these acts. The taboo helped to eliminate these practices from social life. And it helped to instill in us a psychological revulsion for such acts.

Might rumination and the unwillingness to forget the injustices of a genocide serve a similar function? Might it help in establishing a taboo against harming helpless people? Milgram points out that "Of all moral principles, the one that comes closest to being universally accepted is this: one should not inflict suffering on a helpless person who is neither harmful nor threatening to oneself" (Milgram, 1974, p. 13). Still, as Milgram's experiments show, people will inflict suffering on a helpless person depending on the context.

In growing up, most of us have learned to suppress actions that go against social expectations. But the culture has failed in teaching us internal controls on destructive actions stemming from social obligations, group values, or familial legacies. Establishing a taboo against genocidal acts might help in teaching us internal controls in carrying out deliberate and systematic aggressive actions against other ethnic groups. It might create a sense of utter repugnance similar to our sense about incest and cannibalism. And this sense of repugnance could serve as an inner control.

With terrorism, continued conflict in the Middle East, and upheaval in almost every pocket of the globe, the issue of planned massacres in the name of social obligations or group values or familial legacies has taken on a new urgency, as has the need for controls against carrying out such massacres. As the social psychologist Myers notes, because of our social identifications, we conform to our group norms. We sacrifice ourselves for family, nation, religion. "We dislike outgroups. The more important our social identity and the more strongly attached we feel to a group, the more we react prejudicially to threats from another group" (Myers, 2002, p. 348).

Paradoxically, as pointed out in a document by the Pontifical Council for Justice and Peace (2002, p. 1), although globalization is growing, and countries, economies, and cultures are drawing closer together and becoming more universal and blended, ethnic violence is increasing. The violence has escalated to such a degree that, at times, barbarous acts are committed against ethnic groups. So, perhaps, establishing a taboo that prohibits genocidal acts could work toward creating a more fraternal society.

Memorializing the Holocaust is essential because later generations will find evidence of the genocidal acts inflicted on helpless people. This, in turn, may help to develop a repugnance for undeserved suffering. And it may help to elevate the plight of genocidal victims into the world's consciousness. As Holocaust survivors die, it becomes increasingly important for their testimonies to be preserved for future generations. There are many who still deny the Holocaust and many who want to try to draw discussion of the Holocaust to a conclusion. There is a generational shift within Germany toward a society with no experience in the war. As the decades go by, the injustices of the Holocaust appear to recede more and more into the past.

Memorials, memoir projects, Spielberg's Survivors of the Shoah Visual History Foundation, which has videotaped 50,000 interviews since 1994, and Fortunoff Video Archives for Holocaust Testimonies at Yale University, among other projects, are all important for memorializing the past. Similarly, Germany's memorials, war museums, and the planned Holocaust Memorial in Berlin and also the Holocaust Museum in Washington are all important for enhancing awareness and for drawing attention to the atrocities of calculated genocide.

Yet, there is one caveat. In memorializing the past, there is the tendency to overestimate a groups' unanimity. As Niven points out, this may happen because historical museums and memorials "distort . . . history to make it appear better than it really was, or play down the negative episodes" (Niven, 2002, p. 202). And from a psychological viewpoint, this may happen because of a group-serving bias. In other words, we grant members of our own group the benefit of the doubt. But when explaining acts by members of other groups, we assume the worst, "Germans were evil anti-Semites." Positive behavior by outgroups members is often dismissed. It may be seen as a "special case."

Fifty years of research in prejudice teaches us it can be dangerous to categorize an entire group's actions and attitudes. It can lead to more anger and resentment. Some of today's Germans feel a blanket moral condemnation of all Germans is unfair. Thus, they may resent, as many other Germans do, being categorized as evil anti-Semites. Some of today's Germans feel that the memorials "represent the institutionalization of negative moral emotion and the raising of historical guilt to a state creed, forever blocking attempts by Germans to derive strength and orientation from a history that had more to it than National Socialism" (Niven, 2002, p. 194). If our goal, therefore, is to engage people in reflecting and contemplating the past crimes it is important to establish "the most appropriate form of bridge between past [injustice] and present reflection" (Niven, 2002, p. 197).

The descendants of those who suffered injustices tend to perpetuate categorizing an entire group's actions and attitudes, the data from the conference suggested. The danger is that overestimating a group's unanimity may contribute to the escalatory dynamic of conflict interactions. The daughter of a survivor who insists that her parents' past suffering entitles her to hate all Germans and who feels all Germans are indebted to her, can it must be

understood, encourage an unpleasant response. The child of a German sol-
dier, for example, may realize that the daughter of the survivor hates him or
her as a representative of the "German people," and the German child resents
this, and resents "them—the Jews." And then comes the clincher. Does this
spark anti-Semitism? "That question can be read either way: as a projection
of resentment ('anti-Semitism is caused by Jews') . . . or as an honest diag-
nosis" (Joffe, 1988, pp. 226–227). Either way, it is reasonable to argue, based
on years of research on prejudice, that collective accusations strike a nerve
that contributes to negative relations.

Initially, the relations between Nazis' children and survivors' children in the
conference were based on the assumption that the Nazis' children had a moral
debt to the survivors' children. Survivors' children expressed directly a feeling
of being owed something in return for the injustices their families suffered.
Sitting face to face with people they considered to be on the opposite side of
the victimizing barricade provoked deep emotional reactions. There were
moments when survivors' children accused—indeed in some ways attacked—
the Nazis' children sitting opposite them. It was hard for survivors' children to
control their negative emotional reactions, the data suggested.

Ulysses chained himself to the ship's mast before coming within earshot of
the Sirens. "He did so not because he feared the Sirens per se, but because he
feared his own reaction to their singing. In effect, he took a precaution against
himself, because he knew . . . what he would be likely to do if he heard the
Sirens" (Dawes, 1988, p. 142). Since this was the first time survivors' children
and Nazis' children were meeting each other, unlike Ulysses, they did not
know what they would likely do in reaction to sitting face to face with people
they considered "the enemy."

The good news is a cessation of reproaches and accusations occurred when
some survivors' children and Nazis' children discussed their own hurts. The
act of entering into and sharing their own hurts and feelings and being sensitive to and affected by the other's emotions, experiences, and especially
sorrows produced a shift in their interactions. As they talked about their own
hurts, rather than their parents' hurts and histories, they showed compassion
for the other and, by that, restored equal moral relations.

An important implication of this finding is that compassion can lead to
changes at the level of individuals—in the form of experiencing transformations in their feelings and categorizations. Compassion can inhibit negative
feelings like resentment and transform the categorizations left by the inheritance of one's past. Instead of judging a whole people, one is more likely to
see diversity. These individual transformations can then become vehicles for
changes at the interpersonal level.

When some survivors' children gave up the unqualified right to the moral condemnation of all Germans and acknowledged that the Nazis' children at the conference could not be made guilty for the Holocaust, then normal dialogue was possible, and Nazis' children resentments deriving from being incorrectly categorized overcome. Instead of looking back with anger, resentment, and shame, some survivors' children and Nazis' children shifted toward looking forward in moral determination to prevent future genocide. In the relations between survivors' children and Nazis' children, then, a new interaction was visible. In essence, they created a legacy of responsibility for the future (Weissmark et al., 1993).

There is no simple remedy for preventing future genocides. But, we can anticipate techniques for creating a more fraternal society. In an essay titled "Compassion," Lawrence Blum tells us, "Characteristically . . . compassion requires the disposition to perform beneficent actions, and to perform them because the person has had a certain sort of imaginative reconstruction of someone's condition and has a concern for his good. The steps that the person takes to ameliorate the condition are guided by and prompted by that imaginative reconstruction and concern" (Blum, 1980, p. 513).

Blum points out, however, that while compassion typically prompts kindly action or a search for ways of helping where none was evident before, it also often prompts precipitous action, or makes more difficult the sort of cold, professional behavior that may be necessary. Blum points out that compassion can also be "misguided grounded in a superficial understanding of the situation" (cited in Solomon, 1990, p. 35).

But this limitation does not give too much to the cynical critics, writes Solomon (1990).

> The limitations of compassion hardly undermine its virtue or the overall utility of compassionate actions. Blum rightly concludes that "because compassion involves an active and objective interest in another's welfare, it is characteristically a spur to deeper understanding than rationality alone could ensure. A person who is compassionate by character is in principle committed to as rational and as intelligent course of action as possible." Compassion without intelligence is no virtue, and intelligence without compassion is not justice. The significance of compassion is that it forms the core of our sense of justice and provides rationality with a heart. (Solomon, 1990, p. 235)

Milgram's famous experiments on obedience confirms Solomon's assertion that compassion prompts kindly behavior. Milgram (1974) chose 80 ordinary people of various ages and occupational backgrounds and asked them to take part in what he said was an important scientific experiment on learning.

The subjects were required to teach a list of word pairs to a "learner" (the experimenter's confederate) and to punish errors by delivering shock of increasing intensity. The subjects were urged by the experimenter to raise the amount of electricity higher and higher—and most did, even though the "learner" shouted that the shocks were painful and later began to groan and finally scream in pain.

But a few people refused and took the critical step of disobeying the authority. Interestingly, if we examine the transcript closely, we can see that those who disobeyed did so out of compassion and concern for the victim's good.

Here is an example of one such woman named Gretchen who defied the experimenter's orders to shock the learner. Gretchen was a medical technician who worked at Yale University Medical School. She had emigrated from Germany 5 years before and spoke with a thick German accent (Milgram, 1974, p. 85). She told the experimenter firmly but politely that she would not continue to shock the learner.

EXPERIMENTER: The experiment requires that you go on until he learned all the words correctly.
GRETCHEN: He has a heart condition, I'm sorry. He told you before.
EXPERIMENTER: The shocks may be painful but they are not dangerous.
GRETCHEN: Well, I'm sorry, I think when shocks continues like this, they are dangerous. You ask him if he wants to get out. It's his free will.
EXPERIMENTER: It is absolutely essential that we continue. . . .
GRETCHEN: I like you to ask him. We came here of our free will. If he wants to continue I'll go ahead. He told you he had a heart condition. I'm sorry, I don't want to be responsible for anything happening to him. I wouldn't like it for me either.
EXPERIMENTER: You have no other choice.
GRETCHEN: I think we here are on our own free will. I don't want to be responsible if he has a heart condition if anything happens to him. Please understand that.

The woman refuses to go further and the experiment is stopped. Ironically, the woman grew up in Hitler's Germany. When asked about the possible effect of her background, she said, "Perhaps we have seen too much pain." Milgram writes, "The woman's straightforward, courteous behavior in the experiment, . . . and total control of her own actions seems to make disobedience a simple and rational deed. Her behavior is the very embodiment of what I had initially envisioned would be true for all subjects" (Milgram, 1974, p. 85).

The journey from resentment to compassion is a long and arduous one. It involves transforming feelings of anger and resentment into a willingness to "hear the other side." The price of hearing the other side is a gnawing sense of faithlessness. Most participants who attended the meetings were troubled that they had disrupted their family and group legacy. Understanding why disrupting the legacy is so difficult, the deep, emotional, and psychological pull of attachment and belongingness, is essential.

We turn now to consider diversity and nations.

9
Diversity and Nations

What Is a Nation?

What is a nation? According to some scholars, no term in social science is more ambiguous than "the nation." Since Ernest Renan's famous essay "What Is a Nation? ("Qu'est-ce qu'une nation?") was delivered as a lecture at the Sorbonne in 1882, scholars have been debating the concept of a nation.

Scholars have pointed out that although many attempts have been made to define a nation, none have been successful because there is no methodical or scientific way any social theoretical definition can justify the state of nationhood in one case and deny it in the other. When discussing the terms or the relations between nation, nationhood, statehood, civic identity, ethnic identity, national identity, nationalism, and patriotism in today's world, few concepts—including the terms used—are clear-cut or uncontroversial. The definitions used, unlike those in science, have not, until recently, been studied by experimental repetition; they have relied on historical evidence to test their validity.

In addition to the difficulty in defining the concepts and terms, sociologists and political scientists have encountered difficulties in explaining the origins of nations. Several competing theories have been proposed. These competing theories have received much attention in nationalism studies, an interdisciplinary academic field devoted to the study of nationalism and related issues.

Briefly, the first, "primordialism theory," claims that nations and nationalism are natural phenomena. The theory underscores the long-term significance of kinship in small kin groups and cultural bonds. It holds that although the concept "nationhood" may be recent, nations have always existed. The theory purports that the nation is a primordial category based on primordial relations with kin groups. These may be genetic or cultural (Geertz, 1973; Shils, 1957; Van den Berghe, 1995).

The second, "perennialist theory," claims that nations are ancient, but not necessarily "natural," as claimed by primordialism theory (Hastings, 1997). Perennialist theory purports that nations, whether natural or not, have existed as long as humans have lived in "society." According to perennialist theory, the

The Science of Diversity. Mona Sue Weissmark, Oxford University Press (2020). © Oxford University Press.
DOI: 10.1093/oso/9780190686345.001.0001

Figure 9.1 White globe

history of nations and nationalism can be found by tracing the development of the cultural bonds in each nation over time.

The theory contends that nations are a basic form of human association and identity throughout history. Even where the cultural characteristics are considered symbolic or mythical, according to this theory, they are believed to preexist in the consciousness of the members of the nation (Hastings, 1997).

The third, "modernist theory" claims that nations and nationalism are modern phenomena. The theory contends that nations and nationalism appeared from the 18th century onward. According to this view, they are the products of the emergence of capitalism, industrialization, urbanization, secularism, and the bureaucratic state. The theory asserts that nations and nationalism are not given in nature, but rather are an outcome of industrial society. When people moved to the cities, populations had to be mobile, literate, and homogeneous. So, according to modernist theory, the nation and nationalism act as a method for linking mobile populations in industrial societies (Gelner, 1983).

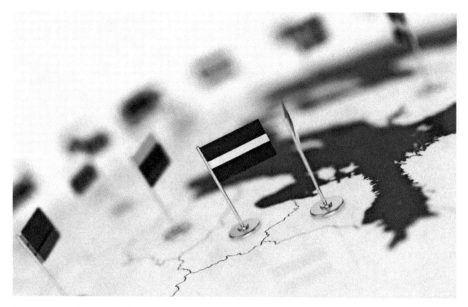

Figure 9.2 Flags on globe

Whereas in the village local customs had reinforced social bonds and structures, in the impersonal life of the city, "culture replaced structure." In the city, a new literate, linguistic, culture replaced the traditional structure of role expectations. According to modernist theory, only a literate culture could bind the great mass of immigrants to the city, and turn them into citizens. This could only be done through a mass, standardized, public education system. Public education systems turned villagers into national citizens and a culturally homogeneous workforce (Gellner, 1983).

According to the modernist theory, the nation became the most important agent of social control in the time of capitalism. Upper classes manipulated the feelings of the masses into new forms of status systems and new kinds of community bonds by engineering "invented traditions" of a made-up national history, symbolism, and mythology, according to modernist theory. Modernist theory claims that the invention of printing and mass-produced vernacular books made it possible to create "nations."

Books and newspapers united readers who would never have met or known one another into the new imagined community of the nations. It was the combination of new technical print inventions, new systems of production, and

Figure 9.3 People in shape of the U.S.

capitalism that ensured the success of binding citizens to nations across the globe, according to modernist theory (P. Anderson, 1991).

The fourth theory, "ethnosymbolism," claims that the previous three theories fail to provide a distinct and precise sociohistorical account of the formation and character of nations that sustained themselves as well as those that did not (Smith, 2000). According to ethnosymbolism theory, nation formation must be understood by considering the importance of heritages, myths, memories, values, symbols, and the vital role of ethnic ties and ethnic communities, or *ethnies*, for providing the basis for the emergence and persistence of nations (Armstrong, 1982; Smith, 2000).

According to ethnosymbolism theory, an *ethnie* is defined as a named human population with a common myth of descent, shared historical memories, one or more elements of common culture, a link with a historic territory, and a measure of solidarity. All these factors, according to ethnosymbolism theory, play a crucial part in arousing subjective ties and collective emotions, and ensuring cultural differentiation (Armstrong, 1982; Smith, 1986).

The fifth, "postmodernist theory," argues that nations and nationalism are narrative and conversational constructions (ways of thinking, talking about,

Figure 9.4 Drawing of printing press

and acting in, the world) and should be understood as such, whatever their agreement with material reality (Hearn, 2006, p. 244). According to postmodernist theory, a nation is a particular way of thinking about what it means to be a people (Calhoun, 1997). This theory has grown into a view of "imagined communities."

According to this view, nations rest on the attachments of individuals who might be scattered and never meet each other but who share customs, language, traditions, culture, or residence within a set of borders. Because individuals and groups imagine these attachments, neither nations nor the identities attached to them can be presumed to be fixed or permanent. "Instead, according to this view, nations today are thought to be imagined, constructed, and negotiated" (Miller-Idriss & Bracho, 2011).

Although all five theories define the term "nation" and the origins of nations differently, all imply that people form emotional attachments to a group and to a locale. As mentioned in chapter 6, people went from living in small nomadic hunter-gatherer kinship groups to farming groups to urban groups to more elaborate structures of a nation. History is the story of how people adapted to living together in greater numbers—from tribes to cities to nations. At each stage, people built social infrastructures needed for the operation of a community, society, or enterprise.

History shows that humanity has always pushed to come together in greater numbers to achieve more and to improve lives in ways people could not do in smaller groups. Each type of group required new ways of regulating social life and interpersonal behaviors that depended on the emotional and psychological process of attachment. The attachment bonds that bind a group of people into a family group or farming group or an urban group or a national group hold true.

National bonds do not dictate that members of a nation should all be alike or share an ethnicity, but only that the members should feel a bond of attachment to the nation and other members of their nation. For example, members of some nations share an ethnicity (e.g., almost everyone in South Korea is Korean, and in Argentina 97% of the country is white and more than 9-in-10 Argentines are at least nominally Roman Catholic). But other nations consist of ethnically diverse groups of people (e.g., the United States, Australia, the United Kingdom, Singapore, etc.) (Pew Research Center [PRC], 2013).

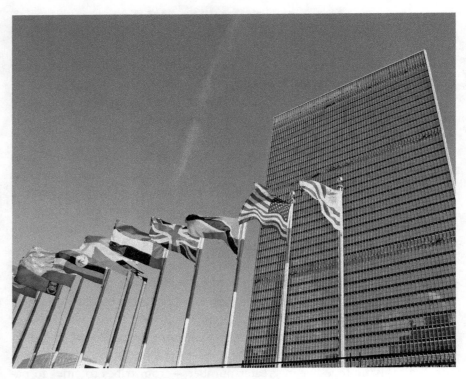

Figure 9.5 Flags in front of UN headquarters in NY

A nation, therefore, consists of a distinct population of people who feel bound together and who are typically concentrated within a specific geographic region, though not necessarily so. The point is that members of a nation see themselves as connected, often take pride in being a part of a nation, and may celebrate their nation. Sharing a national identity generates an emotional bond among fellow nationals. This sentiment is referred to as nationalism.

Nationalism

Two Dichotomous Types of Nationalism: Civic Versus Ethnic

In recent years, the study of nationalism has attracted growing attention from scholars in a range of disciplines—sociology, anthropology, history, politics, psychology, literature, and philosophy—that have produced a set of various theoretical approaches.

Although scholars from these different disciplines have been debating the term "nationalism," most theoretical definitions tacitly imply that nationalism entails feelings of belongingness and attachment. Scholars have distinguished different types of nationalism, according to the nature of belonging. Hans Kohn, a philosopher and historian and one of the earlier writers on nationalism, proposed two dichotomous types of nationalism, civic nationalism and ethnic nationalism, that scholars continue to apply today (Kohn, 1944).

Kohn classified the nationalism in Western societies as "civic nationalism," characterized as citizens *belonging to a political community* consisting of people with equal rights and duties. People can join and belong to a nation as long as they accept and are loyal to a set of political principles that embody the nation's values and respect its institutions (Kohn, 1944, 1956, 1982).

By contrast, Kohn defined and classified the nationalism in Eastern societies that developed in Germany and countries in Central and Eastern Europe and the periphery of Western Europe, such as Ireland and Spain as "ethnic nationalism." Ethnic nationalism is characterized as citizens *belonging to an ethnic community* based on blood ties. Ethnic nationalism considers membership in a nation to be ascriptive and based on descent (Janmaat, 2006); citizenship and belonging, therefore, rests on blood ties (Montgomery, 2005).

The distinction between ethnic and civic nationalism is a one of the best-known contributions to investigations into nationalism, and is still considered instructive (Jeong, 2016). After Kohn, other scholars have continued to apply the dichotomy civic-ethnic nationalism to compare and explain the

Figure 9.6 Drawing of people in a crowded room

differences in nationalism and belonging in different countries (Greenfeld & Chirot, 1994; Jeong, 2016; Ignatieff, 1993; Jeong, 2016; Kolstø, 2000; Rusciano, 2003; Schøpflin, 1996; Smith, 1991).

For example, Ignatieff (1993) builds on Kohn's dichotomy. Ignatieff describes civic nationalism as a community of equal, rights-bearing citizens who belong to a political community voluntarily based on a patriotic attachment to a shared set of patriotic practices and values. Ignatieff contrasts this with ethnic nationalism, where citizens' attachments are inherited, not chosen. According to Ignatieff, it is the nationalist community that defines the individual not the individual who defines the national community (Ignatieff, 1993, pp. 7–8).

According to Ignatieff (1993), civic nationalism assumes a more "rational attachment" of national belonging. By contrast, according to Ignatieff "the psychology of belonging" of ethnic nationalism may have "greater depth" because it is inherited, but it is not realistic. Ignatieff argues that most societies are not monoethnic; and even when they are, common ethnicity does not of itself eradicate divisions, because ethnicity is only one of the many claims on an individual's loyalty.

The law should hold a society together, not common ethnic roots, according to Ignatieff. By supporting democratic procedures and values, citizens, according to Ignatieff, can reconcile their right to shape their own lives with their need to belong to a community. This in turn assumes that national belonging can be a kind of rational attachment. Nevertheless, Ignatieff asserts that ethnic nationalism is the world's primary way of belonging today.

In brief, the division into "civic nationalism" and "ethnic nationalism" assumes that civic nationalism is voluntary, inclusive, rational, and based on chosen attachments, whereas ethnic nationalism is inherited, exclusionary, and irrational and is based on hereditary attachments. Also, the dichotomy assumes that civic nationalism is democratic in the sense that a civic nation is in principle a community of equal, rights-bearing citizens united in patriotic attachment to a shared set of political practices and values regardless of ethnicity or race, color, religion, gender, or language, whereas ethnic nationalism uses some set criteria such as descent as its basis for inclusion and exclusion. It does not allow individuals to choose which nation they belong to but holds that membership is decided at birth.

According to Janmatt (2006), the ethnic–civic dichotomy still gets scholarly attention, especially in relation to present-day immigration issues. Although scholars have criticized the dichotomy, its basic ideas that civic meanings of nationhood promote a positive attitude toward immigrants while ethnic-based meanings of the nation contribute to xenophobia still holds interest for scholars as well as policymakers.

It has been assumed that East and West countries in Europe that are typically associated with ethnic nationalism tend to exclude immigrants as members of the nation, as nationals or citizens, while Western countries associated with civic nationalism tend to have more positive attitudes toward immigrants (Hobsbawn, 1992; Maddens et al., 2000; Nieguth, 1999; Pehrson et al., 2009; Reijerse et al., 2013). Scholars have often pointed to the United States as the exemplary civic state (Kohn, 1957; Lipset, 1968). And some scholars have suggested that the United States is "an example of a state built around 'constitutional patriotism' where identities are already 'cosmopolitan,' 'postmodern,' 'intersectional,' and 'multiple'" (Kuzio & Magocsi, 2007, p. 13).

Many scholars, however, have criticized the civic-ethnic nationalism dichotomy. For example, Yack (2012) asserts that the notion of a civic nation is a myth that exaggerates a person's independence from the contingencies of birth and cultural heritage. Yack claims that many Western intellectuals and policymakers share the myth of a civic nation. The myth, according to Yack, suggests that liberal democratic nations' freely chosen principles have replaced cultural heritage as the basis of solidarity. And according to Yack, if only, so the fiction goes, Serbians, Kosovars, Hindus, or Quebecers would exchange their ethnic or cultural unit with the idea of civic solidarity, then nationalism would not lead to ethnic violence and intolerance.

According to Yack, there are problems with the view of liberal democracies as purely civic communities. First, Yack contends, it gets the history wrong. Liberal democratic nations like France, Canada, and the United States may have become relatively open societies that offer citizenship rights to all peoples, but they did not start that way. They all began with restricted core communities that were white or Catholic or British or European and then expanded outward.

Second, according to Yack, the celebration of civic nationalism distorts liberal democratic communities as they are presently, not just in the past. Yack contends that however much their citizens may associate these communities with a set of political principles, each of these nations gets its identity from a heritage associated with their peculiar histories and from an intergenerational community that plays an important role in modern national life.

Finally, according to Yack, even if modern liberal democratic communities were to change themselves into purely civic nations, the change would introduce different forms of exclusion and intolerance just as powerful as those they were trying to eliminate. So, according to Yack, the myth of the civic nation distorts the value as well as the existence of the form of the community that it celebrates.

In a similar manner, Kuzio (2002) asserts that the division into "civic Western" and "ethnic Eastern" does not reflect historical reality. Kuzio challenges the Kohn dichotomy as idealized and argues that it does not reflect historical reality and is out of step with contemporary theories of nationalism. Kuzio contends that its continued use ignores, for example, the evolution from communist to civic states that has taken place in central-eastern Europe during the 1990s. Kuzio challenges the assumption that Western nation-states were always "civic" from their start in the 18th century.

Also, Kuzio contends that in times of crisis such as immigration, foreign wars, domestic secessionism, and terrorism, the civic factors of the nations may continue to be dominated by ethnic particularistic factors. According to Kuzio, the balanced structure of a nation's ethnic particularism and civic universalism is always in tension and is dependent not on geography but on two aspects the historic stage from ethnic to civic nationhood and the degree of democratic consolidation.

Kuzio (citing Smith) claims that each nationalism and nation has elements and dimensions that include both types of nationalism explained by Kohn ("organic, ethnic" and "voluntary, civic"). " 'No nation, no nationalism, can be seen as purely the one or the other, even if at certain moments one or other of these elements predominate in the ensemble of components of national identity' " (Kuzio, 2002, cited by Smith, 2000, p. 25).

In a similar vein, Medrano (2005) asserts that people do not divide nations' attributes into ethnic and civic dimensions but position them along a single continuum ranging from postnationalism to credentialism. Likewise, Smith

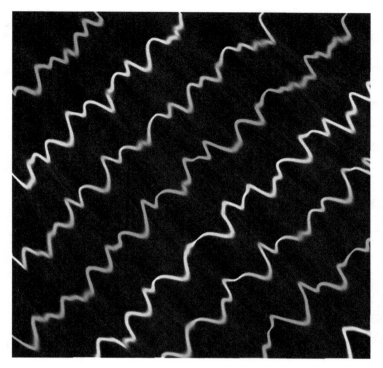

Figure 9.7 pink, yellow, blue wavelines

(1991) asserts that the ethnic–civic framework should be regarded as a continuum of both civic and ethnic nationalism rather than as a binary typology.

All civic states, whether in the West or East, are based, according to Smith, on an ethnocultural core.

Other scholars have argued that every government works to build a sense of national identity among its citizens, and sometimes governments even carefully create or construct that identity. For this reason, some scholars argue the concepts of nations and nationalism should be understood as being more about perceptions and feelings of identity, belongingness, and attachment than concrete facts.

Measuring Nationalism

Despite the voluminous theoretical literature on nationalism and critiques of the dichotomous types of nationalism, there has been little empirical research.

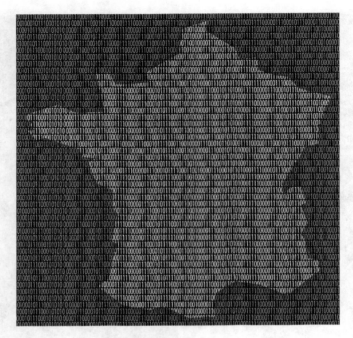

Figure 9.8 France shaped with binary digits

Figure 9.9 Holding hands

There is scant empirical research investigating the dichotomy ethnic-civic nationalism in Western and Eastern countries or nationalist sentiments among its citizens. Also, there has been little empirical research on the relationship between nationalist sentiments and attitudes toward immigrants and diversity.

Only recently have empirical studies examined the East/Ethnic–West/Civic dichotomy of national identity and extended the analysis to selected Asian countries as well. To this end, a recent study used data from the 2005 to 2007 rounds of the World Values Survey (Jeong, 2016). The sample size was over a thousand people in the United States, Norway, Sweden, Taiwan, China, and South Korea.

In the study, national identity was measured using questions asking people to rate the importance of the requirements needed to be recognized as citizens of their countries. The question was phrased as follows: "In your opinion, how important should the following be as requirements for somebody seeking citizenship of your country? Specify for each requirement if you consider it as very important, rather important or not important." The requirements

Figure 9.10 Australian passport

were: "(1) Having ancestors from my country, (2) Being born on my country's soil, (3) Adopting the laws of my country, and (4) Abiding by my country's laws." The importance rating was based on a three-point scale ranging from 1, "not at all important" to 3, "very important" (Jeong, 2016, pp. 209–210).

In the study, the variable ethnic identity was created by getting the average of those who considered requirements 1 and 2 as important and very important. The variable civic identity was constructed from the average of those who considered requirements 3 and 4 as important and very important. The researcher (Jeong, 2016) notes that the creation of these two key variables was derived from the literature on ethnic and civic ideas of citizenship (Brubaker, 1990; Hjerm, 1998; Kohn, 1944; Smith, 1991).

Peoples' attitudes toward immigration-related issues were based on three questions asking whether people would accept foreign workers/immigrants as neighbors, what the government should do about people from other countries coming to their country to work, and whether priority for employment should be given to immigrants over native people.

The fourth question asked about peoples' views on multicultural societies. Focusing on the question of ethnic diversity, people were asked which of the following views they agreed with and to use a scale to indicate their position. "Ethnic diversity enriches life." "Ethnic diversity erodes a country's unity" (Jeong, 2016, p. 210).

The results of the study showed that most countries had above-average scores for both types of national identities. That is to say, people in Asia and Western countries had moderate to high levels of each type of national identity. The results indicated that the differences between countries or between the Asia and the West were not substantial (Jeong, 2016, p. 211). Both ethnic and civic conceptions of the nation were found in all the states examined. So, the results indicated that civic and ethnic identities are not mutually exclusive and can be present simultaneously in societies.

Also, the results of the multivariate analysis that examined individuals' attitudes toward immigration and national identity suggested that in most countries, except Taiwan, those with stronger ethnic identity were more reluctant to accept foreigners/immigrants as their neighbors. However, civic identity was also found to be associated with anti-immigration sentiments in two Western countries (the United States and Sweden) and one Asian country (Taiwan).

Regarding the link between national identity and individuals' attitudes toward policies on foreign workers, the data showed that those with stronger ethnic identity expressed negative attitudes toward policies on foreign workers among all countries in Asia and the West. However, in all Western countries those with a stronger civic identity were also more likely to take un-yielding stances against foreign-worker policies too.

Finally, the data showed that in all three Western countries, both ethnic and civic identity negatively affected support for multicultural societies. However, in the three Asian countries, only ethnic identity registered as a consistently negative association.

According to the researcher, the results of the empirical analysis yield several important implications. The results both confirm and depart from previous findings. On average, respondents from Asian countries accorded more weight to the ethnic dimension and less to the civic, while Western respondents attached more importance to the civic dimension than the ethnic. The results, however, showed that civic and ethnic identities are not mutually exclusive and can be present simultaneously in societies (Jeong, 2016).

The researcher notes that some previous studies (e.g., Hjerm, 1998) suggest that in countries where nationalism is based on ethnic identity anti-immigrant sentiment is stronger than in countries where it is based on civic identity. However, the researcher notes that in his study it was remarkable to find a negative association not only between ethnic identity and immigrant attitudes in Western and Eastern countries, confirming the previous literature, but also between civic identity and sentiments toward immigrants in Western countries (Jeong, 2016). In conclusion, the researcher says, "The common assumption (Birnbaum, 1996; Gellner, 1983; Nodia, 1994) that it is desirable to emphasize civic identity because of its association with positive social attitudes, including attitudes towards immigrants, might be reconsidered" (Jeong, 2016, p. 217).

Resurgence of Nationalism

A limitation of the study mentioned earlier is that it used the World Values Survey, which is a cross-sectional survey carried out at a single point in time. So, it cannot account for the process of change in peoples' national identities or its relation to changes in attitudes on diversity and immigration. As mentioned before, some scholars have suggested that the formation of a national identity and nationalist sentiments (including both ethnic and civic aspects) is a dynamic process and under certain conditions may change or reemerge (Auer, 2000; Kaufmann, 1999, 2000; Kuzion, 2002).

Indeed, nationalist sentiments, once thought by many scholars to be a declining motivating force, have, according to scholars, apparently returned with renewed strength in recent decades. Over the past 75 years, scholars

Figure 9.11 Refugee children near watchtower

argued that Western nations were moving toward cooperation and interconnectedness, as their shared economic and political interests joined during this era called globalization.

For example, Ignatieff states, "With blithe lightness of mind, we assumed that the world was moving irrevocably beyond nationalism, beyond tribalism, beyond the provincial confines of the identities inscribed in our passports, toward a global market culture that was to be our new home. In retrospect, we were whistling in the dark. The repressed has returned, and its name is nationalism" (Ignatieff, 1993, p. 1).

Similarly, in a recent *New York Times* interview, Mark Zuckerberg the American computer programmer and cofounder of Facebook, states, "When I started Facebook, the idea of connecting the world was not controversial," ... "The default assumption was that the world was incrementally just moving in that direction. So I thought we can connect some people and do our part in helping move in that direction." But now, Zuckerberg said, whether it was wise to connect the world was "actually a real question" (Manjoo, 2017, p. 7). Zuckerberg also expressed doubt about Facebook's global role. "Giving everyone a voice has historically been a very positive force for public discourse

Figure 9.12 Mark Zuckerberg talking

because it increases the diversity of ideas shared," . . . "But the past year has also shown it may fragment our shared sense of reality" (Manjoo, 2017, p. 7).

Many commentators have noted, as a backlash to globalization there are signs of a new age of nationalism emerging in the United States and Europe, that according to some could undermine democracy and postwar security and unity. For example, critics point out that Donald Trump won the 2016 US presidential election in part by promising to "Make America Great Again," a general slogan that supports an isolationist, protectionist, "America First" attitude toward the world.

According to Trump's critics, Trump's campaign rhetoric criticizing Muslims and Mexicans, and advocating limiting trade and immigration has moved the United States toward a period of antiglobalization and exclusionary ethnonationalism. Some commentators have argued that with Donald Trump's presidency—and politics in the United Kingdom, France, and Germany moving toward anti-immigration attitudes and policies—the Western model of democracy and inclusionary nationalism unexpectedly looks unstable. Critics maintain that Trump's election and Britain's exit from the European Union (EU) may have encouraged nationalist groups across

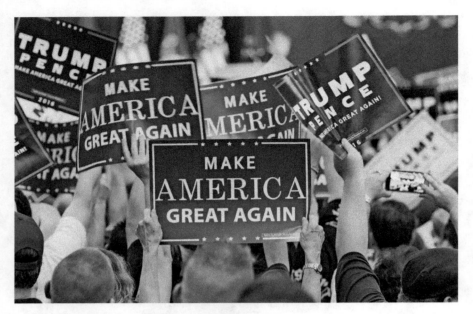

Figure 9.13 Make America Great Again signs

Europe, as there has been a change away from international collaboration, sharing power, building international relations and organizations, to focusing on the national rights of individual countries.

As mentioned before, some scholars argue that nationalism is not a rigid dichotomy between civic and ethnic aspects but rather a mix of both strains. Some strains are more inclusive than others, based on a person's emotional attachment and subjective identification with a nation. Ethnic-driven nationalism is often about a common ancestry, religion, language, and dissent. Scholars contend that despite some public perceptions, populism and exclusionary ethnonationalism have not suddenly surged in the United States and Europe since Trump's ascendancy.

Rather, critics maintain that many US and European exclusionary nationalist parties have been around for decades, with varying levels of success. For instance, nationalism in France has been on the rise since the 1980s, when the National Front party's founder, Jean-Marie Le Pen, won a seat in European Parliament in 1984. Since then, the French National Front has placed itself against globalization and immigration. And populist-nationalist parties on the far right have been on the rise in Hungary, Poland, Slovakia, and Croatia as well.

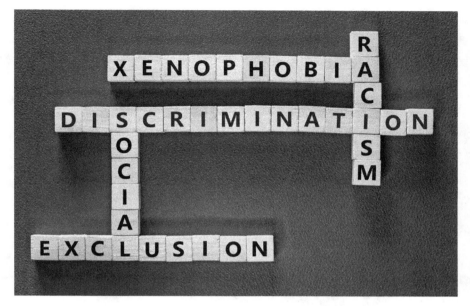

Figure 9.14 Scrabble words

Also, some critics point out that Trump first found his political popularity in 2011 after he claimed President Barack Obama was born in Kenya and was not a legitimately elected president. Trump's critics contend that Trump appeared to fuel exclusionary nationalistic sentiments among his mainly white supporters and was slow to reject endorsements by white nationalists, including the Ku Klux Klan. According to some critics, organized ethnonationalist fringe groups wishing to remake the United States as a white, nationalist state have long existed on the margin of American politics and society, but the Trump campaign's spread of an agenda that aligned with theirs brought some extremist ethnonationalist groups into the mainstream.

Other critics, however, underscore that approximately 63 million voters and the vast majority backed Trump were not extremist nationalists, but Americans with traditional nationalist values that wanted change. These commentators claim there is a segment of the US population that does not define the nation in ethnocultural terms per se; they are not all members of neo-Nazi groups, for instance. They just have a personal felt understanding of what America is and should continue to be, which is a white, Christian America. And with the "Make America Great Again" agenda, for the first time in a long time they feel they have been allowed to be part of the conversation.

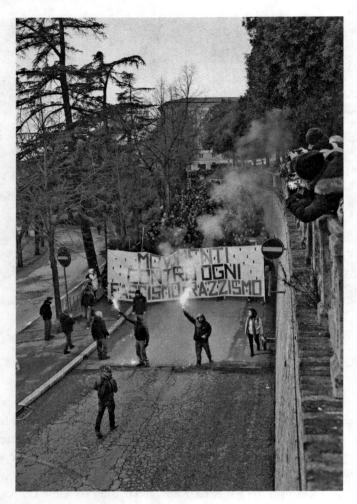

Figure 9.15 Demonstration after a shooting

According to this view, the "Make America Great Again" agenda gives these citizens a degree of increased legitimacy adding to the sense that there is a broad nationalist wave moving around America.

Thus, some scholars contend that the nationalist sentiments among the millions of traditional American white working-class centers more on the dynamics of recognition: how much place those groups are given in social and cultural debates about issues like public bathrooms and sexual orientation and climate change. According to this view, the surge in nationalistic sentiment derives from a backlash to the liberal obsession with diversity and

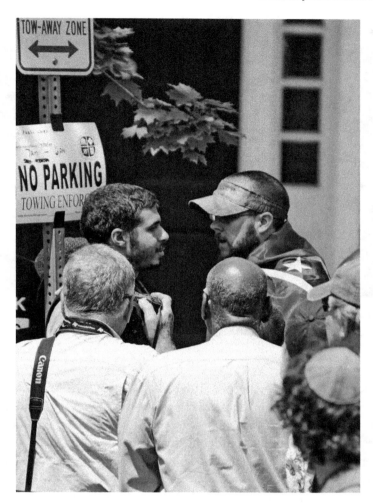

Figure 9.16 Protester and KKK

identity politics. This has caused white, rural, religious Americans to think of themselves as a disadvantaged, victimized group whose identity is being threatened or ignored. Such people, according to this view, are not actually reacting against globalization or the reality of a diverse America. They are reacting against the ubiquitous rhetoric of identity liberalism and "political correctness" (e.g., Hochschild, 2016; Lilla, 2016).

Thus, some scholars have concluded that what has changed is the salience of these nationalist sentiments. Citizens are giving more value to their nationalist sentiments because of certain contextual factors: globalization and

Figure 9.17 Trump hats

liberal identity politics being two such factors. But according to this line of reasoning, there are other contextual factors too: persistent economic inequality stemming out of neoliberalism and globalization, demographic changes, an influx of immigrants, concerns about terrorism, along with political events like obstructionism in Washington, and the perceived corruption or nonrepresentativeness of the EU governance system.

All of these factors have generated some level of anxiety among mainly white, native-born populations and a perceived status loss at the group level among these citizens. This in turn, makes nationalist claims—and, especially, nationalist-anti-immigrant and antiglobalization claims—more appealing and more salient than they had been in the past.

Inequality and Nationalism

Despite the sizable critical and theoretical literature on the rise of nationalism and the various explanations, the relationship between the hypothesized factors in a country and nationalist sentiments among its citizens has not been directly investigated empirically. Indeed, there has been relatively little cross-national empirical research on the causes of nationalism at all.

As Solt (2011) points out, the literature on nationalism leaves a lot of room for more empirical research on nationalism's causes. To date most of the literature has failed to frame hypotheses clearly and test the hypotheses against empirical evidence. So, the literature on the causes of the rise of nationalism leaves many questions unresolved. To remedy this, Solt provided a first test of whether greater economic inequality causes more nationalism by examining evidence from the world's advanced democracies (Solt, 2011).

The main measure of individuals' nationalism was drawn from the five waves of the World Values Survey (WVS), conducted from 1981 to 2007, as well as the International Social Survey Program (ISSP) survey on national identity conducted in 2003–2004. These surveys asked people the extent of their pride in their respective nations: "How proud are you to be French [or Albanian, or Belgian, etc.]?" Answers were on a 4-point scale recoded to range from (1) not at all proud, through (2) not very proud and (3) quite proud, to (4) very proud.

The surveys used provided data on national pride in 78 countries, in one to six different years each, for a total of 222 different country-year contexts (Solt, 2011). Two additional measures of nationalism were also examined. Both were based on the 2003–2004 ISSP survey on national identity as well as an

Figure 9.18 Bastille day

earlier version of that survey. People were first asked "How close—how emotionally attached—do you feel to France [or Australia, etc.]?" with answers on a 4-point scale from "not close at all" to "very close." On the 4-point, "not at all proud" to "very proud" scale, the ISSP respondents were asked to rate their pride in each of five areas: (1) their country's achievements in the arts, (2) its achievements in sports, (3) its achievements in science and technology, (4) its armed forces, and (5) its history. Responses to these five questions were used to create an index of national-cultural pride (for details, see Solt, 2011).

To measure economic inequality, the study used the Standardized World Income Inequality Database (SWIID). The results showed that across the countries and over time, where economic inequality was greater, nationalist sentiments were substantially more widespread. The researcher concludes that the results add to our understanding of nationalism by demonstrating that domestic inequality is an important stimulus for the generation of nationalist sentiments.

In addition, the researcher contends that the results of the study also help to elucidate the relationship between economic inequality and democratic politics. According to the researcher, it helps explain the fact that democracies with higher levels of inequality do not consistently respond with more wealth redistribution. Rather than allowing redistribution to be decided through the democratic process, democratic nations often respond to higher levels of inequality with more nationalism. Nationalism then, according to the researcher, may work to divert attention from inequality. So many citizens neither realize the extent of inequality nor demand redistributive policies (Solt, 2011, p. 829).

Other studies have expanded on investigating the relationship between income inequality and nationalistic sentiments to see whether nationalistic sentiments may, perhaps, be shaped by other social features such as the level of migration (Han, 2013). Although historical evidence suggests nationalistic sentiments increase when levels of migration are higher, the question has rarely been answered with empirical studies.

To this end, Han (2013) conducted an empirical study examining the relationship between national pride, income inequality, and migration. The dependent variable national pride was measured using the data set from the WVS and the European Value Survey (EVS) from the survey waves of 1995, 2000, and 2005. The independent variable income inequality was measured by using the Gini coefficient from the Standardized World Income Inequality Database. The data on the number of migrants came from the World Bank, World Development Indicators.

The results of the study showed that national pride of poor people rises as income inequality increases, especially in countries where there are many migrants in the lower class. According to the researcher, the results are consistent with the social identification theory by Shayo (2009).

According to social identification theory, poor people become more nationalistic because they do not want to identify themselves with the lower class, whose material value and status has declined. International migration, especially the inflow of migrants lacking higher education and skills, drives the inclination more because it increases the perceived distance that poor people feel between themselves and other members in the lower class.

The results of the study, according to the researcher, suggest that the link between income inequality and national pride is indeed shaped by international migration. International migration, according to the researcher, reduces class-consciousness, weakens working-class movements, and impairs political parties that are based on class identity. According to the researcher, the results support the idea that increases in international migration, together with rising income inequality, drives poor people to look for another social identity (national identity) (Han, 2013).

Nationalism and Inequality: A Threat to Democracy?

Some scholars have speculated that the rise of nationalism and inequality may pose a threat to democracy. Noam Chomsky, an American MIT professor sometimes described as "the father of modern linguistics," argues that inequality in all its forms today threatens democracy in the United States. Chomsky cites the research findings of the Princeton political scientist Martin Gilens's study (2014) showing the inequality in power that low- and middle-income Americans have on affecting government policy in any form.

Gilens's multivariate analysis demonstrates that economic elites and organized groups representing business interests have large independent impacts on US government policy, while average citizens and mass-based interest groups have little or no independent influence.

Gilens (2014) looked at thousands of proposed governmental policy changes, and the degree of support for each among poor, middle-class, and affluent Americans. His findings showed that when preferences of low- or middle-income Americans diverged from those of the affluent, there was almost no relationship between policy outcomes and the wishes of less advantaged groups. In contrast, affluent Americans' wishes show a strong relationship with policy outcomes whether lower-income groups share their wishes or not.

Figure 9.19 US capitol

According to Gilens, the results provide considerable support for theories of economic-elite domination and for theories of biased pluralism, but not for theories of majoritarian electoral democracy or majoritarian pluralism. In short, average citizens are powerless when it comes to influencing governmental policies.

Chomsky and other scholars have questioned whether a country can be a true democracy if its government only responds to the preferences of the rich. In an ideal democracy, all citizens should have equal influence on government policy—but as the data show, America's policymakers respond almost exclusively to the preferences of the economically advantaged.

According to some commentators, this powerlessness has translated in the discourse seen during the US 2016 election. Researchers contend that there is a correlation between powerlessness and voting behaviors that has been noted for years.

For example, Burnham conducted a study of the socioeconomic character of nonvoters in the United States. What he found was that increasing numbers of average Americans are no longer motivated to vote for parties that do not represent their interests (Burnham, Ferguson, 2014), retrieved on February 21, 2017, from http://www.alternet.org/americans-are-sick-death-both-parties-why-our-politics-worse-shape-we-thought). Direct poll evidence

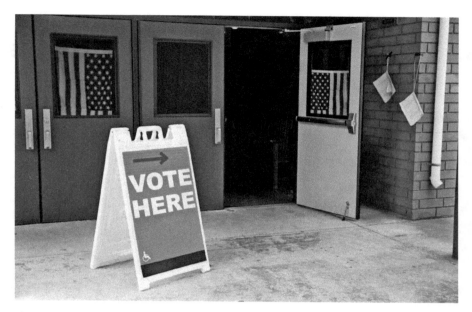

Figure 9.20 Vote here polling sign

confirms that huge numbers of Americans are now wary of both major political parties, and increasingly upset about prospects in the long term. Many are
convinced that a few big interest groups control governmental policy and they
lack the power to influence governmental policy.

According to Chomsky, powerlessness and alienation among average
Americans is increasing as large sectors of the population are cast by the way-
side in the course of neoliberal programs. In the past workers would organize
and effectively do something about their economic situations, as in the 1930s
with the militant labor movement. But according to Chomsky, now their only
recourse is to get angry, frustrated, xenophobic, racist, and destructive.

Chomsky contends that alienation, powerlessness, and inequality in all its
forms continue to threaten democracy in the United States. Chomsky's most
recent documentary, *Requiem for the American Dream* (2016) focuses on
income and power inequality. But unlike fellow system critic Robert Reich
(discussed next), Chomsky does not suggest saving democracy through economic reshuffling or revitalized democratic elections. Rather Chomsky
suggests that ultimately learning how the system works will greatly help in
changing it.

Robert Reich, professor of public policy at the University of California at
Berkeley, contends that wealth inequality is even more of a problem than

Figure 9.21 Immigration protest

income inequality. Half of the United States' total assets are now owned by 400 people—and, Reich argues that this is not just a threat to the economy, but also to democracy.

The documentary *Inequality for All* (2013) is based on Robert Reich's book *Aftershock: The Next Economy and America's Future* (2010). The film explores the widening wealth inequality—currently at record highs—and examines what effects this increasing gap has on the US economy and on American democracy. The film addresses these questions: What role does the widening wealth gap play in the decline of the nation's economic health and democracy? And does the widening wealth gap undermine a just society?

Reich points out that over the last 30 years, before the latest recession, the US economy doubled. But, according to economists, these gains went to a very few: the top 1% of earners take in more than 20% of all income—three times what they did in 1970. Inequality is extreme at the very top, according to Reich. The 400 richest Americans own more wealth than the bottom 150 million combined. Reich and other scholars have concluded that the concentration of wealth and power among a small elite has polarized American society. Also, they maintain that it has brought about the decline of the middle class and has produced a corrosive effect on democracy.

Figure 9.22 Rooftop depicting rich and poor

While, according to Reich, this level of inequality poses a serious risk to all Americans, regardless of income level, researchers contend that this inequality has fueled anger and resentment from an alienated middle class who feels their birthright—the American Dream—has been taken away from them.

In psychology, surprisingly little empirical work has been conducted on income inequality in the general US population. What are the psychological effects of income inequality? Are people happier when national wealth is allocated more evenly?

To address these questions psychology researchers used General Social Survey (GSS) data (Oishi, Kesebir, & Diener, 2011). The participants were 53,043 respondents to the GSS (National Opinion Research Center, 2010) from 1972 to 2008 (29,675 females, 23,368 males; 43,323 self-identified as white, 7,314 self-identified as black, and 2,406 self-identified as an ethnicity other than white or black; age ranged from 18 to 89 years, with a mean of 45.52 years. Of the total sample, 48,318 provided valid responses to the happiness item on the GSS.

The data suggested that Americans were on average happier in the years with less national income inequality than in the years with more national income inequality. Moreover, the data demonstrated that the inverse relation between income inequality and happiness was explained by perceived fairness and general trust. That is to say, the data showed that Americans trusted other people less and thought other people to be less fair in the years with more national income inequality than in the years with less national income inequality.

The negative association between income inequality and happiness held for lower-income respondents, but not for higher-income respondents. According to the researchers, the most important finding they found was that the negative link between income inequality and the happiness of lower-income respondents was explained not by the lower income, but by perceived unfairness and lack of trust.

The results are correlational, so the researchers note that they cannot be sure that the income gap directly caused unhappiness, but according to the researchers an examination of the data turned up a plausible explanation. When the income gap grew, low- and middle-class people became increasingly distrustful of their fellow Americans. They were also less likely to believe that fair and just treatment from others was the norm. According to the researchers, this social fracturing could explain the drop in happiness during these times.

If the results hold, the researchers maintain, they explain why countries with lower income gaps, such as Denmark and Germany, have become happier as their wealth has grown, while Americans have not (Oishi et al., 2011). "The implications are clear: If we care about the happiness of most people, we need to do something about income inequality" says the researcher (Oishi, Kesebir, & Diener, 2011).

In sum, nationalism is both old and contemporary. The resurgence of nationalistic sentiments is happening around the globe. Some scholars have noted it appears that every expression in some ways resembles expressions elsewhere, leading researchers to think some common factors are fueling the phenomenon. The parallels between the slogans "Make America Great Again!" and "France for The French" and "Take Back Control!" (adopted by the Brexit campaign) suggest that appeals to citizens' nationalistic sentiments are vote-winners.

Research suggests that many factors have contributed to the resurgence of nationalistic sentiments including economic, cultural, social, and political factors driven by economic inequality, globalization, and immigration. Scholars contend that economic inequality and the increase in immigration have caused many lower- and middle-class native-born citizens to view themselves as the designated victim class living in social disaffection that has been overlooked (Krueger, 2016).

Lower- and middle-class native citizens in the United States and Europe have seen their earning power decline. Many feel that the new arrivals, particularly Muslim immigrants and refugees from the Middle East, are leap-frogging over them economically by coming in and taking their resources. So, for many native-born citizens it is a sense of social displacement and state pecking order. Some scholars argue that this sense among many lower- and middle-class native-born citizens has justified and legitimized political parties in the United States and Europe to advocate banning immigration.

Some scholars contend that the resurgence of nationalistic sentiments has exposed not only the economic gap between winners and losers of global-ization; but also a cultural divide between those comfortable with the pace of change, from technology to same-sex marriage to transgender rights and those wanting to slow down the clock and rediscover their roots in ethnicity, religion, and nationality. These citizens feel as though outside influences such as immigration threaten their sense of national identity.

This cultural divide, according to scholars, helps explain the appeal of Trump's pledge to build a "beautiful" wall on the Mexican border and his ex-ecutive order to close the nation's borders to certain refugees and to grant pri-ority to Christian over Muslim refugees (Shear & Cooper, 2017). Also, it helps explain Britain's prime minister Theresa May's statement on politically correct multiculturalism: "If you believe you are a citizen of the world, you are a citizen of nowhere." And it helps to explain the French National Front (FN) political party leader Marine Le Pen's vow to defend France against "rampant globali-zation." "The main thing at stake in this election is the rampant globalization

Figure 9.23 World map with infographics

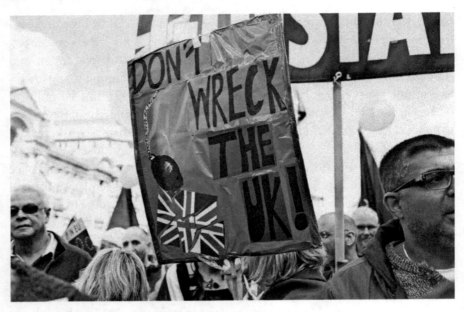

Figure 9.24 UK EU Protest

that is endangering our civilization," Le Pen stated, urging French voters "to shake off the shackles of an "arrogant elite." (as cited in Thomas, 2017).

Between the Obama 2008 election and the Trump 2016 election, America changed from being a majority white Christian nation (54%) to a minority white Christian nation (43%). The choice between the 2016 US presidential candidates, according to some scholars, was blatantly clear. Donald Trump's Republican Party looked back nostalgically to a monochromatic image of 1950s America. By contrast, Hillary Clinton's Democratic Party looked ahead to a pluralistic, feminist future of 2050, when the Census Bureau first predicted the United States would become a majority nonwhite nation.

Survey data suggests that a shared sense of American national identity is on the decline. Seven in 10 Americans say the United States is losing its national identity. (Connelly, Malato, Tompson, & Benz 2017). Retrieved from http://www.apnorc.org/projects/Pages/HTML%20Reports/points-of-pride-conflicting-views-and-a-distinct-culture.aspx. At the center of this decline, are citizens' opposing reactions to the changing demographics and culture with two mutually exclusive viewpoints emerging along party lines.

Figure 9.25 French sign

Democratic citizens are more likely than Republican citizens to view the nation's diversity and the ability of people to immigrate to the United States as important, while Republican citizens are more inclined to view the importance of the use of English and sharing a culture, ideally founded on Christian beliefs and European customs.

When asked what kind of culture is important for American identity, 66% of Democratic citizens, compared with only 35% of Republican citizens, said the mixing of cultures and values from around the world was extremely or very important to American identity. Whereas 64% of Republican citizens,

Figure 9.26 1950s office staff photo

"compared with 32% of Democratic citizens, saw a culture grounded in Christian religious beliefs as extremely or very important" (cited in Jones, 2017). These contrasting viewpoints underscore that US citizens are divided between opposing poles of cultural pluralism versus cultural monism.

In conclusion, scholars agree that the last 30 years have been a period of dramatic economic and cultural changes. Not all citizens, however, in the traditional societies of the United States and Europe want to embrace the changes. Getting use to iPhones, activity trackers, and other items that go with material modernization is one thing. But for many citizens, questions of what is going to happen with religion, with traditional families, with traditional curricula in schools, and with the history of their country have left many citizens feeling unmoored. The resurgence of nationalistic sentiments is driven by the need for meaning, identity, and emotional connection that citizenship—a relationship between a person and a nation—may provide.

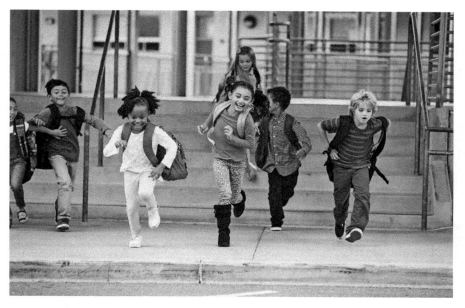

Figure 9.27 Kids running out of school

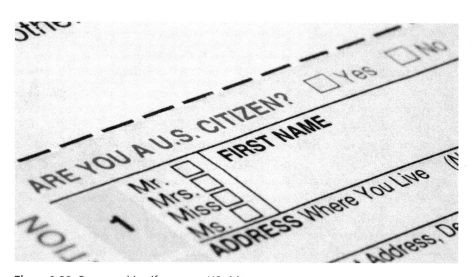

Figure 9.28 Survey asking if you are a US citizen

10
Concluding Remarks

Diversity is a central feature of all social systems. Whether we are discussing individuals, groups, or nations differences exists. History shows that from the beginning of time philosophers and scientists have tried to explain the differences.

Many thinkers throughout early history thought factors like geography and climate explained the diversity in the physical appearances of different people. Later, Greek philosophers and European and Americans scientists thought factors like different types of souls, skull sizes, and brain sizes explained the diversity. Scientists then used these explanations to devise categorization systems that divided the human species into separate races.

Darwin, one might say, tried to put the human races together again. The evolutionary unity of all humans (and animals) was the central message of Darwin's theory. We are part of nature, Darwin contended. But Darwin did not negate human differences and uniqueness.

Darwin used the tree of life image in the context of his theory of evolution, so that we could visualize our differences and our interconnections. The tree of life is a key image because it presents Darwin's central organizing vision of shared descent. It portrays the idea that species are related and ultimately evolved from a common ancestor in the distant past. The different branches portray the changes in populations. From a single starting point in the tree of life, we can see how differences emerge.

Broadly speaking, Darwin showed that the phenotypic racial differences had no inherent value because all human beings shared a single, common ancestor. The idea that all species are related by common descent from a single ancestor was a transformative idea and unlike other ideas about our differences that had come before. (Alfred Russel Wallace, another British naturalist independently presented a similar theory.)

This is probably the feature of Darwin's theory that has been opposed the most. If all life is related by common descent, what does this imply about humanity and our place in the world? According to evolutionary theory, it means all humans are connected and are a part of the natural environment, rather than in a separate, superior position to the environment or to one another. Darwin's theory was and still is controversial.

The Science of Diversity. Mona Sue Weissmark, Oxford University Press (2020). © Oxford University Press.
DOI: 10.1093/oso/9780190686345.001.0001

Understanding our differences has not been a unilinear development of progress.

Scientists and the public did not just accommodate their thinking in light of Darwin's new evolutionary theory about diversity. Rather, the reception of Darwin's ideas met with rebuke even hostility (and continues today to arouse heated religious and scientific debates). After Darwin, scientists continued to devote their research to studying differences in populations and its implications.

Throughout the 19th and 20th century scientists hit on the idea that differences in human populations could be explained by superior genes. According to this line of reasoning, it followed that human populations could be improved by halting the reproduction of so-called lesser genes. This way, it was believed, more suitable races or strains of blood would produce a highly gifted race of "men" that was different and better than lesser races. This view of human differences culminated in the Final Solution under Nazi policy.

In total, the Final Solution consisted of gassings, shootings, terrorism, torture, starvation, and disease that accounted for the deaths of millions of people

Figure 10.1 Prisoners in line at concentration camp

from "lesser races" such as Jews, Romani, Poles, Slavs, Jehovah's Witnesses, the disabled, homosexuals, the incurably ill, and other groups of people. The "lesser races" were viewed as useless to society, a threat to Aryan genetic racial purity, and, basically, unworthy of life.

Partly as result of the genocide of Nazism, the United Nations Educational, Science and Cultural Organization (UNESCO) was established with the mission to build the defenses of peace in the minds of "men." Its Constitution states: "Since wars begin in the minds of men, it is in the minds of men that the defenses of peace must be constructed." Afterward, UNESCO published several statements on human differences that proved to be controversial.

The first statement supported Darwin's evolutionary theory, underscoring that "all men belong to the same species," but it also included the view that human groups differed because of innate genetic biological differences for intellectual and emotional capacities. The final UNESCO document, however, unlike the previous documents revised its view on innate genetic differences. The revised document declared that all peoples of the world possessed equal faculties and any differences are due to historical, political, economic, social, and cultural factors, not biological factors.

It also stressed that the solution to the problems between different races of people rested on the shoulders of an individual. The individual was responsible for creating a culture of peace, respect, and tolerance. Education, according to

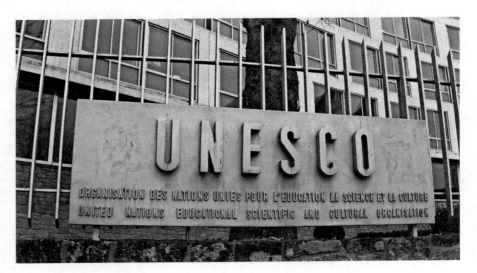

Figure 10.2 UNESCO sign

UNESCO, can transform minds, lives, and drives the development of an individual. This document still defines the mission of UNESCO today.

The history of how we revised our thinking about our differences demonstrates that education can, indeed, transform minds. Today, scholars and the public agree that factors like geography and climate cannot explain the diversity in the physical appearances of different people. Also, researchers agree that factors like soul quality, nose configuration, skull capacity, and brain size cannot scientifically be used to categorize people into different racial or ethnic groups. Likewise, there is widespread agreement that a "final solution" to destroy the so-called lesser races to produce a highly gifted race cannot be justified.

Learning and Flexibility

Our ability to learn from mistakes confirms that human beings possess the flexibility required for development. Human development resides in our ability to educate and to learn. The influence of individuals on the world has

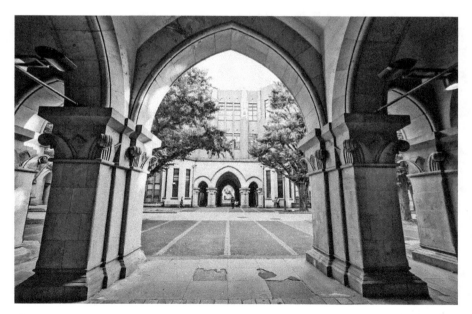

Figure 10.3 Arch at Tokyo University

been immense because humans invented a new type of evolution—cultural evolution.

Cultural evolution maintains the transmission across generations of learned knowledge and behaviors. It is expressed in societies and cultures built on our learned knowledge. Whatever one generation learns it can pass to the next by writing, instructions, socialization, rituals, norms, traditions, and many other methods that humans have developed to assure continuity in culture.

History shows that individuals adapted to being members of hunter-gatherer groups, tribes, cities, nations, and global online communities because of cultural evolution. These adaptations are a testimony to flexibility as the hallmark of human behavior. It shows that people's behaviors are an expression of general rules that can be adapted to specific interactions and environments. Why should people have the ability to be mentally and behaviorally flexible?

The flexibility to change is important because environments can change and unexpected outcomes can occur. Human mental and behavioral flexibility demonstrates biological potentiality versus biological determinism (Katseneliboigen, 1984). For instance, a person has the potential to act aggressively in one kind of interaction or environment and compassionate in

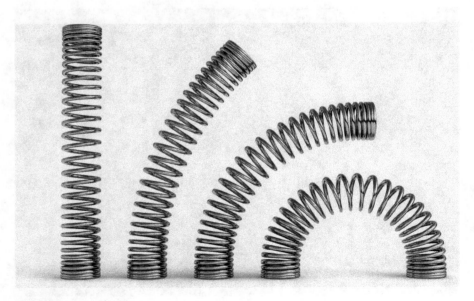

Figure 10.4 Metal springs

another. Or citizens of a nation have the potential to revert back and forth between acting violently under an authoritarian government or peacefully under a democratic government.

The English social scientist Gregory Bateson defined flexibility as the "uncommitted potential for change" (Bateson, 1972, p. 497). Bateson describes a healthy system, flexibility-wise, by comparing it with an acrobat on a high wire:

> To maintain the ongoing truth of his basic premise ("I am on the wire"), he must be free to move from one position of instability to another, i.e., certain variables such as the position of his arms and the rate of movement of his arms must have great flexibility, which he uses to maintain the stability of other more fundamental and general characteristics. If his arms are fixed or paralyzed (isolated from communication), he must fall. (Bateson, 1972, p. 498)

The human ability to be flexible is the ability to adapt to changes in an unprogrammed manner. Like the acrobat who must be flexible to change positions in relation to the movement of the wire and gravity, flexibility allows people to learn and adapt their thinking and behaviors to the circumstances. There are constraints to flexibility. We know that the acrobat's wide range of balancing behaviors arises from the interaction between two physical rules, gravity and the frictional resistance of the wire. Still, this interaction can generate many different ways of balancing. The acrobat has many degrees of freedom at his or her disposal.

Similarly, our attachment needs, our propensity to categorize, and to judge, our very sense of self, sets constraints on our thinking and behaviors. But they do not eliminate our potential to develop. Human development lies in the flexibility of our ability to learn (and also unlearn). Indeed one might claim that what makes humans so intelligent lies in our potential flexibility to think and act in an unprogrammed manner.

Evolutionary biologists stress that our intelligence is what sets us apart among organisms and that it is why natural selection acted to maximize the flexibility of our behavior. Our ability to face problems in an unprogrammed or we might say in a creative manner is a valuable tool. Imagine if we had genes selected for revenge, aggression, racism, and xenophobia rather than the flexibility to learn to generate revenge and aggression in appropriate situations and peacefulness and compassion in others.

We are learning animals. Our development occurs in the process of learning. Because one individual cannot learn for another, development cannot be done for, or imposed on, another individual. The only type of development that is possible is self- development. But it can be nurtured and facilitated by others (Ackoff, 2005).

Learning and Education

UNESCO is correct in stating that education is essential for development, but it is incorrect in assuming that education and schooling and that being taught and learning, are the same things. Progressive educators such as John Dewey, Paulo Freire, Jonathan Kozol, Ivan Illich, Maria Montessori, and Jean-Jacques Rousseau, among others, have pointed out that there are at least two types of education. Both types are needed for the study of the science of diversity. (For example, when teaching about the history of the science of diversity the first type, the banking method, may be helpful.)

One type, "the banking method" of education, considers students as vessels to be filled by teachers. The more completely the teachers fill the vessel, the better the teachers. The more submissively the vessels allow themselves to be filled, the better students they are. This type of education becomes an act

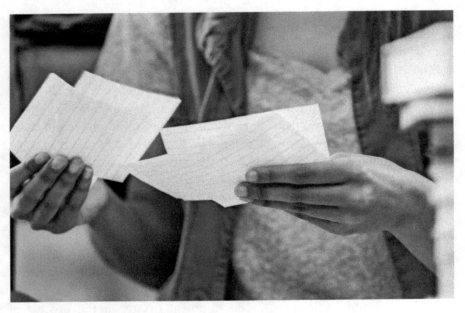

Figure 10.5 Student with notepads

of depositing. Instead of communicating, teachers make deposits and the students receive, memorize, and repeat information.

In the banking concept of education, knowledge is a thing given by those who consider themselves knowledgeable. Teachers are the epistemological authority in this system, and students' preexisting knowledge is ignored. This reinforces a lack of critical thinking, commitment, and knowledge ownership in students.

By contrast, the other type of education rejects the banking concept and replaces it with the idea of "problem-solving" education. Education, according to this method is "the participation of the individual in the social consciousness of the race" (Dewey, 1897, para. 1). As such, this method takes into account that the student is a social being. Knowledge is a social condition and students are helped to construct their own learning (Shermer, 2016). Since it is difficult to prepare students for a precise set of conditions, problem-solving education focuses on preparing students to have ready use of their judgments in social situations.

Problem-solving education consists in acts of cognition, not transferals of information. The problem-solving method does not dichotomize the activity of the teacher and student. Problem-solving education responds to the dialectic: people studying people. It exemplifies communication and self-reflection.

Figure 10.6 People putting together a puzzle

The students are no longer docile listeners. They are now critical co-investigators in dialogue with the teacher. The teacher presents the materials to the students for their evaluations, and re-evaluates his or her earlier evaluations as the students express their own. Problem-solving education responds to the essence of evaluations. It epitomizes the special characteristic of making evaluations: turning in on itself to reflect on one's own evaluations.

The dialogue that takes place is not a debate. Debates are won through a blend of persuading the opponent, proving one's view correct, and proving the opponent's view incorrect. Indeed, the calls for "national conversations" and town hall meetings to talk about race relations, or "personal biases" or discrimination generally end up being debates and politicized. Individuals get locked into positions they already have. People do more clashing and defending than discoursing. It fosters a debate society where thousands of national conversations are masked behind screen handles on Twitter. And few subjects start more online wars than race, bias, and discrimination (Weissmark, 2016, 2017, 2018, 2019, 2020).

What tends to go missing from national conversing is a facilitated dialogue using the dialectical method. This is the method used in problem-solving

Figure 10.7 Globe

Figure 10.8 Kids talking in a classroom

education. The dialogue that takes place in problem-posing education is the scientific dialectical method. It is a dialogue between students and teachers holding different points of view about a subject but wishing to understand the other and test the views. Personal views are the starting points of a working hypothesis. The outcome of such dialectic might be the refutation of a relevant view, or of a synthesis, or an integration of the opposing views, or a qualitative improvement of the dialogue.

During this dialogue, students are increasingly presented with hypotheses relating to themselves and others and will feel increasingly challenged and obliged to understand the scientific challenge. Because they understand the challenge as relevant to them and their lives, not just as a theoretical hypothesis, the resulting comprehension tends to be critical and meaningful. Their responses to the scientific challenge evoke new challenges, followed by new understandings; and gradually some students and teachers come to regard themselves as committed to authentic reflection.

Learning by Unlearning

Science advances, as do people, from refuting older ideas in the light of a different view about the nature of things and differences. This requires learning by unlearning. We do not learn by doing things right because we already know how to do them. What we get by so doing is validation of what we already know. This has value, but it is not learning.

We learn from our mistakes, by identifying them, determining their source, and correcting them. According to legend, Thomas Edison tried 999 times to invent the light bulb, before actually doing so on his 1,000th try. After Edison revealed his earth-shattering invention, a reporter asked, "Mr. Edison, how did it feel to fail 999 times?" As the story goes, Edison smiled and replied, "Young man, I have not failed 999 times. I have simply found 999 ways how not to create a light bulb."

"Unlearning is not about forgetting" (Boncheck, 2016, p. 1). It is about the ability to choose an alternative mental view, model, or paradigm. When we learn, we add new skills or knowledge to what we already know (Weissmark & Giacomo, 2008). When we unlearn, we step outside the mental model in order to choose a different one.

Darwin had to step outside the mental model that races were separate species to create the common-descent view. It takes unlearning to see the model as invalid or one possibility rather than canonical truth. The process of unlearning has several aspects.

First, we have to identify that the old mental model is no longer relevant or effective. This is a challenge because we are typically unconscious of our mental models. Our mental models are the familiar water to the fish. Also, we might be afraid to acknowledge that the existing model is growing outdated or is invalid. Letting go can seem like starting over and losing our sense of self and belonging to a community.

Second, we might need to find or create a new model that can better reflect our revised view. And third, we might need to instill the new mental model. This process is similar to creating a new behavioral habit. The tendency will be to fall back into the old way of thinking and therefore the old way of doing. But practicing unlearning makes it easier and quicker to make the changes as our brain adjusts. We can see this process at work in an experiment by Sandler and his "backwards bicycle." (Sandlin, 2015, https://www.youtube.com/watch?v=MFzDaBzBlL0&t=57s).

At the end of the video, you can see the unlearning process work. Is not a unilinear development of progress. One moment he cannot ride the backward bicycle and then the next moment he can and then the next moment he cannot. The process of unlearning is an inner journey that requires patience and tolerance for ourselves.

Sometimes our old views will be the right ones. But other times we might need to unlearn these views and replace them with new ones. Albert Einstein

Figure 10.9 Hand reaching for a key

said it effectively, "We cannot solve our problems with the same thinking we used when we created them."

If we desire a more peaceful earth, the place to start is with ourselves. We have much to learn about ourselves from the science of diversity. My message, as I trust I have conveyed it, is optimistic. I offer this book in the hope of further developing our human potential for the good of all human beings.

References

Aberson, C. L., Shoemaker, C., & Tomolillo, C. (2004). Implicit bias and contact: The role of interethnic friendships. *Journal of Social Psychology, 144*(3), 335–347.

Acevedo, B. P., Aron, A., Fisher, H. E., & Brown, L. L. (2012). Neural correlates of long-term intense romantic love. *Social Cognitive and Affective Neuroscience, 7*(2), 145–159. https://doi.org/10.1093/scan/nsq092

Adams, G., Biernat, M., Branscombe, N. R., Crandall, C. S., & Wrightsman, L. S. (2008). Beyond prejudice: Toward a sociocultural psychology of racism and oppression. In G. Adams, M. Biernat, N. R. Branscombe, C. S. Crandall, & L. S. Wrightsman (Eds.), *Commemorating Brown : The social psychology of racism and discrimination* (1st ed., pp. 215–246). Washington, DC: American Psychological Association.

Adamson, L. B., & Frick, J. E. (2003). The still face: a history of a shared experimental paradigm. *Infancy, 4*(4), 451–473.

Adorno, T. E. (1950). The authoritarian personality. New York, NY: Harper.

Ainsworth, M. S., & Bowlby, J. (1991). An ethological approach to personality development. *American Psychologist, 46*(4), 333–341.

Akande, A., & Lester, D. (1994). Suicidal preoccupation, depression and locus of control in Nigerians and Americans. *Personality and Individual Differences, 16*(6), 979.

Altemeyer, B. (1988). *Enemies of freedom: understanding right-wing authoritarianism.* San Francisco, CA: Jossey-Bass Publishers.

Altemeyer, B., & Hunsberger, B. (1992). Authoritarianism, religious fundamentalism, quest, and prejudice. *The International Journal for the Psychology of Religion, 2*(2), 113–133.

Alexander, P. C. (1992). Application of attachment theory to the study of sexual abuse. *Journal of Consulting and Clinical Psychology, 60*(2), 185–195.

Allport, G. W. (1954). *The nature of prejudice.* Cambridge, MA: Addison-Wesley.

Almada, L. F., Pereira, A., Jr., & Carrara-Augustenborg, C. (2013). What affective neuroscience means for science of consciousness. *Mens Sana Monographs, 11*(1), 253.

Aloise, P. A. (1993). Trait confirmation and disconfirmation: The development of attribution biases. *Journal of Experimental Child Psychology, 55*(2), 177–193.

Anderson, C. (1982). Inoculation and couterexplanation: debiasing techniques in the perseverance of social theories. *Social Cognition, 1*(2), 126–139.

Anderson, C. A., Lepper, M. R., & Ross, L. (1980). Perseverance of social theories: The role of explanation in the persistence of discredited information. *Journal of Personality and Social Psychology, 39*(6), 1037–1049.

Anderson, C. A., & Sechler, E. S. (1986). Effects of explanation and counterexplanation on the development and use of social theories. *Journal of Personality and Social Psychology, 50*(1), 24–34.

Anderson, P. (1991). Nation-states and national identity [Review of the book *The Identity of France. Vol. II: People and Production*, by Fernand Braudel, Translated by Sian Reynolds]. *London Review of Books, 13*(9), 3–8.

Anderson, S. W., Bechara, A., Damasio, H., Tranel, D., & Damasio, A. R. (1999). Impairment of social and moral behavior related to early damage in human prefrontal cortex. *Nature Neuroscience, 2*(11), 1032–1037.

Andersen, S. M., & Glassman, N. S. (1996). Responding to significant others when they are not there: effects on interpersonal inference, motivation, and affect. In R. M. Sorrentino & E. T. Higgins (Eds.), *Handbook of motivation and cognition, Vol. 3., The interpersonal context* (pp. 262–321). New York, NY: Guilford Press.

Arendt, H. (1964). *Eichmann in Jerusalem*. London, UK: Penguin.

Aristotle. (1981). *The politics* (T. J. Saunders, Rev., & T. A. Sinclair, Trans.). Harmondsworth, UK: Penguin Books.

Aristotle, Thomson, J. A. K. (1955). *The ethics of Aristotle: the nicomachean ethics*. Harmondsworth, England: Penguin Books.

Armstrong, J. A. (1982). *Nations before nationalism*. Chapel Hill: University of North Carolina Press.

Aron, A., Aron, E. N., & Smollan, D. (1992). Inclusion of Other in the Self Scale and the structure of interpersonal closeness. *Journal of Personality and Social Psychology, 63*(4), 596–612.

Aron, A., Fisher, H., Mashek, D. J., Strong, G., Li, H., & Brown, L. L. (2005). Reward, motivation, and emotion systems associated with early-stage intense romantic love. *Journal of Neurophysiology, 94*(1), 327–337.

Aronson, E., & Mills, J. (1959). The effect of severity of initiation on liking for a group. *Journal of Abnormal and Social Psychology, 59*(2), 177–181.

Asch, S. E. (1952). *Social psychology*. New York, NY: Prentice-Hall.

Ashton, M. C., Paunonen, S. V., Helmes, E., & Jackson, D. N. (1998). Kin altruism, reciprocal altruism, and the Big Five personality factors. *Evolution and Human Behavior, 19*(4), 243–255.

Auer, S. (2000). Nationalism in central Europe—A chance or a threat for the emerging liberal democratic order? *East European Politics and Societies, 14*(2), 213–245. https://doi.org/10.1177/0888325400014002001

Baker, M. J., & Swope, K. (2005). *Sharing, gift-giving, and optimal resource use incentives in hunter-gatherer society*. United States Naval Academy Working Paper, 8.

Baker, W. E., & Levine, S. S. (2013). Mechanisms of Generalized Exchange: Towards an Integrated Model. *SSRN Electronic Journal*. doi: 10.2139/ssrn.1352101

Bales, K. L., van Westerhuyzen, J. A., Lewis-Reese, A. D., Grotte, N. D., Lanter, J. A., & Carter, C. S. (2007). Oxytocin has dose-dependent developmental effects on pair-bonding and alloparental care in female prairie voles. *Hormones and Behavior, 52*(2), 274–279.

Bandura, A. (1979). The social learning perspective: Mechanisms of aggression. In H. Toch (Ed.), *Psychology of crime and criminal justice* (pp. 298–336). New York, NY: Holt, Rinehart, and Winston.

Bandura, A. (2016). The power of observational learning through social modeling. In R. J. Sternberg, S. T. Fiske, & D. J. Foss (Eds.), *Scientist making a difference: One hundred eminent behavioral and brain scientists talk about their most important contributions* (p. 33). New York, NY: Cambridge University Press.

Banaji, M. R., & Hardin, C. D. (1996). Automatic Stereotyping. *Psychological Science, 7*(3), 136–141.

Bar-Haim, Y., Ziv, T., Lamy, D., & Hodes, R. M. (2006). Nature and nurture in own-race face processing. *Psychological Science, 17*(2), 159–163.

Bargh, J. A. (1999). The cognitive monster: The case against the controllability of automatic stereotype effects. In S. Chaiken & Y. Trope (Eds.), *Dual-process theories in social psychology* (pp. 361–382). New York, NY: Guilford Press.

Barnett, R. C., & Hyde, J. S. (2001). Women, men, work, and family: An expansionist theory. *American Psychologist, 56*(10), 781.

Barrett, P. H., Gautrey, P. J., Herbert, S., Kohn, D., & Smith, S. (Eds.). (1987). *Charles Darwin's notebooks, 1836–1844: Geology, transmutation of species, metaphysical enquiries* (1st ed.). Cambridge, UK: Cambridge University Press.

Bar-Tal, D. (2000). From intractable conflict through conflict resolution to reconciliation: Psychological analysis. *Political Psychology, 21*(2), 351–365.

Bartels, A., & Zeki, S. (2000). The neural basis of romantic love. *NeuroReport, 11*(17), 3829–3834.

Bartels, A., & Zeki, S. (2004). The neural correlates of maternal and romantic love. *NeuroImage, 21*(3), 1155–1166. https://doi.org/10.1016/j.neuroimage.2003.11.003

Bates, C. (1995). Race, caste and tribe in central India: The early origins of Indian anthropometry. In P. Robb (Ed.), *The concept of race in South Asia* (pp. 219–259). India: Delhi.Oxford University Press. http://www.research.ed.ac.uk/portal/en/publications/race-caste-and-tribe-in-central-india-the-early-origins-of-indian-anthropometry(648413d8-c58e-4078-8629-3b500ccecdfc)/export.html

Bateson, G. (1972). *Steps to an ecology of mind: Collected essays in anthropology, psychiatry, evolution, and epistemology.* Chicago, IL: University of Chicago Press.

Baumeister, R. F., Bratslavsky, E., Finkenauer, C., & Vohs, K. D. (2001). Bad is stronger than good. *Review of General Psychology, 5*(4), 323370.

Baumeister, R. F., & Leary, M. R. (1995). The need to belong: Desire for interpersonal attachments as a fundamental human motivation. *Psychological Bulletin, 117*(3), 497–529.

Bean, R. B. (1906). Some racial peculiarities of the Negro brain. *American Journal of Anatomy, 5*(4), 353–432. https://doi.org/10.1002/aja.1000050402

Bean, R. B. (1913). The nose of the Jew and the quadratus labii superioris muscle. *Anatomical Record, 7*(2), 47–49. https://doi.org/10.1002/ar.1090070205

Benassi, V. A., Sweeney, P. D., & Dufour, C. L. (1988). Is there a relation between locus of control orientation and depression? *Journal of Abnormal Psychology, 97*(3), 357–367. https://doi.org/10.1037/0021-843X.97.3.357

Benoit, D., & Parker, K. C. (1994). Stability and transmission of attachment across three generations. *Child Development, 65*(5), 1444–1456.

Benson, M. (2016). *Lifestyle migration: Expectations, aspirations and experiences.* London, UK: Routledge.

Berndt, R. M., & Tonkinson, R. (2018). Australian aboriginal peoples. In Encyclopaedia Britannica. Retrieved from https://www.britannica.com/topic/Australian-Aborigine.

Bernier, F. (1684). *Memoirs read before the Anthropological Society.* London, UK: Trubner and Co. Retrieved May 18, 2017, from https://archive.org/stream/memoirsreadbefor01anth#page/356/mode/2up

Berntson, G. G., Boysen, S. T., & Cacioppo, J. T. (1993). Neurobehavioral organization and the cardinal principle of evaluative bivalence. *Annals of the New York Academy of Sciences, 702*(1), 75–102.

Berridge, K., & Winkielman, P. (2003). What is an unconscious emotion? (The case for unconscious "liking"). *Cognition and Emotion, 17*(2), 181–211.

Bhopal, R. (2007). The beautiful skull and Blumenbach's errors: The birth of the scientific concept of race. *BMJ : British Medical Journal, 335*(7633), 1308–1309. Retrieved from https://doi.org/10.1136/bmj.39413.463958.80

Bieneck, S., & Krahé, B. (2011). Blaming the victim and exonerating the perpetrator in cases of rape and robbery: Is there a double standard? *Journal of Interpersonal Violence, 26*(9), 1785–1797.

Bies, R. J., & Moag, J. F. (1986). Interactional justice: communication criteria of fairness. In R. J. Lewicki, B. H. Sheppard & M. H. Bazerman (Eds.), *Research on negotiations in organizations* (pp. 43–55). Greenwich, England: JAI Press.

Binder, J., Zagefka, H., Brown, R., Funke, F., Kessler, T., Mummendey, A., . . . Leyens, J. P. (2009). Does contact reduce prejudice or does prejudice reduce contact? A longitudinal test of the contact hypothesis among majority and minority groups in three European countries. *Journal of Personality and Social Psychology, 96*(4), 843–856.

Birnbaum, P. (1996). From multiculturalism to nationalism. *Political Theory, 24*(1), 33–45. https://doi.org/10.1177/0090591796024001003

Blum, L. (1980). "Compassion." In A. O. Rorty (Ed.), *Explaining emotions.* Berkeley: University of California Press.

Blumenbach, J. F., Bendyshe, T., Flourens, P., Hunter, J., Marx, K. F. H., & Wagner, R. (1865). *The anthropological treatises of Johann Friedrich Blumenbach.* London, UK: Publication for the Anthropological Society of London, by Longman, Green, Longman, Roberts, & Green. Retrieved from http://www.biodiversitylibrary.org/bibliography/50868

Blumenfeld, L. (2002). *Revenge: A story of hope.* New York, NY: Simon & Schuster.

Bodenhausen, G. V. (1988). Stereotypic biases in social decision making and memory: Testing process models of stereotype use. *Journal of Personality and Social Psychology, 55*(5), 726–737.

Bodenhausen, G. V., Kramer, G. P., & Susser, K. (1994). Happiness and stereotypic thinking in social judgement. *Journal of Personality and Social Psychology, 66*(4), 621–632.

Bodenhausen, G. V., & Macrae, C. N. (1998). *Advances in Social Cognition: Vol. 11. Stereotype activation and inhibition* (pp. 1–52). Retrieved from https://www.scholars.north-western.edu/en/publications/stereotype-activation-and-inhibition-advances-in-social-cognition

Boiten, F. A., Frijda, N. H., & Wientjes, C. J. (1994). Emotions and respiratory patterns: Review and critical analysis. *International Journal of Psychophysiology, 17*(2), 103–128.

Bowlby, J. (1977). The making and breaking of affectional bonds. *The British Journal of Psychiatry, 130*(1), 421–431.

Bonchek, M. (2016, November 3). *Why the problem with learning is unlearning.* Retrieved June 1, 2017, from https://hbr.org/2016/11/why-the-problem-with-learning-is-unlearning

Borgida, E., & Brekke, N. (1985). Psycholegal research on rape trials. In A. W. Burgess (Ed.), *Rape and Sexual Assault: A Research Handbook* (pp. 313–342). Garland Reference Library of Social Science, vol. 203. New York, NY: Garland.

Bornstein, M. (1984). A descriptive taxonomy of psychological categories used by infants. In C. Sophian & Carnegie-Mellon University (Eds.), *Origins of cognitive skills: The eighteenth annual Carnegie Symposium on Cognition* (pp. 313–338). Hillsdale, NJ: Erlbaum.

Borod, J. C., Haywood, C. S., & Koff, E. (1997). Neuropsychological aspects of facial asymmetry during emotional expression: A review of the normal adult literature. *Neuropsychology Review, 7*(1), 41–60.

Bothwell, R. K., Brigham, J. C., & Malpass, R. S. (1989). Cross-racial identification. *Personality and Social Psychology Bulletin, 15*(1), 19–25.

Bottomore, T., Frisby, D., & Simmel, G. (2004). *Philosophy of money.* London, UK: Routledge.

Bowlby, J. (1951). Maternal care and mental health. *Bulletin of the World Health Organization, 3*(3), 355–533.

Bowlby, J. (1977). The making and breaking of affectional bonds: II. Some principles of psycho-therapy; The fiftieth Maudsley Lecture. *British Journal of Psychiatry: The Journal of Mental Science, 130,* 421–431.

Bowlby, J. (1979). *The making and breaking of affectional bonds.* London, UK: Tavistock.

Bretherton, I. (1992). The origins of attachment theory: John Bowlby and Mary Ainsworth. *Developmental Psychology, 28*(5), 759–775.

Brewer, M. B. (1988). A dual process model of impression formation. In T. K. Srull & R. S. Wyer (Eds.), *A dual process model of impression formation* (pp. 1–36). Hillsdale, NJ: Erlbaum.

Brewer, M. B., & Caporael, L. R. (2006). An evolutionary perspective on social iden-tity: Revisiting groups. In M. Schaller & J. A. Simpson (Eds.), *Evolution and Social Psychology* (pp. 143–160). New York, NY: Psychology Press.

Brewer, M. B., & Miller, N. (1984). Beyond the contact hypothesis: Theoretical perspectives on desegregation. In N. Miller & M. B. Brewer (Eds.), *Groups in contact: The psychology of desegregation* (pp. 281–302). Orlando, FL: Academic Press.

Brown, S. L., & Brown, R. M. (2006). Selective investment theory: Recasting the functional significance of close relationships. *Psychological Inquiry, 17*, 1–29. doi: 10.1207/s15327965pli1701_01

Brubaker, W. R. (1990). Immigration, citizenship and the nation-state in France and Germany: A comparative historical analysis. *International Sociology, 5*(4), 379–407. Retrieved from https://doi.org/10.1177/026858090005004003

Bruce, V., & Young, A. (1986). Understanding face recognition. *British Journal of Psychology, 77*(3), 305–327.

Bruner, J. (1990). *Acts of meaning* (Jerusalem-Harvard lectures). Cambridge, MA: Harvard University Press.

Bruner, J. S. (1957). On perceptual readiness. *Psychological Review, 64*(2), 123–152. https://doi.org/10.1037/h0043805

Burnham, W. D., & Ferguson, T. (2014). Americans are sick to death of both parties: Why our politics is in worse shape than we thought. *AlterNet.* Retrieved from http://www.alternet.org/americans-are-sick-death-both-parties-why-our-politics-worse-shape-we-thought

Bushman, B. J., & Anderson, C. A. (2001). Is it time to pull the plug on hostile versus instrumental aggression dichotomy? *Psychological Review, 108*(1), 273–279.

Bushman, B. J., & Huesmann, L. R. (2010). Aggression. In S. T. Fiske, D. T. Gilbert & G. Lindzey (Eds.), *Handbook of social psychology.* Hoboken, NJ: John Wiley.

Bushnell, I. (2001). Mother's face recognition in newborn infants: Learning and memory. *Infant and Child Development, 10*(1–2), 67–74.

Bushnell, I., Sai, F., & Mullin, J. (1989). Neonatal recognition of the mother's face. *British Journal of Developmental Psychology, 7*(1), 3–15.

Buss, A. H. (1961). *The psychology of aggression.* New York, NY: Wiley.

Buss, D. M. (1994). *The evolution of desire: Strategies of human mating.* New York, NY: Basic Books.

Buss, D. (1995). Psychological sex differences: Origins through sexual selection. *American Psychologist, 50*(3), 164–168.

Buss, D. M. (2007). The evolution of human mating. *Acta Psychologica Sinica, 39*(3), 502–512.

Buss, D. M., Larsen, R. J., Westen, D., & Semmelroth, J. (1992). Sex differences in jealousy: Evolution, physiology, and psychology. *Psychological Science, 3*(4), 251–256.

Buss, D. M., Shackelford, T. K., Kirkpatrick, L. A., & Larsen, R. J. (2001). A half century of mate preferences: The cultural evolution of values. *Journal of Marriage and Family, 63*(2), 491–503.

Bussey, K., & Bandura, A. (1999). Social cognitive theory of gender development and differentiation. *Psychological Review, 106*(4), 676.

Cacioppo, J. T., & Berntson, G. G. (1994). Relationship between attitudes and evaluative space: A critical review, with emphasis on the separability of positive and negative substrates. *Psychological Bulletin, 115*(3), 401.

Cacioppo, J. T., Gardner, W. L., & Berntson, G. G. (1997). Beyond bipolar conceptualizations and measures: The case of attitudes and evaluative space. *Personality and Social Psychology Review, 1*(1), 3–25.

Calhoun, C. (1997). *Nationalism and the public sphere.* In J. A. Weintraub & K. Kumar (Eds.), *Public and private in thought and practice: Perspectives on a grand dichotomy.* Chicago, IL: University of Chicago Press.

Camus, A. (1957). Reflections on the guillotine. *Evergreen Review, 1*(3), 5.

Carli, L. L. (1989). Gender differences in interaction style and influence. *Journal of Personality and Social Psychology*, 56(4), 565–576.

Carli, L. L. (1999). Gender, interpersonal power, and social influence. *Journal of Social Issues*, 55(1), 81–99.

Carlson, Neil R., & Heth, C. Donald (2010). *Psychology: The Science of Behaviour*. Ontario: Pearson Education Canada. pp. 20–22.

Carroll, J. S., Nelson, D. A., Yorgason, J. B., Harper, J. M., Ashton, R. H., & Jensen, A. C. (2010). Relational aggression in marriage. *Aggressive Behavior*, 36(5), 315–329.

Carter, C. S. (1998). Neuroendocrine perspectives on social attachment and love. *Psychoneuroendocrinology*, 23(8), 779–818.

Caspi, A., McClay, J., Moffitt, T. E., Mill, J., Martin, J., Craig, I. W., . . . Poulton, R. (2002). Role of genotype in the cycle of violence in maltreated children. *Science*, 297(5582), 851–854.

Cassidy, J., & Shaver, P. R. (1999). *Handbook of attachment: Theory, research, and clinical*. New York, NY: Guildford Press.

Cauvin, J. (2000). *The birth of the Gods and the origins of agriculture*. Cambridge, UK: Cambridge University Press.

Chakravarti, A. (2015). Perspectives on human variation through the lens of diversity and race. *Cold Spring Harbor Perspectives in Biology*, 7(9), a023358. https://doi.org/10.1101/cshperspect.a023358

Champagne, F. A., Chretien, P., Stevenson, C. W., Zhang, T. Y., Gratton, A., & Meaney, M. J. (2004). Variations in nucleus accumbens dopamine associated with individual differences in maternal behavior in the rat. *Journal of Neuroscience*, 24(17), 4113–4123.

Champagne, F., Diorio, J., Sharma, S., & Meaney, M. J. (2001). Naturally occurring variations in maternal behavior in the rat are associated with differences in estrogen-inducible central oxytocin receptors. *Proceedings of the National Academy of Sciences*, 98(22), 12736–12741.

Chance, J. E., & Goldstein, A. G. (1996). The other-race effect and eyewitness identification. In S. L. Sporer, R. S. Malpass, & G. Koehnken (Eds.), *Psychological issues in eyewitness identification*. Mahwah, NJ: Erlbaum.

Chang, L., Wang, Y., Shackelford, T. K., & Buss, D. M. (2011). Chinese mate preferences: Cultural evolution and continuity across a quarter of a century. *Personality and Individual Differences*, 50(5), 678–683.

Cheng, C., Cheung, S., Chio, J. H., & Chan, M. S., & Stephen, P (2013). Cultural meaning of perceived control: A meta-analysis of locus of control and psychological symptoms across 18 cultural regions. *Psychological Bulletin*, 139(1), 152–188.

Chiaburu, D. S., Thundiyil, T., & Wang, J. (2014). Alienation and its correlates: A meta-analysis. *European Management Journal*, 32(1), 24–36.

Childe, V. G. (1950). The urban revolution. *Town Planning Review*, 21(1), 3–17.

Chomsky, N., & Trivers, R. (2006, August 31). Robert Trivers and Noam Chomsky [Video File]. Retrieved from https://www.youtube.com/watch?v=WJe5UmBlxdE

Christie, D. J., & Louis, W. R. (2012). Peace interventions tailored to phases within a cycle of intergroup violence. In L. R. Tripp (Ed.), *The Oxford handbook of intergroup conflict*. (pp. 252–269) New York, NY: Oxford University Press.

Clark, A. (1998). Being there: Putting mind, world, and body back together. Cambridge, MA: MIT Press.

Clark, A. (2008). *Supersizing the mind: Embodiment, action, and cognitive extension*. New York, NY: Oxford University Press.

Clark, D. A. (2005). Focus on "cognition" in cognitive behavior therapy for OCD: Is it really necessary? *Cognitive Behaviour Therapy*, 34(3), 131–139.

Cohen, A. (2016). *Imbeciles: The Supreme Court, American eugenics, and the sterilization of Carrie Buck*. New York, NY: Penguin Press.

Cohn, J. F., & Tronick, E. Z. (1988). Discrete versus scaling approaches to the description of mother-infant face-to-face interaction: convergent validity and divergent applications. *Developmental Psychology, 24*(3), 396–397.

Cole, P. M., Teti, L. O., & Zahn-Waxler, C. (2003). Mutual emotion regulation and the stability of conduct problems between preschool and early school age. *Development and Psychopathology, 15*(1), 1–18.

Compassion [Def. 1]. (n.d.). English Oxford Living Dictionaries. In Oxford Dictionaries.

Connelly, M., Malato, D., Tompson, T., & Benz, J. (2017). *The American identity: Points of pride, conflicting views, and a distinct culture.* Retrieved from http://apnorc.org/PDFs/American%20Identity/APNORC_American_Identity_2017.pdf

Conroy-Beam, D., Buss, D. M., Pham, M. N., & Shackelford, T. K. (2015). How sexually dimorphic are human mate preferences? *Personality and Social Psychology Bulletin, 41*(8), 1082–1093.

Cooper, J. (1999). Unwanted consequences and the self: In search of the motivation for dissonance reduction. In E. Harmon-Jones & J. Mills (Eds.), *Cognitive dissonance: Progress on a pivotal theory in social psychology* (pp. 149–173). Washington, DC: American Psychological Association.

Cooper, J. (2007). *Cognitive dissonance: 50 years of a classic theory.* London, UK: SAGE.

Corneille, O., Huart, J., Becquart, E., & Brédart, S. (2004). When memory shifts toward more typical category exemplars: Accentuation effects in the recollection of ethnically ambiguous faces. *Journal of Personality and Social Psychology, 86*(2), 236–250.

Corneille, O., Klein, O., Lambert, S., & Judd, C. M. (2002). On the role of familiarity with units of measurement in categorical accentuation: Tajfel and Wilkes (1963) revisited and replicated. *Psychological Science, 13*(4), 380–383.

Cox, L., & Wood, S. (2017). "Got him": Revenge, emotions, and the killing of Osama bin Laden. *Review of International Studies, 43*(1), 112–129.

Craig, A. D., & Craig, A. (2009). How do you feel—now? The anterior insula and human awareness. *Nature Reviews Neuroscience, 10*(1), 59–70.

Crandall, C. S., Eshleman, A., & O'Brien, L. (2002). Social norms and the expression and suppression of prejudice: The struggle for internalization. *Journal of Personality and Social Psychology, 82*(3), 359–378.

Cropanzano, R., & Greenberg, J. (1997). Progress in Organizational Justice: Tunneling through the Maze. In: C. L. Cooper & I. T. Robertson (Eds.), *International Review of Industrial and Organizational Psychology* (Vol. 12, pp. 317–372). John Wiley & Sons, New York.

Cummings, V., Jordan, P., & Zvelebil, M. (2014). *The Oxford handbook of the archaeology and anthropology of hunter-gatherers.* Oxford, UK: Oxford University Press.

Curie, M., Kellogg, C., & Kellogg, V. L. (1923). *Pierre Curie.* New York: Macmillan Co.

Daly, M., Wilson, M. (1983). *Sex, evolution and behavior.* San Francisco, CA: Wadsworth Publishing.

Damasio, A. R. (1994). *Descartes' error: Emotion, reason and the human brain.* New York, NY: Putnam.

Damasio, A. R. (2000). A second chance for emotion. In R. Lane & L. Nadel (Eds.), *Cognitive neuroscience of emotion* (pp. 12–23). New York, NY: Oxford University Press.

Darby, B. W., & Schlenker, B. R. (1982). Children's reactions to apologies. *Journal of Personality and Social Psychology, 43*(4), 742–753.

Darley, J. M., & Gross, P. H. (1983). A hypothesis-confirming bias in labeling effects. *Journal of Personality and Social Psychology, 44*(1), 20–33.

Darwin, C. (1859). *On the origin of species by means of natural selection, or, the preservation of favoured races in the struggle for life.* London, UK: J. Murray.

Darwin, C. (1871). *The descent of man, and selection in relation to sex.* London, UK: J. Murray.

Davidson, R. J., & Sutton, S. K. (1995). Affective neuroscience: The emergence of a discipline. *Current Opinion in Neurobiology, 5*(2), 217–224.

Davies, K., & Aron, A. (2016). Friendship Development and Intergroup Attitudes: The role of interpersonal and intergroup friendship processes. *Journal of Social Issues, 72*(3), 489–510.

Davies, K., Tropp, L. R., Aron, A., Pettigrew, T. F., & Wright, S. C. (2011). Cross-group friendships and intergroup attitudes: A meta-analytic review. *Personality and Social Psychology Review, 15*(4), 332–351.

Davies, M. F. (1997). Belief persistence after evidential discrediting: The impact of generated versus provided explanations on the likelihood of discredited outcomes. *Journal of Experimental Social Psychology, 33*(6), 561–578.

Davis, K. E., & Jones, E. E. (1960). Changes in interpersonal perception as a means of reducing cognitive dissonance. *Journal of Abnormal and Social Psychology, 61*(3), 402–410.

Dawkins, M. S. (1989). Time budgets in Red Junglefowl as a baseline for the assessment of welfare in domestic fowl. *Applied Animal Behaviour Science, 24*(1), 77–80.

Dawkins, R. (1976). Hierarchical organisation: A candidate principle for ethology. In P. P. G. Bateson & R. A. Hinde (Eds.), *Growing points in ethology* (pp. 7–54). Cambridge, UK: Cambridge University Press.

Dawkins, R. (1982). Replicators and vehicles. In *Current problems in sociobiology* (pp. 45–64). New York, NY: Cambridge University Press.

Dawkins, R. (1986). *The blind watchmaker: Why the evidence of evolution reveals a universe without design.* New York, NY: Norton.

Dean, D. G. (1961). Alienation: Its meaning and measurement. *American Sociological Review, 26*(5), 753–758.

Decasper, A. J., & Spence, M. J. (1986). Prenatal maternal speech influences newborns' perception of speech sounds. *Infant Behavior and Development, 9*(2), 133–150.

Decasper, A. J., & Fifer, W. P. (1980). Of human bonding: newborns prefer their mothers' voices. *Science, 208*(4448), 1174–1176.

Deci, E. L., & Ryan, R. M. (2000). The "what" and "why" of goal pursuits: Human needs and the self-determination of behavior. *Psychological Inquiry, 11*(4), 227–268.

De Jaegher, H., & Di Paolo, E. (2007). Participatory sense-making. *Phenomenology and the Cognitive Sciences, 6*(4), 485–507.

Denham, S. A. (1993). Maternal emotional responsiveness and toddlers' social-emotional competence. *Journal of Child Psychology and Psychiatry, and Allied Disciplines, 34*(5), 715–728.

Denke, C., Rotte, M., Heinze, H.-J., & Schaefer, M. (2014). Belief in a just world is associated with activity in insula and somatosensory cortices as a response to the perception of norm violations. *Social Neuroscience, 9*(5), 514–521.

Dennett, D. C. (1995). Darwin's dangerous idea. *Sciences, 35*(3), 34–40.

Dershowitz, A. M. (2000). *Just revenge.* New York, NY: Grand Central Publishing.

Desmond, A., & Moore, J. (1991). *Darwin: The life of a tormented evolutionist.* New York, NY: Norton.

Desmond, A., & Moore, J. (2009). *Darwin's sacred cause: Race, slavery and the quest for human origins.* London, UK: Penguin.

DeSteno, D., Bartlett, M. Y., Braverman, J., & Salovey, P. (2002). Sex differences in jealousy: Evolutionary mechanism or artifact of measurement? *Journal of Personality and Social Psychology, 83*(5), 1103–1116.

Devine, P. G. (1989). Stereotypes and prejudice: Their automatic and controlled components. *Journal of Personality and Social Psychology, 56*(1), 5.

Dewey, J. (1897). My pedagogic creed. *The School Journal, 54*, 77–80.

De Waal, F. B. M. (1989). *Peacemaking among primates.* Cambridge, MA: Harvard University Press.

De Waal, F. (1989). *Chimpanzee politics: Power and sex among apes.* Baltimore, MD: John Hopkins University Press.

De Waal, F. B. (1989). Food sharing and reciprocal obligations among chimpanzees. *Journal of Human Evolution, 18*(5), 433–459.

De Waal, F. B. (1996). *Good natured: The origins of right and wrong in humans and other animals.* Cambridge, MA: Harvard University Press.

Di Paolo, E. A., Rohde, M., & De Jaegher, H. (2010). Horizons for the enactive mind: values, social interaction, and play. In *Enaction: toward a new paradigm for cognitive science* (pp. 33–87). Cambridge, MA: MIT Press.

Diamond, G., Russon, J., & Levy, S. (2016). Attachment-based family therapy: A review of the empirical support. *Family Process, 55*(3), 595–610.

Dijken, S. V. (1998). *John Bowlby: His early life; A biographical journey into the roots of attachment therapy.* London, UK: Free Association Books.

Dimberg, U., & Öhman, A. (1996). Behold the wrath: Psychophysiological responses to facial stimuli. *Motivation and Emotion, 20*(2), 149–182.

Di Paolo, E., & De Jaegher, H. (2012). The interactive brain hypothesis. *Frontiers in Human Neuroscience, 6,* 163.

Dovidio, J. F., Evans, N., & Tyler, R. B. (1986). Racial stereotypes: The contents of their cognitive representations. *Journal of Experimental Social Psychology, 22*(1), 22–37.

Dovidio, J. F., & Gaertner, S. L. (2000). Aversive racism and selection decisions: 1989 and 1999. *Psychological Science, 11*(4), 315–319.

Dovidio, J. F., Gaertner, S. L., & Saguy, T. (2009). Commonality and the complexity of "we": Social attitudes and social change. *Personality and Social Psychology Review, 13*(1), 3–20.

Dovidio, J. F., Glick, P. E., & Rudman, L. A. (2005). *On the nature of prejudice: Fifty years after Allport.* Malden, MA: Blackwell.

Dovidio, J. F., Hewstone, M., Glick, P., & Esses, V. M. (2010). Prejudice, stereotyping and discrimination: Theoretical and empirical overview. In *The SAGE handbook of prejudice, stereotyping and discrimination* (pp. 3–29). London, UK: SAGE.

Dubois, N. (2010). Theory of the social value of persons applied to organizations: Typologies of "good" leaders and recruitment. *Revue Européenne de Psychologie Appliquée/European Review of Applied Psychology, 60*(4), 255–266.

Duchaine, B., Cosmides, L., & Tooby, J. (2001). Evolutionary psychology and the brain. *Current Opinion in Neurobiology, 11*(2), 225–230.

Dumas, G., Nadel, J., Soussignan, R., Martinerie, J., & Garnero, L. (2010). Inter-brain synchronization during social interaction. *PloS One, 5*(8), e12166.

Dumas, J. E., LaFreniere, P. J., & Serketich, W. J. (1995). "Balance of power": A transactional analysis of control in mother-child dyads involving socially competent, aggressive, and anxious children. *Journal of Abnormal Psychology, 104*(1), 104–113.

Durkheim, E. (1951). *Suicide: A study in sociology.* Glencoe, IL: Free Press.

Durkheim, E., & Schmidts, L. (1984). *Die elementaren Formen des religiösen Lebens.* Frankfurt am Main, Germany: Suhrkamp.

Edwards, K., & Smith, E. E. (1996). A disconfirmation bias in the evaluation of arguments. *Journal of Personality and Social Psychology, 71*(1), 5–24.

Egan, L. C., Santos, L. R., & Bloom, P. (2007). The origins of cognitive dissonance. *Psychological Science, 18*(11), 978–983.

Ehrlich, P., &Feldman, M. (2003). Genes and cultures: What creates our behavioral phenome? *Current Anthropology, 44*(1), 87–107.

Ehrlich, P. R., & Levin, S. A. (2005). The evolution of norms. *PLoS Biology, 3*(6), e194.

Einstein, A. (2010). *Ideas And Opinions.* Broadway Books.

Eklund, A., Nichols, T. E., & Knutsson, H. (2016). Cluster failure: Why fMRI inferences for spatial extent have inflated false-positive rates. *Proceedings of the National Academy of Sciences, 113*(28), 7900–7905.

Eller, A., & Abrams, D. (2004). Come together: Longitudinal comparisons of Pettigrew's reformulated intergroup contact model and the common ingroup identity model in Anglo-French and Mexican-American contexts. *European Journal of Social Psychology, 34*(3), 229–256.

Enzi, B., De Greck, M., Prösch, U., Tempelmann, C., & Northoff, G. (2009). Is our self nothing but reward? Neuronal overlap and distinction between reward and personal relevance and its relation to human personality. *PLoS One, 4*(12), e8429.

Erikson, E. (1963). *Children and society.* (35th anniversary ed.). New York, NY: Norton.

Erikson, E. (1968). *Youth: Identity and crisis.* (1st ed.) New York, NY: Norton.

Erikson, E. H. (1950). Growth and crises of the "healthy personality." In C. Kluckhohn & H. A. Murray (Eds.), *Personality in nature, society, and culture* (1st ed.) . New York, NY: Knopf.

Erikson, E. H. (1964). Identity and uprootedness in our time. In *Insight and Responsibility: Lectures on the ethical implications of psychoanalytic insight* (1st. ed., pp. 81–107). New York, NY: Norton.

Erikson, E. H. (1970). Autobiographic notes on the identity crisis. *Daedalus, 99*(4), 730–759.

Esses, V. M., Haddock, G., & Zanna, M. P. (1993). Values, stereotypes, and emotions as determinants of intergroup attitudes. In D. Mackie & D. L. Hamilton (Eds.), *Affect, cognition and stereotyping: Interactive processes in group perception* (pp. 137–166). San Diego, CA: Academic Press.

European Union, Directorate-General for Communication. (2015). *Flash Eurobarometer 423: Citizens' awareness and perceptions of EU regional policy.* https://data.europa.eu/euodp/en/data/dataset/S2055_423_ENG

Fantz, R. L. (1963). Pattern vision in newborn infants. *Science (New York, N.Y.), 140*(3564), 296–297.

Fehr, E., & Gächter, S. (2001). *Do incentive contracts crowd out voluntary cooperation?* London, UK: Centre for Economic Policy Research.

Feldman, R., Weller, A., Zagoory-Sharon, O., & Levine, A. (2007). Evidence for a neuroendocrinological foundation of human affiliation: Plasma oxytocin levels across pregnancy and the postpartum period predict mother-infant bonding. *Psychological Science, 18*(11), 965–970. Retrieved from https://doi.org/10.1111/j.1467-9280.2007.02010.x

Ferguson, J. N., Young, L. J., Hearn, E. F., Matzuk, M. M., Insel, T. R., & Winslow, J. T. (2000). Social amnesia in mice lacking the oxytocin gene. *Nature Genetics, 25*(3), 284–287.

Ferrari, G. A., Nicolini, Y., Demuru, E., Tosato, C., Hussain, M., Scesa, E., . . . Ferrari, P. F. (2016). Ultrasonographic investigation of human fetus responses to maternal communicative and non- communicative stimuli. *Frontiers in Psychology, 7.* Retrieved from https://doi.org/10.3389/fpsyg.2016.00354

Ferris, C. F., Kulkarni, P., Sullivan, J. M., Harder, J. A., Messenger, T. L., & Febo, M. (2005). Pup suckling is more rewarding than cocaine: evidence from functional magnetic resonance imaging and three-dimensional computational analysis. *Journal of Neuroscience, 25*(1), 149–156.

Ferry, F., Bunting, B., Murphy, S., O'Neill, S., Stein, D., & Koenen, K. (2014). Traumatic events and their relative PTSD burden in Northern Ireland: A consideration of the impact of the "Troubles." *Social Psychiatry and Psychiatric Epidemiology, 49*(3), 435–446.

Feshbach, S. (1964). The function of aggression and the regulation of aggressive drive. *Psychological Review, 71*(4), 257–272.

Festinger, L. (1957). *A theory of cognitive dissonance*. Evanston, IL: Row, Peterson.

Festinger, L., & Carlsmith, J. M. (1959). Cognitive consequences of forced compliance. *Journal of Abnormal and Social Psychology, 58*(2), 203–210.

Feynman, R. (1966, April). What is Science? *National Science Teachers Association*. New York City. Retrieved from http://www.feynman.com/science/what-is-science/

Feynman, R. P. (1999). *The Pleasure of Finding Things Out*. Cambridge, MA: Perseus.

Field, T., Healy, B. T., Goldstein, S., & Guthertz, M. (1990). Behavior-state matching and synchrony in mother-infant interactions of nondepressed versus depressed dyads. *Developmental Psychology, 26*(1), 7–14. https://doi.org/10.1037/0012-1649.26.1.7

Field, T., & Fogel, A. (1982). *Emotion and Early Interaction*. Hillsdale, NJ: Lawrence Erlbaum Associates Publishers.

Field, T. M., Cohen, D., Garcia, R., & Greenberg, R. (1984). Mother-stranger face discrimination by the newborn. *Infant Behavior and Development, 7*(1), 19–25.

Fifer, W. P., Monti, L. M., Myers, M. M., & Yongue, B. G. (1987). Autonomic response to mother's voice in newborns. *Pediatric Research, 21*(4), 181A–181A.

Fifer, W. P., & Moon, C. (1989). Psychobiology of newborn auditory preferences. *Seminars in Perinatology, 13*(5), 430–433.

Fifer, W. P., & Moon, C. M. (1995). The effects of fetal experience with sound. In *Fetal Development, A Psychobiological Perspective* (pp. 351–366). Hillsdale, NJ: Lawrence Erlbaum Associates Publishers.

Figley, C. R. (1985). *Trauma and its wake: Vol. 1*. New York, NY: Brunner/Mazel.

Fisher, H., Aron, A., & Brown, L. L. (2005). Romantic love: An fMRI study of a neural mechanism for mate choice. *Journal of Comparative Neurology, 493*(1), 58–62.

Fisher, H. E. (1992). *Anatomy of love: The natural history of monogamy, adultery, and divorce*. New York, NY: Norton.

Fiske, S. T. (1989). Examining the role of intent: toward understanding its role in stereotyping and prejudice. In J. S. Uleman & J. A. Bargh (Eds.), *Unintended thought* (pp. 253–283). New York, NY: Guilford Press.

Fiske, S. T. (1998). Stereotyping, prejudice, and discrimination. In D. T. Gilbert, S. T. Fiske & G. Lindzey (Eds.), *Handbook of social psychology* (p. 366). New York, NY: McGraw-Hill.

Fiske, S. T. (2000). Stereotyping, prejudice, and discrimination at the seam between the centuries: Evolution, culture, mind, and brain. *European Journal of Social Psychology, 30*(3), 299–322.

Fiske, S. T., & Neuberg, S. L. (1990). A continuum of impression formation, from category-based to individuating processes: Influences of information and motivation on attention and interpretation. *Advances in Experimental Social Psychology, 23*(C), 1–74. https://doi.org/10.1016/S0065-2601(08)60317-2

Fogel, A. (1993). *Developing through relationships*. New York, NY: Harvester Wheatsheaf.

Frankl, V. E. (1963). *Man's search for meaning: An introduction to logotherapy*. Boston, MA: Beacon Press.

Freud, S. (1950). Totem and taboo: Some points of agreement between the mental lives of savages and neurotics (J. Strachey, Trans.). London, UK: Routledge & K. Paul.

Freud, S. (1961). The ego and the id. In J. Strachey (Ed. and Trans.), *The standard edition of the complete psychological works of Sigmund Freud* (Vol. 19, pp. 3–66). London, UK: Hogarth Press. (Original work published 1923.)

Fromm, E. (1941). *Escape from freedom*. New York, NY: Holt, Rinehart & Winston of Canada Limited.

Fromm, E. (1955). The present human condition. *The American Scholar, 25*(1), 29–35.

Fuchs, T., & De Jaegher, H. (2009). Enactive intersubjectivity: Participatory sense-making and mutual incorporation. *Phenomenology and the Cognitive Sciences, 8*(4), 465–486.

Furnham, A. (2003). Belief in a just world: Research progress over the past decade. *Personality and Individual Differences, 34*(5), 795–817.

Furnham, A., & Gunter, B. (1984). Just world beliefs and attitudes towards the poor. *British Journal of Social Psychology, 23*(3), 265–269.

Furnham, A., & Procter, E. (1989). Belief in a just world: Review and critique of the individual difference literature. *British Journal of Social Psychology, 28*(4), 365–384.

Gaertner, S. L., Dovidio, J. F., & Bachman, B. A. (1996). Revisiting the contact hypothesis: The induction of a common ingroup identity. *International Journal of Intercultural Relations, 20*(3), 271–290.

Gaertner, S. L., Mann, J., Murrell, A., & Dovidio, J. F. (1989). Reducing intergroup bias: The benefits of recategorization. *Journal of Personality and Social Psychology, 57*(2), 239–249.

Galton, F. (1883). *Inquiries into human faculty and its development.* London: Macmillan.

Ganzach, Y. (1995). Attribute scatter and decision outcome: Judgment versus choice. *Organizational Behavior and Human Decision Processes, 62*(1), 113–122.

Geary, D. C. (1998). *Male, female: The evolution of human sex differences* (2nd ed.). Washington, DC: American Psychological Association.

Geary, D. C., Rumsey, M., Bow-Thomas, C. C., & Hoard, M. K. (1995). Sexual jealousy as a facultative trait: Evidence from the pattern of sex differences in adults from China and the United States. *Ethology and Sociobiology, 16*(5), 355–383.

Geertz, C. (1973). *The interpretation of cultures: Selected essays.* New York: Basic Books.

Gellner, E. (1983). *Nations and nationalism.* Ithaca, NY: Cornell University Press.

Gervais, W. M., & Norenzayan, A. (2012). Analytic thinking promotes religious disbelief. *Science (New York: NY), 336*(6080), 493–496.

Gianino, A., & Tronick, E. Z. (1988). The mutual regulation model: the infant's self and interactive regulation and coping and defensive capacities. In *Stress and coping across development* (p. 264). Hillsdale, NJ: Erlbaum.

Gibbs, N., & Duffy, M. (2007). *The preacher and the presidents: Billy Graham in the White House* (1st ed.). New York, NY: Center Street.

Gilbert, D. T., & Hixon, J. G. (1991). The trouble of thinking: Activation and application of stereotypic beliefs. *Journal of Personality and Social Psychology, 60*(4), 509–517. https://doi.org/10.1037/0022-3514.60.4.509

Glass, D. C. (1964). Changes in liking as a means of reducing cognitive discrepancies between self-esteem and aggression. *Journal of Personality, 32*(4), 531–549.

Golby, A. J., Gabrieli, J. D., Chiao, J. Y., & Eberhardt, J. L. (2001). Differential responses in the fusiform region to same-race and other-race faces. *Nature Neuroscience, 4*(8), 845.

Gollan, T., & Witte, E. H. (2008). "It was right to do it, because . . . ": Understanding justifications of actions as prescriptive attributions. *Social Psychology, 39*(3), 189–196.

González, R., & Brown, R. (2003). Generalization of positive attitude as a function of subgroup and superordinate group identifications in intergroup contact. *European Journal of Social Psychology, 33*(2), 195–214.

Goodall, J. (1979). Intercommunity interactions in the chimpanzee population of the Gombe National Park. In D. Hamburg, E. R. McCown, & Society for the Study of Human Evolution (Eds.), *The great apes* (pp. 13–53). Menlo Park, CA: Benjamin/Cummins.

Gordon Childe, V. (1936). *Man makes himself.* London, UK: Watts.

Goren, C. C., Sarty, M., & Wu, P. Y. (1975). Visual following and pattern discrimination of face-like stimuli by newborn infants. *Pediatrics, 56*(4), 544–549.

Gould, S. J. (2007). *The richness of life: The essential Stephen Jay Gould* (S. Rose, Ed.). New York, NY: Norton.

Gove, P. B. (Ed.). (1981). *Webster's third new international dictionary of the English language, unabridged.* Springfield, MA: Merriam-Webster.

Granier-Deferre, C., Ribeiro, A., Jacquet, A.-Y., & Bassereau, S. (2011). Near-term fetuses process temporal features of speech. *Developmental Science, 14*(2), 336–352.

Green, W. J. (2000). Left liberalism and race in the evolution of Colombian popular national identity. *The Americas, 57*(1), 95–124.

Greenfeld, L., & Chirot, D. (1994). Nationalism and aggression. *Theory and Society, 23*(1), 79–130.

Greenwald, A. G., & Banaji, M. R. (1995). Implicit social cognition: Attitudes, self-esteem, and stereotypes. *Psychological Review, 102*(1), 4.

Greenwald, A. G., McGhee, D. E., & Schwartz, J. L. (1998). Measuring individual differences in implicit cognition: The implicit association test. *Journal of Personality and Social Psychology, 74*(6), 1464.

Greenwald, A. G., Poehlman, T. A., Uhlmann, E. L., & Banaji, M. R. (2009). Understanding and using the Implicit Association Test: III. Meta-analysis of predictive validity. *Journal of Personality and Social Psychology, 97*(1), 17–41.

Hafer, C. L., & Bègue, L. (2005). Experimental research on just-world theory: Problems, developments, and future challenges. *Psychological Bulletin, 131*(1), 128–167.

Haggbloom, S. J., Warnick, R., Warnick, J. E., Jones, V. K., Yarbrough, G. L., . . . Monte, E. (2002). The 100 most eminent psychologists of the 20th century. *Review of General Psychology, 6*(2), 139–152.

Haidt, J. (2010). Moral psychology must not be based on faith and hope: Commentary on Narvaez (2010). *Perspectives on Psychological Science, 5*(2), 182–184.

Haller, J. S. (1970). Concepts of race inferiority in nineteenth-century anthropology. *Journal of the History of Medicine and Allied Sciences, 25*(1), 40–51. https://doi.org/10.1093/jhmas/XXV.1.40

Hamilton, D. L., & Sherman, J. W. (1994). Stereotypes. In R. S. Wyer & T. K. Srull (Eds.), *Handbook of social cognition, second edition: Volume 2: Applications* (pp. 1–36). New York, NY: Erlbaum Associates.

Hampshire, S. (2000). *Justice is conflict* (Vol. 5). Princeton, NJ: Princeton University Press.

Han, K. J. (2013). Income inequality, international migration, and national pride: A test of social identification theory. *International Journal of Public Opinion Research, 25*(4), 502–521.

Harlow, H. F. (1958). The nature of love. *American Psychologist, 13*(12), 673.

Harlow, H. F. (1961). The development of affectional patterns in infant monkeys. In B. M. Foss (Ed.), *Determinants of infant behaviour* (pp. 75–88). Wiley.

Harlow, H., & Zimmermann, R. (1958). The development of affectional responses in infant monkeys. *Proceedings of the American Philosophical Society, 102*(5), 501–509.

Harlow, H. F., & Mears, C. (1979). *The human model: Primate perspectives*. Washington, DC: V. H. Winston.

Harris, C. R. (2000). Psychophysiological response to imagined infidelity: The specific innate modular view of jealousy reconsidered. *Journal of Personality and Social Psychology, 78*(6), 1082–1091.

Hart, J., Nailling, E., Bizer, G. Y., & Collins, C. K. (2015). Attachment theory as a framework for explaining engagement with Facebook. *Personality and Individual Differences, 77*, 33–40. https://doi.org/10.1016/j.paid.2014.12.016

Hart, W., Albarracín, D., Eagly, A. H., Brechan, I., Lindberg, M. J., & Merrill, L. (2009). Feeling validated versus being correct: A meta-analysis of selective exposure to information. *Psychological Bulletin, 135*(4), 555–588.

Hartup, W. W. (1974). Aggression in childhood: Developmental perspectives. *American Psychologist, 29*(5), 336.

Haselhuhn, M. P., & Mellers, B. A. (2005). Emotions and cooperation in economic games. *Cognitive Brain Research, 23*(1), 24–33.

Hastings, A. (1997). *The construction of nationhood: Ethnicity, religion and nationalism.* Cambridge, UK: Cambridge University Press.

Hazan, C., & Diamond, L. M. (2000). The place of attachment in human mating. *Review of General Psychology*, 4(2), 186–204. Retrieved from https://doi.org/10.1037/1089-2680.4.2.186

Hazan, C., & Shaver, P. (1987). Romantic love conceptualized as an attachment process. *Journal of Personality and Social Psychology*, 52(3), 511–524.

Hazan, C., & Shaver, P. R. (1994). Attachment as an organizational framework for research on close relationships. *Psychological Inquiry*, 5(1), 1–22.

Hearn, J. (2006). *Rethinking nationalism: A critical introduction.* Basingstoke, UK: Palgrave Macmillan.

Heider, F. (1958). *The psychology of interpersonal relations.* New York, NY: Wiley.

Helmreich, W. (1992). *Against all odds: Holocaust survivors and the successful lives they made in America.* New York, NY: Simon & Schuster.

Henrich, J. (2009). The evolution of costly displays, cooperation and religion: Credibility enhancing displays and their implications for cultural evolution. *Evolution and Human Behavior*, 30(4), 244–260.

Henrich, J., & Gil-White, F. J. (2001). The evolution of prestige: Freely conferred deference as a mechanism for enhancing the benefits of cultural transmission. *Evolution and Human Behavior*, 22(3), 165–196.

Heradstveit, D. (1979). *The Arab-Israeli conflict: Psychological obstacles to peace.* Oslo, Norway: Universitetsforlaget.

Hetherington, M. J., & Weiler, J. D. (2009). *Authoritarianism and Polarization in American Politics.* New York, NY: Cambridge University Press.

Hippocrates, A. (400AD, Originally written). *On airs, waters, and places.* Retrieved May 18, 2017, from http://classics.mit.edu/Hippocrates/airwatpl.mb.txt

Hirt, E. R., & Markman, K. D. (1995). Multiple explanation: A consider-an-alternative strategy for debiasing judgments. *Journal of Personality and Social Psychology*, 69(6), 1069–1086.

Hjerm, M. (1998). National identities, national pride and xenophobia: A comparison of four western countries. *Acta Sociologica*, 41(4), 335–347. Retrieved from https://doi.org/10.1177/000169939804100403

Hobsbawm, E. (1992). *Nations and nationalism since 1870: Programme, myth, reality* [Book Review]. *Ibero-Americana Pragensia*, 26, 323.

Hochschild, A. R. (2016). *Strangers in their own land: Anger and mourning on the American Right.* New York, NY: The New Press.

Hoffman, E. (2008). Abraham Maslow: A biographer's reflections. *Journal of Humanistic Psychology*, 48(4), 439–443. Retrieved from https://doi.org/10.1177/0022167808320534

Hogg, M. A., & Williams, K. D. (2000). From I to we: Social identity and the collective self. *Group Dynamics: Theory, Research, and Practice*, 4(1), 81.

Hojjat, M., & Cramer, D. (2013). *Positive psychology of love.* London: Oxford University Press.

Holder, E. E., & Levi, D. J. (1988). Mental health and locus of control: SCL-90-R and Levenson's IPC scales. *Journal of Clinical Psychology*, 44(5), 753–755.

Holy Bible, King James Version. (2010). Zondervan.

Hornsey, M. J., & Hogg, M. A. (2000). Assimilation and diversity: An integrative model of subgroup relations. *Personality and Social Psychology Review*, 4(2), 143–156.

Horwitz, M. J. (1984). *Progressive legal historiography.* Eugene: University of Oregon.

Hosken, D. J., & House, C. M. (2011). Sexual selection. *Current Biology*, 21(2), R62–R65.

Hunt, M. (1993). *The story of psychology.* New York, NY: Doubleday.

Hunt, P. S., & Campbell, B. A. (1997). Developmental dissociation of the components of conditioned fear. In M. E. Bouton & M. S. Fanselow (Eds.), *Learning, motivation, and cognition: The functional behaviorism of Robert C. Bolles* (pp. 53–74). Washington, DC: American Psychological Association.

Hunter, J. A., Stringer, M., & Watson, R. (1991). Intergroup violence and intergroup attributions. *British Journal of Social Psychology, 30*(3), 261–266.

Hyman, A., & Walsh, J. J. (1973). *Philosophy in the Middle Ages: The Christian, Islamic, and Jewish traditions.* Indianapolis, IN: Hackett.

Ignatieff, M. (1993). *Blood and belonging: Journeys into the new nationalism.* New York, NY: Farrar, Straus and Giroux.

Insel, T. R., & Young, L. J. (2001). The neurobiology of attachment. *Nature Reviews. Neuroscience, 2*(2), 129–136. Retrieved from https://doi.org/10.1038/35053579

Ito, T. A., Larsen, J. T., Smith, N. K., & Cacioppo, J. T. (1998). Negative information weighs more heavily on the brain: The negativity bias in evaluative categorizations. *Journal of Personality and Social Psychology, 75*(4), 887–900.

Jacoby, S. (1983). *Wild justice: The evolution of revenge.* New York, NY: Harper & Row.

Jankowiak, W. R., & Fischer, E. F. (1992). A cross-cultural perspective on romantic love. *Ethnology, 31*(2), 149–155.

Janmaat, J. G. (2006). Popular conceptions of nationhood in old and new European member states: Partial support for the ethnic-civic framework. *Ethnic and Racial Studies, 29*(1), 50–78.

Jarcho, J. M., Berkman, E. T., & Lieberman, M. D. (2011)). The neural basis of rationalization: Cognitive dissonance reduction during decision-making. *Social Cognitive and Affective Neuroscience, 6*(4), 460–467.

Jeong, H. O. (2016). A new comparison of the East and West: National identity and attitudes toward immigration. *Asian and Pacific Migration Journal, 25*(2), 206–219. Retrieved from https://doi.org/10.1177/0117196816640972

Joffe, J. (1988). Tocqueville revisited: Are good democracies bad players in the game of nations? *Washington Quarterly, 11*(1), 161–172.

Joffe, J. (1998). *The great powers.* London, UK: Phoenix.

Johnson, M. H., Dziurawiec, S., Ellis, H., & Morton, J. (1991). Newborns' preferential tracking of face-like stimuli and its subsequent decline. *Cognition, 40*(1), 1–19.

Jones, R. (2017). The Collapse of American Identity. *India Abroad*, p. 7,30.

Jones, J. M., Dovidio, J. F., & Vietze, D. L. (2014). *The psychology of diversity: Beyond prejudice and racism.* Chichester, UK: Wiley-Blackwell.

Kahneman, D., & Riepe, M. W. (1998). Aspects of investor psychology. *Journal of Portfolio Management, 24*(4), 52–65.

Kagan, J. (1981). *The second year: the emergence of self-awareness.* Cambridge, MA: Harvard University Press.

Kagan, J. (2015). Amen. *Psychological Inquiry, 26*(3), 244–246. https://doi.org/10.1080/1047840X.2015.1019392

Kagan, J., & Segal, J. (1968). *Psychology, an introduction.* New York, NY: Harcourt Brace Jovanovich.

Kaplan, H., Hill, K., Lancaster, J., & Hurtado, A. M. (2000). A theory of human life history evolution: Diet, intelligence, and longevity. *Evolutionary Anthropology: Issues, News, and Reviews, 9*(4), 156–185.

Karpinski, A., & Hilton, J. L. (2001). Attitudes and the implicit association test. *Journal of Personality and Social Psychology, 81*(5), 774–788.

Katsenelinboïgen, A. (1984). *Some new trends in systems theory.* Seaside, CA: Intersystems Publications.

Katz, J., Street, A., & Arias, I. (1997). Individual differences in self-appraisals and responses to dating violence scenarios. *Violence and Victims, 12*(3), 265–276.

Kaufman, J., & Zigler, E. (1987). Do abused children become abusive parents? *American Journal of Orthopsychiatry, 57*(2), 186–192.

Kaufmann, E. (1999). American exceptionalism reconsidered: Anglo-Saxon ethnogenesis in the "universal" nation, 1776–1850. *Journal of American Studies, 33*(3), 437–457.

Kawanaka, K., & Nishida, T. (1975). Recent advances in the study of inter-unit-group relationships and social structure of wild chimpanzees of the Mahale Mountains. In S. Kondo, M. Kawai, A. Ehara, & S. Kawamura (Eds.), *Proceedings from the Symposium of the 5th Congress of the International Primatology Society* (pp. 173–186). Tokyo: Japan Science Press.

Kelly, D. J., Quinn, P. C., Slater, A. M., Lee, K., Gibson, A., Smith, M. . . . Pascalis, O. (2005). Three-month-olds, but not newborns, prefer own-race faces. *Developmental Science, 8*(6), F31–F36.

Kendrick, K. (2000). Oxytocin, motherhood and bonding. *Experimental Physiology, 85.*

Kenrick, D. T. (1987). Gender, genes, and the social environment: A biosocial interactionist perspective. In P. Shaver & C. Hendrick (Eds.), *Review of personality and social psychology, Vol. 7., Sex and gender* (pp. 14–43). New York, NY: Sage Publications.

Kenrick, D. T., & Keefe, R. C. (1992). Age preferences in mates reflect sex differences in human reproductive strategies. *Behavioral and Brain Sciences, 15*(1), 75–91.

Kenrick, D. T., Neuberg, S. L., & White, A. E. (2013). Relationships from an evolutionary life history perspective. In J. A. Simpson, & L. Campbell (Eds.), *Oxford handbook of close relationships* (pp. 13–38). New York: Oxford University Press.

Kerber, L. K. (1988). Separate spheres, female worlds, woman's place: The rhetoric of women's history. *Journal of American History, 75*(1), 9–39.

Kiely, R. (1996). *The good heart: A Buddhist perspective on the teachings of Jesus.* Boston, MA: Wisdom Publications.

Kisilevsky, B. S., Hains, S. M. J., Lee, K., Xie, X., Huang, H., Ye, H. H., . . . Wang, Z. (2003). Effects of experience on fetal voice recognition. *Psychological Science, 14*(3), 220–224. Retrieved from https://doi.org/10.1111/1467-9280.02435

Kisilevsky, B. S., & Low, J. A. (1998). Human fetal behavior: 100 years of study. *Developmental Review, 18*(1), 1–29. https://doi.org/10.1006/drev.1998.0452

Kite, M. E., & Whitley, B. E. (2010). *The Psychology of Prejudice and Discrimination.* Boston, MA: Wadsworth Cengage Learning.

Klein, J. G. (1996). Negativity in impressions of presidential candidates revisited: The 1992 election. *Personality and Social Psychology Bulletin, 22*(3), 288–295.

Klein, J. G. (1991). Negativity effects in impression formation: a test in the political arena. *Personality and Social Psychology Bulletin, 17*(4), 412–418.

Koffka, K. (1935). *Principles of gestalt psychology.* New York, NY: Harcourt Brace.

Kohler, K. (1929). *The origins of the synagogue and the church.* New York, NY: Macmillan.

Kohn, H. (1944). *The idea of nationalism: A study in its origins and background.* New York, NY: Macmillan.

Kohn, H. (1957). *American nationalism : An interpretative essay.* New York: Macmillan.

Kohn, H. (1956). A new look at nationalism. *Virginia Quarterly Review, 32*(3), 321.

Kohn, J. (1994). Introduction to H. Arendt, "Some questions of moral philosophy." *Social Research, 61*(4), 739–764.

Kolstø, P. (2000). *Political construction sites: Nation-building in Russia and the post-Soviet states.* Boulder, CO: Westview Press.

Krahé, B. (2013). *The social psychology of aggression.* Hove, UK: Psychology Press.

Krueger, Alan B. (2016). *Where have all the workers gone? An inquiry into the decline of the U.S. labor force participation rate.* Conference draft, Brookings Papers on Economic Activity.

Kruglanski, A. W., & Fishman, S. (2006). Terrorism between "syndrome" and "tool." *Current Directions in Psychological Science, 15*(1), 45–48.

Kuhn, D., & Lao, J. (1996). Effects of evidence on attitudes: Is polarization the norm? *Psychological Science, 7*(2), 115–120.

Kurth, F., Zilles, K., Fox, P. T., Laird, A. R., & Eickhoff, S. B. (2010). A link between the systems: Functional differentiation and integration within the human insula revealed by meta-analysis. *Brain Structure and Function, 214*(5), 519–534.

Kuzio, T. (2000). Nationalism in Ukraine: Towards a new framework. *Politics, 20*(2), 77–86. https://doi.org/10.1111/1467-9256.00115

Kuzio, T. (2002). The myth of the civic state: a critical survey of Hans Kohn's framework for understanding nationalism. *Ethnic and Racial Studies, 25*(1), 20–39. doi:10.1080/01419870120112049

Kuzio, T., & Magocsi, P. (2007). Theoretical and comparative perspectives on nationalism : New directions in cross-cultural and post-communist studies (Soviet and post-soviet politics and society ; 71). Stuttgart: Ibidem-Verlag.

Lama, D. (1999). *Ethics for the new millennium*. New York: Riverhead Books.

Lama, D. (2000). *The Dalai Lama's book of transformation*. London: Thorsons.

Lama, D. (2002). *Understanding our fundamental nature*. In R. Davidson & A.

Lama, D. (2000). A little compassion will do the trick. *Sunday Tribune*. December 10, 2000.

Lama, D. (2002). *An open heart: Practicing compassion in everyday life*. Hachette UK.

Langmuir, G. I. (1996). *Toward a definition of antisemitism*. Berkeley: University of California Press.

Leary, M. R., Diebels, K. J., Jongman-Sereno, K. P., & Fernandez, X. D. (2015). Why seemingly trivial events sometimes evoke strong emotional reactions: The role of social exchange rule violations. *Journal of Social Psychology, 155*(6), 559–575.

Leary, M. R., Kelly, K. M., Cottrell, C. A., & Schreindorfer, L. S. (2013). Construct validity of the need to belong scale: Mapping the nomological network. *Journal of Personality Assessment, 95*(6), 610–624. https://doi.org/10.1080/00223891.2013.819511

LeDoux, J. E. (1995). Emotion: Clues from the brain. *Annual Review of Psychology, 46*(1), 209–235.

Lefebvre, H. (2003). *The urban revolution*. Minneapolis: University of Minnesota Press.

Lepore, L., & Brown, R. (1997). Category and stereotype activation: Is prejudice inevitable? *Journal of Personality and Social Psychology, 72*(2), 275–287. https://doi.org/10.1037/0022-3514.72.2.275

Lerner, M. (1980). *Belief in a just world: A fundamental delusion*. Boston: Springer.

Lerner, M. J. (2003). The justice motive: Where social psychologists found it, how they lost it, and why they may not find it again. *Personality and Social Psychology Review, 7*(4), 388–399.

Lerner, M. J., & Katz, D. (1965). Evaluation of performance as a function of performer's reward and attractiveness. *Journal of Personality and Social Psychology, 1*(4), 355–360.

Lerner, M. J., & Miller, D. T. (1978). Just world research and the attribution process: Looking back and ahead. *Psychological Bulletin, 85*(5), 1030–1051.

Levin, S., Van Laar, C., & Sidanius, J. (2003). The effects of ingroup and outgroup friendships on ethnic attitudes in college: A longitudinal study. *Group Processes and Intergroup Relations, 6*(1), 76–92.

Levine, M., Prosser, A., Evans, D., & Reicher, S. (2005). Identity and emergency intervention: How social group membership and inclusiveness of group boundaries shape helping behavior. *Personality and Social Psychology Bulletin, 31*(4), 443–453.

Levine, R., Sato, S., Hashimoto, T., & Verma, J. (1995). Love and marriage in eleven cultures. *Journal of Cross-Cultural Psychology, 26*(5), 554–571.

Levine, R. A., & Campbell, D. T. (1972). *Ethnocentrism: Theories of conflict, ethnic attitudes and group conflict.* New York, NY: John Wiley & Sons.

Levenson, R. (1996). Biological substrates of empathy and facial modulation of emotion: two facets of the scientific legacy of john lanzetta. *Motivation and Emotion, 20*(3), 185–204.

Levitt, A., & Leonard, K. E. (2013). Relationship-specific alcohol expectancies and relationship-drinking contexts: reciprocal influence and gender-specific effects over the first 9 years of marriage. *Psychology of Addictive Behaviors: Journal of the Society of Psychologists in Addictive Behaviors, 27*(4), 986–996. doi:10.1037/a0030821

Levy Paluck, E. (2010). The promising integration of qualitative methods and field experiments. *The Annals of the American Academy of Political and Social Science, 628*(1), 59–71.

Lewin, K. (1946). Action research and minority problems. *Journal of Social Issues, 2*(4), 34–46.

Lickel, B. (2012). Retribution and revenge. In *The Oxford handbook of intergroup conflict.* New York: Oxford University Press.

Lieberman, M. D., Ochsner, K. N., Gilbert, D. T., & Schacter, D. L. (2001). Do amnesics exhibit cognitive dissonance reduction? The role of explicit memory and attention in attitude change. *Psychological Science, 12*(2), 135–140.

Lifton, R. J. (1986). *The Nazi doctors: Medical killing and the psychology of genocide.* New York, NY: Basic Books.

Lilla, M. (2016). *The reckless mind: Intellectuals in politics: With a new afterword* (new ed.). New York, NY: New York Review Books.

Lindenberger, U., Li, S.-C., Gruber, W., & Müller, V. (2009). Brains swinging in concert: Cortical phase synchronization while playing guitar. *BMC Neuroscience, 10*(1), 22.

Linnaeus, C. (1758). *Systema naturae per regna tria naturae : Secundum classes, ordines, genera, species, cum characteribus, differentiis, synonymis, locis.* Holmiae: Impensis Direct. Laurentii Salvi. Retrieved from https://www.biodiversitylibrary.org/bibliography/542

Lipset, S. M. (1968). *Revolution and counterrevolution: Change and persistence in social structures.* New York: Basic Books, Inc.

Lorberbaum, J. P., Newman, J. D., Horwitz, A. R., Dubno, J. R., Lydiard, R. B., Hamner, M. B., Bohning, D. E., & George, M. S. (2002). A potential role for thalamocingulate circuitry in human maternal behavior. *Biological Psychiatry, 51*(6), 431–445.

Londerville, S., & Main, M. (1981). Security of attachment, compliance, and maternal training methods in the second year of life. *Developmental Psychology, 17*(3), 289–299. https://doi.org/10.1037/0012–1649.17.3.289

Lord, C. G., Lepper, M. R., & Preston, E. (1984). Considering the opposite: A corrective strategy for social judgment. *Journal of Personality and Social Psychology, 47*(6), 1231–1243.

Lord, C. G., Ross, L., & Lepper, M. R. (1979). Biased assimilation and attitude polarization: The effects of prior theories on subsequently considered evidence. *Journal of Personality and Social Psychology, 37*(11), 2098–2109.

Lovgren, S. (2006). Sex-based roles gave modern humans an edge, study says. *National Geographic News.* Retrieved from http://news.nationalgeographic.com/news/ 2006/12/061207-sex-humans.html

Lumley, A. J., Michalczyk, Ł., Kitson, J. J., Spurgin, L. G., Morrison, C. A., Godwin, J. L., . . . Chapman, T. (2015). Sexual selection protects against extinction. *Nature, 522*(7557), 470–473.

Lupfer, M. B., Weeks, K. P., Doan, K. A., & Houston, D. A. (2000). Folk conceptions of fairness and unfairness. *European Journal of Social Psychology, 30*(3), 405–428.

Luthar, S. S. (1991). Vulnerability and resilience: A study of high-risk adolescents. *Child Development, 62*(3), 600–616.

Luthar, S. S. (2006). Resilience in development: A synthesis of research across five decades. In D. Ciccetti & D. J. Cohen (Eds.), *Developmental psychopathology* (2nd ed., pp. 739–795). Hoboken, NJ: John Wiley & Son.

Luthar, S. S., & Goldstein, A. (2004). Children's exposure to community violence: Implications for understanding risk and resilience. *Journal of Clinical Child and Adolescent Psychology, 33*(3), 499–505.

Luthar, S. S., & Zelazo, L. B. (2003). Research on resilience: An integrative review. In S. Luthar, M. M. Wong (Eds.), *Resilience and vulnerability: Adaptation in the context of childhood adversities* (pp. 510–549), Cambridge, UK: Cambridge University Press.

Lyons-Padilla, S., Gelfand, M. J., Mirahmadi, H., Farooq, M., & van Egmond, M. (2015). Belonging nowhere: Marginalization and radicalization risk among Muslim immigrants. *Behavioral Science and Policy, 1*(2), 1–12.

MacDonald, G., Marshall, T. C., Gere, J., Shimotomai, A., & Lies, J. (2012). Valuing romantic relationships: The role of family approval across cultures. *Cross-Cultural Research, 46*(4), 366–393.

Macfarlane, A. (1975). Olfaction in the development of social preferences in the human neonate. *Ciba Foundation Symposium*, (33), 103–117.

Mackie, D. M., Hamilton, D. L., Susskind, J., & Rosselli, F. (1996). Social psychological foundations of stereotype formation. In C. N. Macrae, C. Strangor, & M. Hewstone (Eds.), *Stereotypes and stereotyping* (pp. 41–78). New York: Guilford.

Maddens, B., Billiet, J., & Beerten, R. (2000). National identity and the attitude towards foreigners in multi-national states: The case of Belgium. *Journal of Ethnic and Migration Studies, 26*(1), 45–60.

Maes, J. (1998). Eight stages in the development of research on the construct of belief in a just world? In L. Montada & M. J. Lerner (Eds.), *Responses to victimizations and belief in a just world* (pp. 163–185). Boston, MA: Springer US.

Maier, C. S. (1998). *The unmasterable past: History, Holocaust, and German national identity.* Cambridge, MA: Harvard University Press.

Malinowski, B. (1921). The primitive economics of the Trobriand Islanders. *The Economic Journal, 31*(121), 1–16.

Malinowski, B. (1922). *Argonauts of the western pacific: an account of native enterprise and adventure in the archipelagoes of Melanesian New Guinea.* Long Grove, IL: Waveland Press.

Manjoo, F. (2017, April 25). Can Facebook fix its own worst bug? Retrieved June 1, 2017, from https://www.nytimes.com/2017/04/25/magazine/can-facebook-fix-its-own-worst-bug.htm

Marshall, T. C. (2008). Cultural differences in intimacy: The influence of gender-role ideology and individualism—collectivism. *Journal of Social and Personal Relationships, 25*(1), 143–168.

Marx, K. (1867). *Capital* (Vol. 1).

Marx, K. F. H. (1846). *The moral aspects of medical life* (J. Mackness, Trans.). London, England: John Churchill.

Marx, V., & Nagy, E. (2015). Fetal behavioural responses to maternal voice and touch. *PLOS ONE, 10*(6), e0129118. https://doi.org/10.1371/journal.pone.0129118

Maslow. A. H. (1943). A theory of human motivation. *Psychological Review, 50*(4), 370–396.

Masten, A. S. (2007). Resilience in developing systems: Progress and promise as the fourth wave rises. *Development and Psychopathology, 19*(3), 921–930.

Matt, D. (2004). *The Zohar: 1.* Stanford, CA: Stanford University Press.

Maturana, H. R. (1990). The biological foundations of self consciousness and the physical domain of existence. In N. Luhmann (Ed.), *Beobachter: Konvergenz der Erkenntnistheorien?* (pp. 47–117). Munich, Germany: Wilhelm Fink Verlag.

Maturana, H. R., & Verden-Zoller, G. (2008). *The origin of humanness in the biology of love.* Exeter, UK: Imprint Academic.

Maurer, D., & Young, R. E. (1983). Newborn's following of natural and distorted arrangements of facial features. *Infant Behavior and Development, 6*(1), 127–131.

McCullough, M. E. (2000). Forgiveness as human strength: Theory, measurement, and links to well-being. *Journal of Social and Clinical Psychology, 19*(1), 43–55.

McCullough, M. E., Bellah, C. G., Kilpatrick, S. D., & Johnson, J. L. (2001). Vengefulness: Relationships with forgiveness, rumination, well-being, and the big five. *Personality and Social Psychology Bulletin, 27*(5), 601–610.

McCullough, M. E., Hoyt, W. T., & Rachal, K. C. (2000). What we know (and need to know) about assessing forgiveness constructs. In M. E. McCullough, K. I. Pargament, & C. E. Thoresen (Eds.), *Forgiveness: Theory, research, and practice* (pp. 65–88). New York, NY: Guilford Press.

McCullough, M. E., Worthington, E. L., Maxey, J., & Rachal, K. C. (1997). Gender in the context of supportive and challenging religious counseling interventions. *Journal of Counseling Psychology, 44*(1), 80–88.

McKean, E. (2005). *The new Oxford American dictionary* (2nd ed.). New York, NY: Oxford University Press.

Medrano, J. D. (2005). Nation, citizenship and immigration in contemporary Spain. *International Journal on Multicultural Societies, 7*(2), 133–156.

Meissner, C. A., & Brigham, J. C. (2001). Thirty years of investigating the own-race bias in memory for faces: A meta-analytic review. *Psychology, Public Policy, and Law, 7*(1), 3–35.

Mellor, D., Stokes, M., Firth, L., Hayashi, Y., & Cummins, R. (2008). Need for belonging, relationship satisfaction, loneliness, and life satisfaction. *Personality and Individual Differences, 45*(3), 213–218.

Mennella, J. A., & Beauchamp, G. K. (1999). Smoking and the flavor of breast milk. *Pediatrics, 103*(6), 48.

Merton, R. K. (1948). The self-fulfilling prophecy. *Antioch Review, 8*(2), 193–210.

Mesman, J., van IJzendoorn, M. H., & Bakermans-Kranenburg, M. J. (2009). The many faces of the still-face paradigm: A review and meta-analysis. *Developmental Review, 29*(2), 120–162. https://doi.org/10.1016/j.dr.2009.02.001

Migration Policy institute. (2014). Top 10 Migration Issues of 2014. *Originally published on the Migration Policy Institute's Migration Data Hub.* Retrieved from: www.migrationpolicy.org/programs/migration-data-hub

Mikula, G. (1986). The experience of injustice. In J. Greenberg, H. Bierhoff, & R. Cohen (Eds.), *Justice in social relations* (pp. 103–123). New York, NY: Plenum Press.

Mikula, G., Scherer, K. R., & Athenstaedt, U. (1998). The role of injustice in the elicitation of differential emotional reactions. *Personality and Social Psychology Bulletin, 24*(7), 769–783.

Mikulincer, M., & Shaver, P. R. (2007). *Attachment in adulthood: Structure, dynamics, and change.* New York, NY: Guilford Press.

Mikulincer, M., Shaver, P. R., & Berant, E. (2013). An attachment perspective on therapeutic processes and outcomes. *Journal of Personality, 81*(6), 606–616. Retrieved from https://doi.org/10.1111/j.1467-6494.2012.00806.x

Milgram, S. (1963). Behavioral study of obedience. *Journal of Abnormal and Social Psychology, 67*(4), 371–378.

Milgram, S. (1964). Group pressure and action against a person. *Journal of Abnormal and Social Psychology, 69*(2), 137–143.

Miller, D. T. (2001). Disrespect and the experience of injustice. *Annual Review of Psychology, 52*(1), 527–553.

Miller, G. (2000). *The mating mind: How sexual selection shaped the evolution of human nature* (1st ed.). New York, NY: Doubleday.

Miller, G. A. (1956). The magical number seven plus or minus two: Some limits on our capacity for processing information. *Psychological Review, 63*(2), 81–97.

Miller-Idriss, C., & Bracho, C. (2011). Nationalism. Sociology, Sociology. Retrieved from http://www.oxfordbibliographies.com/view/document/obo-9780199756384/obo-9780199756384-0037.xml

Miller, G. F., & Penke, L. (2007). The evolution of human intelligence and the coefficient of additive genetic variance in human brain size. *Intelligence, 35*(2), 97–114. Retrieved from https://doi.org/10.1016/j.intell.2006.08.008

Miller, J. A. (1993). Rationalizing injustice: The Supreme Court and the property tax. *Hofstra Law Review, 22*(1), 79–144.

Miller, N. E. (1961). Some recent studies of conflict behavior and drugs. *American Psychologist, 16*(1), 12–24. https://doi.org/10.1037/h0048720

Minow, M. (1998). Between vengeance and forgiveness: South Africa's truth and reconciliation commission. *Negotiation Journal, 14*(4), 319–355.

Minow, M. (1991). *Identities.* New Haven, CT: Yale University Press.

Moffitt, T. E. (2003). Life-course-persistent and adolescence-limited antisocial behavior: A 10-year research review and a research agenda. In B. B. Lahey, T. E. Moffitt, & A. Caspi (Eds.), *Causes of conduct disorder and juvenile delinquency* (pp. 49–75). New York, NY: The Guilford Press.

Molina, C. D., & Molina, J. M. (1995). Blood lead levels among children in a managed-care organization - California, October-1992 March-1993. *Journal of the American Medical Association, 274*(16), 1262–1263.

Montgomery, K. (2005). Banal race-thinking: Ties of blood, Canadian history textbooks and ethnic nationalism. *Paedagogica Historica, 41*(3), 313–336.

Moon, C., Cooper, R. P., & Fifer, W. P. (1993). Two-day-olds prefer their native language. *Infant Behavior and Development, 16*(4), 495–500.

Moon, C. M., & Fifer, W. P. (2000). Evidence of transnatal auditory learning. *Journal of Perinatology, 20*(1), 37–44.

Moore, J. (1996). Savanna chimpanzees, referential models and the last common ancestor. In W. C. McGrew, L. F. Marchant, & T. Nishida, *Great ape societies* (pp. 275–282). New York, NY: Cambridge University Press.

Morton, S. G. (1849). *Observations on the size of the brain in various races and families of man.* Philadelphia: [s.n.]. Retrieved from http://archive.org/details/b24924921

Morton, S. G., & Combe, G. (1839). *Crania Americana; or, A comparative view of the skulls of various aboriginal nations of North and South America. To which is prefixed an essay on the varieties of the human species.* Philadelphia: J. Dobson; London: Simpkin, Marshall & Co. Retrieved from http://archive.org/details/Craniaamericana00Mort

Mukherjee, S. (2016, August 18). Same but different: How epigenetics can blur the line between nature and nurture. *New Yorker.* Retrieved May 18, 2017, from http://internationalpsychoanalysis.net/2016/08/18/same-but-different-how-epigenetics-can-blur-the-line-between-nature-and-nurture/

Munro, G. D., & Ditto, P. H. (1997). Biased assimilation, attitude polarization, and affect in reactions to stereotype-relevant scientific information. *Personality and Social Psychology Bulletin, 23*(6), 636–653.

Murphy, G. L. (2002). *The big book of concepts.* Cambridge, MA: MIT Press.

Murphy, J. G. (1988). Forgiveness, mercy, and the retributive emotions. *Criminal Justice Ethics, 7*(2), 3–15.

Murphy, J. G., & Hampton, J. (1988). *Forgiveness and mercy.* Cambridge, UK: Cambridge University Press.

Myers, D. G. (2002). *Social psychology* (7th ed.). Boston: McGraw-Hill.

Myers, J. E., Madathil, J., & Tingle, L. R. (2005). Marriage satisfaction and wellness in India and the United States: A preliminary comparison of arranged marriages and marriages of choice. *Journal of Counseling and Development, 83*(2), 183–190.

Nagda, B. (Ratnesh) A., & Zúñiga, X. (2003). Fostering meaningful racial engagement through intergroup dialogues. *Group Processes and Intergroup Relations, 6*(1), 111–128.

Neafsey, E. J., Terreberry, R. R., Hurley, K. M., Ruit, K. G., & Frysztak, R. J. (1993). Anterior cingulate cortex in rodents: Connections, visceral control functions, and implications for emotion. In B. Vogt & M. Gabriel, *Neurobiology of cingulate cortex and limbic thalamus: A comprehensive handbook* (pp. 206–223). Boston, MA: Birkhäuser.

Netting, N. S. (2010). Marital ideoscapes in 21st-century India: Creative combinations of love and responsibility. *Journal of Family Issues, 31*(6), 707–726.

New World Encyclopedia. (2014). Natural law. In *New World Encyclopedia*. Retrieved from http://www.newworldencyclopedia.org/entry/Natural_law

Ng, W.-J., & Lindsay, R. C. (1994). Cross-race facial recognition: Failure of the contact hypothesis. *Journal of Cross-Cultural Psychology, 25*(2), 217–232.

Nichols, A. L., & Webster, G. D. (2013). The single-item need to belong scale. *Personality and Individual Differences, 55*(2), 189–192.

Nieguth, T. (1999). Beyond dichotomy: Concepts of the nation and the distribution of membership. *Nations and Nationalism, 5*(2), 155–173.

Nier, J. A., Gaertner, S. L., Dovidio, J. F., Banker, B. S., Ward, C. M., & Rust, M. C. (2001). Changing interracial evaluations and behavior: The effects of a common group identity. *Group Processes and Intergroup Relations, 4*(4), 299–316.

Nishida, T. (1983). Alpha status and agonistic alliance in wild chimpanzees (Pan troglodytes schweinfurthii). *Primates, 24*(3), 318–336.

Nishida, T., & Kawanaka, K. (1985). Within-group cannibalism by adult male chimpanzees. *Primates, 26*, 274–284. https://doi.org/10.1007/BF02382402

Niven, B. (2002). *Facing the Nazi past: United Germany and the legacy of the Third Reich.* London, UK: Routledge.

Nodia, G. (1994). Nationalism and democracy, In L. Diamond & M. F. Plattner (Eds.), *Nationalism, Ethnic Conflict, and Democracy.* Baltimore, MD: Johns Hopkins University Press.

Norenzayan, A., & Gervais, W. M. (2012). The cultural evolution of religion. In E. G. Slingerland & M. Collard (Eds.), *Creating consilience: Integrating science and the humanities* (pp. 243–265). New York, NY: Oxford University Press.

Northoff, G., Heinzel, A., de Greck, M., Bermpohl, F., Dobrowolny, H., & Panksepp, J. (2006). Self-referential processing in our brain: A meta-analysis of imaging studies on the self. *NeuroImage, 31*, 440–457.

Nourse, V. (2016). History of science: When eugenics became law: Victoria Nourse reviews a study on a historic US misuse of biology, the case of Buck v. Bell. *Nature, 530*(7591), 418. Retrieved from https://doi.org/10.1038/530418a

Nussbaum, M. (1994). Pity and mercy: Nietzsche's stoicism. In R. Schacht (Ed.), *Nietzsche, genealogy, morality: Essays on Nietzsche's genealogy of morals.* Berkeley: University of California Press.

Nussbaum, M. (2001). Can patriotism be compassionate? *The Nation, 273*(20), 11–12.

Nussbaum, M. C. (2016). *Not for profit: Why democracy needs the humanities.* Princeton, NJ: Princeton University Press.

Ockleford, E. M., Vince, M. A., Layton, C., & Reader, M. R. (1988). Responses of neonates to parents' and others' voices. *Early Human Development, 18*(1), 27–36. https://doi.org/10.1016/0378-3782(88)90040-0

Ohbuchi, K., Kameda, M., & Agarie, N. (1989). Apology as aggression control: Its role in mediating appraisal of and response to harm. *Journal of Personality and Social Psychology, 56*(2), 219–227.

Ohman, A., & Soares, J. F. (1993). On the automatic nature of phobic fear: conditioned electrodermal responses to masked fear-relevant stimuli. *Journal of Abnormal Psychology, 102*(1), 121–132.

Öhman, A., & Soares, J. J. (1998). Emotional conditioning to masked stimuli: Expectancies for aversive outcomes following nonrecognized fear-relevant stimuli. *Journal of Experimental Psychology: General, 127*(1), 69–82.

Oishi, S., Kesebir, S., & Diener, E. (2011). Income inequality and happiness. *Psychological Science, 22*(9), 1095–1100.

Olsavsky, A. K., Telzer, E. H., Shapiro, M., Humphreys, K. L., Flannery, J., Goff, B., & Tottenham, N. (2013). Indiscriminate amygdala response to mothers and strangers after early maternal deprivation. *Biological Psychiatry, 74*(11), 853–860.

Olson, J. M., & Stone, J. (2005). The influence of behavior on attitudes. In D. Albarracín, B. T. Johnson, & M. P. Zanna (Eds.), *The handbook of attitudes* (pp. 223–271). Lawrence Erlbaum Associates Publishers.

Ono, M., Kikusui, T., Sasaki, N., Ichikawa, M., Mori, Y., & Murakami-Murofushi, K. (2008). Early weaning induces anxiety and precocious myelination in the anterior part of the basolateral amygdala of male Balb/c mice. *Neuroscience, 156*(4), 1103–1110.

Ortigue, S., Bianchi-Demicheli, F., Hamilton, A. de C., & Grafton, S. T. (2007). The neural basis of love as a subliminal prime: An event-related functional magnetic resonance imaging study. *Journal of Cognitive Neuroscience, 19*(7), 1218–1230.

Ostrom, T. M., & Sedikides, C. (1992). Out-group homogeneity effects in natural and minimal groups. *Psychological Bulletin, 112*(3), 536–552. https://doi.org/10.1037/0033-2909.112.3.536

Paluck, E. L. (2006). Diversity training and intergroup contact: A call to action research. *Journal of Social Issues, 62*(3), 577–595.

Paluck, E. L. (2009). Reducing intergroup prejudice and conflict using the media: a field experiment in rwanda. *Journal of Personality and Social Psychology, 96*(3), 574–587.

Paluck, E. L. (2010). The promising integration of qualitative methods and field experiments. *Annals of the American Academy of Political and Social Science, 628*(1), 59–71.

Paluck, E. L. (2012). Interventions aimed at the reduction of prejudice and conflict. In L. Troop (Ed.), *The Oxford handbook of intergroup conflict* (pp. 179–192). New York, NY: Oxford University Press.

Paluck, E. L., & Cialdini, R. B. (2014). Field research methods. In H. T. Reis & C. M. Judd (Eds.), *Handbook of research methods in social and personality psychology* (pp. 81–97). New York, NY: Cambridge University Press.

Panksepp, J. (2001). The long-term psychobiological consequences of infant emotions: Prescriptions for the twenty-first century. *Neuropsychoanalysis, 3*(2), 149–178.

Panksepp, J. (2004). *Affective neuroscience: The foundations of human and animal emotions.* Oxford, England: Oxford University Press.

Panksepp, J. (2005). Affective consciousness: Core emotional feelings in animals and humans. *Consciousness and Cognition, 14*(1), 30–80.

Paolini, S., Hewstone, M., Cairns, E., & Voci, A. (2004). Effects of direct and indirect cross-group friendships on judgments of Catholics and Protestants in Northern Ireland: The mediating role of an anxiety-reduction mechanism. *Personality and Social Psychology Bulletin, 30*(6), 770–786.

Pape, R. A. (2003). The strategic logic of suicide terrorism. *American Political Science Review, 97*(3), 343–361.

Park, J., & Banaji, M. R. (2000). Mood and heuristics: The influence of happy and sad states on sensitivity and bias in stereotyping. *Journal of Personality and Social Psychology, 78*(6), 1005–1023. https://doi.org/10.1037/0022-3514.78.6.1005

Parrott, D. J., & Giancola, P. R. (2007). Addressing "The criterion problem" in the assessment of aggressive behavior: Development of a new taxonomic system. *Aggression and Violent Behavior, 12*(3), 280–299.

Pascalis, O., de Haan, M., & Nelson, C. A. (2002). Is face processing species-specific during the first year of life? *Science, 296*(5571), 1321–1323.

Pascalis, O., & de Schonen, S. (1994). Recognition memory in 3-to 4-day-old human neonates. *Neuroreport, 5*(14), 1721–1724.

Pascalis, O., de Schonen, S., Morton, J., Deruelle, C., & Fabre-Grenet, M. (1995). Mother's face recognition by neonates: A replication and an extension. *Infant Behavior and Development, 18*(1), 79–85.

Pedersen, C. A. (1997). Oxytocin control of maternal behavior Regulation by sex steroids and offspring stimuli. *Annals of the New York Academy of Sciences, 807*(1), 126–145.

Pedersen, C. A., & Prange, A. J. (1979). Induction of maternal behavior in virgin rats after intracerebroventricular administration of oxytocin. *Proceedings of the National Academy of Sciences of the United States of America, 76*(12), 6661–6665.

Pedersen, C. A., Ascher, J. A., Monroe, Y. L., & Prange, A. J. (1982). Oxytocin induces maternal behavior in virgin female rats. *Science, 216*(4546), 648–650.

Peeters, G., & Czapinski, J. (1990). Positive-negative asymmetry in evaluations: The distinction between affective and informational negativity effects. *European Review of Social Psychology, 1*(1), 33–60.

Pedersen, P. E., & Blass, E. M. (1982). Prenatal and postnatal determinants of the 1st suckling episode in albino rats. *Developmental Psychobiology, 15*(4), 349–355.

Pehrson, S., Brown, R., & Zagefka, H. (2009). When does national identification lead to the rejection of immigrants? Cross-sectional and longitudinal evidence for the role of essentialist in-group definitions. *British Journal of Social Psychology, 48*(1), 61–76.

Pettigrew, T. F., & Tropp, L. R. (2006). A meta-analytic test of intergroup contact theory. *Journal of Personality and Social Psychology, 90*(5), 751–783.

Perrett, D., Hietanen, J., Oram, M., Benson, P., & Rolls, E. (1992). Organization and functions of cells responsive to faces in the temporal cortex. *Philosophical Transactions of the Royal Society of London. Series B: Biological Sciences, 335*(1273), 23–30.

Pew Research Center. (2013). The most (and least) culturally diverse countries in the world. Retrieved from: https://www.pewresearch.org/fact-tank/2013/07/18/the-most-and-least-culturally-diverse-countries-in-the-world/

Pfeiffer, U. J., Timmermans, B., Bente, G., Vogeley, K., & Schilbach, L. (2011). A non-verbal turing test: differentiating mind from machine in gaze-based social interaction (non-verbal turing test). *PLoS ONE, 6*(11), 1–12.

Piaget, J. (1971). The theory of stages in cognitive development. In D. Green, M. P. Ford, G. B. Flamer (Eds.), *Measurement and Piaget: Proceedings of the CTB/McGraw-Hill Conference on Ordinal Scales of Cognitive Development*. New York, NY: McGraw-Hill.

Piaget, J. (1972). Development and learning. In C. S. Lavatelly & F. Stendler & W. E. William (Eds.), *Reading in child behavior and development* (3rd. ed, pp. 7–20). New York, NY: Harcourt Brace Jovanovich.

Piaget, J., & Cook, M. (1952). *The origins of intelligence in children* (Vol. 8). New York, NY: International Universities Press.

Pickett, C. L., Gardner, W. L., & Knowles, M. (2004). Getting a cue: The need to belong and enhanced sensitivity to social cues. *Personality and Social Psychology Bulletin, 30*(9), 1095–1107. https://doi.org/10.1177/0146167203262085

Pietrzak, R. H., Laird, J. D., Stevens, D. A., & Thompson, N. S. (2002). Sex differences in human jealousy: A coordinated study of forced-choice, continuous rating-scale, and physiological responses on the same subjects. *Evolution and Human Behavior, 23*(2), 83–94.

Pinker, S. (1997). *How the mind works*. New York, NY: Norton.

Pinker, S. (2003). *The blank slate: The modern denial of human nature*. New York: Penguin.

Plato. (1968). *The Republic of Plato*. New York, NY: Basic Books.

Plato. (1980). *Laws* (L. Thomson, Trans.). New York: Basic Books.

Pratto, F., Sidanius, J., Stallworth, L. M., & Malle, B. F. (1994). Social dominance orientation: A personality variable predicting social and political attitudes. *Journal of Personality and Social Psychology, 67*(4), 741–763. https://doi.org/10.1037/0022-3514.67.4.741

Querleu, D., Renard, X., Versyp, F., Paris-Delrue, L., & Crèpin, G. (1988). Fetal hearing. *European Journal of Obstetrics, Gynecology, and Reproductive Biology, 28*(3), 191–212.

Quinn, P. C., & Bomba, P. C. (1986). Evidence for a general category of oblique orientations in 4-month-old infants. *Journal of Experimental Child Psychology, 42*(3), 345–354.

Rakison, D. H., & Oakes, L. M. (2003). *Early category and concept development: Making sense of the blooming, buzzing confusion.* Oxford, UK: Oxford University Press.

Rawls, J. (1971). *A theory of justice.* Cambridge, MA: Belknap Press of Harvard University Press.

Redcay, E., Dodell-Feder, D., Pearrow, M. J., Mavros, P. L., Kleiner, M., Gabrieli, J. D., & Saxe, R. (2010). Live face-to-face interaction during fMRI: A new tool for social cognitive neuroscience. *Neuroimage, 50*(4), 1639–1647.

Reijerse, A., Van Acker, K., Vanbeselaere, N., Phalet, K., & Duriez, B. (2013). Beyond the ethnic-civic dichotomy: Cultural citizenship as a new way of excluding immigrants. *Political Psychology, 34*(4), 611–630.

Robinson-Whelen, S., Kim, C., MacCallum, R. C., & Kiecolt-Glaser, J. K. (1997). Distinguishing optimism from pessimism in older adults: Is it more important to be optimistic or not to be pessimistic? *Journal of Personality and Social Psychology, 73*(6), 1345–1353.

Rokeach, M., & Mezei, L. (1966). Race and Shared Belief as Factors in Social Choice. *Science, 151*(3707), 167–172. Retrieved January 31, 2020, from www.jstor.org/stable/1717292

Rosch, E. (1978). Principles of categorization. In E. Rosch & B. B. Lloyd (Eds.), *Cognition and Categorization* (p. 2748). Hillsdale, NJ: Erlbaum.

Rosenthal, D. M. (2002). Persons, minds, and consciousness. In M. G. Grene, R. E. Auxier, & L. Hahn (Eds.), *The philosophy of Marjorie Grene.* Chicago, IL: Open Court; Publishers Group West.

Rosenthal, R. (1994). Science and ethics in conducting, analyzing, and reporting psychological research. *Psychological Science, 5*(3), 127–134.

Rosenthal, R., & Fode, K. L. (1963). The effect of experimenter bias on the performance of the albino rat. *Systems Research and Behavioral Science, 8*(3), 183–189.

Rosenthal, R., & Rosnow, R. (2009). Characteristics of the volunteer subject. *Artifacts in Behavioral Research,* 677–744.

Rosenthal, R., & Rubin, D. B. (1978). Interpersonal expectancy effects: The first 345 studies. *Behavioral and Brain Sciences, 1*(3), 377–386.

Rosnow, R., & Rosenthal, R. (1997). *People studying people: Artifacts and ethics in behavioral research.* New York, NY: Freeman.

Rotter, J. B. (1966). Generalized expectancies for internal versus external control of reinforcement. *Psychological Monographs: General and Applied, 80*(1), 1.

Roughgarden, J. (2004). Evolution and the embodiment of gender. *GLQ: A Journal of Lesbian and Gay Studies, 10*(2), 287–291.

Roughgarden, J., Oishi, M., & Akçay, E. (2006). Reproductive social behavior: Cooperative games to replace sexual selection. *Science, 311*(5763), 965–969.

Rouhana, N. N., & Bar-Tal, D. (1998). Psychological dynamics of intractable ethnonational conflicts: The Israeli–Palestinian case. *American Psychologist, 53*(7), 761–770.

Rousseau, J. J. (1762). *The social contract.* London, England: J. M. Dent & Sons.

Rozin, P., & Royzman, E. B. (2001). Negativity bias, negativity dominance, and contagion. *Personality and Social Psychology Review, 5*(4), 296–320.

Rubinow, D. R., & Schmidt, P. J. (1996). Androgens, brain, and behavior. *American Journal of Psychiatry, 153*(8), 974–984.

Rusciano, F. L. (2003). The construction of national identity—A 23-nation study. *Political Research Quarterly, 56*(3), 361–366. https://doi.org/10.1177/106591290305600310

Russell, M. J. (1976). Human olfactory communication. *Nature, 260*(5551), 520–522.

Russell, M. J., Mendelson, T., & Peeke, H. V. S. (1983). Mother's identification of their infant's odors. *Ethology and Sociobiology, 4*(1), 29–31. https://doi.org/10.1016/0162-3095(83)90005-5

Ryan, A. A. (1984). *Quiet neighbors: Prosecuting Nazi War criminals in America* (1st ed.). San Diego, CA: Harcourt Brace Jovanovich.

Sandlin, D. [SmarterEveryDay]. (2015, April 24). *The Backwards Brain Bicycle - Smarter Every Day 133* [Video file] . Retrieved from https://www.youtube.com/watch?v=MFzDaBzBlL0&t=57s

Sangrigoli, S., Pallier, C., Argenti, A.-M., Ventureyra, V., & De Schonen, S. (2005). Reversibility of the other-race effect in face recognition during childhood. *Psychological Science, 16*(6), 440–444.

Sanquirgo, N., Oberle, D., & Chekroun, P. (2012). The need to belong scale: french validation and impact on reactions to deviance. *Annee Psychologique, 112*(1), 85–113.

Sartre, J.-P. (1948). Existentialism and humanism (1947). Brooklyn: Haskell House. P. 115.

Scheck, B., Neufeld, P., Dwyer, J., & Schwartz, A. (2001). Actual innocence: Five days to execution and other dispatches from the wrongly convicted. *Punishment and Society, 3*(3), 446–447.

Schilbach, L., Wohlschlaeger, A. M., Kraemer, N. C., Newen, A., Shah, N. J., Fink, G. R., & Vogeley, K. (2006). Being with virtual others: Neural correlates of social interaction. *Neuropsychologia, 44*(5), 718–730.

Schindehette, S., & Seaman, D. (2002). Settling the score. *People, 57*(14), 129–131.

Schmitt, D. P. (2005). Sociosexuality from Argentina to Zimbabwe: A 48-nation study of sex, culture, and strategies of human mating. *Behavioral and Brain Sciences, 28*(2), 247–275.

Schopenhauer, A. (1995). *On the basis of morality*. Indianapolis, IN: Hackett.

Schöpflin, G. (1996). The politics of national identities. *International Review of Sociology, 6*(2), 219–230.

Searle, J. R. (1990). Is the brain's mind a computer program. *Scientific American, 262*(1), 26–31.

Seeman, M. (1959). On the meaning of alienation. *American Sociological Review, 24*(6) 783.

Seeman, M. (1975). Alienation studies. *Annual Review of Sociology, 1*(1), 91–123.

Seeman, M. (2001). Alienation: Psychosociological tradition. In N. Smelser & P. B. Baltes (Eds.), *International encyclopedia of social and behavioral sciences* (1st ed., pp. 385–388). Amsterdam, The Netherlands: Elsevier.

Segev, T. (2000). *The seventh million: The Israelis and the Holocaust*. New York, NY: Macmillan.

Seligman, M. (1975). *Helplessness: On depression, development, and death*. San Francisco, CA: Freeman.

Seligman, M. E. (1972). Learned helplessness. *Annual Review of Medicine, 23*(1), 407–412.

Seneca, L. (2010). *Anger, mercy, revenge* (R. A. Kaster & M. C. Nussbaum, Trans.). Chicago, IL: University of Chicago Press.

Senekal, B. A. (2008). Alienation as a fictional construct in four contemporary. British novels: A literary-theoretical study (Unpublished PhD thesis). University of the Free State. Retrieved from http://scholar.ufs.ac.za:8080/xmlui/handle/11660/1636

Shackelford, T. K., Buss, D. M., & Bennett, K. (2002). Forgiveness or breakup: Sex differences in responses to a partner's infidelity. *Cognition and Emotion, 16*(2), 299–307.

Shackelford, T. K., Voracek, M., Schmitt, D. P., Buss, D. M., Weekes-Shackelford, V. A., & Michalski, R. L. (2004). Romantic jealousy in early adulthood and in later life. *Human Nature, 15*(3), 283–300.

Shariff, A. F., & Norenzayan, A. (2011). Mean gods make good people: Different views of God predict cheating behavior. *International Journal for the Psychology of Religion, 21*(2), 85–96.

Shayo, M. (2009). A model of social identity with an application to political economy: Nation, class, and redistribution. *American Political Science Review, 103*(02), 147–174.

Shear, M. D., & Cooper, H. (2017, January 27). Trump bars refugees and citizens of 7 Muslim countries. *New York Times (New York)*, p. A1.

Sherman, J. W., Lee, A. Y., Bessenoff, G. R., & Frost, L. A. (1998). Stereotype efficiency reconsidered: Encoding flexibility under cognitive load. *Journal of Personality and Social Psychology, 75*(3), 589–606.

Shermer, M. (2016). *The moral arc: how science makes us better people.* New York: St. Martins Griffin.

Shils, E. A. (1957). The intellectuals, public opinion, and economic development. *Economic Development and Cultural Change, 6*(1), 55–62.

Shin, S. J. (2012). *Bilingualism in schools and society: Language, identity, and policy.* New York, NY: Routledge.

Sidanius, J., Levin, S., Liu, J., & Pratto, F. (2000). Social dominance orientation, antiegliratianism and the political psychology of gender: an extension and cross cultural replication. *European Journal of Social Psychology, 30*(1), 41–67.

Sidanius, J., & Pratto, F. (1999). *Social dominance: an intergroup theory of social hierarchy and oppression.* Cambridge, England: Cambridge University Press.

Simmel, G., & Frisby, D. (2004). *The philosophy of money.* New York, NY: Routledge.

Simmel, G. (1903). The metropolis and mental life. In G. Bridge & S. Watson (Eds.), *The Blackwell reader.* Oxford, UK: Wiley-Blackwell.

Simmel, G. (1950). Individual and society. In G. Simmel & K. H. Wolff, *The Sociology of Georg Simmel.* Human Relations Collection. Glencoe, IL: Free Press.

Simmel, G. (1971). The stranger. In D. Levine (Ed.), *Some individuality and social forms* (pp. 143–149). Chicago, IL: University of Chicago.

Simpson, J. A. (1993). *Oxford English dictionary.* Oxford: Clarendon Press.

Singer, T., Seymour, B., O'Doherty, J. P., Stephan, K. E., Dolan, R. J., & Frith, C. D. (2006). Empathic neural responses are modulated by the perceived fairness of others. *Nature, 439*(7075), 466–469.

Skarlicki, D. P., & Folger, R. (1997). Retaliation in the workplace: The roles of distributive, procedural, and interactional justice. *Journal of Applied Psychology, 82*(3), 434–443. https://doi.org/10.1037/0021-9010.82.3.434

Skinner, B. F. (1951). How to teach animals. *Scientific American, 185*(6), 26–29.

Skowronski, J. J., & Carlston, D. E. (1989). Negativity and extremity biases in impression formation: A review of explanations. *Psychological Bulletin, 105*(1), 131–142.

Smith, A. (1976). *The theory of moral sentiments.* Ed. David D. Raphael and Alec L. MacFie. New York: Oxford University Press.

Smith, A. D. (1986). Conflict and collective identity: Class, ethnie and nation. In J. Burton & E. Azar (Eds.), *International conflict resolution: Theory and practice.* Boulder, CO: Lynne Rienner.

Smith, A. D. (1991). *National identity.* Reno: University of Nevada Press.

Smith, A. D. (2000). Theories of nationalism. In M. Leifer, *Asian Nationalism: Alternative Models of Nation-Formation* (pp. 1–20). London: Routledge.

Smith, E. R., & Decoster, J. (1998). Knowledge acquisition, accessibility, and use in person perception and stereotyping: Simulation with a recurrent connectionist network. *Journal of Personality and Social Psychology, 74*(1), 21–35.

Smith, E. E., & Medin, D. L. (1981). *Categories and concepts.* Cambridge, MA: Harvard University Press. Retrieved from http://www.cs.indiana.edu/~port/teach/sem08/Smith.Medin.1983.ch1.2.3.pdf

Smith, E. R., & Zarate, M. A. (1992). Exemplar-based model of social judgment. *Psychological Review*, 99(1), 3–21.

Smith, H. J., & Tyler, T. R. (1997). Choosing the right pond: The impact of group membership on self-esteem and group-oriented behavior. *Journal of Experimental Social Psychology*, 33(2), 146–170.

Snyder, M., Tanke, E. D., & Berscheid, E. (1977). Social perception and interpersonal behavior: On the self-fulfilling nature of social stereotypes. *Journal of Personality and Social Psychology*, 35(9), 656–666.

Solomon, Z. (1990). Does the war end when the shooting stops? The psychological toll of war. *Journal of Applied Social Psychology*, 20(1), 1733–1745.

Solt, F. (2011). Diversionary nationalism: Economic inequality and the formation of national pride. *Journal of Politics*, 73(3), 821–830.

Smotherman, W. P., & Robinson, S. R. (1987). Prenatal influences on development: Behavior is not a trivial aspect of fetal life. *Journal of Developmental & Behavioral Pediatrics*, 8(1), 171–176.

Smotherman, W. P. (1982). Odor aversion learning by the rat fetus. *Physiology & Behavior*, 29(5), 769–771.

Spence, M. J., & Decasper, A. J. (1987). Prenatal experience with low-frequency maternal-voice sounds influence neonatal perception of maternal voice samples. *Infant Behavior and Development*, 10(2), 133–142.

Sporer, S. L. (2001). Recognizing faces of other ethnic groups: An integration of theories. *Psychology, Public Policy, and Law*, 7(1), 36–97.

Sroufe, L. A., Egeland, B., Carlson, E., & Collins, W. A. (2005). Placing early attachment experiences in developmental context. In K. E. Grossmann, K. Grossmann, & E. Waters (Eds.), *The power of longitudinal attachment research: From infancy and childhood to adulthood* (pp. 48–70). New York: Guilford.

Stangor, C. (2000). *Stereotypes and prejudice: Essential readings*. Philadelphia, PA: Psychology Press.

Stangor, C., Sechrist, G. B., & Jost, J. T. (2001). Changing racial beliefs by providing consensus information. *Personality and Social Psychology Bulletin*, 27(4), 486–496.

Stanley, M. (1974). *Obedience to authority: An experimental view*. New York, NY: Harper & Row.

Stathi, S., & Roscini, C. (2016). Identity and acculturation processes in multicultural societies. In N. Ferguson, R. Haji, & S. McKeown, *Understanding peace and conflict: Through social identity theory* (pp. 55–69). Cham, Switzerland: Springer International.

Staub, E. (2002). Emergency helping, genocidal violence, and the evolution of responsibility and altruism in children. In *Visions of compassion: Western scientists and Tibetan Buddhists examine human nature* (pp. 165–81). New York, NY: Oxford University Press.

Steel, M., & Penny, D. (2010). Origins of life: Common ancestry put to the test. *Nature*, 465(7295), 168–169.

Stern, D. N. (1974). Mother and infant at play: the dyadic interaction involving facial, vocal and gaze behaviors. In *The effect of the infant on its care-giver* (pp. 187–215). New York, NY: John Wiley & Sons.

Stern, D. N. (1985). *The interpersonal world of the infant: a view from psychoanalysis and developmental psychology*. New York, NY: Basic Books.

Stewart, J., Gapenne, O., & Di Paolo, E. A. (2010). *Enaction: toward a new paradigm for cognitive science*. Cambridge, MA: MIT Press.

Strathearn, L., Fonagy, P., Amico, J., & Montague, P. R. (2009). Adult attachment predicts maternal brain and oxytocin response to infant cues. *Neuropsychopharmacology*, 34(13), 2655–2666. https://doi.org/10.1038/npp.2009.103

Strathearn, L., Li, J., Fonagy, P., & Montague, P. R. (2008). What's in a smile? Maternal brain responses to infant facial cues. *Pediatrics, 122*, 40–51. doi: https://doi.org/10.1542/peds.2007-1566

Stroessner, S. J., & Mackie, D. M. (1993). Affect and perceived group variability: Implications for stereotyping and prejudice. In D. M. Mackie & D. L. Hamilton (Eds.), *Affect, Cognition, and Stereotyping: Interactive Processes in Group Perception* (pp. 63–86). San Diego, CA: Academic Press.

Stuurman, S. (2000). Francois Bernier and the invention of racial classification. *History Workshop Journal: HWJ, (50)*, 1–21.

Subrahmanyam, K., Smahel, D., & Greenfield, P. (2006). Connecting developmental constructions to the Internet: Identity presentation and sexual exploration in online teen chat rooms. *Developmental Psychology, 42*(3), 395–406.

Summers, G., & Feldman, N. S. (1984). Blaming the victim versus blaming the perpetrator: An attributional analysis of spouse abuse. *Journal of Social and Clinical Psychology, 2*(4), 339–347.

Sumner, W. G. (1906). *Folkways: A study of the sociological importance of usages manners customs mores and morals*. Boston, MA: Ginn and Company.

Suomi, S. J., Eisele, C. D., Grady, S. A., & Harlow, H. F. (1975). Depressive behavior in adult monkeys following separation from family environment. *Journal of Abnormal Psychology, 84*(5), 576–578.

Swain, J. E., Lorberbaum, J. P., Kose, S., & Strathearn, L. (2007). Brain basis of early parent-infant interactions: psychology, physiology, and in vivo functional neuroimaging studies. *Journal of Child Psychology and Psychiatry, 48*(3), 262–287.

Tabibnia, G., & Lieberman, M. D. (2007). Fairness and cooperation are rewarding. *Annals of the New York Academy of Sciences, 1118*(1), 90–101.

Tajfel, H. (1959). Quantitative judgement in social perception. *British Journal of Psychology, 50*(1), 16–29.

Tajfel, H. (1969). Cognitive aspects of prejudice. *Journal of Biosocial Science, 1*(S1), 173–191.

Tajfel, H. (1978). *Differentiation between social groups: Studies in the social psychology of intergroup relations* (European monographs in social psychology ; 14). London: Published in co-operation with European Association of Experimental Social Psychology by Academic Press.

Tajfel, H., Sheikh, A. A., & Gardner, R. C. (1964). Content of stereotypes and the inference of similarity between members of stereotyped groups. *Acta Psychologica, 22*, 191–201.

Tajfel, H., & Wilkes, A. (1964). Salience of attributes and commitment to extreme judgments in the perception of people. *British Journal of Clinical Psychology, 3*(1), 40–49.

Tajfel, H., & Wilkes, A. L. (1963). Classification and quantitative judgement. *British Journal of Psychology, 54*(2), 101–114.

Taylor, S. E. (1981). The interface of cognitive and social psychology. In J. Harvey, *Cognition, Social Behavior, and the Environment* (pp. 189–211). Hillsdale, NJ: Erlbaum.

Taylor, S. E. (1991). Asymmetrical effects of positive and negative events: The mobilization-minimization hypothesis. *Psychological Bulletin, 110*(1), 67.

Tetlock, P. E., & Mitchell, G. (2008). Calibrating prejudice in milliseconds. *Social Psychology Quarterly, 71*(1), 12–16.

Thelen, E., & Smith, L. (1994). *A dynamic systems approach to the development of cognition and action*. MIT Press/Bradford Books Series in Cognitive Psychology. Cambridge, MA: MIT Press.

Thomas, L. (2017, April 23). Le Pen says will defend France against globalization. *U.S. News & World Report*. Retrieved from https://www.usnews.com/news/world/articles/2017-04-23/le-pen-says-will-defend-france-against-globalization?src=usn_tw

Thompson, E. (2010). *Mind in life: Biology, phenomenology, and the sciences of mind*. Cambridge, MA: Harvard University Press.

Thompson, P. (2012). Both dialogic and dialectic: "Translation at the crossroads". *Learning, Culture and Social Interaction, 1*, 90–101.

Thompson, J. N. (2014). *Interaction and coevolution*. Chicago, IL: University of Chicago Press.

Tobin, S. J., & Raymundo, M. M. (2010). Causal uncertainty and psychological well-being: The moderating role of accommodation (secondary control). *Personality and Social Psychology Bulletin, 36*(3), 371–383.

Todorovic, D. (2008). Gestalt principles. *Scholarpedia, 3*(12), 5345. Retrieved from http://www. scholarpedia.org/article/Gestalt_principles

Todrank, J., Heth, G., & Restrepo, D. (2011). Effects of in utero odorant exposure on neuroanatomical development of the olfactory bulb and odour preferences. *Proceedings. Biological Sciences, 278*(1714), 1949–1955. https://doi.org/10.1098/rspb.2010.2314

Tooby, J., & Cosmides, L. (1992). The psychological foundations of culture. In J. Barkow, L. Cosmides, & J. Tooby, *The adapted mind: Evolutionary psychology and the generation of culture* (pp. 19–136). New York, NY: Oxford University Press.

Tottenham, N., Hare, T. A., Quinn, B. T., McCarry, T. W., Nurse, M., Gilhooly, T., . . . Eigsti, I. (2010). Prolonged institutional rearing is associated with atypically large amygdala volume and difficulties in emotion regulation. *Developmental Science, 13*(1), 46–61.

Trevarthen, C. (1984). Chapter IIIa: How control of movement develops. *Advances in Psychology, 17*(C), 223–261. https://doi.org/10.1016/S0166-4115(08)61374-6

Trivers, R. (1972). *Parental investment and sexual selection*. Cambridge, MA: Biological Laboratories, Harvard University.

Tronick, E. Z. (1989). Emotions and emotional communication in infants. *American Psychologist, 44*(2), 112–119.

Tronick, E. (2009, Nov 30). Still face experiment: Dr. Edward Tronick [Video File]. Retrieved from https://www.youtube.com/watch?v=apzXGEbZht0

Tronick, E., Als, H., Adamson, L., Wise, S., & Brazelton, T. B. (1978). The infant's response to entrapment between contradictory messages in face-to-face interaction. *Journal of the American Academy of Child Psychiatry, 17*(1), 1–13. https://doi.org/10.1016/S0002-7138(09)62273-1

Tronick, E. Z., & Cohn, J. F. (1989). Infant-mother face-to-face interaction: age and gender differences in coordination and the occurrence of miscoordination. *Child Development, 60*(1), 85–92.

Tucker, D. H., & Rowe, P. M. (1979). Relationship between expectancy, causal attributions, and final hiring decisions in the employment interview. *Journal of Applied Psychology, 61*(1), 27–34.

Turner, R. (1981). Social support as a contingency in psychological well-being. *Journal of Health and Social Behavior, 22*(4), 357–367.

Turner, J., & Hogg, M. (1987). Intergroup behavior, self-stereotyping and the salience of social categories. *British Journal of Social Psychology, 26*(4), 325–340.

Turner, J. C. (1981). The experimental social psychology of intergroup behavior. In J. Turner & H. Giles (Eds.), *Intergroup behavior* (p. 346). Oxford, England: Blackwell.

Turner, J. C. (1987). *Rediscovering the social group. A self-categorization theory* (pp. 282, 346). New York: Basil Blackwell.

Turner, J. C., & Onorato, R. S. (1999). Social identity, personality, and the selfconcept. A self-categorizing perspective. In T. R. Tyler, R. M. Kramer, & O. R. John (Eds.), *The psychology of the social self* (p. 346). Mahwah, NJ: Erlbaum.

Turner, J. C., Hogg, M. A., Oakes, P. J., Reicher, S. D., & Wetherell, M. S. (1987). *Rediscovering the social group: A self-categorization theory*. Cambridge, MA: Basil Blackwell.

UNESCO, & Conference for the Establishment of an Educational, Scientific and Cultural Organization of the United Nations. (1945). *Constitution of the United Nations Educational, Scientific and Cultural Organization*. London, UK: UNESCO.

United Nations Educational, Scientific, and Cultural Organization. (1950). *The Race Question*. Paris. Retrieved from https://unesdoc.unesco.org/ark:/48223/pf0000128291

United Nations Educational, Scientific, and Cultural Organization. (1952). *The race concept: Results of an inquiry*. Paris. Retrieved from https://unesdoc.unesco.org/ark:/48223/pf0000073351

United Nations Educational, Scientific, and Cultural Organization (1965). A document of paramount importance: The biological facts of the race question. *The UNESCO Courier, 18*(4), 8.

United Nations Educational, Scientific, and Cultural Organization (1969). *Four statements on the race question*. Paris. Retrieved from https://unesdoc.unesco.org/ark:/48223/pf0000122962

United Nations Educational, Scientific, and Cultural Organization. (1979). Declaration on race and racial prejudice : Adopted by the General Conference of Unesco at its twentieth session Paris, 27 November 1978. Paris.

United Nations, Department of Economic and Social Affairs, Population Division. (2014). *World urbanization prospects: The 2014 revision, highlights*. United Nations. Retrieved from https://www.un.org/en/development/desa/publications/2014-revision-world-urbanization-prospects.html

Valenza, E., Simion, F., Cassia, V. M., & Umiltà, C. (1996). Face preference at birth. *Journal of Experimental Psychology: Human Perception and Performance, 22*(4), 892–903.

Vallone, R. P., Ross, L., & Lepper, M. R. (1985). The hostile media phenomenon: Biased perception and perceptions of media bias in coverage of the Beirut massacre. *Journal of Personality and Social Psychology, 49*(3), 577–585.

Van den Berghe, P. L. (1995). Does race matter? *Nations and Nationalism, 1*(3), 357–368.

Van Dijken, S. (1998). *John Bowlby: his early life: a biographical journey into the roots of attachment theory*. New York, NY: Free Association Books.

Van Overwalle, F. (2009). Social cognition and the brain: A meta-analysis. *Human Brain Mapping, 30*(3), 829–858.

Van Veen, V., Krug, M. K., Schooler, J. W., & Carter, C. S. (2009). Neural activity predicts attitude change in cognitive dissonance. *Nature Neuroscience, 12*(11), 1469–1474.

Vanderwert, R. E., Marshall, P. J., Nelson, C. A., Zeanah, C. H., & Fox, N. A. (2010). Timing of intervention affects brain electrical activity in children exposed to severe psychosocial neglect. *PLoS One, 5*(7), E11415. https://doi.org/10.1371/journal.pone.0011415

Varela, F. J., Thompson, E., & Rosch, E. (1991). *The embodied mind: cognitive science and human experience*. Cambridge, MA: MIT Press.

Varshney, A. (2003). *Ethnic conflict and civic life: Hindus and Muslims in India*. New Haven, CT: Yale University Press.

Von Hippel, W., Sekaquaptewa, D., & Vargas, P. (1995). On the role of encoding processes in stereotype maintenance. In M. P. Zanna (Eds.), *Advances in experimental social psychology* (Vol. 27, pp. 177–254). Cambridge, MA: Academic Press.

Vygotsky, L. (1978). Interaction between learning and development. In M. Gauvain & M. Cole (Eds.), *Readings on the development of children* (pp. 34–41). New York, NY: Scientific American Books.

Waldman, E. A. (2003). Healing hearts or righting wrongs: A meditation on the goals of restorative justice. *Hamline Journal of Public Law and Policy, 25*(2), 355–373.

Walton, G. E., Bower, N. J. A., & Bower, T. G. R. (1992). Recognition of familiar faces by newborns. *Infant Behavior and Development, 15*(2), 265–269. https://doi.org/10.1016/0163-6383(92)80027-R

Wang, D., Wang, Y., & Zhang, Y. (1992). The relationship between locus of control, depression, shame, and self-esteem. *Chinese Mental Health Journal, 6*(5), 207–210.

Weinberg, M. K., & Tronick, E. Z. (1996). Infant affective reactions to the resumption of maternal interaction after the still-face. *Child Development, 67*(3), 905–914.

Weiner, B. (1993). On sin versus sickness: A theory of perceived responsibility and social motivation. *American Psychologist, 48*(9), 957–965.

Weissmark, M. (1995, June 29). Coming to the table - Part 1 [Video File]. Retrieved from https://youtu.be/NRB--qC7Zeo

Weissmark, M. (1995, June 29). Coming to the table - Part 2 [Video File]. Retrieved from https://youtu.be/IdQnNWfrtZM

Weissmark, M. S. (2004). *Justice matters: Legacies of the holocaust and World War II*. New York, NY: Oxford University Press.

Weissmark, M. S. (2016, July 12). Lessons learned from Auschwitz. [Blog post]. Retrieved from https://www.psychologytoday.com/us/blog/justice-matters/201607/lessons-learned-auschwitz

Weissmark, M. S. (2017, July 28). Why are conversations on race often futile? [Blog post]. Retrieved from https://www.psychologytoday.com/us/blog/justice-matters/201707/why-are-conversations-race-often-futile

Weissmark, M. S. (2017, August 17). The virtues of science-based thinking in the post-truth age. [Blog post]. Retrieved from https://www.psychologytoday.com/us/blog/justice-matters/201708/the-virtues-science-based-thinking-in-the-post-truth-age

Weissmark, M. S. (2017, November 4). Teaching and writing about diversity: Worldwide Students respond to diversity taught through a scientific lens. [Blog post]. Retrieved from https://www.psychologytoday.com/us/blog/justice-matters/201711/teaching-and-writing-about-diversity

Weissmark, M. S. (2018, January 9). Why do diversity programs fail? [Blog post]. Retrieved from https://www.psychologytoday.com/us/blog/justice-matters/201801/why-do-diversity-programs-fail

Weissmark, M. S. (2018, February 7). Outlawing bias is doomed to fail [Blog post]. Retrieved from https://www.psychologytoday.com/intl/blog/justice-matters/201802/outlawing-bias-is-doomed-fail

Weissmark, M. S. (2018, May 8). Are there any solutions to group polarization? [Blog post]. Retrieved from https://www.psychologytoday.com/us/blog/justice-matters/201805/are-there-any-solutions-group-polarization

Weissmark, M. S. (2018, August 8). Evaluating psychology research [Blog post]. Retrieved from https://www.psychologytoday.com/us/blog/justice-matters/201808/evaluating-psychology-research

Weissmark, M. S. (2018, November 14). Are there effective ways to reduce bias and prejudice? [Blog post]. Retrieved from https://www.psychologytoday.com/us/blog/justice-matters/201811/are-there-effective-ways-reduce-bias-and-prejudice

Weissmark, M. S. (2019, February 12). Reducing polarization: What works? [Blog post]. Retrieved from https://www.psychologytoday.com/us/blog/justice-matters/201902/reducing-polarization-what-works

Weissmark, M. S. (2019, April 29). If banning bias doesn't work, what will? [Blog post]. Retrieved from https://www.psychologytoday.com/us/blog/justice-matters/201904/if-banning-bias-doesnt-work-what-will

Weissmark, M. S. (2019, July 10). What is justice? [Blog post]. Retrieved from https://www.psychologytoday.com/us/blog/justice-matters/201907/what-is-justice

Weissmark, M. S. (2019, August 22). Can We Teach Diversity Without an Agenda? [Blog post]. Retrieved from https://www.psychologytoday.com/intl/blog/justice-matters/201908/can-we-teach-diversity-without-agenda

Weissmark, M. S. (2019, October 22). Are Diversity Activists Focused on the Wrong Solution? [Blog post]. Retrieved from https://www.psychologytoday.com/intl/blog/justice-matters/201910/are-diversity-activists-focused-the-wrong-solution

Weissmark, M. S. (2020, January 29). The Perils of Apathy [Blog post]. Retrieved from https://www.psychologytoday.com/us/blog/justice-matters/202001/the-perils-apathy

Weissmark, M. S., Giacomo, D. A., & Kuphal, I. (1993). Psychosocial themes in the lives of children of survivors and Nazis. *Journal of Narrative and Life History, 3*(4), 319–335.

Weissmark, M. S., & Giacomo, D. A. (2008). *Doing psychotherapy effectively.* Chicago, IL: University of Chicago Press.

Wertheimer, M. (1923). Laws of organization in perceptual forms. In W. D. Ellis (Ed.), *A source book of gestalt psychology.* London, UK: Routledge & Kegan Paul.

Westermann, R., Stahl, G., & Hesse, F. (1996). Relative effectiveness and validity of mood induction procedures: A meta-analysis. *European Journal of Social Psychology, 26*(4), 557–580.

Whitehouse, H. (2000). *Arguments and icons: Divergent modes of religiosity: Divergent modes of religiosity.* Oxford, UK: Oxford University Press.

Whitehouse, H. (2004). *Modes of religiosity: A cognitive theory of religious transmission.* Walnut Creek, CA: AltaMira Press.

Widom, C. S. (1989). Does violence beget violence? A critical examination of the literature. *Psychological Bulletin, 106*(1), 3–28.

Wierda-Boer, H. H., Gerris, J. R., & Vermulst, A. A. (2009). Managing multiple roles: Personality, stress, and work-family interference in dual-earner couples. *Journal of Individual Differences, 30*(1), 6–19.

Wilder, D. A. (1981). Perceiving persons as a group: Categorization and intergroup relations. In D. Hamilton, *Cognitive processes in stereotyping and intergroup behavior* (pp. 213–258). Taylor and Francis: New York.

Wilder, D. A. (1978). Reduction of intergroup discrimination through individuation of the out-group. *Journal of Personality and Social Psychology, 36*(12), 1361–1374. https://doi.org/10.1037/0022-3514.36.12.1361

Wilson, M. L., & Wrangham, R. W. (2003). Intergroup relations in chimpanzees. *Annual Review of Anthropology, 32*(1), 363–392.

Winslow, J. T., Hastings, N., Carter, C. S., Harbaugh, C. R., & Insel, T. R. (1993). A role for central vasopressin in pair bonding in monogamous prairie voles. *Nature, 365*(6446), 545–548.

Wirth, L. (1938). Urbanism as a way of life. *American Journal of Sociology, 44*(1), 1–24.

Word, C. O., Zanna, M. P., & Cooper, J. (1974). The nonverbal mediation of self-fulfilling prophecies in interracial interaction. *Journal of Experimental Social Psychology, 10*(2), 109–120.

Worthington, E. L., Sandage, S. J., & Berry, J. W. (2000). Group interventions to promote forgiveness. In M. McCullough, K. Pargament, & C. Thoresen (Eds.), *Forgiveness: Theory, research, and practice* (pp. 228–253). New York, NY: Guilford Press.

Worthington, E. L., Jr., Kurusu, T. A., Collins, W., & Berry, J. W. (2000). Forgiving usually takes time: A lesson learned by studying interventions to promote forgiveness. *Journal of Psychology and Theology, 28*(1), 3–20.

Wrangham R., Pilbeam D. (2001). African apes as time machines. In B. M. F. Galdikas, N. E. Briggs, L. K. Sheeran, G. L. Shapiro, & J. Goodall (Eds.), *All apes great and small: Developments in primatology; Progress and prospects* (pp. 5–18). Boston, MA: Springer.

Wrangham, R. W. (1999). Evolution of coalitionary killing. *American Journal of Physical Anthropology, 110*(S29), 1–30.

Xu, X., Aron, A., Brown, L., Cao, G., Feng, T., & Weng, X. (2011). Reward and motivation systems: A brain mapping study of early-stage intense romantic love in Chinese participants. *Human Brain Mapping, 32*(2), 249–257.

Yack, B. (2012). *Nationalism and the moral psychology of community.* Chicago, IL: University of Chicago Press.

Yang, Y., & Raine, A. (2009). Prefrontal structural and functional brain imaging findings in antisocial, violent, and psychopathic individuals: A meta-analysis. *Psychiatry Research: Neuroimaging, 174*(2), 81–88.

Ybarra, O., & Stephan, W. G. (1996). Misanthropic person memory. *Journal of Personality and Social Psychology, 70*(4), 691–700.

Yehuda, R. (2002). Post-traumatic stress disorder. *New England Journal of Medicine, 346*(2), 108–114.

Younger, B. A. (2010). Categorization and concept formation in human infants. In D. Mareschal, P. Quinn, & S. Lea, *The making of human concepts* (pp. 245–263). Oxford, UK: Oxford University Press.

Younger, J., Aron, A., Parke, S., Chatterjee, N., & Mackey, S. (2010). Viewing pictures of a romantic partner reduces experimental pain: Involvement of neural reward systems. *PloS One, 5*(10), E13309.

Yudkin, D. A., Rothmund, T., Twardawski, M., Thalla, N., & Van Bavel, J. J. (2016). Reflexive intergroup bias in third-party punishment. *Journal of Experimental Psychology,* 145(11):1448–1459.

Zarate, M. A., & Smith, E. R. (1990). Person categorization and stereotyping. *Social Cognition, 8*(2), 161–185.

Zhang, S., & Kline, S. L. (2009). Can I make my own decision? A cross-cultural study of perceived social network influence in mate selection. *Journal of Cross-Cultural Psychology, 40*(1), 3–23.

Figure Credit Lines

Figure 1.1 https://www.shutterstock.com/image-illustration/babel-tower-concept-3d-rendering-583264918

Figure 1.2 https://www.shutterstock.com/image-photo/socrates-statue-athens-academy-221652247

Figure 1.3 https://www.shutterstock.com/image-vector/type-cranial-given-by-spurzheim-profile-154876247

Figure 1.4 https://www.shutterstock.com/image-photo/brain-tape-measure-isolated-on-white-431970499

Figure 1.5 https://www.shutterstock.com/image-vector/may202019-charles-robert-darwin-naturalist-geologist-1404662372

Figure 1.6 https://www.shutterstock.com/image-illustration/large-group-people-seen-above-gathered-245469079

Figure 1.7 https://www.shutterstock.com/image-vector/family-tree-genealogy-diagram-stick-figure-136701419

Figure 2.1 https://www.shutterstock.com/image-vector/human-fetus-inside-womb-1-9-499432027

Figure 2.2 https://www.shutterstock.com/image-photo/image-pregnant-woman-touching-her-belly-111643082

Figure 2.3 https://www.shutterstock.com/image-vector/molecule-body-concept-human-dna-eps10-251639014

Figure 2.4 https://www.shutterstock.com/image-photo/newborn-baby-sleep-first-days-life-653105200

Figure 2.5 https://www.shutterstock.com/image-photo/pretty-woman-holding-newborn-baby-her-566796565

Figure 2.6 https://www.shutterstock.com/image-photo/no-little-african-baby-boy-crying-390076054

Figure 2.7 https://www.shutterstock.com/image-photo/black-white-portrait-sad-lonely-child-137011292

Figure 2.8 https://www.shutterstock.com/image-photo/professional-female-psychologist-working-teenage-girl-672818578

Figure 2.9 https://www.shutterstock.com/image-vector/vector-flat-design-illustrated-maslow-pyramid-416861629

Figure 2.10   https://www.shutterstock.com/image-photo/friends-community-chill-out-together-561407323

Figure 2.11   https://www.shutterstock.com/image-photo/top-view-people-meeting-old-wooden-323566982

Figure 3.1   https://www.shutterstock.com/image-photo/concept-racism-misunderstanding-barrier-relations-denial-692329723

Figure 3.2   https://www.shutterstock.com/image-vector/visualized-simplified-sort-process-792427462

Figure 3.3   https://www.shutterstock.com/image-vector/male-hand-pointing-above-finger-directed-672496219

Figure 3.4   https://www.shutterstock.com/image-photo/artists-lay-figure-represents-leader-addressing-587846414

Figure 3.5   https://www.shutterstock.com/image-photo/wire-nails-looks-like-davlenie-authoritarianism-546092608

Figure 3.6   https://www.shutterstock.com/image-photo/child-therapist-observing-how-girl-interacts-649306726

Figure 3.7   https://www.shutterstock.com/image-photo/womens-hands-guiding-child-help-him-236959759

Figure 3.8   https://www.shutterstock.com/image-illustration/folder-open-papers-3d-render-518120560

Figure 3.9   https://www.shutterstock.com/image-photo/rat-corner-maze-during-experiment-46094989

Figure 3.10   https://www.shutterstock.com/image-photo/interracial-friends-greeting-each-other-handshaking-494209579

Figure 3.11   https://www.shutterstock.com/image-photo/sad-little-child-boy-hugging-his-390037516

Figure 3.12   https://www.shutterstock.com/image-vector/cross-section-through-brain-showing-limbic-327400424

Figure 3.13   https://www.shutterstock.com/image-illustration/fiddler-on-roof-344410550

Figure 3.14   https://www.shutterstock.com/image-photo/close-hands-bride-groom-holding-together-570524407

Figure 4.1   https://www.shutterstock.com/image-vector/bible-serpent-fruit-325934918

Figure 4.2   https://www.shutterstock.com/image-vector/adam-eve-artnouveau-style-124564579

Figure 4.3   https://www.shutterstock.com/image-vector/modern-flat-thin-line-design-vector-687778612

Figure 4.4   https://www.shutterstock.com/image-illustration/3d-xray-human-brain-computer-chip-165213380

Figure 4.5   https://www.shutterstock.com/image-photo/programming-code-on-computer-screen-source-422924974

Figure 4.6   https://www.shutterstock.com/image-illustration/human-emotion-mood-disorder-tree-shaped-273373235

Figure 4.7   https://www.shutterstock.com/image-illustration/subconscious-mind-concept-brain-under-water-246587989

Figure 4.8   https://www.shutterstock.com/image-photo/man-prepares-run-digital-interface-414995995

Figure 4.9   https://www.shutterstock.com/image-vector/best-friends-vector-icon-friendship-agreement-304239890

Figure 4.10   https://www.shutterstock.com/image-photo/hand-drawing-geometry-categorize-on-chalkboard-602143955

Figure 4.11   https://www.istockphoto.com/photos/684540232?license=rf&phrase=684540232)&assettype=image&sort=best

Figure 4.12   https://www.shutterstock.com/image-illustration/excluded-group-business-concept-birds-on-460275331

Figure 4.13   https://www.shutterstock.com/image-photo/business-group-seminar-meeting-concept-397451767

Figure 4.14   https://www.shutterstock.com/image-vector/business-man-activity-110588132

Figure 4.15   https://www.shutterstock.com/image-illustration/psychologists-session-two-men-sitting-blue-394394557

Figure 4.16   https://www.shutterstock.com/image-vector/four-temperaments-sanguine-choleric-melancholic-phlegmatic-272046833

Figure 4.17   https://www.shutterstock.com/image-photo/two-cheetah-hunting-catching-impala-antelope-173037086

Figure 5.1   https://www.shutterstock.com/image-photo/big-bang-theory-very-high-density-512836666

Figure 5.2   https://www.shutterstock.com/image-photo/two-different-color-moths-small-dusty-710460175

Figure 5.3   https://www.shutterstock.com/image-vector/old-engraved-illustration-two-hands-quadrumana-92898526

Figure 5.4   https://www.shutterstock.com/image-photo/monkey-hanging-on-tree-15006187

Figure 5.5   https://www.shutterstock.com/image-photo/microscopic-photograph-ciliate-protozan-phylum-ciliophora-553842106

Figure 5.6   https://www.shutterstock.com/image-illustration/twocell-embryo-3d-illustration-115167925

Figure 5.7   https://www.shutterstock.com/image-photo/family-portrait-24283168

Figure 6.6 https://www.shutterstock.com/image-photo/drawing-cave-drawn-by-prehistoric-man-651017017

Figure 6.7 https://www.shutterstock.com/image-vector/ancient-greece-scene-black-figure-pottery-577810900

Figure 6.8 https://www.shutterstock.com/image-vector/rocky-seashore-classic-minoan-colony-bay-249766660

Figure 6.9 https://www.shutterstock.com/image-vector/large-collection-greek-songs-on-white-356460515

Figure 6.10 https://www.shutterstock.com/image-vector/old-eastern-persian-orient-scenic-view-524504116

Figure 6.11 https://www.istockphoto.com/ca/vector/vector-illustration-of-social-disparity-gm187890299-24103812

Figure 6.12 https://www.shutterstock.com/image-illustration/rich-cynical-industry-captain-takes-advantage-644029255

Figure 6.13 https://www.shutterstock.com/image-photo/close-blacksmith-manually-forging-molten-metal-601870478

Figure 6.14 https://www.shutterstock.com/image-vector/business-concept-illustration-leader-pointing-wrong-615528884

Figure 6.15 https://www.shutterstock.com/image-vector/business-concept-illustration-chained-businessman-612156089

Figure 6.16 https://premier.shutterstock.com/image/detail-352941977/cityscape-and-sunset-at-evening-time

Figure 6.17 https://www.shutterstock.com/image-photo/mumbaii-india-march-24-2015-mumbai-403396726

Figure 6.18 https://www.shutterstock.com/image-illustration/humiliation-harassment-crowd-people-chase-sad-648801862

Figure 6.19 https://www.istockphoto.com/ca/photo/british-newspaper-frontpages-following-brexit-vote-result-gm542321314-97105255

Figure 6.20 https://www.shutterstock.com/image-photo/serious-teen-boy-surrounded-by-darkness-666328516

Figure 6.21 https://www.shutterstock.com/image-photo/teamwork-couple-hiking-help-each-other-250176199

Figure 6.22 https://www.istockphoto.com/ca/photo/girl-crying-gm108226209-8644259

Figure 6.23 https://www.shutterstock.com/image-vector/male-heads-silhouette-depression-schizophrenia-paper-522145147

Figure 6.24 https://www.shutterstock.com/image-photo/woman-stands-front-crowd-angry-mob-1012104691

Figure 7.1   https://www.shutterstock.com/image-photo/berlin-may-19-dalai-lama-speaks-64829506

Figure 7.2   https://www.shutterstock.com/image-photo/buddha-sculpture-659455243

Figure 7.3   https://www.shutterstock.com/image-photo/brussels-belgium-july-26-2012-adam-198468671

Figure 7.4   https://www.shutterstock.com/image-photo/noah-released-dove-1-le-sainte-94379629

Figure 7.5   https://www.shutterstock.com/image-photo/s-wife-salts-statue-near-dead-48383098

Figure 7.6   https://www.shutterstock.com/image-photo/abraham-sends-hagar-ishmael-away-picture-97130927

Figure 7.7   https://premier.shutterstock.com/image/detail-94224790/the-murder-of-abel-1-le-sainte-bible-traduction-nouvelle-selon-la-vulgate-par-mm-j-j-bourasse-et-p-janvier-tours-alfred-mame-et-fils-2-1866-3-france-4-gustave-dore

Figure 7.8   https://www.shutterstock.com/image-illustration/visual-perception-impact-computer-use-on-310753076

Figure 7.9   https://www.shutterstock.com/image-photo/building-look-symmetry-565127815

Figure 7.10   https://www.istockphoto.com/ca/photo/connected-together-and-forever-gm646407158-117224981

Figure 7.11   https://www.istockphoto.com/ca/photo/doctor-and-patient-using-digital-tablet-in-hospital-gm838723420-136614599

Figure 7.12   https://www.shutterstock.com/image-vector/mechanism-icon-vector-simple-flat-symbol-365118002

Figure 7.13   https://www.shutterstock.com/image-vector/vector-business-concepts-flat-style-hands-227876281

Figure 7.14   https://www.shutterstock.com/image-photo/statue-justice-lady-iustitia-justitia-roman-645714523

Figure 7.15   https://www.shutterstock.com/image-photo/auschwitz-poland-february-10-2019-museum-585719252

Figure 7.16   https://www.istockphoto.com/ca/photo/silhouette-cutout-men-standing-next-to-each-other-as-one-pushes-another-off-the-edge-gm859608004-142047553

Figure 7.17   https://www.shutterstock.com/image-photo/nazi-concentration-camp-auschwitz-poland-unesco-576657064

Figure 7.18   https://www.shutterstock.com/image-photo/holocaust-remembrance-day-1061755361

Figure 7.19   https://www.shutterstock.com/image-vector/law-legal-business-accessory-themis-lady-373233997

Figure 8.1   https://www.shutterstock.com/image-vector/guillotine-sketch-style-vector-illustration-old-472664524

Figure 8.2 https://www.shutterstock.com/image-photo/primitive-stone-ax-man-lies-on-726742765

Figure 8.3 https://www.shutterstock.com/image-photo/liberated-prisoners-wobbelin-concentration-camp-taken-249574036

Figure 8.4 https://www.shutterstock.com/image-photo/law-wooden-gavel-barrister-justice-concept-594894248

Figure 8.5 https://www.shutterstock.com/image-photo/chess-pieces-metaphor-racism-bullying-one-389099977

Figure 8.6 https://www.istockphoto.com/ca/photo/stop-violence-over-women-gm523694708-92027521

Figure 8.7 https://www.istockphoto.com/ca/photo/closed-society-gm172247612-3980751

Figure 8.8 https://www.shutterstock.com/image-vector/crowd-behaviors-measuring-social-sampling-statistics-689023369

Figure 8.9 https://www.shutterstock.com/image-photo/hand-black-glove-pushing-on-scale-689385859

Figure 8.10 https://www.shutterstock.com/image-photo/young-brothers-talking-tin-can-telephone-116233960

Figure 8.11 https://www.shutterstock.com/image-photo/oswiencim-poland-january-14-2017-portraits-567048193

Figure 8.12 https://www.shutterstock.com/image-photo/palm-youth-adults-321800429

Figure 8.13 https://www.shutterstock.com/image-photo/relationship-problems-frustrated-young-african-couple-561618586

Figure 8.14 https://www.istockphoto.com/ca/photo/two-halves-heart-embroidered-red-thread-on-black-fabric-two-halves-heart-sewn-with-gm691600518-127561987

Figure 8.15 https://www.shutterstock.com/image-photo/germany-circa-1988-stamp-printed-shows-103974272

Figure 8.16 https://www.shutterstock.com/image-illustration/anxiety-solution-freedom-fear-depression-group-357485966

Figure 8.17 https://www.shutterstock.com/image-photo/family-tree-genealogy-399516166

Figure 8.18 https://www.shutterstock.com/image-illustration/global-relations-concept-group-white-peace-214923151

Figure 8.19 https://www.istockphoto.com/ca/photo/creative-office-gm642980978-116693911

Figure 8.20 https://www.istockphoto.com/ca/photo/woman-during-a-psychotherapy-session-gm814596226-131841947

Figure 8.21 https://www.shutterstock.com/image-photo/group-therapy-patients-standing-holding-hands-688611787

Figure 8.22 https://www.shutterstock.com/image-photo/resentful-man-talking-angrily-relationship-psychologist-675831163

Figure 8.23   https://www.shutterstock.com/image-vector/dialoguecontact-conversational-exchange-between-two-individuals-126723503

Figure 8.24   https://www.istockphoto.com/ca/photo/censorship-gm468867990-60165354

Figure 8.25   https://www.shutterstock.com/image-photo/mens-muscles-reality-expectation-sports-training-609800483

Figure 8.26   https://www.shutterstock.com/image-illustration/integration-concept-two-groups-running-people-431065036

Figure 8.27   https://www.shutterstock.com/image-photo/view-crowd-covering-ears-146263625

Figure 8.28   https://www.shutterstock.com/image-photo/story-time-121083364

Figure 8.29   https://www.shutterstock.com/image-photo/mother-handing-key-daughter-135523697

Figure 8.30   https://www.shutterstock.com/image-photo/linking-entities-networking-social-media-sns-588813473

Figure 8.31   https://www.shutterstock.com/image-illustration/hand-holding-polygonal-lamp-on-grey-773293384

Figure 8.32   https://www.shutterstock.com/image-photo/head-clouds-minimalist-concept-536001130

Figure 8.33   https://www.shutterstock.com/image-photo/red-text-what-paper-question-mark-431153836

Figure 9.1   https://www.shutterstock.com/image-illustration/white-globe-extruded-continents-national-borders-299323850

Figure 9.2   https://www.shutterstock.com/image-illustration/latvia-flag-focus-europe-map-countries-507187507

Figure 9.3   https://www.shutterstock.com/image-illustration/large-group-people-seen-above-gathered-286867178

Figure 9.4   https://www.shutterstock.com/image-vector/marinoni-printing-press-vintage-engraving-old-82645594

Figure 9.5   https://www.shutterstock.com/image-photo/united-nations-headquarters-new-york-city-202309894

Figure 9.6   https://www.shutterstock.com/image-vector/illustration-large-mass-people-perspective-grey-686048416

Figure 9.7   https://www.shutterstock.com/image-illustration/pink-yellow-blue-energetic-waves-over-349728953

Figure 9.8   https://www.shutterstock.com/image-illustration/illustration-silhouette-france-binary-digits-on-718482712

Figure 9.9   https://www.shutterstock.com/image-photo/view-senior-people-holding-hands-dancing-285424514

Figure 9.10   https://www.shutterstock.com/image-photo/australian-passport-application-citizenship-form-408460138

Figure 9.11   https://www.shutterstock.com/image-photo/refugee-children-concept-silhouette-two-refugees-457657579

Figure 9.12   https://www.shutterstock.com/image-photo/barcelona-march-02-facebook-ceo-mark-258044801

Figure 9.13   https://www.shutterstock.com/image-photo/manheim-pa-october-1-2016-people-530768224

Figure 9.14   https://www.shutterstock.com/image-photo/discrimination-xenophobia-racism-social-exclusion-words-531750853

Figure 9.15   https://www.shutterstock.com/image-photo/maceratamarcheitalyfebruary-102018-people-demonstrate-against-fascism-1091598758

Figure 9.16   https://www.shutterstock.com/image-photo/charlottesville-8-2017-counter-protester-kkk-1082661191

Figure 9.17   https://www.shutterstock.com/image-photo/new-york-july-16-selection-donald-685378291

Figure 9.18   https://www.istockphoto.com/ca/photo/military-parade-in-bastille-day-gm458293067-23654651

Figure 9.19   https://www.istockphoto.com/ca/photo/close-up-dollar-bill-gm647444330-117504585

Figure 9.20   https://www.istockphoto.com/ca/photo/polling-place-gm538475150-95759001

Figure 9.21   https://www.shutterstock.com/image-photo/new-york-city-november-13-2016-516305989

Figure 9.22   https://www.istockphoto.com/ca/photo/view-from-rooftop-in-morocco-division-between-rich-and-poor-gm640345778-115954839

Figure 9.23   https://www.istockphoto.com/ca/photo/strategic-world-map-with-infographics-gm875327078-244373223

Figure 9.24   https://www.shutterstock.com/image-photo/birmingham-united-kingdom-october-2-2016-492419296

Figure 9.25   https://www.shutterstock.com/image-photo/strasbourg-france-may-7-2017-sticker-635188049

Figure 9.26   https://www.shutterstock.com/image-photo/usa-circa-1950s-vintage-photo-shows-224163778

Figure 9.27   https://www.shutterstock.com/image-photo/group-elementary-school-kids-rushing-out-388630366

Figure 9.28   https://www.istockphoto.com/ca/photo/citizenship-requirement-gm171241063-2079797

Index

For the benefit of digital users, indexed terms that span two pages (e.g., 52–53) may, on occasion, appear on only one of those pages.

Abraham (Biblical), 192–96
accommodation, 75–81, 270, 274
acting, "requiredness" of, 198–206
action research, 100–2
Adorno, Theodor, 54–56
affective systems evolution, 108–9
aggression, human tendency towards, 148–50, 302–3
agreeableness, 229
Agricultural Revolution, 155–59
Ainsworth, Mary, 47
Albania, 226
Aleichem, Sholem, 77
alienation. *See* social alienation
Allen, Woody, 148
Allport, Gordon, 53, 93, 94
amygdala, 72–73, 107, 139–40
Anderson, C., 268–69, 281
anger/resentment, 241–43
anonymous social relations, 155–58
anterior cingulate cortex, 205–6
apology dynamic, 299, 301. *See also* forgiveness, promotion of
Arendt, Hannah, xxi, 245–46
Arias, I., 300–1
Aristotle, 5, 241
Aron, A., 139
Aryan certificate, 22
Asch, Solomon, 202, 209
assimilation, 75–81, 270, 274
ataraxia, 103–4
attachment. *See also* development
    amygdala in, 72–73
    behavioral orienting response and, 38
    cross-race effect, 73–75
    emotional care link, 135–37
    emotion regulation and, 38–43
    Harlow experiments, 135–37

mother–infant, 35–38, 72, 134–35
neural activation studies, 74–78
neurobiological basis of, 38, 51–52, 72–73
psychological theories of, 44–52
psychotherapy, 45–47
social media engagement, 50–51
trust *vs.* mistrust, 180, 181
attitude change, imaging, 206
auditory stimulation in fetal development, 28–29
auid alteram partem, 279–81
Authoritarian Personality, The (Adorno), 54–56
authority, obedience to, 306–7, 384
authority acceptance, 235
autonomy *vs.* shame, 180, 181–82
Avraham Avinu, 194

band societies, 151–53
banking method, 350–51
Bateson, Gregory, 349
Baumeister, R. F., 49–50, 271
Bean, Robert, 13–15
Begin, Menachem, 245–46
behavioral orienting response
    adaptive nature of, 129
    affective systems evolution, 108–9
    attachment and, 38
    fetal, 32–33
    learning, flexibility and, 347–50
behaviorism, 53, 56–58, 92–93, 134–35
behaviors
    expectancy-confirming, 62–64
    implicit bias in predicting, 68–69
    interpretation, stereotypes and, 62
    stranger anxiety, 70–71
being-in-the-world interactions, 90–95
belief perseverance, 266, 269, 298–99

belongingness
   adolescence and, 183
   cooperation and, 134
   emotions/feelings in, 108, 271
   Gemeinshcaft/Gesellschaft, 167
   gender roles in, 125
   group identity/loyalty, 151, 170–71, 176,
      235, 272–74, 317, 319
   Marxist alienation, 165
   nationalism and, 315, 316
   need to, studies of, 48–50, 271–77
   one-dimensional views and,
      271–77, 282–83
   in online contexts, 50
   rational attachment, 316
Bernier, François, 6–7
Berry, J. W., 299–300
Bhopal, R., 9
bias
   activation of, xi, 204
   biased pluralism, 333–34
   categorization and, 304
   hearing the other side, 279–81
   implicit in predicting behaviors, 68–69
   in-/ *vs.* out-groups, 97, 232–34, 303
   negativity, 110–11
biology of cognition, 102
Blum, Lawrence, 293, 306
Blumenbach, Johann Friedrich, 8–10
Blumenfeld, Laura, 248–50
Bowlby, John, 44–45, 46–47, 137–38
brain measurements
   Bean, 13–15
   Morton, 10–13
brotherhood of man, 128–29
Bruner, Jerome, 58–59, 84–85, 87–88
Buck v. Bell 1927, 22
Buddha (Siddharta Guatama), 189–90
Buddhism, 147–48, 190
Burnham, W. D., 361
Bush, Barbara, 148
Buss, A. H., 122

Cain/Abel (Biblical), 195–96
Campbell, B. A., 108
capitalism, 165–66, 170, 171, 311
categorization
   accentuation effects, 64–65
   adaption to new information, 77–81
   adverse effects of, 304–5

assimilation/accommodation, 75–81,
   270, 274
background, 53–59
cognitive approach limitations, 84–89
cross-race effect, 73–75
development and, 70–73
expectancy effects, 63–64
information processing, 53, 59, 62, 76–77,
   84–85, 93–94
information retrieval, 60
in-/ *vs.* out-groups, 62–63, 75–76,
   97, 234–35
mother-stranger distinction, 70–72
novel stimuli and, 60, 69
short-term memory capacity and, 93–94
studies on, 60–69
Catholicism, on compassion, 147
caudate, love studies, 139
change by common descent, 17
Childe, C. Gordon, 160–63
childhood maltreatment, 150
childhood neglect, 43
childhood separation studies, 44
chimpanzees studies
   cooperation, 145–46
   revenge, 225
Chomsky, Noam, 130, 333, 334, 335
Christianity, 190–94
classification systems
   Aristotle, 5
   Bean, 13–15
   Bernier, 6–7
   Blumenbach, 8–10
   Linnaeus, 7–8
   Morton, 10–13
   natural selection, 16–20, 21
   use of, 21–23
class separation, Socrates on, 4–5
Clinton, Hillary, 340
closure, law of, 200
cognitive approach limitations, 84–89,
   105–6. *See also* categorization
cognitive dissonance theory, 203–6
cognitive recategorization, 67
collective punishment/responsibility, 214
communication of scientific knowledge,
   x–xi, xii–xiii
compassion. *See also* sympathy
   characterization/limitations of,
      146–48, 306

discussing here/now stage, 283, 288–89
distinguishing stage, 283, 287–88
generalizing stage, 283, 285–86
justice as, 283–97
relationship based on, 297
revealing stage, 283, 286–87
sharing hurts stage, 283, 289–93, 305
transformation stage, 283, 293–97
transformation to, 284–97, 298, 305
concentration camp survivors offspring
    case study, 215–24. See also face to face
    meetings
context-free psychology, 88–89
craniometry, 14
cross-race effect, 73–75
cultural evolution, 347–50
cupboard love, 135, 136–37
Curie, Marie, ix–x, xi

Dalai Lama, 189–90
Damasio, Antonio, 106–8
Darwin, Charles, 16–20, 111–12, 114, 123–
    24, 125–31, 133–34, 146, 197–98, 209,
    344, 354
Dean, D. G., 171
deaths by mass unpleasantness, 148
decategorization strategies, 66
decision-making processes, cognitive
    dissonance reduction, 206
decision rationalization, imaging, 206
"Declaration on Race and Racial
    Prejudice," 25–26
degenerative theory (Blumenbach), 8–10
Descartes, René, 105
devaluation, 205
development. See also attachment
    categorization and, 70–73
    emotion regulation, 38–43
    fetal, 28–29
    indiscriminate behaviors, 73
    mother–infant attachment, 35–38
    newborn, 33–35
    recognition processes in, 35–36
De Waal, F., 225
dialectical method, 352–53
diligence in scientific thinking, xiii
diversity
    Biblical origins of, 1–2, 190–91
    biological vs. cultural basis of, 23–27
    Greek mythology on, 2–3

Greek philosophers on, 3–5
Hippocrates on, 3
dopaminergic reward-processing system in
    attachment, 37, 141
dorsolateral PFC, 139–40
double victim phenomena, 219–20, 222–23,
    239–40, 249, 260, 292, 294–95
Dreyfus, Hubert, 88–89
Dukagjini, Leke, 226

ecological validity, 96–97
economic-elite domination, 333–35
economic exchange, influences on civil
    life, 166–67
economic exchange games, 208–9
Edison, Thomas, 354
education, learning and, 350–53
Eichmann, Adolf, 245
Einstein, Albert, ix–x, xi, 354–55
embodied cognition, 90–95, 102
emotions. See also judgment
    affective revolution, 106
    ethics/virtues and, 104–5, 111–12
    evil acts as intergenerational
        influence, 213–14
    evolution of, 108–13
    fairness impacts on, 209
    humours, 104
    mentalizing, 140
    mind/body dualism, 105
    moral/social, 111–12, 133–34, 197–206
    natural selection in development of, 108–9
    negative, 241–43
    negativity bias, 110–11
    positivity, 111–12
    reason and, clinical studies, 106–7
    reason–emotion distinction, 105
    research historically, 102–7, 112–13
    of vengeful people, 229
empathy deficits, 229
empirical research, xii
enacting the world, 90–95
enaction, 91–92, 102
enforced sterilizations, 22, 31
epigenetics, 31–32
Erikson, Erik, 177–79, 235
ERP studies
    love, 138
    negativity bias, 110
error in scientific thinking, xiii

Escape from Freedom (Fromm), 169–70
ethnic conflicts
  Blumenfeld/Khatib interaction, 248–50
  collapsed sense of time, 231–32, 237
  in-groups *vs.* out-groups, 303
  injustice, legal redress, 243–50
  justice, mutual awareness/reason
    in, 248–50
  justice as interpersonal, 238–52
  revenge and, 210–13, 225–37
ethnic identification, 218, 222, 234–36
ethnosymbolism theory, 312
eugenics movement historically, 21–23, 31
European Value Survey (EVS), 332
evolution (Darwinian). *See* natural selection
evolutionary psychology limitations, 125–31
excommunication, 236
existing views, power of, 267–69

Facebook, 50–51, 324–25
face to face meetings
  accomplishments/gains, 262–63, 305–6
  anger/resentment, 242–43
  assimilation/accommodation, 75–81,
    270, 274
  cathartic experiences, 262–65, 292, 293–97
  compassion (*see* compassion)
  disbelief, 258–59
  disinterest in, 254
  distrust, 257
  don't listen, 259–60
  double victim phenomena, 260
  emotional bonding, 261
  existing views, power of, 267–69
  hearing the other side, 279–81
  Holocaust legacy perspectives, 238–40
  hypothetical reasoning, 277–79, 281–82
  interpersonal behavior study, 252–55
  interpersonal justice, 252–55
  legacies, betrayal of, 255, 271
  legacy, adherence to, 275–76
  methodology, 215–17
  moral relations equality, 250–52
  motivations for, 254
  Nazi death-camp stories, 256
  need to belong, 271–77
  negative emotions/unequal moral
    relations, 263–65
  never said anything bad about Jews, 258
  no restitution, 260

not just the Germans, 259
one-dimensional views, 271–77, 282–83
rationality/intellectual activity,
    275–77, 282
real-world contexts applicability, 281–82
rebuilding of lives, 250–52
resentment/rage, 256, 306
resistance, 261, 265
respondent themes, 217–24
restorative justice, 265
retaliation, fear of, 256–57
retribution seeking, 257
social pressures, 273–75, 282
wartime stories, 256
we are different, 260–61
facial recognition studies
  in infants, 34, 70, 74
  mother's love, 140
  romantic love, 138–40
family violence, 148
farming/pastoralist groups, 155–59, 313
feelings of indignation, 221–22
Festinger, Leon, 203, 209
fetal development/embryology, 28–33
Feynman, Richard, ix–x, xi
Fiddler on the Roof, 77–79
fidelity, 184
Fisher, Ronald, 24
flexibility, learning and, 347–50
fMRI studies
  cognitive dissonance theory, 205–6
  justice-world belief, 208
  love, 138, 139–40, 142
  same-race effect, 75
forgiveness, promotion of, 299–302
Fortunoff Video Archives for Holocaust
    Testimonies, 304
Frankl, Viktor, 227–28
Freud, Sigmund, 235–36, 302–3
Fromm, Eric, 169–71, 177
F scale, 54–56
furor brevis, 104

Gage, Phineas, 106–7
Galilei, Galileo, xviii
Galton, Francis, 21–22
Gandhi, Mohandas, 233–34
Garden of Eden, 82–84, 190–91
Gemeinshcaft/Gesellschaft, 167
General Social Survey (GSS), 337–38

generativity *vs.* stagnation, 180
genocide, Biblical stories of, 191–94
genu/intellectual capacity/personality
    hypothesis, 13–15
Gestalt perception, 198–202
Giacomo, Daniel, 254–55
gift economy, 152–53
Gilens, Martin, 333–34
globalization, 186, 303, 324–25, 339
Goodall, Jane, 145
Graham, Ruth, 148
great chain of being, 5, 17
groups
    alienation, identity and, 176–79, 267
    attachment bonds in, 313–15
    authoritarianism, 169–71
    belongingness, identity/loyalty and, 151,
        170–71, 176, 235, 272–74, 317, 319
    economic inequality, 164–65
    evolutionary advantages of, 145–46, 151
    farming/pastoralist, 155–59, 313
    hunter-gatherers, 151–55, 313
    migration, urbanization/alienation
        and, 173–76
    modern consumption-capitalism, 168
    money, influences on civil life, 166–67
    multicultural societies, 187
    powerlessness/helplessness, 171–72
    property rights, 164–65
    rational calculation relationships,
        162–63, 167
    religious, 151, 157–58
    salesmanship mentality, 168–69
    social alienation, urbanization
        and, 163–73
    social hierarchy development, 158–59, 161
    unanimity of, 304–5
    urban, 160–63
    white-collar workers, 168–69

Hagar, expulsion of, 194
Hampshire, 234
Hampshire, Stuart, 279
Han, K. J., 332–33
happiness/income inequality
    relationship, 337–38
Harlow, Harry, 135–37
Hawkins, Stephen, x
hearing the other side, 279–81
Heidegger, Martin, 245

Heider, Fritz, 198–203, 209, 228
hierarchy of needs (Maslow), 48–49
Himmler, Heinrich, 245
Hippocrates, 3
Holocaust
    children of survivors case study, 215–24,
        238–40, 242–43 (*see also* face to face
        meetings)
    evaluations, effects of, 86
    injustices, intergenerational effects of, 213
    injustices, negative feelings of, 210–11
    justice, concepts of, 197
    legal redress, 210–11, 245–46
    lives, reconstruction of, 250–52
    memorialization of, 303–4
    personal history of, xix, 146
    reparations system, 243–44
    revenge/retribution, desire for, 211–13
hostile aggression, 149
humanism, on compassion, 148
Hunt, P. S., 108
hunter-gatherer groups, 151–55, 313
hypothetical reasoning, 266–67,
    277–79, 281–82

IAT studies/prejudice, 67–68
identity development
    Erikson, 179–88
    ethnic (*see* ethnic identification)
    identity crisis, 177–79, 187
    identity *vs.* role confusion, 180, 183–88
    social identity theory, 65, 236
ideology of separate spheres, 125
Ignatieff, M., 316, 324
imagined communities, 312–13
immune system, 35–36
indignation, feelings of, 221–22
Industrial Revolution, 161
industry *vs.* inferiority, 180, 183, 185–86
Inequality for All, 336
inferior frontal gyrus, 206
information processing, 53, 59, 62, 76–77,
    84–85, 93–94
inherited guilt, 301–2
initiative *vs.* guilt, 180, 182–83, 185–86
injustice. *See also* justice
    case study, 215–24, 238–40, 242–43
        (*see also* face to face meetings)
    dislike, 208–13
    experience of, 240–43

injustice (*cont.*)
  intergenerational effects of, 213
  legal redress, 243–50
  negative feelings of, 210–11
  parental experiences, children's
    internalization of, 298
  people's responses to, 244–47
  ruminative thinking, revenge and, 228–29,
    299, 302, 303
instrumental aggression, 149
insula, 205–6, 208
integrity *vs.* despair, 180
interactional justice, 241
intergroup relations studies, 101–2
International Social Survey Program
    (ISSP), 331–32
interpersonal communications, 240–41
interpreter effect, 9–10
intimacy *vs.* isolation, 180
in-/ *vs.* out-groups
  bias, 97, 232–34, 303
  categorization by, 62–63, 75–76,
    97, 234–35
  ethnic conflicts, 303
  punishment studies, 97
IOS Scale studies, 140–41
Isaac/Ishmael (Biblical), 194–95
Islam, 147, 194

Jacob (Biblical), 193, 195–96
Jacobs, Lizbeth, xiv
Janmaat, J. G., 317
Jesus Christ, 189–90
jihad, 175
Judaism, 146–47, 194, 233
judgment. *See also* emotions
  action research, 100–2
  Biblical end of unity, 82–84
  cognitive approach limitations, 84–89
  hearing the other side, 279–81
  human awareness/identity, 84
  hypothetical reasoning, 277–79, 281–82
  laboratory studies limitations, 96–100
  negative, neural inactivation of, 141
  rationality/intellectual activity, 275–77
  symbolism in, 82–84, 88–89, 95, 210
justice. *See also* injustice
  as compassion, 283–84
  described, 196–98

existing views, power of, 267–69
  group identity impacts, 267
  as intergenerational, 213–14, 238–40
  justice motive, 207–13
  mutual awareness/reason in, 248–50
  origins of, 189–98
  "ought" sense, 198–206, 223, 245
  personal sense of, 222, 223
  two sides of, 266–69
justice-world belief, 207–13

Kandel, Eric, 69
Kant, Immanuel, 150
kapos, 220, 222–23, 256, 260–61, 265
Katz, J., 300–1
Khatib, Omar, 248–50
kinship, 153–55, 157, 158, 170, 313
Kiwai-Papuans, 225–26
knowledge deficit model, x–xi
Koffka, Kurt, 198, 200
Köhler, Wolfgang, 198, 200
Kohn, Hans, 315, 318
Kuzio, T., 318

laboratory studies limitations, 96–100
Lady Justice, 210
Langmuir, G. I., 62–63
learned helplessness theory, 172
learning
  assimilation/accommodation, 75–81,
    270, 274
  education and, 350–53
  flexibility and, 347–50
  hypothetical reasoning, 277–79, 281–82
  by unlearning, 353–55
Leary, M. R., 49–50, 271
Lebensunwertes Leben, 23
legal redress
  ethnic conflicts injustice, 243–50
  Holocaust survivors, 210–11, 245–46
  injustices, redress of, 243
  Nazi Germany, 210–11, 243–44
  revenge and, 210–11, 230–31
Le Pen, Jean-Marie, 326, 339
Lepper, M. R., 280–81
Lepper, Mark, 267–69
Lerner, Melvin, 207–8, 209
Lewin, Kurt, 100–1, 198
Ley, Robert, 245

Linnaeus, Carl, 7–8
locus of control (LOC), 171–72
Lord, C. G., 280–81
love needs, 48–50

majoritarian electoral democracy/
    pluralism, 333–35
Malthus, Thomas Robert, 127
marriage. *See* relationships
Marx, Karl, 165–66
Maslow, Abraham, 48–49
Maturana, Humberto, 102, 134
May, Theresa, 339
McCullough, M. E., 299
medial frontoparietal region, 206
Medrano, J. D., 318–19
Meet the Patels, 79–81
megacities, 173
Mein Kampf, 233
memory/learning, fetal, 32
mentalizing, 140
Merton, Robert, 62
Metzger, W., 200
Milgram, Stanley, 303, 306–7
Miller, George, 53, 58–59–59, 69, 93–94, 110
Mills, Wright, 168–69
Minow, Martha, 126
modernist theory, 310–12
Mohammed (Prophet), 190, 194
monogenism, 8, 12, 18–20
moral conscience, 111–12, 133–34, 197–206
Morton, Samuel George, 10–13
mother–infant attachment, 35–38, 72, 134–35
Mother Teresa, 144
Mukherjee, S., 31
Murphy, Jeffrie, 302
Muselmanner, 220

nations/nationalism. *See also*
    belongingness; groups
    antiglobalization, 325–28
    anti-immigration attitudes/
        policies, 325–26
    civic *vs.* ethnic, 315–19, 326
    contextual factors, 329–30
    described, 309–15
    economic inequality and, 330–33,
        338–39
    economic inequality as threat, 333–42

exclusionary ethnonationalism, 325–28
foreign workers policy
    attitudes, 322–23
    immigration attitudes, 322, 323,
        332–33, 338–39
    measurement of, 319–23
    multiculturalism attitudes, 322,
        323, 339–40
    national identity loss and, 340–42
    powerlessness/alienation, 333–42
    recognition dynamics, 328–29, 340
    resurgence of, 323–30, 338–39
natural selection
    classification systems, 16–20, 21
    Darwinian theory of, 16–20, 114–15, 344
    Darwin on love, 133–34
    emotions, development of, 108–9
    evolution through, 16–20, 21
    sex/sexual reproduction, 115–20,
        123–24, 125–31
natural slavery theory, 5
Nazi Germany
    authoritarianism, rise of, 169–71
    children of Nazis case study, 215–24,
        238–40, 242–43 (*see also* face to face
        meetings)
    eugenics in, 22–23, 31, 345–46
    genocide in, 148
    Hitler's justification of, 233
    legal redress, 210–11, 243–44
    lives, reconstruction of, 250–52
    victims, indignation/need for
        revenge, 210–13
negative affectivity, 229
negativity bias, 110–11
Neolithic Revolution, 155–59
neuroticism, 229
newborn development, 33–35
Nishida, Toshisada, 145
nonvoters studies, 334

obedience to authority, 306–7, 384
Ohman, A., 108
Old Testament, on justice, 190–96
olfactory preference, in newborns, 34–35
On the Origin of Species (Darwin), 16–20
"ought" sense, 198–206, 223, 245
out-groups. *See* in-/ *vs.* out-groups
Out of Africa hypothesis, 27

own-race effect, 75
oxytocinergic system in attachment,
    37–38, 141

Palestinians/Israelis conflicts, 231–32
Paluck, E. L., 98, 100, 101–2
parental investment theory, 120–21
perennialist theory, 309–10
personalization strategies, 66
personal sense of justice, 222, 223
physical aggression, 149
Piaget, Jean, 76–77, 81, 92, 270
planned revenge, 225–26
Plato, 3, 214
polygenism, 12, 18, 19
postmodernist theory, 312–13
post-truth discourse, x–xi
poverty
    identity formation influences, 185–86
    Victorian-era solutions to, 127–28
prägnanz, law of, 199–200
prefrontal cortex studies
    aggression, 149–50
    love, 139–40, 141
prejudgments, 267–69
prejudice
    as adaptive process, 94–95
    authoritarian personality and, 54–56
    behaviorism, 53, 56–58, 92–93, 134–35
    categorization in development
        of, 53–54
    changes in expression of, 67
    cognitive psychology on, 58–59, 60–61
    Freudian psychoanalysis on, 53–54
    implicit, studies of, 67–68
    real-world interventions, 100–2
    reduction of, 98, 99–100
    social dominance orientation, 56
    stereotypes effects on, 61–62, 65, 69, 93
    studies on, 60–61
Preston, E., 280–81
primordialism theory, 309
problem-solving education, 351–52
Protestant doctrine, 170
pseudospecies, 235
psychopathy, 106–7
psychosocial identity development
    (Erikson), 179–88

punishment studies, in-groups *vs.*
    out-groups, 97
punitive reciprocity, 225–26

race, UNESCO statements on, 23–26,
    346–47, 350
race classifications. *See* classification systems
racism defined, 25
radicalization, 175
Rawls, John, 241
reasoning, hypothetical, 277–79, 281–82
recognition processes in development, 35–36
Reich, Robert, 335–37
relational aggression, 149
relationships
    affectional system, 135–37
    arranged marriages, 124
    cooperation and, 143–50
    cultural change influences, 130–31
    evolutionary perspective, 114–25
    love factor and, 131–43
    mate choice theory, 120–23, 131
    negative emotions and, 242
    sexual/emotional infidelity, 123–24
    sexual selection hypothesis,
        115–20, 123–24
    sexual selection hypothesis
        limitations, 125–31
revenge
    chimpanzees studies, 225
    ethnic conflicts and, 210–13, 225–37
    planned, 225–26
    ruminative thinking and, 228–29, 299,
        302, 303
    as symbolism, 228
    victims, indignation/need for, 210–13,
        227–28, 232–34, 240–43
rewards/punishments system, 236
romantic love studies, 138–40
Rosenthal, Robert, 63–64, 98–99
Rosnow, R., 98–99
Ross, Lee, 267–69
Rousseau, Jean-Jacques, 163–65
ruminative thinking, revenge and, 228–29,
    299, 302, 303

same-race effect, fMRI studies, 75
Sandage, S. J., 299–300

Sardinia, 226
Sartre, J. P., 63
scientific integrity, xii
scientific thinking, ix–x, xi–xiv
Searle, John, 88
Seebass, Julius, xix, 146
Seeman, Melvin, 171
self-awareness in scientific thinking, xiii
self-definition by opposition, 234
self-determination theory, 171–72
self-fulfilling prophecy, 62–64
self-interests vs. fellow feeling, 143–45
self-worth, 241, 244–45
Seneca, 104
sexual selection hypothesis, 19–20
Simmel, Georg, 161–63, 166
Skinner, B. F., 56–58, 134
skull volume/intellectual capacity
        hypothesis, 10–13
Smith, Adam, 143, 146
social alienation
    identity and, 176–79, 267
    identity vs. role confusion, 180, 183–88
    migration, urbanization and, 173–76
    nationalism, powerlessness in, 333–42
    urbanization and, 163–73
social identity theory, 65, 236, 283–84, 333
social interactive brain hypothesis, 92
social justice. See justice
social networking sites, belongingness
        studies, 50–51
Socrates, 3–5, 103
Solomon, Robert, 105, 293, 306
Solt, F., 331
somatic marker hypothesis, 107
somatosensory cortices, 208
Standardized World Income Inequality
        Database (SWIID), 332
Staub, Ervin, 293
Stephen, James, 243
stereotyping
    as adaptive process, 94–95
    prejudice, effects on, 61–62, 65, 69, 93
still face experiments, 41–43
Street, A., 300–1
Sufism, on compassion, 147
Survivors of the Shoah Visual History
        Foundation, 304

symbolism
    ethnosymbolism theory, 312
    in judgment, 82–84, 88–89, 95, 210
    revenge as, 228
symmetry, law of, 200–1
sympathy, 112, 133–34

taboos, 302–3
Tajfel, H., 65
Taylor, S. E., 110
terrorism, 175–76, 303
therapist–patient relationship, 45–47
thermal pain/love studies, 139–40
Tower of Babel, 1–2
tradition as barrier to change, 203
Tree of Life, 17–18
Trobrianders, 153
Trump, Donald, 325–28, 339, 340
trust vs. mistrust, 180, 181

UNESCO statements on diversity, 23–26,
        346–47, 350
unity of humankind, 128–29
unlearning, learning by, 353–55
Untermeschen/Übermenschen, 22
urbanization, migration/social alienation
        and, 173–76, 313
Urban Revolution, 160–63

Vallone, Robert, 267
Van Veen, V., 205
vendetta, 226
ventral striatum, 206
ventral tegmental area, love
        studies, 139, 141
verbal aggression, 149
Vergangenheitsbewältigung, 223
victim blaming, 205, 207, 228, 261
victims, indignation/need for
        revenge, 210–13, 227–28,
        232–34, 240–43
violence/aggression, human tendency
        towards, 148–50, 302–3
violent extremism, 175–76
VMPFC studies, emotion/reason, 106–7
voice recognition, fetal, 29–33
volunteers in studies, 98–100
Vygotsky, Lev, 92

Wallace, Alfred Russell, 17
Weiner, Bernard, 241–42
Wertheimer, Max, 198, 199, 200
Wiedergutmachung, 243–44
Wilkes, A., 65
World Values Survey, 321–22, 323, 331–32

Worthington, E. L., 299–300

Yack, B., 317–18

Zuckerberg, Mark, 324–25